The Levy Family

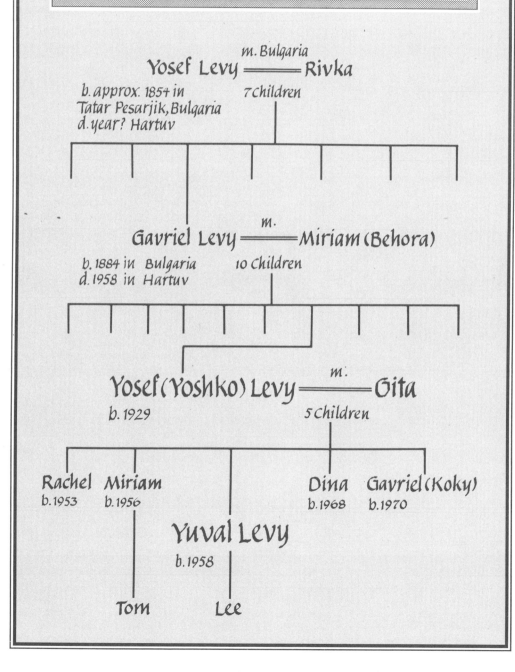

Yosef Levy ══ m. Bulgaria ══ **Rivka**

b. approx. 1854 in
Tatar Pesarjik, Bulgaria
d. year? Hartuv

7 children

Gavriel Levy ══ m. ══ **Miriam (Behora)**

b. 1884 in Bulgaria
d. 1958 in Hartuv

10 Children

Yosef (Yoshko) Levy ══ m. ══ **Gita**

b. 1929

5 Children

Rachel
b. 1953

Miriam
b. 1956

Dina
b. 1968

Gavriel (Koky)
b. 1970

Yuval Levy
b. 1958

Tom

Lee

THEIR PROMISED LAND

Grateful acknowledgment is given for permission to use material from
the following sources:

Excerpts from "The Insult and the Fury" in *In The Land of Israel* by Amos Oz,
copyright © 1983 by Amos Oz and Am Oved Publishers Ltd., English translation
copyright © 1983 by Amos Oz, reprinted by permission of Harcourt Brace Jovano-
vich, Inc. Excerpt from *The Birth of Israel: The Drama As I Saw It* by Jorge García-
Granados, copyright © 1948 by Alfred A. Knopf, Inc. Used by permission of Alfred
A. Knopf, Inc. Excerpts from *A History of Israel: From the Rise of Zionism to Our Time*
by Howard M. Sachar, copyright © 1976 by Howard M. Sachar. Used by permission
of Alfred A. Knopf, Inc. English translation of excerpts from "Hartuv Under Siege"
by Mattiyahu Peled in *Ma'arachot*, No. 61 (Feb. 1950), copyright © 1950. Used by
permission of *Ma'arachot*. *Ma'ariv* articles on Hartuv, Sept. 20, 1968; Sept. 9, 1977; May
16, 1966. Copyright © 1968, 1977, 1986. Used by permission of *Ma'ariv*. Clarence S.
Fisher notes, entries for August 26 and 27, 1929 (Box 7, Folder 8); "Valley east of Ishwa,
Beit Mahsir, April 11, 1930." Photographs, Vol. II (1930 Campaign), p. 117 (Box 8, Folder
6). University Museum Archives, University of Pennsylvania. Expedition Records—
Near East—Syria-Palestine—Ain Shems. Used by permission of The University
Museum Archives, University of Pennsylvania, Philadelphia.

Published by Crown Publishers, Inc., 201 East 50th Street,
New York, New York 10022. Member of the Crown Publishing Group.

CROWN is a trademark of Crown Publishers, Inc.
Manufactured in the United States of America
Library of Congress Cataloging-in-Publication Data

Kunstel, Marcia.
Their promised land / by Marcia Kunstel and Joseph Albright.—1st ed.
p.   cm.
1. Sorek River Valley (Israel)—Ethnic relations.   2. Jewish-Arab
relations—1917-   3. Israel-Arab War, 1948–1949—Israel—Sorek River Valley.
I. Albright, Joseph.   II. Title.
DS110.S67A43   1989
956.04′2—dc20   89-71260
                                                     CIP

Book design by Deborah Kerner

ISBN 0-517-57231-1
10 9 8 7 6 5 4 3 2 1
First Edition

THEIR PROMISED LAND

ARAB VERSUS JEW IN HISTORY'S CAULDRON—
ONE VALLEY IN THE JERUSALEM HILLS

◆　◆　◆

MARCIA KUNSTEL
AND
JOSEPH ALBRIGHT

CROWN PUBLISHERS, INC.
NEW YORK

CONTENTS

v

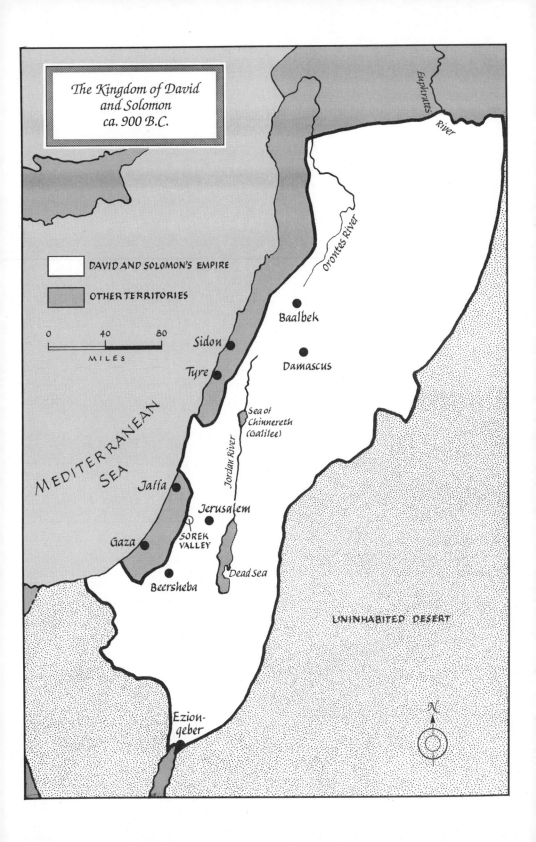

The Kingdom of David and Solomon ca. 900 B.C.

DAVID AND SOLOMON'S EMPIRE

OTHER TERRITORIES

0   40   80
MILES

MEDITERRANEAN SEA

Euphrates River

Orontes River

Baalbek

Sidon

Damascus

Tyre

Sea of Chinnereth (Galilee)

Jordan River

Jaffa

Jerusalem

SOREK VALLEY

Gaza

Dead Sea

Beersheba

UNINHABITED DESERT

Ezion-geber

N

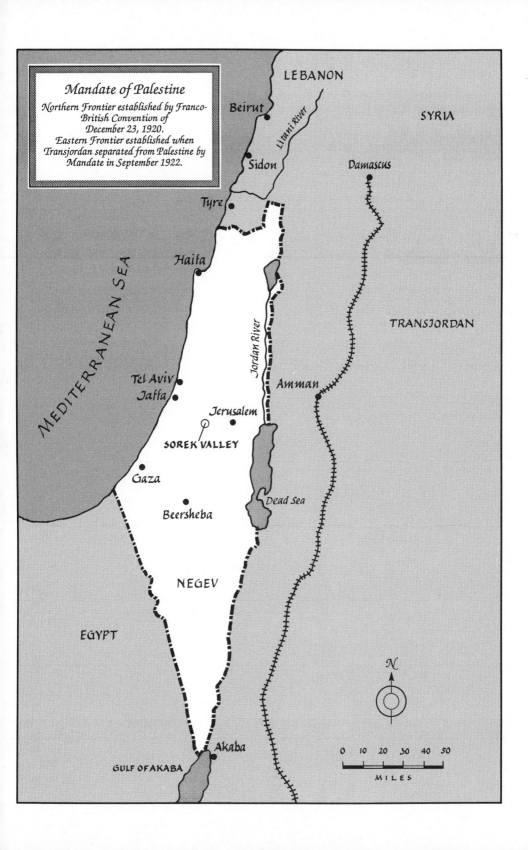

Mandate of Palestine

Northern Frontier established by Franco-British Convention of December 23, 1920.
Eastern Frontier established when Transjordan separated from Palestine by Mandate in September 1922.

LEBANON

Beirut

SYRIA

Litani River

Sidon

Damascus

Tyre

Haifa

TRANSJORDAN

Jordan River

MEDITERRANEAN SEA

Tel Aviv
Jaffa

Amman

Jerusalem

SOREK VALLEY

Gaza

Dead Sea

Beersheba

NEGEV

EGYPT

N.

Akaba

GULF OF AKABA

0   10   20   30   40   50
MILES

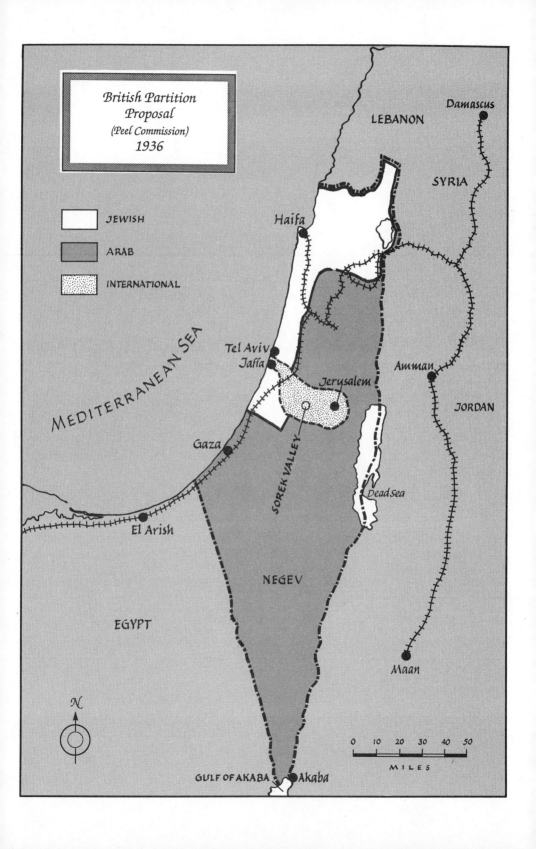

British Partition
Proposal
(Peel Commission)
1936

JEWISH

ARAB

INTERNATIONAL

MEDITERRANEAN SEA

LEBANON

Damascus

SYRIA

Haifa

Tel Aviv
Jaffa

Jerusalem

Amman

JORDAN

Gaza

SOREK VALLEY

Dead Sea

El Arish

NEGEV

EGYPT

Maan

N

0 10 20 30 40 50

MILES

GULF OF AKABA Akaba

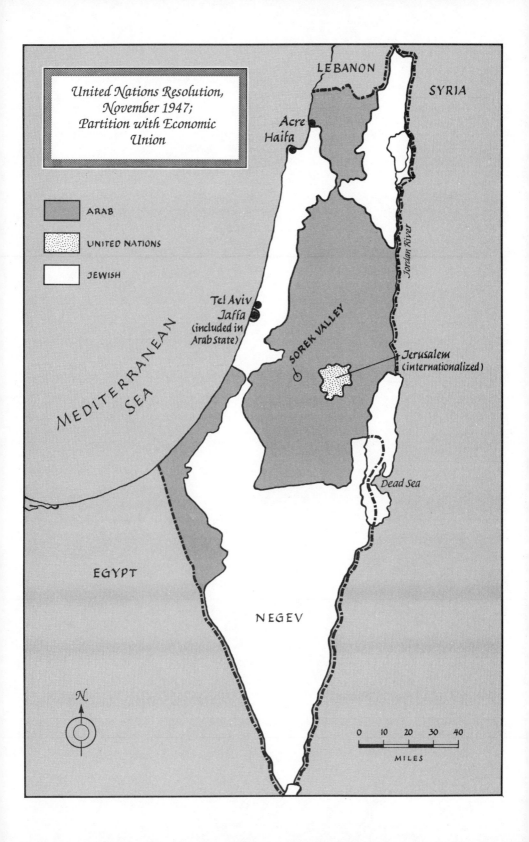

United Nations Resolution,
November 1947;
Partition with Economic
Union

ARAB

UNITED NATIONS

JEWISH

LEBANON

SYRIA

Acre
Haifa

Jordan River

Tel Aviv
Jaffa
(included in
Arab State)

SOREK VALLEY

Jerusalem
(internationalized)

MEDITERRANEAN
SEA

Dead Sea

EGYPT

NEGEV

N

0   10   20   30   40

MILES

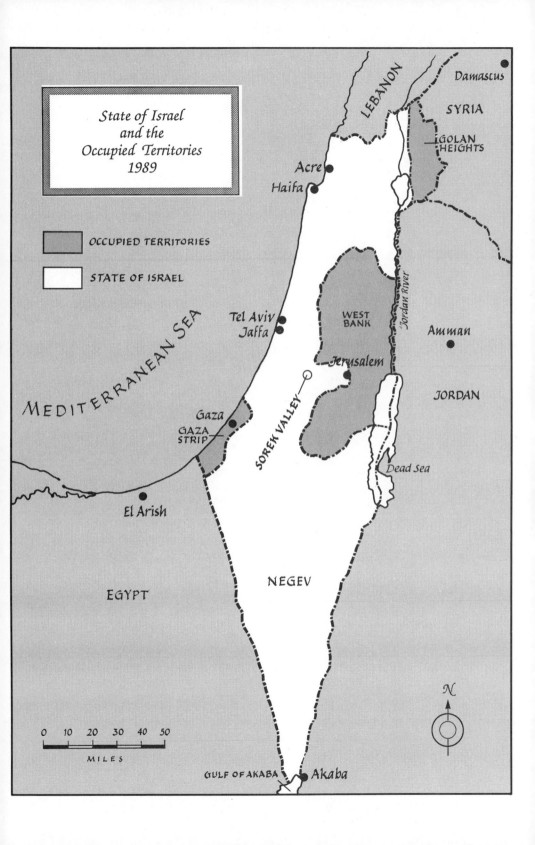

State of Israel
and the
Occupied Territories
1989

OCCUPIED TERRITORIES

STATE OF ISRAEL

MEDITERRANEAN SEA

LEBANON

Damascus

SYRIA

GOLAN
HEIGHTS

Acre

Haifa

Jordan River

Tel Aviv
Jaffa

WEST
BANK

Amman

Jerusalem

JORDAN

Gaza

GAZA
STRIP

SOREK VALLEY

Dead Sea

El Arish

NEGEV

EGYPT

N

0 10 20 30 40 50
MILES

GULF OF AKABA   Akaba

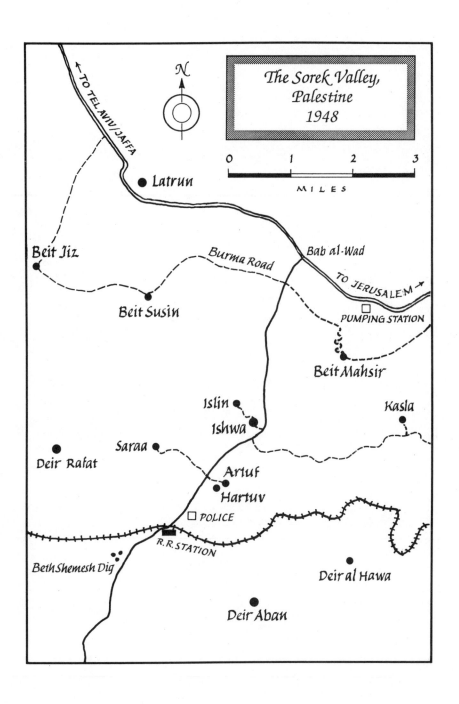

The Sorek Valley,
Palestine
1948

0 1 2 3
MILES

N

← TO TEL AVIV/JAFFA

Latrun

Beit Jiz

Burma Road

Bab al-Wad

TO JERUSALEM →

Beit Susin

PUMPING STATION

Beit Mahsir

Islin

Kasla

Ishwa

Saraa

Deir Rafat

Artuf

Hartuv

POLICE

R.R. STATION

Beth Shemesh Dig

Deir al Hawa

Deir Aban

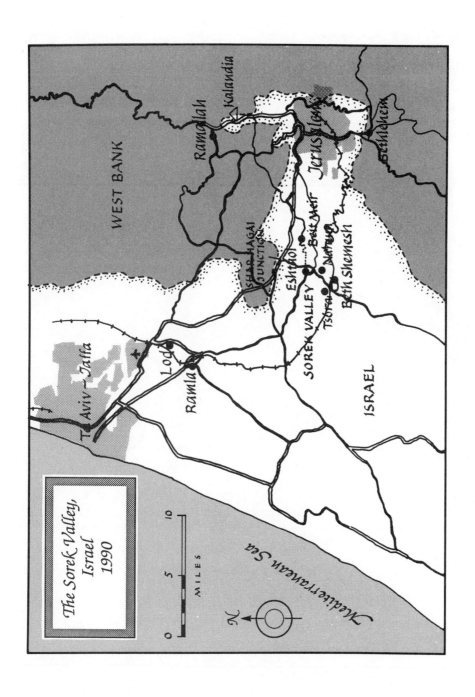

The Sorek Valley,
Israel
1990

MILES

0   5   10

MEDITERRANEAN SEA

WEST BANK

ISRAEL

Tel Aviv — Jaffa

Lod

Ramla

SHAAR HAGAI
JUNCTION

Eshtaol

Beit Meir

Nahum

SOREK VALLEY

Tsora

Beth Shemesh

Ramallah

Kalandia

JERUSALEM

Bethlehem

INTRODUCTION:
WHY?

*T*he conflict between Israelis and Palestinians is hard to release from mind once you step onto its dramatic soil. It is a struggle of such hurtful emotion, of so many rights and such grievous wrongs, that it draws in even the outsider who is neither Arab nor Jew to try to reach the knot clenched at its core.

That is what seized us, two American foreign correspondents who began spending time in the Middle East a decade ago. We walked into a land of claims and counterclaims, of sorrowful people, injured people, angry people. With each visit, each interview, we pried off another layer only to reveal multiple layers below. As we explored this "glass onion" of history, we realized that millions of others, especially Americans, had even less understanding of what was really going on than we did.

Our posting abroad in 1983 coincided with a time of accelerated terrorist incidents, with the crisis of conscience in Israel after its invasion of Lebanon, with the tragedy of the U.S. Marines in Beirut, the American bombing of Libya, and the murder of Leon Klinghoffer. All these stories had roots twined into the history of a territory that saw centuries of conflict even *before* it became a holy land for Judaism, Christianity, and Islam. How were we to understand the crush of emotion bound up in these events—and in those that surely loomed in the 1990s—if the history behind them remained impenetrable?

And so we set out to learn as much as we could about the origin and progression of the conflict over this land sacred to so many people. We decided to pursue one slice of history, to trace one community back through thousands of years in a way that would explain to us the broader story. We went about it retro-spectively, talking to people who are alive today to find out what happened to them, why they fought, and how they bled, asking them to unravel their bit of the story. And then we started looking further back, finding records that told about their place before they were born, and further and further back, before their parents and grandparents were there to pass down the story. We found real people from a real valley not far from Jerusalem whose recorded history goes back at least to 3000 B.C. Nothing we have written is fictionalized, including the names of the people. This is their story, in their words.

THEIR
PROMISED
LAND

• 1 •

HOME

*T*he rusted hulks of armored cars are lonely sentries on Route 1, the link binding Jerusalem to Tel Aviv. They are reminders that Palestinians and Israelis fought each other here in fierce personal combat in the days before there were big guns and trained soldiers in the surrounding hills, when adversaries could look into each other's eyes before they discharged—or crumpled into—a fatal blast of gunfire. The aging relics on the roadside were victims of the prewar war, the battles in a civil war between Zionist Jews and Palestinian Arabs. There was no Israel then, only Palestine, and that, of course, is what the fighting was about. The armored cars were homemade "sandwiches" of steel sheeting tacked onto ordinary trucks with slits left up front to view the road and along the sides so guards could poke out the muzzles of their carbines. They were used to convoy food and guns up what was then just a skinny two-lane road from Tel Aviv to the Jews isolated in Jerusalem. In the skirmishes and terrorism waged by both sides in the first months of 1948, the convoys became targets of Palestinian farmers turned fighters.

Today the road is a four-lane highway, gliding east from the urbanized coast through flat farmland and finally wriggling over steep hills that open up to Jerusalem. An Israeli driving down the road today still may feel an aching swell in his throat when he reaches the foothills and the armored cars pop into view. To Israelis, the war remnants littering the shoulders of the highway are shrines to the more than forty young troops who died on this road in 1948. They raise hard memories of how the Jews almost lost the heart of their dream when they lost the road and the ability to supply besieged Jerusalem. The leaders of Israel chose to leave the relics there at the roadside so they would evoke exactly those memories and serve warning that a lifeline taken for granted is tenuous. They warn that the Jews must keep alert and strong or risk, again, losing what they consider the capital of their homeland or perhaps even the homeland, the nation itself. They carry one other message: if you want something badly enough, are forceful enough, and are willing to sacrifice enough, you can take it, even with the rest of the world against you.

Riding down Route 1 with a Palestinian, one sees the same terrain, but the view is different. The flaking orange steel in the grass is a glimpse of fleeting victory. Each date scrawled on the fractured skeletons of war is the date of a triumph. Each marks a time when the Palestinians were winning the battles they fought to save their homeland from being sliced into bits by the decision of diplomats they'd never seen in places they'd never been. Jerusalem was a holy city for them as well. Their leaders were not willing to give it up or any of the territory their ancestors had tended for centuries. They would not give up any of it, but they were unable to defend it, and eventually they lost it all. For a Palestinian, too, there is a lesson buried in the metal scraps on Route 1: fight as well as you can, but know your enemy, know yourself, and know when the times demand compromise.

Mahmoud Asad Hamdan is a Palestinian who knows the story of those armored wrecks. He is a quiet man who seems to have made peace with himself and with the calamitous twists that have encumbered his life's path. He and his generation may have accommodated, but he is quick to point out when passing down the road the symbols of momentary Palestinian success. To him they raise memories of a time when the countryside belonged to his people and they were fighting to keep it. "I never came here to attack, but when the convoys came to pass by the village, I was with the *mujahideen.*" He speaks with neither pride nor apology of those times. It is how a fifty-three-year-old refugee describes events that happened when he was thirteen and there was war, and his people lost everything without him having much to do with it.

Just east of the wasted armored cars on Route 1 is the turnoff for the biblical Valley of Sorek, the road where the teenage Mahmoud Hamdan joined the fighters in attacking Jewish supply convoys. It used to be the turnoff for his home. Three miles down that road was Mahmoud's village, Ishwa, and a mile farther was the tiny Jewish settlement of Hartuv, which convoys coming from Jerusalem were trying to resupply with provisions from the city's dwindling stash of food and arms. It was that small Jewish colony, a lonely outpost in a Palestinian Arab landscape, that brought the valley into the periphery of war. It was Hartuv that gave the leaders of the Jewish community of Palestine a stake in this valley during the prewar skirmishing. But ultimately it was the battle for Jerusalem, for an Israeli state bigger than the boundaries the diplomats had drawn, that would bring real war to the valley.

The history of this bit of valley is in many ways the story of the Palestinian-Israeli conflict. The valley contributed celebrated warriors to early chapters of the struggle three thousand years ago, among them the lusty avenger Samson. Yet in the modern conflict the place and its people were rather reluctant players. It did not supply the preeminent personalities of either side, but day-to-day life here was driven by decisions being made by Arab leaders in Jerusalem and Jews in Tel Aviv, as well as by officials in London, Berlin, Cairo, Washington, Manila, Moscow, and a dozen other capitals. The valley is not a perfect reflection of every development in the agonizing relationship between Arab and Jew, perhaps because the people who lived

here in the crucial fifty-odd years before their first modern war
were not militantly political. They tried harder than most to get
along. Some of them sustained neighborly bonds even when the
tide of events turned most other Jews and Arabs into deadly
enemies, though most of them, too, finally acted as enemies. The
lives of the average, regular people here are the flesh on the
skeletal facts of history, the humanity of conflict that extends till
today. In this case the history expands from the place, because
in the end this conflict had a change of venue. The people who
were here, all the people, were violently separated from their
homes and replaced by newcomers. The Jews had the option to
come back, but most of them did not, and none of them stayed.
The Palestinians had no such option, and they kept an angry
longing that seeded a storm of outrage in their descendants forty
years later.

The geographical Sorek Valley twists fifty miles all the way
from the inland Jerusalem Hills to the Mediterranean coastal
plain. For millennia, one focal point of human activity in this
valley had been the bowl of hillsides twelve miles west-south-
west of Jerusalem, where by the end of the nineteenth century
a cluster of four Palestinian Arab villages, one Arab town, and
a young Jewish colony were spread in settlement. One of the
Palestinian villages claimed position in the continuum of history, carrying the same name and sitting on the same site as a
village storied in biblical tales. Through at least five thousand
years people managed to farm survival off their land, a fifty-
square-mile piece of valley that was often dry and sometimes
impossibly parched. They would plant grain in the flattest
parts—the valley bottom and gentler slopes that collected the
most water—and usually lodged themselves in the most defensible positions higher up the hillsides that they shared with olive
groves, vineyards, and fruit trees. One species of vine grew well
enough to give the valley its name—the Sorek, an especially
succulent grape. This was the pattern of life in the valley from
biblical times until 1948.

By the turn of the twentieth century the villagers here were
close. There were social divisions, but not huge ones. Whoever

had more didn't have much more. When Mahmoud was growing up, the closest wealthy *sheikh* lived ten miles out of the valley
up the road toward Jerusalem. Perhaps the greatest differences
were between the villages and the town, a place called Deir
Aban that was nearly four times bigger than any of the villages
and sat a mile down a side road running south. It was scarcely
in the valley, but its influence would be felt.

The villages all had been aligned with one of the two factions
into which Arabs divided themselves for hundreds of years, up
into the twentieth century. That meant village feuds chafed
relations less often than in some parts of Palestinian Arab society. It made it easier for men and women to intermarry among
villages, so clans became vines with shoots twining them together. When they got a school, it would be one school for all
the Arab boys of the four Palestinian villages, a place where
boys made friendships that lasted them through weddings and
feast days and funerals. When the railroad ran its tracks along
the southern edge of the valley bowl in the 1890s, it further
encapsulated these villages, creating a physical boundary that
cut them from the town, Deir Aban, where politics and nationalism would begin to stir some men to angry radical thoughts
after they rounded the twentieth century. At times, that anger
would sweep into the valley in a fury.

The biggest of the four villages was Ishwa. By the 1945 census
it claimed 620 people, who lived midway up a hillside in houses
laid out in the shape of a star. It was the first village encountered
by a traveler walking or riding horseback or, later, driving down
the valley from the Jerusalem–Tel Aviv road. Ishwa was important because it had water. The best well in the valley was there,
and its bounty was shared with everyone. Ishwa was prosperous
enough to have a few stores and a guest house, and when the
valley school was built, it was on Ishwa land.

Just a few hundred yards northwest of Ishwa an offshoot
village called Islin lay closer to the top of the hill. Islin's 260
people were as prideful as their Ishwa neighbors; its peasant
farmers readily boasted years later about their land and their
crops and most of all about their ingenuity in rigging up piped

water to some of the town's stone and mud-mortared houses.

West and a bit north, the highest and longest-inhabited point was the village Saraa. Though its 560 people delighted in their panoramic view of the valley and beyond, their immediate environs were the least congenial in the neighborhood of villages. Saraa was almost barren. It faced south and sat fully exposed to a Middle Eastern sun that gave no mercy all summer long. At night the people often slept outside on the ground to escape the heat of their homes. The best place for respite during the day was the ancient grove of olives that they tended, trees standing low on trunks grown fifteen feet around, with fat gnarled limbs and slender dusky leaves that can be described as no color but olive green.

The three villages looked down from hillsides that formed the northern rim of the valley. Facing them from across the valley on a hill a bit farther west was Artuf. Settled so it missed some of the worst hours of sun, Artuf sat amid greenery from trees of olives and fruits and almonds. Still, it grew only to a population of 350 by 1945. It was the closest of the villages to the British police fortress, which was no more than half a mile west, and to the train station, just beyond the police.

Artuf also was closest of all the Arab villages to the Jewish settlement, a colony that came to renew the Jewish claim to the valley more than seventeen hundred years after the last Jew had left it at the insistence of a Roman emperor. At its founding in 1895 the Jewish colony took the same name as its Arab neighbor. In spoken Hebrew, it came to be called Hartuv. The two at one time were so close, with the Jews sitting just below the Arabs on the hillside, that they would have been a single town had their people not been so culturally divided. In 1945 only eighty people lived in Hartuv. It always was the smallest entity in the valley.

Hartuv was founded by pioneering Bulgarians who came to make a farm out of rocks and dry dirt. Both Arabs and Jews from the valley like to remember the quiet years of coexistence. The Arabs in Artuf were by far the closest and most friendly of the Arabs, though other villagers also worked with and—at some desperate moments—aided the Jews. The valley was decidedly more tolerant of this foreign presence than were Arabs from more distant places, including those in the dominating big town of Deir Aban, just two miles southwest. Even within the valley, however, conflict repeatedly interrupted what in retrospect was not a deep-seated peace. The discord existed, and it grew more harsh under prodding by outsiders from both camps, Arab and Jew. Perhaps the people of the valley could have outlasted their squabbles, but then 1948 and the battle for Jerusalem carried real war into the valley.

What happened in the valley in 1948 has never been told in detail in any of the hundreds of books chronicling the war. A cadre of Jewish soldiers and a few remaining families held Hartuv for five and a half bleak months, then abruptly were ordered to evacuate. By then a third generation was taking command of Hartuv and fighting in its defense. One of them was Yosef "Yoshko" Levy, the grandson of original Bulgarian settlers who grew up in the colony a mile from Mahmoud Hamdan's Arab village. Forty years later he remembered well the frustration and fear of those months of siege in Hartuv. "We sat in the Independence War isolated, completely detached. It was hard." It was a hard place of hard battles over decades, but the Jews did conquer this plot of land when they won their nation. The Israelis as a country won it, but the Jews of Hartuv did not. Like the Palestinians, they too had to leave.

Back in 1948, wheat and barley fields filled the valley bottom in good years, and green clusters of olive, fig, and carob trees broke the unrelenting brown of bare or brush-covered hillsides. There were plenty of years that were not so good, when drought or locusts ravaged fields and left sorry, wilting trees. Yet it has been remembered almost as a paradise by Yoshko Levy and Mahmoud Hamdan, who never knew each other back then or later. After forty years, Yoshko spoke with animation about the attacks against his colony, the days when food ran low and spirits lower. But he spoke lovingly of the row of palm trees that used to line a path from his uncle's big stone home to his own, of bicycling down country roads as a boy, of the graveyard in

the valley bottom where his parents were buried. He was sad-
dened and distressed that only a few shells of houses mark the
place where his settlement stood.

Mahmoud Hamdan was just as reverent about the place he
spent his boyhood, a place where his family had lived for so
many generations they did not even know when they arrived.
For forty years now it had been in Israel, not Palestine. Mahmoud still could point to every field that his family farmed
back when it was Palestine, to the best place for grazing the
goats he herded, to the precise spot where his stone house with
a red-tiled roof had stood low on the hillside. Arid winds that
have toughened Mahmoud Hamdan's face and hands over decades of work in quarries and construction sites almost seem to
have buffed a hard skin on his heart, too. He stores his anger
there, Mahmoud said, and no emotion breaks into his matter-of-
fact description of a countryside forty years ago dominated by
Palestinian farmers.

In four decades the valley has burst out of its rural garb.
Forests climb over the hills, small industries dot the bottom, and
foul smells bubble out of the Brook of Sorek. Jews who have
come from Yemen raise chickens in long tin-roofed sheds in a
suburban settlement that covers every trace of the village where
Mahmoud Hamdan was born. A few boarded-up houses still
stand at Yoshko Levy's colony, and above it on the hillside is
another postwar settlement of Yemenite Jews. Down the road
across the railroad tracks is an entire new city of fifteen thousand. Both Mahmoud and Yoshko consider this place their real
home, but both are a bit confounded at the changes. After trips
to the place where he grew up, Yoshko Levy drives off to a
bright house in Udim, a town up north near the coast. After the
Israelis won, his family came back to Hartuv for a while, but
finally resettled in Udim's more hospitable landscape. For his
part, Mahmoud Hamdan returns after visiting the valley to a
rather less hospitable environment. His people were among the
Palestinian losers pushed out in 1948 and collected, destitute,
into refugee camps.

Mahmoud Hamdan's current home is not so far in distance,

only twenty-two miles away, past Jerusalem and then north into the West Bank. But Kalandia refugee camp is a world away from what the village of Ishwa was. Concrete-block houses climb back to back up the sides of potholed roads that become mud channels in winter rain and raise dust devils under passing vehicles in summertime. Waste water from the packed houses runs down the lanes, because there are no sewer pipes there. The luckiest families have made a compound, walling themselves into some privacy from the moil of people surrounding them. Mahmoud Hamdan has accommodated. He has kept probing the edges of his wound with visits to the Sorek Valley, somehow seeing or smelling or breathing his home through its altered state. But he has still tried to make life work in the camp. His plodding years as a stonecutter have enabled him to affix small luxuries to his family's life. There is a black-and-white television set now, and an indoor latrine. He has made a few larger advances: the gravel truck he wriggles through the camp's skinny, ruptured paths, the son who finished teachers' school.

But after forty years of trying to remake a life, he wondered what his sweaty labors have guaranteed for his children. The main entrances to his refugee camp were blocked in early 1988 by a fifteen-foot-high wall of iron barrels filled with concrete, topped with barbed wire and guarded day and night by Israeli soldiers carrying guns and clubs and tear gas. Schools had been mostly closed, jobs were scarce, and prisons seemingly were mounted with revolving doors for young Palestinians. The camp was one of hundreds of sites that had become the new battlegrounds for Palestinians and Israelis. It is the sons of men like Mahmoud who resumed the struggle for a homeland, and sons of men like Yoshko who tried to stop them. The Palestinians called the latest chapter in their long-running war against Israelis their *intifada,* an uprising for liberation. Many Israelis said it was an outbreak of terrorism that must be crushed.

Yet beyond these angry descriptions, something else was changing at the dawn of the 1990s. Though this was hard to see sometimes, there were faint signs that the silent moderates in two communities—the men of temperate politics like Yoshko and Mahmoud—were gradually coming closer to sharing the same view of the future. Israelis and Palestinians of the middle were thinking that somehow there must be room for both of their people, no matter what the extremists on either side might shout in their ears. If those howling voices could be screened out so the words of men like Mahmoud and Yoshko could be heard, their message would surprise the world.

"CANAANITES WERE IN THE LAND"

*T*he Old Testament celebrates a man called Samson with gigantic shoulders and maimed legs who could uproot mountains and rub them together like pebbles. He grew up in the hills overlooking the Sorek Valley to become the chieftain of a tribe of Israelites. Around 1100 B.C., Samson helped the Israelites end their wandering and solidify their first foothold in the green pastures of Palestine. One day, according to the Bible, Samson killed a thousand of the neighboring Philistine tribesmen with the jawbone of an ass. So terrifying were Samson's power-lifter muscles that the elders of the Philistines dispatched their secret weapon, Delilah, on a Mata Hari mission. "Cajole him and find out where his great strength comes from," the chiefs of the Philistines had told her. "In return we will each give you eleven hundred silver shekels."

What happened next would put the Sorek Valley on the map down to modern days. Suspecting nothing, Samson fell into Delilah's arms near the Brook of Sorek. Three times Delilah pressed Samson for the secret of what it would take to bind and tame him. Seven new bowstrings, her lover replied. Believing him, Delilah tied him with bowstrings while he slept, but he

awoke and burst the bonds. She asked again and Samson answered: "If I were bound tightly with new ropes that have never
been used, I should lose my strength." She tried that, too, but
he snapped the ropes like thread. Samson kept feeding her lies
until Delilah, her mission verging on disaster, complained,
"How can you say you love me when you do not trust me? Three
times you have laughed at me and have not told me where your
great strength comes from." She tried one more time. Near the
instant of sexual fulfillment, she pulled away from Samson and
again asked him his secret. And finally he blurted it out: he
belonged to the Nazarene cult, which held that a person's hair
must never be shorn.

Eavesdropping nearby, Philistine agents burst in on the lovers. They sheared seven of Samson's locks and his strength
vanished. They poked out his eyes and took him to prison—in
a place that even then was called Gaza. But after his hair had
grown back, Samson was led by his captors into a temple to
entertain the Philistine congregation. Uttering a prayer to God
for vengeance, Samson thrust apart two pillars with his arms.
He brought down the roof, killing himself and three thousand
Philistines.

The Samson and Delilah story was only a microsecond in the
tribal struggles that have run on for the last three millennia over
this one piece of land. The Book of Judges records the names of
two villages in the Sorek Valley, Eshtaol and Zorah, where
Samson grew up and was infused by the spirit of God. Thirty
centuries later, Samson's Zorah survived as an Arab hilltop
hamlet called Saraa. Its name, as spoken out loud, was still the
same. A mile down the hill from Saraa stood Mahmoud Hamdan's village, Ishwa, which lay close to the ruins of Samson's
ancient Eshtaol. And on the far side of the valley was the Jewish
settlement Hartuv, where Yoshko Levy was born. The struggle
would continue through their days.

In the full sweep of the valley's history, Samson was a Johnny-
come-lately. Zorah was there centuries before he and the Israelites arrived from the desert. Archaeologists have found proof
that another Semitic people called the Canaanites had been liv-

ing in the valley at least since 3300 B.C., about two thousand years before Samson. After drifting in from Syria, the Canaanites settled down, farming and mining copper. About a thousand years before Samson, they had made two of the most consequential discoveries in human history. By developing a twenty-two-character alphabet, the Canaanites swept aside the stultifying Egyptian hieroglyphic technique of representing each word with a separate character. Thus was invented the secret of modern writing. The Canaanites also revolutionized weapon-making when they learned to mix tin and copper to form a harder metal called bronze. Between 3000 and 1100 B.C., Canaanite civilization covered what is today Israel, the West Bank, Lebanon, and much of Syria and Jordan. And it is from these ancient Canaanites that modern Palestinians claim their origins and early attachment to the land.

The Sorek Valley's earliest Canaanite town, established fully six centuries before Egypt's great pyramids, is one of the two or three earliest sites in the Holy Land where nomadic tribesmen stopped their wandering and began to live in towns. Archaeologists discovered this Canaanite temple and a Canaanite village, dating from 3300 B.C., on the banks of the Brook of Sorek. The five-thousand-year-old oblong temple is about forty feet long and is edged by a row of slablike boulders in what looks like a miniature Stonehenge.

Three miles away are the ruins of a Canaanite town from a later period. Here between 2200 and 1700 B.C., Canaanites found prosperity through bronze manufacturing and built a wall and towers as protection. Judging from one inscription found in the ruins, the Canaanite alphabet was in use here by 1700 B.C. So were a furnace for smelting bronze, cisterns for trapping rainwater, and dozens of big storage jars which archaeologists concluded had been imported from Egypt and the Aegean. The town's earliest known name was Ir-Shemesh, meaning Town of the Sun. It covered about nine acres—enough for about seven hundred inhabitants.

A fresh wave of tribes drifted off the desert around 2000 B.C. and began pasturing their herds in the fertile lands of the Canaanites. Among these wanderers were the Hebrews, part of a larger cluster of unsettled tribesmen known as the Apirus or Habirus. They had left what are now the oil fields of southern Iraq and migrated twelve hundred miles up the Euphrates River. The Book of Genesis says they arrived in Canaan and found that "Canaanites were in the land." The Hebrews pitched camp first in what is now the West Bank city of Nablus. Genesis says Yahweh, the God of the Hebrews, appeared to the Hebrew tribal leader Abram and made an astonishing promise: "It is to your descendants that I will give this land." The Hebrews were so awestruck that they built an altar at Nablus. Then they drifted southward through the West Bank, part of the land they would call Judea and Samaria. After being driven into Egypt by a famine, Abram would eventually return to the West Bank, where he would bury his wife, Sarah, in a cave near Hebron. At Hebron, Yahweh gave Abram a new name, Abraham. And with that, Genesis says Yahweh reconfirmed his promise to give Canaan to Abraham's descendants.

So began a four-thousand-year inheritance dispute between Abraham's two sets of descendants. For if Genesis is to be believed, the Arabs are just as much Abraham's descendants as the Jews. Genesis says that when Abraham was still childless at the age of eighty-six, his wife, Sarah, urged him to try having a baby with another woman. As his second wife, Sarah nominated Hagar, her Egyptian slave girl. Abraham straightaway took Hagar, and a son, Ishmael, was born. Fourteen years later, Yahweh "dealt kindly with Sarah." She became pregnant by Abraham and a son, Isaac, was born to Abraham and Sarah. Ishmael and his mother were then expelled from Abraham's household. They settled "east of Egypt on the way to Assyria"—northern Saudi Arabia on today's map. Genesis says that Ishmael lived to father a dozen sons, all of them princes and chiefs of tribes. The Koran accepts the story, calling Abraham a great prophet and Ishmael the progenitor of the Arabian race. One verse of the Koran tells of Allah ordering Abraham and Ishmael to travel to Mecca in order to build a temple to contain the famous black rock from Paradise. That temple, called the Kaaba, is still the center of Moslem pilgrimages.

Isaac's side of the family wandered in and near the land of Canaan while Ishmael's descendants moved farther into the desert. The Bible lost track of Ishmael's clan for a century or two, with all the attention focusing on Isaac's lineage. Among the highlights of their history was an unexpected victory in one desert skirmish, which led Isaac's son Jacob to change his name to Israel. After that, subsequent generations of his Hebrew clansmen began to call themselves Israelites.

Then, in what must have been roughly 1500 B.C., the Israelites crossed paths again with their Arab stepcousins. It happened when Jacob's son Joseph provoked his own brothers to a jealous rage. After tossing Joseph down a well, the brothers peddled him to a caravan of "Ishmaelite" (i.e., Arab) traders who happened to be passing on camels. The Ishmaelites bought him and carried him as their newest slave to Egypt, where they resold him to an Egyptian. Undaunted, Joseph became an adviser and dream interpreter for the Pharaoh. Genesis says they got along so well that the rest of the Israelites decided to pick up stakes and follow him to Egypt from their old camps in the land of Canaan. That was the start of roughly two hundred years when most of the Hebrews toiled in Egypt. According to Exodus, a later Pharaoh decided to "put slave drivers over the Israelites to wear them down with heavy loads" because they had become an internal threat.

While Israelites were building pharaohs' palaces, Canaan was an Egyptian province composed of midget city-states. The Canaanite kings spent much time feuding and rebelling. Historians know this through the study of the Amarna tablets, a clay archive of ancient Egyptian diplomatic correspondence discovered in 1897 by a peasant woman in Egypt. The town of Zorah was described in two of these 3,400-year-old missives as a rebel center dangerous to Egyptian interests. In one letter, Hori, an Egyptian loyalist in Canaan, tried to warn the Pharaoh about the risks of travel in the vicinity of Zorah: "Let him learn of another misery, the crossing of Zorah; he will say it burns more than a hornet's sting." In another letter, Basmatu, a Canaanite queen, pleaded for the Pharaoh's help in rescuing her sons, whom she feared had been taken hostage in Zorah. "Oh King my lord behold," she wrote, "there has been war in the land, and the land of the King my Lord has been wearied by rebels."

The struggle by diverse tribes of Apiru meanderers to capture the valley and the rest of Canaan began about the time of the Amarna letters, in roughly 1400 B.C. In one Amarna letter the Canaanite king of Jerusalem warned the Pharaoh: "If there are no archers, the king's lands will be taken over by the Apiru." The Egyptian empire had begun to collapse, and in the confusion the Canaanite city-states were breaking away from Egypt. Meanwhile, marauders from various Apiru tribes, including the Israelites, were swarming in on the comfortable Canaanites. Around 1300 B.C., the Israelite warrior Joshua swept in from the desert east of the Dead Sea and massacred every Canaanite in Jericho. "They utterly destroyed all that was in the city, both man and woman, young and old, and the ox, and sheep, and ass, with the edge of the sword," the Book of Joshua recounted. There is archaeological evidence that at approximately the same time unknown raiders—presumably Israelites—attacked the Valley of Sorek, thirty miles west of Jericho, and burned the Canaanite town of Ir-Shemesh.

Taking advantage of the spineless government in Egypt, another tribe of Israelites led by Moses escaped from Pharaoh Ramses II's labor gangs in roughly 1250 B.C. Their exodus into the Sinai and on to the promised land would lead to further Israelite penetration of historical Palestine. Although the tribe of Moses numbered only a few thousand, Moses was more important than the earlier invaders because he brought a strategic vision. As his followers set down in the Book of Exodus, Yahweh appeared to Moses on a mountain in the Sinai and promised the Israelites a new homeland that would range from the River Euphrates to the Sea of the Philistines (i.e., the Mediterranean). If Exodus is to be taken literally, God's words to Moses amounted to a long-range plan of conquest:

> I shall spread panic ahead of you. I shall make all your enemies
> turn and run from you. I shall send hornets in front of you to
> drive Hivite and Canaanite and Hittite from your presence. I

shall not drive them out before you in a single year, or the land
would become a desert where, to your cost, the wild beasts would
multiply. Little by little I will drive them out before you until
your numbers grow and you come into possession of the land.

The Book of Exodus made a momentous redefinition of God's
chosen people. No longer was Yahweh portrayed as promising
the land of Canaan to all the descendants of Abraham. Instead,
Yahweh's inheritance had now been restricted to the lineage of
Isaac, namely the Israelites. Between the time of Genesis and
Exodus, the Arab descendants of Abraham had been cut out of
Yahweh's will.

After the destruction of Ir-Shemesh, it took the Israelites
three centuries of hit-and-run warfare to conquer the valley and
the rest of Canaan. Here as elsewhere, the Israelites first en-
camped in the hills, because they couldn't occupy the walled
Canaanite cities or the best farmland of the plains. In Joshua's
time, an agreement among the Israelites had apportioned the
land in the Valley of Sorek to one of the twelve Israelite tribes,
the Tribe of Dan. The Danites' prospects for actually capturing
the allotted territory were so discouraging that the tribe split
up, and some left the valley to scout for new territory in the
north. The Book of Judges recounts that one of the enemy tribes
in Canaan, the Amorites, "forced the children of Dan into the
mountain; for they would not suffer them to come down to the
valley."

The Israelites and the Canaanites were still contending for
control of the valley when another invading tribe called the
Philistines crashed onto the scene from the Aegean Islands
around 1160 B.C. The Israelites were "delivered . . . into the hands
of the Philistines," as the Bible put it. The situation was so bleak
that when Samson's mother got a visit from an angel of Yahweh,
the angel didn't go so far as to promise full deliverance. The
message, according to the Bible, was merely that Samson would
"begin to rescue" the Israelites from the power of the Philistines.

The Philistine warriors, with their crowns of feathers, would dominate the valley for not much more than half a century. Historians don't know exactly how the Israelites pushed the Philistines out. But by around 1050 B.C., Ir-Shemesh was firmly in the hands of the Israelites and they had renamed it Beth Shemesh. The town was just inside the Israelite border, facing the coastal kingdom of the Philistines. The Book of Samuel says that when the Philistines decided to return the Israelite Ark of the Covenant after capturing it in battle, it was to Beth Shemesh that the Philistines sent the Ark, drawn by two oxen in a wooden cart. When the Ark arrived, the Israelites "were reaping their wheat harvest in the valley" near Beth Shemesh.

Around 1000 B.C. the Israelites consolidated their takeover of the promised land. David, their most brilliant strategist and greatest king, pulled together the twelve tribes of Israel to create the United Monarchy. He pushed the Philistines back inside a strip of coastal land around Gaza, at last making the Israelites the rulers of Canaan. Yet the Philistines would leave behind their mark. When the Romans made maps twelve centuries later, they would call this region Syria-Palestina, remembering its ancient Philistine overlords. Today, the Philistines have been extinct as an ethnic group for more than 2,500 years, but the name Palestine lives on.

Under David's son King Solomon, the Israelites rebuilt Beth Shemesh as a fortress. They gave it sturdier walls, a new grain storehouse, and a governor's mansion. For two generations, Beth Shemesh served as one the twelve administrative centers of Israel's United Monarchy. However, the Israelites went into decline after only two kings. Solomon's ineffectual son Rehoboam failed to put down a revolt of the northern Israelite tribes. In 928 B.C. the United Kingdom of Israel split apart into two kingdoms, Judah in the south and Israel in the north. About this time, a mysterious calamity occurred at Beth Shemesh: fire of untraceable origin again devastated the town. Some scholars believe Beth Shemesh was put to the torch by Egyptian invaders under Pharaoh Shishak, who invaded Palestine in 924 B.C. and drove his chariots all the way to Jerusalem. Or perhaps it was a plague. Whatever struck Beth Shemesh, its downfall was so

devastating that it remained uninhabited for several generations, and its fortifications were never to be rebuilt again. In its
place, King Rehoboam, the ruler of the southern Kingdom of
Judah during Pharaoh Shishak's plundering, chose to fortify the
hilltop village of Zorah, two miles northeast of Beth Shemesh.

Instead of protecting their border towns against foreigners,
the rival Israelite kingdoms dissipated their strength squabbling
with each other. In about 786 B.C. the northern kingdom, Israel,
unleashed a punitive raid against the southern kingdom, Judah,
which included the Sorek Valley. Near Beth Shemesh, armies
of the two met in battle. The Book of Chronicles says the northern Israelites won so decisively that the troops of Judah "fled
every man to his tent" and the southern king was seized as a
captive. The rivalry sputtered on while external enemies got
hungrier. By the end of the century, the Assyrian Empire
pushed down from the north, destroyed Israel, and reduced
Judah to a vassal. Under Assyrian pressure, the Jews of Judah
adopted alien rituals, at one point building an idol so big that
it took a thousand men to carry it, according to the Talmud. The
Assyrians gave way to even harsher rulers, the Babylonians,
who came from what is now Iraq. When the puppet king of
Judah tried to revolt against the Babylonians, a vengeful army
marched south in 587 B.C., burning towns and cities, destroying
the Jewish Temple in Jerusalem, and sending thousands of Jews
into exile in Babylon. Thus closed the 425-year reign of the Jews
in the Land of Canaan. Archaeological evidence shows that Beth
Shemesh was among the towns burned and leveled. By then it
was an unwalled village with copper furnaces, grape presses,
and vats of dye and olive oil.

What happened to the Canaanites while the Israelites dominated the Valley of Sorek? They became slave laborers and
concubines for the Israelites and gradually sank into an underclass. Ultimately the Canaanites would mix with wave after
wave of conquerors and bedouins—Israelites, Philistines, Egyptians, Assyrians, Babylonians, Persians, Greeks, Romans, Arabs.
Miscegenation and similarities of language soon broke down the
ethnic margins between the Israelites and the older tribes who

lived in and around Canaan. The Talmud tells of King David praising God for having permitted Israelites to take Ammonite and Moabite women in marriage, since this allowed David, a descendant of the Moabite woman Ruth, to be accepted as an Israelite in "the Assembly of Israel." A generation later, David's son Solomon would keep seven hundred wives and three hundred concubines. These included "many strange women . . . women of the Moabites, Ammonites, Edomites, Zidonians, and Hittites," the Book of Kings records.

Under David and Solomon, the religion of the Israelites became the dominant religion in Palestine. But traces of Canaanite cults would survive for centuries and even insert themselves in odd ways. Scholars in Israel still debate the meaning of one ancient inscription mentioning the Israelite God Yahweh "and his Asherah." To some Israeli experts, the inscription suggests that according to some very early traditions, Yahweh took Asherah—the Canaanite fertility goddess—as his consort. The inscription was found on a goblet at an archaeological site just twenty miles south of the Valley of Sorek. After the Babylonian conquest in 587 B.C., the Jews hung on for another seven hundred years as subjects of conquerors. Sometimes the Jews managed to win a semblance of sovereignty over Palestine, along with a considerable degree of religious independence. But then along came another foreign conqueror to destroy their ambitions of restoring David's kingdom. First the Babylonians, then the Persians, the Greeks, and finally the Romans stormed in. Because the Israelite village of Zorah was high on a defensible ridge, it was one of only a few dozen towns in Palestine where Jews held on during the century and a half when most Jews were captives in Babylon. The Jews of Zorah had to share the valley with neighbors: descendants of the Canaanite tribes that had lived in Palestine since before the time of Exodus as well as Arabs, Samaritans and others who had filtered in from the desert to fill the land left vacant by the exiled Jews.

The Sorek Valley can claim one footnote in the history of primitive Christianity. The first Christian martyr, Saint Stephen, is supposed by Christian tradition to have been buried on

the top of the ridge at Beit Jimal, just south of the valley. The
New Testament described Stephen, a Greek-speaking Jew who
was one of Jesus Christ's disciples, as an evangelist who "did
great wonders and miracles among the people." While living in
Jerusalem he became a vitriolic critic of some rituals then in use
in the Jewish Temple. So outspoken was he that even while
Jesus was alive, the supreme rabbinical court put Stephen on
trial for speaking against the temple establishment. He replied
with insults: "You stiff-necked people, you always resist the
holy spirit." The rabbinical court condemned Stephen to die,
and he was stoned to death, according to the New Testament.
His supposed burial place is occupied today by a Catholic monastery of the Salesian Order.

During and after the time of Jesus, thousands of Jews lived
throughout the Jerusalem Hills. In A.D. 131 they took a momentous gamble. Outraged by Emperor Hadrian's plans to found a
pagan Roman city in Jerusalem, they fomented an armed revolt aimed at re-establishing a Jewish nation. The Jewish guerrilla commander Simeon Bar-Kokhba declared himself the
Messiah and led a holy war against the Romans. The Valley of
Sorek was a no-man's-land. Emperor Hadrian used a road
through the valley in A.D. 133 to rush his Second Legion from
Egypt toward Jerusalem. The Jewish rebels crisscrossed the
valley transporting supplies between their hideouts in the
hills. Finally in A.D. 135 the Romans squashed the rebellion. According to the Roman historian Dio Cassius, the Romans destroyed 985 Jewish villages and settlements to prevent any new
uprising. Except for a few Jewish villages in the Jordan Valley, the entire Jewish population of the province of Judea was
either driven into exile, sold into slavery, or killed. Then, to
remove the traces of a Jewish presence here, Hadrian changed
the name of the region from Judea to Syria-Palestina. Jews living a hundred miles north of the valley, in what is now Israel's
Galilee region, never joined Bar-Kokhba's revolt. As a result,
the Romans did not drive them away, and a few thousand Jews
remained in northern Syria-Palestina through the Middle
Ages and on into the twentieth century. But in the Sorek Val-

ley, Jewish settlement was finished. It would not resume for seventeen centuries.

Life went on in the valley after the Jews were driven out. In the ruins of Beth Shemesh, archaeologists have found three Roman coins that were minted after the Bar-Kokhba revolt. The coins have been identified by American scholars as dating from A.D. 146, 351, and 580. Coins from a spread of centuries are not the only indication that the place remained inhabited. In A.D. 380 a Christian bishop named Eusebius wrote a geography of the Holy Land that took note of towns called Zorah, Eshtaol, and Beth Shemesh.

Those who remained in the Jerusalem Hills after the Romans expelled the Jews were a potpourri: farmers and vineyard growers, pagans and converts to Christianity, descendants of the Arabs, Persians, Samaritans, Greeks, and old Canaanite tribes. The latest of the three coins dated from when Palestine was part of the Byzantine Empire. During those Byzantine times of the fifth century, just after Rome itself had fallen to the Vandals and the Visigoths, a Christian monastery with heavy stone walls and large rooms rose on the ruins of Beth Shemesh. It was during this period that Byzantine monks dug up what they thought were the bones of Saint Stephen while exploring an abandoned Jewish graveyard at Beit Jimal. Stephen's purported relics were carried to Jerusalem and later to Rome.

Armies from deep in the Arabian desert, full of the zeal of the brand-new religion Islam, spread over the Holy Land in the seventh century. It was a lost cause for the Byzantines after the battle of Ajnadayn, when their mercenary army was slaughtered by Arab forces. The battle was fought in A.D. 634 about ten miles north of the Sorek Valley. After that, the Arabs took only six years to squeeze the Byzantine colonialists out of Jerusalem and other walled cities. One of their first acts was to allow Jews to return to Jerusalem. Following their remarkably easy victory, the Arabs settled down in large military camps. Within a few generations, the occupiers bought or seized land around the camps for descendants of the soldiers. In time the Arabs would expand their holdings into the Valley of Sorek itself. As far as historians can tell today, the Arab invaders saw no reason to expel any of the peasants from the valley or even to build fortifications. Instead of spending money on new building, they or the indigenous peasants broke down the walls of the Byzantine monastery and rearranged the stone blocks to make small homes.

The next invading wave, the Christian crusaders of Europe, came to wrestle the Holy Land from the Moslems in A.D. 1099. High on a ridge near ancient Zorah, the crusader troops built a settlement. The crusaders also built a castle to guard the road leading south. By the twelfth century, the villages in the valley had been awarded by the French crusader Godfrey de Bouillon to his favorite charity, the Church of the Holy Sepulcher. A Christian traveler who passed this way in 1280 noted that the biblical town Beth Shemesh was now called Ain Schemes, evidently an Arabization of its name in Old Testament times.

The crusaders's purpose may have been noble, but their record as occupiers of the Holy Land was as ugly as anyone's. They killed or sold into slavery about 25,000 Jews and uncounted thousands of Arabs. And they raped or otherwise impregnated an appreciable number of Arab women. Eventually the crusaders were driven back by the legendary Arab commander Saladin and finally evicted from Palestine in 1291 by a military clique in Egypt called the Mamluks. Six centuries later, a French scholar would conclude that some crusader seed still persisted among the Palestinian peasantry. In 1885 he wrote of "the yellow hair and blue eyes that sometimes even at the present day the astonished traveler may see beneath a Bedaween *kefeeyeh* or a *fellah* turban."

Through the millennia, the tides of events crashing over the valley failed to erase the traces of the first settlers, the Canaanites. Nor did they rub out the later imprint left by the Israelites before they were made refugees by Hadrian. Human habitations in this valley lasted for centuries in the same spots, and so did the same ancient myths. In the year 1322, Isaac Estori ha-Parhi, a French-born physician and amateur geographer, made his way to the valley and found that the biblical villages of Zorah

and Eshtaol still existed. A decade later, another traveler on a
Holy Land expedition made his way up the ridge to Zorah.
Villagers told him it was the grave of Samson. "It is a very
ancient landmark," Rabbi Itzhak Chelo wrote in his journal.
"And on it you have a painting of the jawbone of the ass with
which he hit the Philistines."

· 3 ·

ON THE EVE
OF THE RETURN

Edward Robinson earned his living in the 1830s by teaching theology at the Andover Theological Seminary in Massachusetts. But his real passion was for poking around Palestine, a territory as wild and unknown to Western eyes as the Yukon. After making his way by steamer to Palestine, Robinson would find some horses and enlist the help of a bedouin tracker and of his friend Eli Smith, a missionary who spoke Arabic. Together they would take off across the hills on pack trips. Riding horseback to hundreds of unmapped villages, Robinson inaugurated a new school of biblical research which derived its clues to the location of ancient sites from the folk memories of Arab villagers. That was how he would rediscover the Sorek Valley, which had been unrecorded by any Westerner since the Middle Ages.

The view he brought back was a glimpse at Palestine on the eve of a new chapter in the world's longest-running territorial conflict. The Arab villages he saw were under the dying grip of the six-hundred-year-old Turkish empire. One of those villages in the Sorek Valley would be squeezed so hard to support the Turkish military machine that the Arab villagers would lose their land. When that happened, it would create a historic opening, one that would allow the first Jewish settlers to return to the valley since Jews were expelled by the Romans seventeen centuries before. That, of course, was something Edward Robinson could not see coming. Nor could he anticipate the ethnic melee that has come to be called the Arab-Israeli conflict. All he observed was the precondition that helped bring it about.

During his first Palestine expedition in 1838, Robinson rode through the mountain villages above the south rim of the valley. "We found several of the chief men sitting on carpets under a fig tree in the middle of the village, smoking and holding converse with each other," Robinson wrote in his journal. He talked for a while with an Arab sheikh. "Coffee was served for us," Robinson wrote. "He tried to persuade us to remain all night, saying the people of the village where we expected to lodge were not to be trusted."

Robinson stared down at the villages in the valley and became curious. "The whole tract is full of villages and deserted sites and ruins," he wrote in his memoirs, "and many olive groves appear around the former." Though he didn't have time to ride down from the ridge this trip, he was intrigued enough to return fourteen years later. On an April morning in 1852, Robinson and Smith rode their horses across the opposite rim of the valley. They crossed a low ridge and followed a creek "through rich fields of grain." The creek would lead them toward Saraa, an Arab village that Robinson would realize was the site of Samson's ancient Zorah. "After eight minutes," he wrote in his journal, "we reached the main source of the brook in a noble fountain, walled up square with large hewn stones, and gushing over with fine water. This is the fountain of Zorah, and as we passed on, we overtook no less than twelve females toiling upward toward the village, each with her jar of water on her head. The village, the fountain, the fields, the mountains, and the females bearing water, all transported us back to ancient times; when, in all probability, the mother of Samson often in like manner visited the fountain, and toiled homeward with her jar of water." In an aside to his journal, he called it "inconceivable" that villagers did not use donkeys to haul water; after all, one donkey could carry four jars of water while a woman could carry only one.

Climbing the shoulder of a foothill past the fountain, Robinson found Saraa at the top of a treeless ridge. "It is a miserable village," he wrote, "exposed on this high point to the burning rays of the sun without a trace of shade." From this parched overlook on the northwest rim of the valley, Robinson gazed back in the direction of Jerusalem and saw two streams running out of the Jerusalem Hills and joining to form the Brook of Sorek. "The plains thus shut in are beautiful and fertile," Robinson wrote. He rode down into the valley and stopped first at the village of Artuf. He noted that Artuf was "a poor hamlet of a few houses." After getting directions from a sheikh in Artuf, Robinson decided to ride north through the valley. "At 11:30 [A.M.] we passed close on the left hand of the village, which seemed large, with well-tilled fields and many fruit trees around it." He noted that the village was called Ishwa.

Robinson did not dwell on an enigma he had witnessed: why were the plains "fertile" and the valley's fields "well tilled" while many of the people lived in "miserable" and "poor" villages? Why did some of the villages look to him "deserted, at least for portions of the year"? Modern history wasn't his field. But while acquiring evidence on biblical sites, he was curious enough to store away some impressions that would help resolve the paradox of rich fields and poor villages. First, he noticed an ecological clue: that the top of the ridgeline at Saraa had "not a trace of shade." During Canaanite and Israelite times, the valley was blanketed with evergreens. But over the next three millennia the land of milk and honey had eroded. Generations of inhabitants and conquerors had scraped the ridges almost bare of trees. Since crusader times the erosion had probably accelerated, for evidence now suggests that the climate throughout Palestine changed for the worse in the second half of the sixteenth century. Studies have shown that the level of the Dead Sea began a three-hundred-year decline in the sixteenth century, indicating a long-term drop in rainfall throughout Pales-

tine. By the time Robinson rode over the ridge, the effects of
man and climate combined to turn much of historic Palestine
into a drought-vulnerable savannah interspersed with what
looked like rocky South Dakota badlands. The decline in rainfall
would not reverse itself until the second half of the nineteenth
century.

Robinson formed another impression: Palestine was a tapes-
try of small rural clan dominions set apart by slow-healing
animosities. He learned from the villagers that throughout the
region, the Arab villages were divided into two alliances of
clans, one called the Keis and the other called the Yamenis. "No
person of whom we inquired could tell the origin or the nature
of this distinction," Robinson wrote. "It seems indeed to consist
in little more than the fact that one is the enemy of the other."
Robinson discovered later that the Keis were originally tribesmen from the northern half of the Arabian peninsula and the
Yamenis were from southern Arabia. About twelve hundred
years before, just as the Arabs were conquering Palestine from
the Byzantine overlords, the northern and southern Arab tribes
were torn apart by a civil war over who should succeed the
Prophet Mohammed. Ever since, the Keis and Yamenis had
been enemies. All the villages around the valley owed allegiance
to the Keis. But even in the Keis' territory, local feuds separated
one village from another. That was why the sheikh advised
Robinson not to risk traveling to another nearby village, even
though its people were also Keis. The fighting and suspicions
also contributed to poverty: because there was almost no commerce between the villages, each was forced to live on what it
could grow itself. The feud between the Keis and Yamenis alliances would endure until the early twentieth century, and
even afterward the pattern of clannish fighting continued to
debilitate the Palestinian Arabs.

Robinson's curiosity also led him to remark on the size of the
taxes that governors of the Ottoman Empire managed to extract
from the peasants. He took notes on thirteen kinds of taxes in
one village where his guide lived. The main tax was a share of
a village's harvest, calculated by counting how many oxen the

villagers owned. There were also taxes for each goat, each donkey, each camel, each olive tree, and each fig tree. There were
three kinds of per capita taxes and a tax on homemade wine,
even if the village made no wine. Taxes kept coming due during
good harvests and bad, a relentless drain on the land's output.

Taxes like these were the underpinnings of the Ottoman Empire, one of the most enduring and expensive domains in all
history. From their emerald-encrusted gold throne in the Top-
kapi Palace in Constantinople, now Istanbul, the Ottoman sultans ruled an empire that extended in the early nineteenth century from Algeria to Mecca to Hungary. One of the vital organs
of the empire was Greater Syria, the Ottoman province that
took in Palestine, Syria, and Lebanon. The Sorek Valley was
part of Syria and came under the direct control of the Ottoman
governor of Jerusalem.

The empire had survived since 1326—and had controlled
Palestine since 1516—through its ability to induce poor villagers
to pay taxes. Instead of paying salaries to its military officers, the
imperial treasury awarded them fiefdoms in the territory they
occupied. As long as these fief holders remitted their quota of
taxes, they were entitled to keep whatever extra they could milk
out of the peasants. At first, the fief holders were Turkish cavalrymen who could be called upon by the sultan's governors to
put down peasant rebellions and escort caravans of pilgrims
returning from Mecca. The cavalrymen lost their monopoly on
fiefdoms as the introduction of gunpowder made them prey to
rifle-carrying foot soldiers. At the same time the needs of the
imperial treasury swelled, so the sultan's representatives also
began relying on private enterprise to collect taxes. They began
selling tax-collecting rights on each fief, making the holder a
"tax farmer" for life.

If there was any lasting benefit in this arrangement, it was to
latter-day researchers. By looking at the jumble of old tax registers, scholars working in the Ottoman archives have uncovered
clues to what village life in Palestine was like three centuries
before Robinson's arrival. Compared to the poor and transitory
existence that prevailed in the more low-lying regions of Pales-

tine closer to the coast, life in the Sorek Valley was stable and
fairly prosperous in the Middle Ages. Protected from bedouin
raids by mountain geography, these ancient villages continued
to show the same remarkable resilience that they manifested
from the Canaanites through the Israelites to the crusaders.

Six Arab villages dotted around the Sorek Valley during the
sixteenth century would still exist in 1945. One was Mahmoud
Hamdan's home village of Ishwa. Another would become the
site of the Jewish colony where Yoshko Levy grew up. The
others were called Deir Aban, Islin, Rafat, and Saraa. One of the
most prosperous of these during the Middle Ages, Artuf, clung
to a hillside above the Brook of Sorek. A Turkish census taker
listed twenty adult males as living in Artuf, all of them Moslems. It was an era when the Turkish census counted adult
males only. If women and children had been counted, the village's total population would have come to about a hundred. In
those days the village boasted vineyards, fruit trees, barley and
wheat fields, and vegetable crops. The tax rolls listed Artuf's
income as about 40 percent higher than that of neighboring
Saraa, the biblical village Robinson would write about three
centuries later. Pity the eighty-five Saraa villagers who lived
across the valley from Artuf. They were pictured in the 1596 tax
rolls as having less income from grape arbors and fruit trees, so
they had to depend largely on grain. The largest village in the
neighborhood, Deir Aban, had a half-Moslem, half-Christian
population totaling about 230. These sixteenth-century Christians were probably Arabs whose ancestors had converted to
Christianity either during the Byzantine era or during crusader
times. The five other villages were all-Moslem. Sometime in the
next three centuries or so, the Christians would convert back to
Islam or move away from Deir Aban, perhaps to predominantly
Christian Bethlehem or Ramallah.

By the early eighteenth century the Sorek Valley came under
the Turkish system of selling tax fiefdoms to the highest bidder.
The archives record a decade-long squabble starting in 1705,
which saw two rivals from the same Deir Aban family appeal
up and down the Ottoman chain of command for the right to

be a lifetime tax farmer. Ottoman files show how one tax farmer was dismissed after he was charged by his rival with *kasr-i-yed*—failure to make the payment for the lifetime rights to collect taxes. Not satisfied, the ousted fief-holder lined up well-placed supporters from Jerusalem's Moslem hierarchy, and his appeal went all the way to Constantinople.

By the nineteenth century, the rights to collect taxes in Palestine had long since been sold by Ottoman governors to local Arab notables who took the places of the old Turkish cavalrymen. The sheikh who gave Robinson coffee was not only a village aristocrat but also a minor Ottoman functionary. Often these notables were the heads of the roughly three dozen most powerful and best-connected Palestinian clans, many of which claimed descent from seventh-century Arab conquerors. Tax farming created class differences among Palestinian Arabs that didn't exist in the tradition of Arab desert clans. Under generations of Ottoman patronage, Arab families with tax-farming privileges became petty aristocrats, while other families stayed peasants.

This was only one of the forces combining in the nineteenth century to loosen the peasants' grip on the land. More important, the Ottoman Empire was getting feebler and more pressed for money. After ruling for six centuries, the sultans no longer had the resources to maintain armies big enough to scare off challengers. Along the outer rim of territories, Ottoman governors were breaking away. In fact, during Robinson's first journey, Palestine was temporarily in the hands of the rebellious Ottoman governor in Egypt. Some of the vacant villages Robinson saw may well have been destroyed by his Egyptian troops, who were forced to put down peasant revolts near Jerusalem in the 1830s. There is a ravine south of the valley where these nineteenth-century Egyptians killed a score of Palestinian Arab villagers, according to local legend. By the time Robinson returned in 1852, European powers had forced the Egyptian rebel, Mohammed Ali, to withdraw from Palestine.

That was only a momentary reprieve for the sultans. Every capital in Europe realized that the Ottoman Empire remained vulnerable. The weakness of the Ottomans quickly inspired controversy over control of the holy places of Palestine. France and Russia fell into diplomatic sparring over the rights of the Roman Catholic and Russian Orthodox churches in Jerusalem. Within a year, the dispute would burst into the Crimean War, a three-year struggle on the shores of the Black Sea fought out between the Russians and an alliance of the French, British, and Ottoman Turks. Nothing much was accomplished by the war except the deaths of 500,000 men and the further depletion of the Ottoman treasury. The sultans in Constantinople, seeing their hourglass running toward empty, took ever more desperate steps to raise money. The imperial treasury negotiated loan after loan from Western bankers, even though that meant turning over resources of the empire as collateral to outside financiers. In Palestine and elsewhere throughout the empire, the imperial treasury granted timber-cutting concessions, salt concessions, tobacco concessions, silk concessions, railroad concessions. As debts climbed and resources were mortgaged to foreigners, the sultans came to realize they needed to extract even more money from their oldest asset, the peasants. The result was a series of Ottoman land "reforms" from which the peasants would never recover.

The peasants lost control of the land so gradually that nobody realized it was happening. Up until the early nineteenth century, a Palestinian village was a virtually indivisible unit of property. All the wheat-growing land in the realm was technically owned by the sultan. But in practice, the land was held by the villagers, who in many cases treated it as communally owned property. Every year, these villagers assigned their land among themselves for cultivation in proportion to the number of plowing animals each family owned. The communal form of land ownership was an indispensable safety net for the peasants—the fellaheen, as they were called. It meant that taxes could impoverish them but couldn't force them permanently off the land. Sheikhs who held tax-farming privileges could live more comfortably than peasants, but they couldn't own large blocks of land. But now the pressures on the imperial treasury would cause the peasants' safety net to be dismantled in the name of efficiency.

Sultan Mahmoud II began the unraveling of peasant owner-ship when he ended the old system of lifetime tax fiefs in 1831. The abolition of fiefs brought vast tracts of land back into the hands of the state and disrupted centuries-old feudal relation-ships between peasant farmers and their sheikhs, who had ful-filled a double role as clan protectors and the sultan's bagmen. Now new ways of regulating the land and collecting taxes were being spread throughout the empire. In 1839 the sultan issued the first of several "reform" decrees that, among other things, prom-ised to replace tax farming with a central system of tax collec-tion. What this would mean over the next decade in Palestine was the replacement of old lifetime tax fiefs with annual auc-tions that sold the right to collect taxes to the highest bidder.

A more important rip in the social fabric came in 1858 when a new Ottoman land code was introduced by imperial decree. It was intended to reclaim full government control of land throughout the empire, but it had the opposite effect. For the first time, the law made it feasible for private individuals with no connection to the imperial dynasty to own, inherit, and sell large tracts of land. Two provisions of the new land code in-teracted to put the peasants at a disadvantage. First, the old system of communal landholdings was abolished, and instead each male villager was supposed to enjoy land rights as an indi-vidual. Second and more important, every landowner was put under an obligation to register land with the government. The deeds and the 1858 law permitting land sales made it possible for the first time for anyone with money to speculate on property without having to live in the villages and work the land. It was a consequence the sultan never intended.

The fellaheen didn't automatically avail themselves of the right to register land in their own names. Instead, whole villages were soon recorded in the name of sheikhs, tax farmers, or money lenders. Clan tradition was one reason for the peasants' failure to stake their own claims: by Arab custom going back to bedouin times, they would scarcely question the judgment of their tribal sheikhs. The peasants were also reluctant, right after the Crimean war, to put their names on any Turkish government list. If there was one thing they loathed more than taxes, it was conscription into the Turkish army. In any event, peasants from some poorer villages were not free to register the land in their own names because the land was already encumbered by debts to tax farmers.

Among the first Palestinian Arabs to get sucked into the landless proletariat were the fellaheen who lived in Artuf. Over the previous three centuries Artuf had slipped behind other Arab villages in the valley until it became the "poor hamlet" that Robinson observed. When a drought ruined crops of all the villages in the 1860s, Artuf was pushed into an even more desperate predicament. The villagers fell so far in debt that even after the harvests improved in the next decade, they would still owe 100 percent of their crop each year for unpaid debts and taxes. Finally in about 1877 a Turkish tax collector turned up in Artuf, sealed its grain storage pens, and ordered the villagers not to use any grain until the tax bill was settled.

Some weeks later, another Ottoman functionary descended on Artuf along with a detachment of soldiers. He demanded that the villagers pay off their accumulated debts, but they said they could not. According to village tradition, the Turkish soldiers proceeded to arrest the sheikh of Artuf and at least one other elder. After binding them head and foot, the Turkish soldiers prepared to "torture their soul to make them pay off the debt." To accomplish this, the soldiers are said to have hung the elders head down from a fig tree. As they were dangling in midair, the soldiers piled dry thornbushes under them and made ready to light a fire. Just as the fire was about to be lit, an "angel" is said to have appeared from the edge of the crowd. The "angel" proposed to pay off the accumulated debt—provided the sheikh would turn over the village land to him. With that, the upside-down sheikh is supposed to have agreed to turn over all the wheat fields and meadow land of Artuf to the "angel."

Whether or not the tale of torture is fanciful, there are century-old land records and diplomatic archives in Jerusalem that do confirm that a speculator bought Artuf's land by paying off the taxes. An 1883 diplomatic report by the Austrian consul in Jerusalem identified the "angel" as Sir Iskandar Eifulend, who was a translator and consul in the Spanish consulate in Jerusalem. He may well have sent a middleman to Artuf, although that is not recorded. What the diplomatic account did report was that Sir Iskandar obtained 1,250 acres of Artuf's land by paying the Turkish government a tax debt then equivalent to $1,460.

This and other Austrian records indicate that Sir Iskandar bought the land in 1877 and held it for the next six years. Other records indicate he built a farming estate on the land befitting a country gentleman. In 1883, Sir Iskandar placed the land up for sale when he decided to move back to Spain. During his tenure, the fellaheen of Artuf had been safe. Even though they had lost their ownership rights, Sir Iskandar had allowed them to remain on the land as sharecroppers. But that concession was soon to be threatened by another would-be purchaser. Here in the valley, the struggle between Jews and Arabs was about to begin.

· 4 ·

COME
THE COLONIZERS

*A*ll the Rev. Moses Friedlander wanted to do was to build a little mission outside of Jerusalem where he could convert Jews to Christianity. That is why he turned his eyes toward the Sorek Valley.

Friedlander, an English Jew by birth who had become an Anglican missionary, was the Palestine representative for a musty little do-gooder committee called the London Society for Promoting Christianity Amongst the Jews. Here he was in 1882 in the middle of the biggest spurt of Jewish immigration into Palestine since the Middle Ages. Like his fellow Anglican missionaries in the society, Friedlander was convinced that Jews now arriving from Russia would prove more responsive to the gospel than the roughly 25,000 Jews who already lived in Palestine. Nearly all of these "Old Settlement" Jews lived in the impenetrable orthodox ghettos of Jerusalem, Safed, Tiberias, and Hebron. They spent their days praying and memorizing the Talmud while living on *chalukkah*, the Jewish charitable dole. By contrast the new Jews from Russia seemed ever so much more "liberal-minded," as one of Friedlander's British associates put it. This might be the best chance for the London society to flourish since its founding in 1810 under the patronage of His Highness the Duke of Kent.

But Friedlander's scheme was no more outlandish on its face than the ambition of Rabbi Yechiel Pines, one of a tiny coterie of early dreamers of an obscure new "ism" called Zionism. As a young man in the 1870s still living in the household of his merchant father in Russia, Pines had been influenced by one of the neighborhood Jewish clubs known as Chovevei Zion—Lovers of Zion. Scattered through Russian Poland, Belorussia, and Lithuania, these clubs revolved around courses in Hebrew language, gymnastics, singing, and self-defense. Like many of these local Chovevei Zion enthusiasts, Pines believed that the Jewish people must realize their destiny by assembling in the land of their prophets to build a new Kingdom of David. The early Russian Zionists were impelled more by a yearning than a plan. But it had been powerful enough to cause Rabbi Pines to emigrate to Palestine in 1877. At the age of thirty-five, he jumped at the chance to go as the representative of the Montefiore Fund, a London Jewish charity that aimed to build housing and workshops for Jews in Jerusalem. Full of energy and backed by his family's money, Rabbi Pines turned some of his attention to another project that was too controversial for the Montefiore Fund's taste. Pines explored the intricacies of buying blocks of land in Palestine and reselling them in smaller plots to families from Russia willing to become modern Palestine's first Jewish farmers.

Four years after Pines arrived, an explosion of anti-Semitism in czarist Russia gave Zionism an opportunity to sink its first strong roots in Palestine. Russia was then the heartland of world Jewry. At least half of the Victorian world's eight million Jews were then concentrated in Russia's Pale of Settlement, the zone where the czars had corralled the big Jewish minority that they acquired by annexing most of Poland in the eighteenth century. In this large belt of thirteen provinces along Russia's western frontier, Jews had lived with a measure of tranquillity, with rights comparable to those of the Balts, Poles, and other minorities who were not ethnic Russians. Jews in the Pale were free to worship, they spoke their own language—Yiddish—and they had their own literature, schools, and rabbinical colleges. Some occupations, such as operating hotels and village inns, were blocked to them. As in the rest of Europe, Jews in the Pale had to contend with lurking anti-Semitism.

Within their own communities, though, Jews were generally left alone. They were, that is, until Easter Sunday 1881, when anti-Jewish riots rippled through the Ukraine and then throughout all of western Russia. These pogroms started after an assassin's bomb killed Russian Czar Alexander II. The killer was a Russian nihilist, not a Jew, but rumors percolated that Jews were behind the attack. Within the next two years, Russian mobs attacked Jews and their shops in two hundred towns, killing dozens of them with minimal interference from police. In May 1882 the new czar issued decrees closing the countryside to further Jewish settlement and driving tens of thousands into city slums. The czar made it attractive for Jews to do only one thing: to leave Russia. Thus began a momentous demographic shift, the emigration of 1.5 million Jews over the next quarter of a century from Eastern Europe to Western Europe, North America, and Palestine.

The poorest of these Russian refugees started filing down gangplanks in the Palestinian port of Jaffa in 1882. The handful of Jewish activists already there had almost no resources to resettle them, but they tried. Few were more energetic than Rabbi Pines. In 1882 he and a friend started the Israel Renaissance Society, whose goal was to make a spoken tongue out of scholarly Hebrew. Later that year he founded the Return of the Craftsmen and Smiths Society, a Zionist-oriented committee to resettle Russian refugees and find them productive work. About the same time, Pines began scouting for land where some of the hardier refugees could start an agricultural settlement. He wanted to emulate Petah Tikvah, Palestine's first Jewish farm colony, which he had helped start only four years earlier. Thanks to some land Pines had helped purchase, Petah Tikvah was starting to take hold. The network of Zionist colonies that Pines would play a part in founding would one day trace the outlines of the state of Israel.

Pines had to grapple with a demographic reality: Palestine was not an empty land. Despite what some Zionist visionaries in Russia imagined, the best farmland was already speckled with Arab villages. Approximately 470,000 Arabs lived in Palestine by 1880, which meant there were already twenty Arabs in Palestine for every Jew. As he appraised the situation, the way to build Zionism was to buy any large piece of land that came up for sale and start a Jewish colony on it. If there happened to be Arab tenant farmers on the land, he and most other early Zionist visionaries saw no reason why they should not be evicted.

That is exactly what Rabbi Pines prepared to do when he heard in 1883 that the village of Artuf and its surrounding fields had been put up for sale. Its first owner, the Spanish "angel," had by now sold the property to a Jewish land broker in Jerusalem. Pines and a friend who ran Mikveh Israel, a Jewish agricultural school near Jaffa, made their way to see the village. Encouraged by what they found, Pines conceived of a plan to sell shares of the land to Jewish refugees from Russia. There was one drawback: the land was being farmed by the Arab sharecroppers who had served the Spaniard Sir Iskandar. To resolve this problem, Pines personally added an extra paragraph in a draft of the land purchase contract. His paragraph specified that the Jerusalemite land broker would have to "uproot" the Arab tenant farmers before any sale to the Russian refugees could become final. This was the proviso that Pines spelled out in his cramped Ashkenazic script on March 6, 1883: "The fellaheen who live in the village [of Artuf] will be removed from the village and their dwellings will be uprooted from it without their retaining any rights except their rights to the olive trees."

Three weeks later, Pines dispatched his first prospective buyer in a horse-drawn wagon from Jaffa. He was Yechiel Brill, who had come to Palestine from the heart of the Russian Pale in Minsk. Brill and one of Pines's associates rode by wagon from morning to midnight until they reached the Catholic monastery at Latrun, halfway between Jaffa and Jerusalem. At Latrun they unhitched the wagon and traveled southeast over the ridges on horseback. After two more hours, they passed Saraa and descended into the Sorek Valley. Upon seeing it, Brill was gripped by its possibilities. He described the valley in his journal as a "flat strip of fields between the mountains [that] was good for planting grains, etc." The mountains around the village of Artuf "are covered with grazing land for livestock and trees for firewood," and the village had twenty acres of olive trees and pomegranates. To his mind, even the village itself had its advantages. He noticed several new buildings, evidently built during Sir Iskandar's tenure, along with elaborate cisterns that had been carved out of the mountains much earlier to capture rain water. "If the surface is repaired, they can be good places for rainwater, wine, and olive oil," he wrote. He also saw an abundant spring flowing out of the side of the mountain, but cautioned that it would probably dry up at the end of each summer. Even so, he found a well only twenty minutes from Artuf that gave water all year around. All in all, Artuf did not strike Brill as a "poor hamlet"—the phrase used by biblical scholar Robinson a generation earlier—but rather a place with potential.

Brill also thought the price of 30,000 French francs (equivalent to $6,000) was a bargain. However, his fellow Russian refugees weren't impressed when they accompanied him for a second look. Nine of them rode with him in a wagon from Jaffa past Latrun, then walked another hour and a half while he rode ahead on horseback. From Brill's perspective the nine Russians were ungrateful complainers: "I continued to give these farmers the benefit of my wisdom and advised them to investigate this place further," he wrote, "but my words fell on deaf ears." Brill would remember speaking "softly and harshly" to the farmers, who nonetheless balked on grounds that their colony would be too far from Jerusalem and Jaffa. "If someone would die, where will he be buried?" one man asked him. Brill replied by reminding them the place was good enough to bury one of Judaism's forefathers. "You will bury your dead in Artuf, between Zorah and Eshtaol, at the resting place of our father Samson," Brill said.

It was no use. The Russians turned down the chance to buy Artuf. As a fallback, Pines asked his friend Avraham Koppelman to try to sell Artuf to other potential settlers during his forthcoming trip to Russia. Koppelman tried. He carried the contract, including its eviction clause, on his visits to Kharkov, Minsk, and Moscow in the summer of 1883. The Ezra emigration society in Kharkov did make a down payment on one share of Artuf. So did the emigration society in Minsk. A few individual Jews in Moscow also made pledges, but even with the fear of more pogroms, Koppelman could not raise enough money to meet the price. At least for the moment, Artuf's Arabs were saved from eviction when Rabbi Pines's six-month option expired and the deal collapsed.

That put the land back on the market just when the London Society for the Promotion of Christianity Amongst the Jews was looking for a place to start a Jewish refugee camp. Following the first pogroms, the society tapped charitable feelings among the British upper classes to raise the equivalent of $16,000 in donations for Jewish refugees. The sponsors had a double purpose: to help alleviate their destitution and to keep them from growing "dependent on the Jerusalem rabbinate." As a first step, chief proselytizer Moses Friedlander opened a Christian mission in Jerusalem for refugees. Every day, more than a hundred of these "poor exiles" were handed "the immediate necessities" as well as a Christian prayer service, according to his reports to London. Friedlander wasn't satisfied with merely operating a soup kitchen. With the backing of his London patrons, he also took steps to found a farm community outside Jerusalem where he hoped Jews could settle and eventually become baptized Christians. Toward that end, the society bought Artuf for 45,000 French francs (then about $9,000) in the fall of 1883. The land they acquired was the same 1,250 acres that the "angel" Iskandar had bought at one-sixth the price.

The Artuf mission was inaugurated in October 1883, bringing Jews back to the Jerusalem Hills for the first time since Emperor Hadrian. That milestone went unnoticed as the assemblage of Christian missionaries and Jewish refugees sang hymns and said prayers in English, German, and Hebrew. Twenty-six Jewish families moved into temporary wooden buildings at Artuf the following month. The missionaries promised that they could keep Jewish religious books and hold Jewish prayers in a special room. In exchange, the settlers agreed to listen to weekly sermons and to send their children to a Bible school where both the New and Old Testaments were taught. The missionaries had originally convinced forty-six Jewish refugee families to sign agreements to join the mission, but twenty families dropped out after Jewish newspapers charged that the mission would Christianize Jews by force. Even those Jews who did join the mission were not fully sold on Christianity, as the missionaries soon discovered. In one early report to London, Friedlander admitted that only one-third of the Jewish colonists intended to become Christians. The other two-thirds, he wrote, "are Jews in every sense, and yet do not object to be identified with us."

Like many refugee camps, Artuf was disagreeable and sometimes scary. During the first winter, no fewer than 150 Jewish refugees were packed into temporary sheds the Christians had set up for them. "It requires a stout heart to be happy in such a dwelling, with wife and children," Friedlander reported to London. There weren't enough warm clothes and bedding, he reported, and it was "by no means a pleasant sight" to see barefoot refugee children walking on the dirt floors. Six months later, Friedlander wrote that "the shed they live in is just as much too hot now as it was too cold in the winter." The weather was not their only hardship. As newcomers to Palestine, they had no concept of how to make the farm flourish. "They live for a time in an apparent state of serfdom in which they can call nothing their own," Friedlander wrote. "They have hard work to perform to which they are not used; they do it badly and, of course, get scolded instead of rewarded; they have only very poor fare, never seeing meat the whole week through sometimes."

Having fled to Palestine out of fear of Russian pogroms, the Jewish refugees told the missionaries they were afraid that they might be massacred by their Arab neighbors. Nothing happened, but the Jews took turns serving as night watchmen. They also asked the missionaries to supply them with guns—"so they may look formidable in the eyes of the sons of Ishmael," as

Friedlander put it. He sympathetically endorsed their request for weapons to London. Thus he passed on one of the earliest requests for armaments of the Arab-Jewish conflict. "It is for our purpose, not necessary to have breech-loaders with the latest improvements," Friedlander wrote to his London patrons in January 1884. "Any sort of dangerous-looking and brightly shining weapons will do."

When it came to describing the Arab inhabitants of Artuf, the British missionaries summoned the disdainful tone of a British gentleman describing a visit to some fetid but colorful Egyptian bazaar. "The village is one of the miserable villages in which the fellaheen live," the Rev. A. Hastings Kelk wrote, "but it is finely situated on a hill at the junction of two valleys and just opposite to a third valley. . . . The village, as it is, is of no value to us but we hope to improve it for the fellaheen. . . ." For his part, Friedlander bemoaned the large piles of cow manure that the Artuf peasants collected to fertilize the fields and fuel their bread ovens. "How the fellaheen can exist at all among the dung-hills of many centuries is one of those things nobody outside their circle can understand," he remarked in one of his missionary letters.

Despite all the tribulations, Friedlander reported to London that "the Gospel was preached in Artuf in a manner in which it could not be anywhere else in Palestine, and was really making its way." Still, the effort to Christianize Jews didn't bear much fruit. Kelk baptized seven Jewish converts in the winter of 1883–84. Following the next harvest, the missionaries organized a thanksgiving dinner in the communal dining room to coincide with the Jewish harvest feast of Succoth. After a sermon by Friedlander, the missionaries invited the colonists to step forward for communion. Only one Jew got up and took the sacrament.

Jewish elders in Jerusalem were mortified at the prospect of any Jews converting. To undercut Friedlander's mission, they formed the Society for Assistance for Those Led Astray. The society wrote letters to the Jewish colonists in Artuf suggesting that they go to work instead on a new Jewish-run farm settle-

ment in the lowlands, closer to the Mediterranean coast. Within
the first year, more than half of the Jews in the mission departed.
And over the next three years the Artuf settlement withered
away because of crop failures, diseases, and disputes over the
Jews' desire to worship in their own faith. In all, only eleven
Jews were recorded as converting to Christianity. By the end of
1886 the settlement was empty, and a Jewish newspaper in Jerusalem could report with satisfaction that "the settlement of the
inciters has been dismantled." Binyamin Cohen, one of Friedlander's settlers, would later insist that the Christians threw him
out. "One Saturday they made a sudden visit and found us
praying, as we had in our village in Lithuania," Cohen would
recall in the 1920s. "They were very angry and made us leave the
place. If they hadn't found us, we might still be farmers working
that land."

To the several thousand Arabs of the surrounding villages,
the flow of events must have looked incredibly rapid and strange
in the late nineteenth century. The Christian mission at Artuf
wasn't the only instance of foreigners penetrating the valley.
Back in 1866 the villagers of Saraa on the north rim of the valley
had likewise fallen behind on their taxes and had lost land in a
forced tax sale. Another "angel," a Christian Arab from the Abu
Souwan family of Jerusalem, had purchased several thousand
acres of their farmland on behalf of an Italian monastic order
called the Latin Patriarchate. Then came work crews to build
something never before seen in Palestine, a railroad. By the
early 1890s the crews had set iron rails right across the valley and
then on into the hills toward Jerusalem. The railroad men even
began work on a train station in the Sorek Valley, which until
then was barely accessible by wagon. On December 4, 1891, an
American-made locomotive chugged for the first time from Jaffa
to the station site, which stood between Artuf and Deir Aban.
Trains began steaming from Jaffa to Jerusalem in the summer
of 1892. It wouldn't be long before trains would stop at the Deir
Aban–Artuf station every day en route between Jerusalem and
the coast.

The next set of newcomers would have an even more endur-

ing impact on the valley. They were fifty-five Jews from Bulgaria, coming in 1895 to found one of the early Zionist colonies
in Palestine. The dream of returning to "Zion" sprang out of
Jewish nationalist impulses and from a desire to revive Jewish
culture. It was one of a dozen manifestations of ethnic pride
with which nineteenth-century Europe was awash, from the
Jung Deutschland movement in Berlin to Louis Kossuth's independence movement in Hungary to Pan-Slavism in the Balkans.
Compared to these other isms, Zionism seemed an unlikely candidate for success. Pines and the other proponents had no backing from the Jewish establishment in the West and no ideological manifesto. The Austrian journalist Theodor Herzl would
not write his world-shaking pamphlet *Der Judenstaat* until 1896.
Even after that, most Jews outside Eastern Europe were slow to
embrace Herzl's call for "the restoration of the Jewish state."

But the Bulgarians were true believers. They were fanatical
enough about the cause that each of the twelve families had
agreed they would each give the same first name—Ben-Zion—to
their first sons born in Palestine. They would call their first
daughters either Ziona or Gracia—the latter derived from the
Spanish word for "thanks." So convinced were they that they
were willing to give up safe and prosperous lives to start a farm
in Palestine—even though they knew nothing about farming or
about Palestine. They called themselves the representatives of
the twelve tribes of Israel. Most of them had been merchants in
the larger Bulgarian towns and cities. Among them was Yoshko
Levy's grandfather, Yosef Levy, a merchant from the Bulgarian
provincial town of Tatar-Pazarjik, later Pazardzhik.

One thing that set the Bulgarians apart from virtually all
other early Zionist pioneers in Palestine was that the Bulgarians
were Sephardim—they were descended from Jews who had
been expelled from Spain and Portugal in 1492 and who still
observed Judaism using the old Spanish synagogue rituals. Like
most other Sephardim, they came from families with centuries
of practice in living under Moslem rulers. Most Sephardim had
scattered into the Ottoman Empire after the Spanish expulsion,
since the rest of Europe was closed to them. In Palestine they

were a minority, and this set them a notch below the majority
Ashkenazim—Jews mainly from Central Europe who accepted
the ancient German synagogue ritual and shared centuries of
experience in surviving under Christian kings.

Like Rabbi Pines, the Bulgarians had been touched by the first
stirrings of Zionism. Jewish revival clubs spread into Turkey's
autonomous state of Bulgaria in the 1880s and 1890s. Though
Bulgaria had not been wracked by pogroms, Zionism was just
as strong in the Bulgarian Jewish ghettos as it was in Russia's
Pale of Settlement. Herzl described in his diaries how Bulgarian
Jews came to kiss his hand and greet him as a new Messiah when
he stopped in Sofia in 1896. By then the Bulgarians had already
dispatched several of their members as "messengers" to search
for a tract their whole society could farm, and the colony of
Hartuv had been founded. Their chief messenger, Shabtai
Rifkia, rejected one tract in what would become the heart of Tel
Aviv, having concluded the land had no promise.

He instead fastened on the former Christian mission at Artuf.
After consulting with the manager of the Mikveh Israel agricultural school, the messengers decided the land would accommo-
date all the families in the society. It was big enough, it was only
about a mile from the new railroad station, it was close to Jerusalem. Best of all, it had enough water—or so Rifkia believed. He
might have thought differently if he had seen the valley in August. But he hadn't, and the Bulgarians negotiated a deal with
representatives of the London Christian society by which the
Jews bought the mission property for £1,750 (then $8,750)—a bit
less than the Christians had paid for it in 1883. Along with 1,250
acres, they had acquired twenty-two modest stone buildings,
some of them put up by the Christians or by Sir Iskandar and
some that had been part of Artuf. The mission buildings included two dormitories, a cow shed, a bakery, a laundry, and a
kitchen.

The first three Bulgarian families reached their new land and
founded their settlement on December 18, 1895. It was a settlement based on private-ownership principles, which later would
come to be known in Hebrew as a *moshava*. The Bulgarians

called theirs Hartuv. The name, an adaptation of the old Arabic name Artuf, meant Good Mount in Hebrew. Over the next two years, nine more Bulgarian families arrived to join the first three. In all, about fifty Bulgarian families had put up money to buy plots of land in the moshava, but for the moment the twelve founding families would farm the land in common. The fifty owners were "all people of means with the physical powers necessary for successful colonists," according to an optimistic report in 1897 by a *Jewish Chronicle* correspondent.

The settlement almost died at its inception. The first Bulgarians appeared just as Arab intellectuals and religious leaders were beginning to press the Turks to restrict Jewish immigration. The Palestinians already feared the Jewish claim to an ancestral homeland and what they felt were the Jews' superior financial resources. The first Bulgarians had hardly arrived when one of the Turkish colonial officials in Palestine ordered the Bulgarians to vacate the property within eight days, apparently because they were in violation of an old Turkish restriction on Jewish settlement. The anguished colonists arranged for the *hakham bashi*—the senior Sephardic rabbi in Jerusalem—to deliver a plea to the Sephardic chief rabbi in Constantinople, whose position gave him contacts in the Ottoman court. The entreaty must have reached the top, for a telegram arrived in Palestine a week later from the sultan's grand vizier in Istanbul. As reported at the time, the telegram said, "For what reason do you expel Turkish subjects from their possessions?"

The man whom the settlers would later credit with interpreting the grand vizier's question was a young Palestinian working in the Turkish bureaucracy in Jaffa. His name was Musa Kasem al-Husseini, and he was a member of one of Palestine's most influential families. A generation later, Musa Kasem and others in the Husseini clan were to become the most passionate leaders of Palestinian resistance to the Zionists. Indeed, one of their collateral relatives, Yasser Arafat, would still be fighting the Palestinian cause a century later. But back in the 1890s, Musa Kasem al-Husseini behaved like a loyal bureaucrat. This was how one of the first Hartuvians remembered his contribution to their settlement: "Musa Kasem al-Husseini gathered all the Arab *mukhtars* [village headmen] and told them, 'These Jews are Turkish citizens. By the order of Sultan Abdul-Hamid, they will not have to close their cowsheds. They will not put guards in the fields. They will leave the door open, and nobody will touch them and their property.' "

Even after that victory, the Hartuvians continued to create friction with other Turkish bureaucrats. For a time the Turks in charge of the land registration office flatly refused to issue them a deed for the Artuf land they had purchased. It was a time when Ottoman policy discouraged Jewish immigration and land purchase—unless the price was right. After a while the settlers figured out which palms they needed to lubricate. "Thanks to the *baksheesh* that we gave to the Turks in authority, we succeeded in getting it [the deed]," Avraham Behor wrote in his memoirs.

Their relations with the Arabs were also tenuous. By day they and the Arabs of their village worked side by side, but at night their belongings would from time to time disappear. The most painful episode came after they had planted five thousand mulberry bushes sent by Mikveh Israel. Mulberries would supply not only fruit but also leaves that could support silkworms to give them a silk industry—or so the settlers hoped. One summer morning the Hartuvians woke up to find that unknown Arabs had uprooted all but two of the mulberry bushes. The Artuf Arabs continued to plant and harvest as sharecroppers to the Bulgarians, giving half of the crop to the settlers just as they had done for the Christians. But from the start they disputed the boundaries of the Jewish land. The fellaheen "saw the settlers as exploiters of their lands," wrote Yehuda Appel, who penned a brief handwritten history of the Hartuv settlement in the 1930s.

Yet from time to time the Jews and Arabs did find ways to compromise. One early source of arguments was some land near a streambed that people called the Wadi of the Robbers. The Jews said it was theirs because they had bought it. The Arabs insisted that could not be because it was part of a Moslem religious endowment, or *waqf*. After a year of local bickering, the Jewish and Arab mukhtars from the valley did agree in April 1897 to "partition" the disputed piece of land. For a time, partition solved everyone's problems—a lesson that Arabs and Jews could never quite apply to the larger map of Palestine.

· 5 ·

THRICE-PROMISED LAND

*D*uring the soggy days from December through March, the wadis gorged themselves and the valley would turn phenomenal shades of green. It was nature's trick. In April the rain would stop. In June the valley would turn a drab brown like a chameleon jumping from a vine to a rock pile. As the wadis ran dry, the Arabs would harvest their native wheat as they always had, while the Bulgarians would see their crops wilt. Here in the Jerusalem Hills, the wet season was too short for the seeds they had packed along from Europe.

To survive, these marooned city folk began reaching out to the Arab farmers whom they found as their neighbors. "The settlers did not know in the first years how to plant and how to reap," wrote Avraham Behor, a settler born in Hartuv in 1897. The Bulgarians spoke no Arabic when they came to Palestine. Like many Sephardic Jews, they mainly spoke Ladino, a language derived from archaic Castilian Spanish. They could communicate with the villagers only in Turkish through a few Arab elders who happened to speak the language of the tax collectors. Gradually they picked up the rough Arabic of their fellaheen neighbors. After that, the very Arabs whose former land they had come to occupy taught them how to cajole native wheat from the dry valley bottom. "The Arabs were the ones to guide us in the agricultural work," Behor wrote. "They taught us to plow using an Arab plow that is tied to oxen, to cut the crop, and to thresh the wheat."

Gradually an edgy friendship developed and even spread to the valley around the divided village. The Artuf Arabs and the Hartuv Bulgarians lived across a cow path from each other. On a dusty courtyard between the two halves of the village, Jewish children and Arab children would kick a ball made by stuffing rags into a hat. The Arabs lived in their stone cottages on the top of the hill in the eight-acre enclave of Arab-owned land. The Jews of Hartuv lived just below them in the old missionary buildings. Clustered together, the Jews and Arabs looked down on the fields and hillsides that had been Artuf's land a generation earlier. Now the Jews owned all of these fields and hillsides, all except for seventy acres that included a grove of olive trees. That was waqf land, property of the Moslem religious endowment because it was part of an old Moslem shrine. From their common cow path the Jews and Arabs could look west across the valley and see the Arab village of Saraa up on the ridgeline a mile away, in the direction of the Mediterranean. They could also see the smoke from the cooking fires in Ishwa, the next Arab village one mile to the northeast. Behind their backs was Jerusalem, just twelve miles east of them on a map but invisible behind the crest of a low mountain.

Aside from Artuf, the village on which the Bulgarians depended most was Ishwa. Yoshko Levy's grandparents would have died of thirst if they had had to live on the water that was available on their own property. For the driest several months of the year, their only source of water was the well in the village of Mahmoud Hamdan's late grandfather, Hamdan Asad, who was about fifteen years old when the Bulgarians arrived. The Ishwa well was eighteen feet deep and it yielded water all year around. No one now alive remembers how the Bulgarians got permission from the Arabs of Ishwa to draw their water. All the early settlers wrote down is that they would draw big pots of water from the Ishwa well and carry them back to their settlement on the backs of donkeys. The Ishwa villagers let the Hartuvians take enough water for the fifty-five settlers and their goats and chickens. To Avraham Behor's surprise, the Ishwa people never demanded payment. "They said that the water is the property of Allah, and all the thirsty ones could take however much they wanted," Behor wrote in his memoirs.

It was a friendship of the destitute. The Arabs were not from the landed gentry but rather from the masses of rural peasants who made up three-fourths of Palestine's population. The Jews were no richer. Visiting Hartuv in 1900, a Russian Zionist leader, Achad HaAm, found the Hartuvians living in worse poverty than he had seen in any of the other two dozen Jewish settlements in Palestine:

> The position of the colony in Artuf is the worst of all the settlements of Eretz Israel. They barely support themselves. They don't have clothes and shoes. Bread and vegetables are the only food they have. There is no [stored] food, no mules; the debts of the moshava are heavy, there are no houses except for a big house which twelve families can barely live in; they are extremely poor and they sell their crops for less than the market prices.

Discord murmured in the valley even though these Jewish and Arab farm folk got along most of the time. One of the first-born of the settlers, Ben-Zion Gueron, who was five years old at the time of Achad HaAm's visitation, would remember that the Jews always kept a certain distance from their more numerous Arab neighbors.

"We were very friendly," as he put it. "On the other hand we knew that we shouldn't trust them too much. We were on a tightrope with them." This strain would show itself in its most unpleasant form when it came to boundaries. As long as the Jews and the Arabs would live in the valley together, they could never agree on what land the Bulgarians had purchased and where it met the land of the villages around it.

One dog-eared Turkish document tells of a dispute serious enough to go before the Moslem authorities in Jerusalem. It centered on a grove of olive trees where the Arabs continued to pick even after they lost their land. In 1907, according to a Turkish bureaucrat's report, the Hartuv settlers claimed to own part of the olive grove and took steps to "guard it and prevent the people and the farmers from benefiting from the land and from the olives." A preliminary inquiry by a Turkish police commander found that the Jewish settlers insisted their deed covered the disputed olive grove. A fight trailed on in a Moslem court in Jerusalem for two years. Finally in 1909, a Turkish judge decided the olive grove belonged to the Moslem shrine, as the Arabs contended. The final judgment was a compromise. Instead of ordering the Bulgarians evicted, the Turkish authorities decided that the settlers would be allowed to rent part of the shrine's olive trees and the Arabs could rent the rest.

Bitterness endured. Eighty years after the Turkish judgment, Raphael Ben-Aroya, a grandson of the Hartuv founders, would recall being told as he was growing up that the Arabs falsified the boundaries by knocking down a stone fence and then rebuilding it on Hartuv's property. He acknowledged that a Turkish judge came to inspect the disputed property and took testimony on the spot, then ruled against the Hartuvians. However, by the account he learned when he was a boy, the Arabs hid dirt from their own land inside their shoes so they could mendaciously swear before the judge that they were "standing on Arab soil."

Here, as elsewhere in Palestine, the Jews would cite such stories to justify a speedier form of justice. It was in about 1910, only about a year after the Turkish court decision, when Chelom Behor decided to stop an Arab shepherd from grazing goats in his vineyard. "My father took a big knife from the kitchen," said his son, Avraham Behor. "He went to the herd and slaughtered ten goats before the eyes of the shepherd. He told him, 'If you will enter my vineyard again, I will slaughter twenty goats.' "

But what threatened the colony most was not fights with the

local Arabs but rather dissension between the colonists and their supporters in Bulgaria. In 1903 the colony nearly collapsed because of this. The first arguments started not long after the settlers wrote back to Bulgaria about the sparse crops, which they said could scarcely support the "twelve tribes," let alone the three dozen other Bulgarian families who had put up money to join them. Their differences multiplied when three of the twelve founding families gave up on the Sorek Valley and moved away. In despair, the remaining settlers pleaded for help from the Jewish Colonization Association, a charitable fund in Paris that had been endowed by Baron Maurice de Hirsch. The baron was a Belgian Jew who had made millions building the Trans-Balkan Railroad and later gave a fortune to build colonies in Argentina for Russian Jewish refugees.

Out of what they regarded as Sephardic pride, the Hartuv settlers had always tried to do without handouts. They came to the end of their rope in 1903 and contacted a friend in Jerusalem, Albert Antebi, who led them to de Hirsch's charity in Paris. The settlers got advice they didn't want to hear: abandon Hartuv and move to Argentina. According to files of the Jewish Colonization Association, in 1903 the Paris office approved a loan of roughly $1,200 toward the purchase of the houses and fields of the remaining Hartuvians. The loan stipulated that "all these last ones would emigrate from the colony." The nine families accepted the loan but stayed in Hartuv anyway. Feeling more and more bereft, they appealed again to Antebi in the fall of 1909. "We have never had another person than you who took an interest in our colony," they wrote. "Nobody ever asked whether we are alive or dead." They said the only way they could improve their "miserable state" was to buy out their former partners in Bulgaria, who still owned forty-one parcels of the land the Hartuvians were farming. To raise the money they proposed to sell off part of their land to some new owner. They said they would need a loan of about $1,600 to tide them over during the sale.

Antebi, in a letter to the Jewish Colonization Association, made clear that the settlers had only a precarious legal grip on the property. The "chief obstacle" to the colony's development and prosperity, he wrote, had long been the existence of "dummy holders" and of the shareholders still in Bulgaria. Antebi said it was this obstacle which prevented him from attempting to get the remaining settlers to emigrate:

> I have not wished even to try this disagreeable but possible operation on account of the continuing danger of dummy names, of which there is everything to fear. I would help the colonists in all circumstances but I would refuse any push for basic improvement as long as some Arie or Alajem could one day dispossess legally the actual occupants of the colony.

Antebi advised the association to grant the Bulgarians the loan "to save this colony from a total destruction or from a takeover by the dummy owners." The association's files don't make clear whether the association did approve the loan to help them hold out, but hold out they did. In 1912 the nine families finally found a buyer for three hundred acres of their land, which enabled them to buy out their Bulgarian partners, pay off their debts, and make a new start on farming. "With this money each one of the nine families purchased tools, seeds, two goats, one donkey, and one camel," remembered Avraham Behor.

The new Sorek Valley landowner was from the Ashkenazi mainstream of the political Zionist movement, not the religious Sephardic offshoot that had brought the Bulgarians to Palestine. His name was Itzhak L. Goldberg, and he was already among the few dozen most important leaders of secular Zionism who would eventually become the creators of the state of Israel. He grew up in a prosperous merchant's family in Vilna, then part of Russia's Pale of Settlement and during the twentieth century part of Soviet Lithuania. While in his twenties he had joined underground Zionist cells in Russia and made a mark by trying to bring together the religious and secular Zionist clubs of Vilna. In 1897, when he was thirty-seven, Goldberg was one of the 204 founding delegates at the first world Zionist Congress in Basle, Switzerland. Though Goldberg would not emigrate from

Russia until 1919, he was already buying land in Palestine. In 1906 he made what would be his most important purchase, a block of Jerusalem's Mount Scopus that would become the core of Hebrew University. In 1910, he learned that part of the Bulgarian colony at Artuf was up for sale. He decided to snap it up as an experimental farm.

A few years later the Bulgarians got another lift. In 1914 they got word that Baron Edmond de Rothschild would get off the train to see them during his coming trip to Jerusalem. Rothschild was the anonymous "well-known benefactor" who spent $6 million between 1884 and 1900 to finance Jewish farm settlements in Palestine. At the turn of the century, fifteen of the twenty Jewish farm communities in Palestine were receiving subsidies from Rothschild, but Hartuv wasn't among them. All Rothschild's other projects were Ashkenazi colonies in the flatlands, but now in 1914 someone had interested him in this one lonely Sephardic colony in the Jerusalem Hills. "We received him with bread and salt and we requested his help to build us a school and a place for a doctor and a nurse," Avraham Behor wrote later. "He said 'yes,' and he instructed the clerk in Jaffa to budget this sum of money for the purpose." It meant that still another ancestor of the state of Israel would leave an imprint on this one obscure piece of land. Like Baron de Hirsch, Baron de Rothschild had no intention of contributing to anything so radical as a quest for a Jewish nation in Palestine. Twice he had refused to finance Herzl's scheme to buy a charter for a Jewish state from the hard-pressed Ottoman sultan, believing that Herzl's "political Zionism" was a naive dream. Nonetheless, Hartuv and the other Rothschild-aided settlements would give future political Zionists a geographical base from which to spread into other Palestinian territory.

Rothschild's visit to Hartuv in 1914 coincided with the end of the first modern surge of Jewish immigration to Palestine. In one generation, the Jewish population had more than tripled, but Jews remained only a 12 percent minority in a mainly Arab territory. In 1883, when Rabbi Pines first tried to buy the land at Artuf, there were about 470,000 Moslem and Christian Arabs and 24,000 Jews. By the time the Bulgarians arrived in 1895, the Jewish population had doubled to 47,000, while the Arab population had risen above 500,000. By 1914, Turkish estimates showed that there were about 600,000 Arabs and 85,000 Jews. Of the Jews in Palestine by 1914, only 12,000 lived on farms while the rest lived in Jerusalem, Tel Aviv, and half a dozen other cities. Counting Hartuv, Jews had established only forty-four rural settlements and owned only about 105,000 acres of land—a mere 1.6 percent of all the land in Palestine.

Work was about to begin on Rothschild's school and Goldberg's experimental farm when the Valley of Sorek was sucked up on the fringe of World War I. On August 2, 1914, the future of Palestine was changed for all time when Turkish Grand Vizier Halim Pasha signed a secret alliance with Germany in hopes of safeguarding his Russian border. The battle lines in Europe were just unfolding. Later, some Turkish ministers tried to back out when the cabinet discovered that the British would be arrayed against them, along with Russia and France. But Germany managed to goad the Turks into honoring their alliance by ordering two warships into Turkish waters. On October 31, 1914, three days after Turkey entered the war, the British Admiralty sent a terse wireless message: "Admiralty to all ships: Commence hostilities at once against Turkey." That message would doom the Ottoman Empire and put Palestine up for grabs.

World War I had a paradoxical effect on the valley. While the war was going on, it pulled the Bulgarians and the Arabs closer together. They were drawn by the common need to stay out of harm's way. The Bulgarians, as Turkish citizens, were liable to conscription into the Turkish army, and so were the Arabs. Another shared danger was that they were all liable to be forced to turn over crops and livestock to feed Turkish soldiers. Whenever they could help each other to thwart the Turks, they did. Once early in the war, an Arab sheikh who lived on the way to Jerusalem arranged to slip Avraham Behor through military lines to a Turkish headquarters. With the sheikh's help, Behor got through and bribed a jailer to win the release of half a dozen

Hartuv settlers who were being questioned as possible Allied spies. Later in the war, the Jews repaid the favor. Itzhak Levy was Hartuv's mukhtar—the local headman of either a Jewish settlement or an Arab village chosen by its people for dealings with outside authorities. During the war, Mukhtar Levy used his command of Turkish several times to keep Turkish soldiers from hanging local Arabs accused of stealing or draft evasion. One of the tales the latter-day Hartuvians heard as they were growing up was about a group of Arabs from the town of Deir Aban crying in gratitude because Levy had persuaded the Turks to release one of their sons.

The valley would come under entirely different lines of force after the war. As if two magnets were trying to repel each other, the Jews and Arabs of Palestine found themselves pushed in opposite directions by conflicting promises made by Great Britain in order to win the war. To the Arabs, the French, and the Zionists, Britain held out wildly different visions about what would happen to Palestine if each would help Britain defeat the Turks. Ramsay MacDonald, the British prime minister who inherited the resulting tangle, would lament to the House of Commons in 1922: "We assumed three obligations, each of which contradicts the others."

The pledge to the Arabs came first. In order to weaken Turkey and protect the Suez Canal, British agents set out in 1915 to engineer an Arab revolt in the distant reaches of the Ottoman Empire. They did so by duping Amir Hussein of Mecca into believing he would one day rule virtually all the Middle East. This bit of diplomatic misdirection came about in 1915 when the British high commissioner in Egypt gave Hussein—the great-grandfather of Jordan's latter-day ruler, King Hussein—a written assurance. It spoke of Britain's willingness to "recognize and uphold the independence" of an Arab nation, provided the Arabs would join the war on their side. Hussein had asked the British to recognize everything from the Mediterranean to the southernmost reaches of Arabia as part of an independent "Arab nation." After some hesitation, the British commissioner, Sir Henry McMahon, sent back a note saying Britain was prepared to recognize Arab independence in some parts of the Middle

East but not others. In what turned out to be a crucial exclusion, McMahon wrote: "Portions of Syria lying to the west of the districts of Damascus, Homs, Hama, and Aleppo cannot be said to be purely Arab, and must on that account be excepted from the proposed delimitation." To Hussein, that meant he couldn't rule Lebanon, the territory just west of Damascus, Homs, Hama, and Aleppo. That was all right with him—even Hussein had to admit that the French had a better claim to Lebanon than he. Naively, Hussein assumed that since McMahon hadn't mentioned Palestine as an exclusion, it must be included in the Arab boundaries the British were prepared to recognize. After the war, the British got around to telling him that Palestine was never included in McMahon's pledge. However, in 1923 one Colonial Office official would acknowledge in an in-house commentary that the exclusion of Palestine "was never fully understood by him [Hussein] and is not, in fact, very easy to support in the actual text of the document upon which we rely."

Seven months later, Britain made a second commitment to its weightier wartime Allies, the French and Russians. To them Britain guaranteed that when the Ottoman Empire was dissected after the war, Palestine would *not* be included in Hussein's Arab state after all. In what came to be called the Sykes-Picot agreement of May 1916, the three allies agreed that they would internationalize all of Palestine, including nearly all of what is now Israel and the West Bank. As part of their deal, the Allies agreed to split the rest of the Middle East into spheres of influence. Syria, Lebanon, and most of Turkey were to remain under various degrees of French control or influence. An irregular arc from the Suez Canal to Iraq to the Persian Gulf was to remain under British sway. Imperial Russia was supposed to take the remaining hunk of Turkey, but that pledge was invalidated when the 1917 Russian Revolution dropped Russia out of the war. Hussein lost ground, but his interests were not totally dismissed. The agreement said he was one among the parties entitled to agree on the "form" of any future government for the Holy Land. One party which got nothing from the Sykes-Picot deal was the international Zionist movement.

Eighteen months later, Britain made a third pledge—the one

to the Zionist movement—which turned the Sykes-Picot deal on its head. Instead of talking about internationalizing Palestine, Britain now promised it would try to make Palestine the site for a "national home" for Jews. In what came to be called the Balfour Declaration, Foreign Secretary Arthur Balfour said that Britain was in sympathy with "Jewish Zionist aspirations" and would use its best efforts to create "a national home for the Jewish people" in Palestine. The declaration went on to say that "nothing shall be done which may prejudice the civil and religious rights of existing non-Jewish communities in Palestine."

The cabinet members who approved the Balfour Declaration were inspired by a variety of impulses. Some held a heartfelt sympathy for Jewish refugees, others saw Palestine as a convenient alternative to allowing Jewish immigration into Britain. However, to Prime Minister David Lloyd George the paramount goal was obtaining the support of the international Zionist movement for the war effort—something he was convinced the declaration had achieved. Lloyd George later wrote: "The Zionist leaders gave us a definite promise that, if the Allies committed themselves to . . . a National Home for the Jews in Palestine, they would do their best to rally to the Allied cause . . . Jewish sentiment and support throughout the world. . . . They kept their word in letter and spirit."

Of the three conflicting assurances, the Balfour Declaration of November 2, 1917, was the pledge that mattered. It not only led to Britain's postwar role as Palestine's colonial ruler under a 1922 mandate from the League of Nations. It was also the taproot of the present-day United States commitment to the state of Israel. The draft of the Balfour Declaration had been pre-cleared by President Woodrow Wilson in Washington, thanks to a feat of backstage diplomacy by Louis Brandeis, who was then an incumbent U.S. Supreme Court justice. Before his intervention, the British cabinet had been split on whether to approve the Balfour Declaration. In September 1917 the chief Zionist spokesman in London, Chaim Weizmann, cabled Justice Brandeis asking him to try to win White House support for the declaration. Brandeis, who had been the leader of the American Zionists before he was appointed to the Supreme Court a year earlier, met President Wilson and argued that he should support a Jewish homeland in Palestine under British supervision. Within a week Brandeis sent Weizmann a cable that was just the tool he needed to break the British cabinet deadlock. Brandeis wired: "From talks I have had with President and from expressions of opinion given to closest advisers I feel that I can answer that he is in entire sympathy with [the draft] declaration. . . ."

When Lord Balfour made his indelible pledge, it made no immediate impression in the Valley of Sorek. Neither the Jews nor the Arabs had radios. News traveled by word of mouth, and at that point everyone's biggest worry was whether the valley's familiar protectors, the Turks, would defeat the unknown British Tommies who were approaching. Three days before the Balfour Declaration, British forces under General Edmund Allenby captured Beersheba, about forty miles to the south of Artuf. Next they swept northward along the coast to take Jaffa. In early November, the British began to advance inland toward Jerusalem, and the boom of cannons echoed in the Sorek Valley. From their ridgeline, the Saraa Arabs saw fighting in the distance and told several of the Jews, who rushed up the hill to watch the approaching cannon flashes. A day or so later, a Turkish commander and two other officers appeared at the settlement and asked for provisions. "We received them and supplied what they needed," said Avraham Behor. "They were very pleased."

The Turkish unit spread out along the Saraa ridge, preparing to make a stand to save Jerusalem. One Turk warned the settlers to find a hiding place, because the British troops would probably drive straight across the valley. The settlers found a cave in the hills and began stocking it with food and water. At midnight two days later, the Turks changed their minds. New intelligence convinced the Turkish commander he must retreat toward Jerusalem, because he was in danger of being surrounded. On November 19, the first Allied unit trotted up the Brook of Sorek from the direction of Jaffa and took over the Artuf railroad station without a struggle. It was a detachment of Australian cavalrymen from the 5th Light Horse Brigade.

The settlers would remember one of the cavalrymen offering

to pay them for supplying some fresh bread and eggs. The deal
was struck. "That's how the fear of war ended," Avraham Behor
remembered. On December 9, 1917, Jerusalem surrendered to
the British forces. Two days later, General Allenby walked
through the Jaffa Gate and issued the martial law proclamation
that would begin Palestine's transformation from a Turkish
territory to a British colony.

Compared to most places touched by the Great War, the valley had survived unscratched. The worst thing that happened
between 1914 and 1918 was the locust infestation that had
denuded the vineyards and fields in 1915. For the rest of Palestine
the war had been more onerous. Famine and malaria, as well as
conscription had cut into every sector. The Moslem Arab population had declined by about 4 percent to an estimated 535,000.
The Christian population—Arabs and a few Europeans—had
dropped 13 percent. The decline of the Jewish population was
even steeper. The Turks had expelled more than six thousand
Jews, contending they were citizens of their enemy, Russia.
Between 1914 and 1918, the Jewish population of Palestine fell by
one-third to only 55,000.

The Hartuv Jews had been spared the risk of expulsion because they had never given up their Turkish citizenship. Now
that the war was almost over, the question was how the British
would treat these former Turkish citizens who happened to be
Jews. Better than they were treated by the Turks, as it turned
out. In fact, it was the British army that gave the settlers their
breakthrough toward financial security. "The money was made
during the war," explained Yoshko Levy. "My father was a
contractor to the British army, and he built the road from here
to Bab al-Wad." His father made his leap from the lean prewar
years while General Allenby was preparing his final push to
capture northern Palestine and Damascus in the fall of 1918. The
Artuf train station was a bottleneck that had to be circum-
vented. Supplies poured into the station from as far south as
Cairo, but they all had to be unloaded on the Artuf sidings,
because the track between Artuf and Jerusalem was narrower
than the north-south track that Turkish engineers had pushed

through Palestine in 1914. "Traffic demands to Jerusalem could not be met by the narrow-gauge line," General Allenby wrote in his account of the Palestine campaign. He ordered his engineers to install new standard-gauge tracks through the winding gorges to Jerusalem. During the construction, supply trains kept running at night on the old narrow-gauge tracks, but they couldn't keep up with the supplies jamming into the Artuf siding. Determined to find a second route, the British engineers decided early in 1918 to rush through the construction of a new road that would for the first time link the Artuf railroad station with the Tel Aviv–to–Jerusalem road four miles to the north. That's how Gavriel Levy got a contract and the Sorek Valley got a road connection to Jerusalem.

For about a year after Allenby entered the Jaffa Gate, it seemed that Palestine might be big enough for both the Arabs and the Jews. The high-water mark of their amity may have come in July 1918 when the aging *mufti* of Jerusalem, Kamal al-Husseini, stood side by side with Jewish rabbis and other dignitaries on the Mount Scopus land Itzhak Goldberg had purchased. They had come to dedicate Hebrew University. When it came time to set stones in the ground to commemorate the twelve tribes of Israel, the mufti bent down and laid one of the twelve stones.

This mufti had only another three years to live. By the time he died in 1921, the destinies of the Arabs and Jews in Palestine were no longer anywhere close to being synchronized. At the 1919 Paris Peace Conference, the Zionist Organization laid out its long-range intention to create a Jewish "Commonwealth" that would take in not only all of Palestine but also most of Transjordan, part of Syria, and the southern third of Lebanon. The Zionist yearning for a "Greater Israel" had never been stated more clearly. The British did not endorse the "Greater Israel" notion, or for that matter promise the Jews an independent state on even a part of Palestine. But they did take on an international obligation to carry out Balfour's wartime pledge to create a Jewish national home in Palestine. In 1922 the League of Nations granted Britain a mandate to administer Palestine,

and among its provisions was a clause calling for the establishment of a Jewish national home. As in the Balfour Declaration,
the mandate required Britain to safeguard "the civil and religious rights of all the inhabitants of Palestine, irrespective of
race and religion."

Meanwhile, Palestinian Arab intellectuals were banding together to form nationalist clubs that called for an end to Zionist
immigration and the formation of a national Palestinian parliament for "native" residents—Moslem, Christian, and Jew. "The
Balfour Declaration was made without our being consulted," a
Palestinian Moslem-Christian delegation declared in 1921, "and
we cannot accept it as deciding our destinies."

• 6 •

MOSHAVA ON FIRE

*T*he Arab villages and the Jewish colony of the Sorek Valley began the 1920s protected from the new friction emerging in Palestine. A violent encounter in 1920 between Jerusalem's Arabs and Jews had been contained in the city. By 1921 ethnic tensions were spreading. Arab mukhtars of Saraa and of Deir Ayub, a town five miles to the east, proved the strength of neighborliness when they appeared at Hartuv in May 1921, carrying warnings of trouble and guns for defense. The mukhtar of Deir Ayub had roused a force of thirty villagers to save the Jews here from attacks spreading out to Jewish settlements from clashes that had started in Jaffa, the port city twenty-five miles away. Together at the big fenced home of Itzhak Levy, the Hartuv mukhtar, they planned a defense that in the end was not needed. No assault came, but a detachment of British soldiers did show up with a demonstration of red flares to warn any distant malcontents not to attack here.

Those were the good days, when the weather got better and prosperity edged into the valley and the crooked bureaucrats under Ottoman Turks were replaced by infamously efficient

British civil servants. Rioting was the indulgence of radical city folk, who had time to spend on politics because it wasn't all consumed in survival. The only harm touching the valley during the 1921 riots befell Itzhak Goldberg, who had emigrated from Vilna to Tel Aviv, where he oversaw the experimental farm he had bought at Hartuv. His brother Boris, once an underground Zionist activist in Russia, was wounded in a 1921 clash in Jaffa and later died. Arab nationalism and political Zionism, antagonistic ideologies now that British rule had faced them off in competition for a scrap of land called Palestine, had not yet reached this cranny. It was a peace to be savored, but not forever.

The riots had begun with a fight among Jews, whose ideological divisions broke into violence at a May Day parade of communist Jews in Jaffa. The strife spread to Arab sectors of the city and turned into Arab attacks there, as well as in five rural Jewish settlements. That is what brought the mukhtars to warn Hartuv. In all, forty-seven Jews were killed, mostly by Arabs, while forty-eight Arabs died, mostly at the hands of police.

The fierce Arab reflex was an irrational response to fears that were anything but irrational. The Palestinian Arabs rightly sensed that the British policy of creating a "Jewish national home" in Palestine ultimately would threaten their position as Palestine's dominant people. Unlike the Ottoman Turks, the British were allowing thousands of Jews to immigrate into Palestine. They were coming, and they were buying land. Some Arab villagers feared that Jews "would become so highly organized and so well armed as to be able to overcome the Arabs, and rule over and oppress them," according to a British inquiry into the cause of the 1921 disturbances. The inquiry commission found these fears were based largely on Zionist attitudes expressed not just by radicals but by mainstream Jewish leaders, who said there was room for but one national home in Palestine, and it would be for Jews as soon as enough arrived.

Such thoughts had not entered the Sorek Valley. For now the biggest worry of Arabs and Jews here was making it, and now they were beginning to do that. Indeed, they often were making it together. The Hartuv colonists had bettered their farming skills, but most still had Arab sharecroppers because they were unable to cultivate all their cropland. Some Arab and Jewish neighbors went further than that and started jointly growing vegetables—tomatoes, cabbages, carrots, or beets—that they would market together in Jerusalem or to the west in the Arab town of Zekariya. Itzhak Goldberg had hired five Jews to work his farm, and Arab workers joined them as day laborers. They planted experimental fields of coffee beans and rubber plants, looking for a new cash crop that would thrive in the hard climate. Farming was easier now, in these years when there was plentiful rain not only for the grain fields of wheat and barley but for the grapevines and apricot and almond trees. Rain produced fodder for the cows that children minded in every village in the valley, and it assured grazing grass for goats and sometimes sheep. Ben-Zion Gueron, the settler who would last in Hartuv beyond any other, knew intimately the land and its fickle nature. "If it was raining you had bread," he once said. "If it was not raining you didn't have anything."

Among the most prosperous people in the valley were members of the Levy family, who in wartime had been the lucky ones chosen by the invading British to build the road from the train station to the Tel Aviv–Jerusalem highway. The British army must have paid well, because the Levy brothers afterward started a series of agribusiness enterprises. There was a mill to grind grain, a machine that made cooking oil from hyssop leaves, and a press to squeeze the oil out of olives. Both Arabs and Jews worked for the Levys in their businesses, and both brought their farm products to be processed at the mill and the olive press. Another colonist, Shalom Rebissa, came up with his own cottage industry of drying wild mountain flowers to send to America to sell during holidays, when they could be marketed as fragile bits of the Holy Land. Arab women helped him do it.

Life got better, but it was never cosmopolitan. If young people wanted to see the cinema in Jerusalem, it was a four-hour walk, or two hours and ten minutes on the train—when they could afford it. When someone wanted a newspaper, he might be lucky to talk one out of a traveler passing through the train station. Sometimes the whole valley celebrated an event, such as Avraham Behor's wedding, the first in Hartuv after the war. "All the mukhtars from the Arab villages were invited, and they came riding on their horses. We slaughtered for them in their honor ten sheep and 150 people ate and drank for four days," Behor recounted. The bride and groom got so many presents—including gold coins—that the gifts more than paid the expenses.

Besides demands of survival, the valley people had to contend with a frontier ethic sounding echoes of the American west. Thefts were common in Arab villages as well as in the Jewish colony, and both had to keep guards on call. Friends from surrounding villages would warn if they saw strangers in the hills or heard talk of plans to steal from the Jews. In an emergency they could get to the train-station telephone to call for help from the British police or army. But still the isolation was hard for the Jews, so far from their own people. For years Motza was the closest Jewish colony, and it was just a few miles outside Jerusalem, a seven-hour round trip. Even when the Jewish colony of Kfar Uriah was founded off to the northwest, it still was a two-hour trek away over tiresome brown hills.

In the midst of this quiet, plodding development came another sign of the larger tensions humming through Palestine. In 1926, the Catholic order that owned most of Saraa decided to build on the land. They had bought more than three thousand acres nearly half a century earlier, when the Saraa peasants had been under a tax squeeze. Now they raised Our Lady of Palestine Church and founded their own small town, Deir Rafat, and they wanted to build a convent and school. To finance the development, they put up for sale 250 acres of farmland and 375 acres of mountain land. The Arab farmers of Saraa and Ishwa and Artuf all had been sharecropping and grazing on the Catholics' land for decades. For some, a loss of the use of this land would be a loss of essential income. To the Jews of Hartuv the news of land for sale was a joyful possibility. Itzhak Levy wrote to Goldberg, then in London, that the land had come on the mar-

ket and pleaded on behalf of the Hartuvians that he buy it for
further Jewish settlement. It could bring more Jews so close to
them. But he did not buy it. Nor did the Jewish National Fund,
the agency that was collecting all the land it could afford in
Palestine to be used solely for settlement and work by Jews.

These Arab sharecroppers in the valley were luckier than
many others would be. All over Palestine, more and more land
was passing to the hands of Jewish settlers. More and more
Arabs were ending up as had the fellaheen of Artuf decades
earlier, dispossessed of the land when a rich absentee landlord
sold out. At least the Artuf Arabs had retained their homes and
the use of some grazing land, while many Palestinian Arabs now
were having to leave everything. The Jewish groups and agents
hunting land did not have a plan for buying and settling, or one
centralized vehicle to make purchases. They ended up competing with each other and driving land prices to levels irresistible
to the Arab owners. By the early 1920s, owners of rural land
were getting forty to eighty times what they had paid for it.

Most of the sellers at this stage were not Palestinians, but
absentee owners and landlords with no stake in the future of
some miserable peasant tenants. They were the Arab elite used
to floating from Beirut to Jerusalem to Cairo, sophisticated ur-
banites who saw themselves as citizens of the broader Arab
world. Michel Sursock of Beirut, for example, sold a great swath
of land extending from the sea practically to the border of
Transjordan. A combination of purchases from the Sursocks
and a few other Arab owners in the 1920s put in Jewish hands
sixty thousand acres in the Jezreel Valley, where 688 Arab tenant families worked some of the best agricultural land in Palestine. Some were allowed to stay several years longer and lease
enough land to maintain their families. Others, as did most
displaced tenants, agreed to vacate the land in exchange for cash
payments that sometimes equaled a year's income. It was a
windfall, but the farmers soon found it could not replace the
home, the land, and the livelihood taken from the fellaheen
family. Palestinian Arabs with property succumbed, too, selling
about a fourth of all the land bought legally by Jews in the first

nine years of the British mandate. Some were propelled by
losses suffered under recession and crop failure. Others just
wanted to get richer. Palestinians who sold land in the 1920s did
not understand, or perhaps did not consider, the damage they
would cause future generations.

The ramifications of the land issue may have escaped Palestinian Arabs in these early years, but they did pay attention to
Jewish immigrants. Through much of the decade they had seen
a quickening pace of immigration, a stream they feared would
grow to an irrepressible torrent. What even the British called an
"exceptional volume of immigrants" in 1925 and 1926 helped
bring about an economic depression that lay heavily over Palestine, for a brief time checking the growth of the Jewish national
home. In 1927 more Jews left the country than entered. Then as
the depression lifted the following year, the flow of immigration
resumed. By 1929 the Jewish population had grown to 154,000,
about double its size at the start of the decade. Palestine still was
an overwhelmingly Arab land whose majority was welded by
language, culture, and religion. They outnumbered the Jews by
six to one. The Arab leadership began to realize, however, that
the advantage was slipping.

It was largely immigration that moved the Arabs to new
tactics as the 1920s played out. Ever since the mandate had been
created they had shown only their backs to the British in charge
of Palestine. The Supreme Moslem Council, the body that administered Moslem religious affairs, and the Arab Executive
Committee, which carried out resolutions adopted by periodic
Palestinian Arab congresses, had never cooperated with what
they considered an unjust colonial ruler. They refused even to
recognize the mandate and repeatedly demanded retraction of
the Balfour Declaration. Hoping to throw off the entire mandate structure, they boycotted elections, which the British had
called for a legislative council, and refused to join an advisory
council. They turned down the offer of an Arab Agency, which
would have had lesser powers than the counterpart Jewish
Agency that ran Jewish community affairs.

Finally they saw that the politics of repudiation were losing them ground. They certainly had not convinced the British they should change their policies. A new Palestine Arab Executive was elected in 1928, and its leaders soon signaled to the British that an advisory council might be a desirable forum after all. In meetings they initiated in early 1929 with High Commissioner Sir John Chancellor, they proposed negotiations they hoped would lead to a representative assembly and a democratic government for all the people of Palestine, Jews and Arabs alike. If they could win majority rule, they could wield the power of their numbers and dry up the stream of immigration.

The Jews in Palestine had taken the opposite course. They not only cooperated, but pushed for more participation than the colonial power had in mind. They tried for everything from a Jewish defense force to a commission of Jewish experts to survey the land possibilities. It did not sit well with the Arabs. The Zionists also were quick to organize their Jewish Agency. The document setting up the Palestine mandate had called for such a body to advise the mandatory government and work toward establishing the Jewish national home. Once the Jewish Agency was created, its executive council became the central decision-making body of what was known as Palestine's Yishuv, or Jewish community.

As immigration and land purchasing advanced, the Jewish settlers also developed what was for the Middle East an extraordinary network of social services. The socialist labor federation Histadrut became the dominant protagonist, moving far beyond simple unionization of workers. It was behind cooperatives that purchased and marketed Jewish-produced goods, a bank that financed settlements and urban labor projects, and medical coverage for members through its own doctors, hospitals and clinics. Perhaps its most vital responsibility would be the Haganah, the militia that trained settlers and got them illegal weapons. The Histadrut was building foundations to support a community that it was nudging toward nationhood. All this development was not lost on Arab leaders, for whom socialism was a suspicious alien force. This expanding social system threatened them as a cohesive power in the Jewish community.

Fears among Arab Palestinians were stirred, as well, by a new unity within world Jewry, a new dedication to making the national Jewish home in Palestine. The most visible sign was a 1929 agreement made in Zurich to expand the Jewish Agency to include non-Zionist members. Non-Zionists were uncomfortable with the thought of a Jewish state or political entity. But now they had come around to the notion that a protected piece of land—a Jewish homeland—was the inevitable answer for the poor Jews of Europe subjected to repeated pogroms and discrimination. The wealth of less political and more assimilationist Jews, especially Americans, would be channeled to settlement in Palestine for the first time. With impressive new allies from the West, among them Albert Einstein and the French socialist leader Léon Blum, the movement gained new credibility. It also gained stauncher opposition from the Arabs, who felt themselves threatened now by a growing "world conspiracy."

Arab political figures responded to the swelling Jewish presence with more than a list of demands to the British. The preeminent Arab leader was Hajj Amin al-Husseini, a charismatic Arab nationalist who controlled the most important facets of Moslem life. As the mufti of Jerusalem he not only was interpreter of Koranic law, but controlled Islam's third holiest shrine, the al-Aqsa Mosque, which made him vastly more important than muftis in lesser Arab cities. He also was president of Palestine's Supreme Moslem Council, a power base from which he directed Moslem religious affairs, including schools, courts, and trust funds. The British had found Hajj Amin guilty of inciting the 1920 riots, but he had fled to Transjordan and the British soon pardoned him, reasoning that he would return chastened and indebted and willing to cooperate. He had promised the British he would uphold law and order, but he also came back to Jerusalem dedicated to Palestinian Arab nationalism as a movement that would abort the ambitions of Jewish settlers seeking to cut their own nation from the Arab arena. By the late 1920s, Hajj Amin had followers in key positions as preachers or teachers or in other points of influence. Those who did not agree with Hajj Amin's exhortations against Zionism would not last long in the job.

The British never got to respond to the Arab appeal for a legislative body. Eight months after the request was issued, at the very time the high commissioner was in London to consult about it, the rising swirl of Arab animosities bypassed the bureaucracy and skipped through Palestine with tornadic violence. The harmony of the Sorek Valley was one casualty.

This storm was seeded at the Wailing Wall in Jerusalem, a flint where contentions had sparked between two faiths for the previous decade. Then as now, the Wall was venerated as a relic of the Hebrew Temple, a place where Jews traditionally prayed and wept over their losses of two thousand years before when the Temple was destroyed and Jews driven away. But for centuries it had been Moslem property. It abutted the Haram es-Sharif complex containing the Dome of the Rock and al-Aqsa Mosque. Jews had been granted access to pray at the Wall since the Middle Ages, and the two groups managed to honor their holy sites in relative amity. But after the turn of the twentieth century, some Jews began seeking more than just permission to visit. On several occasions religious Jews had carried to the Wall benches or an ark or a screen to separate men and women, in what the Arabs perceived as an effort to create a synagogue there. In 1919 and 1926, Jews had made queries about buying the Wall from the Moslems. The Arabs would not give up the Wall, which itself was a part of Moslem religious tradition as the place where Mohammed had tethered his horse before he ascended to heaven from the Rock of Abraham's Sacrifice, now covered by the Dome of the Rock. Since the first attempt to buy the Wall, there had been sporadic incidents.

When a Jewish sexton raised a partition at the Wall to separate praying men from women in the fall of 1928, suspicious Moslems protested that the worshipers were taking unauthorized control of the site, and the British agreed the screen must go. There followed months of protests and countercomplaints, agitated by both the Jewish and Arab press. Leaders of the Jewish community renewed talk of buying the Wall and, when that seemed impossible, called on the British to expropriate it from the Moslems. Hajj Amin al-Husseini, the keeper of the Moslem shrines, inflamed the irritation by permitting construction work in the area and noisy ceremonies that disturbed the pious Jews worshiping at the Wall. Outside of Jerusalem, Arab nationalism and warnings of Jewish aspirations were preached in branches of Moslem societies in provincial towns.

Mainstream figure David Ben-Gurion, who already was respected as a leader of the more secular, socialist labor faction of the Jewish community, urged restraint. By making abrasive demands at such a sensitive site the Jews would risk charges that they were a threat to the holy places of Moslems and Christians, he warned. They did not need a religious war added to their agenda of impossible problems. But Vladimir Jabotinsky, a Jewish militant who had been imprisoned for inciting Jews in the 1920 riots, encouraged his right-wing zealots to use the Wall as a call to battle. His radical youth group Betar staged a raucous march at the Wall on August 15, 1929. It was Tisha b'Av, the Jewish day of mourning that commemorates the destruction of the Temple. The young people had a permit, but they violated its terms when they raised the Zionist flag at the Wall and sang the Zionist anthem, "Hatikvah." The demonstration took them right through the Arab quarter.

The radicals' chants that "the Wall is ours" were sufficient provocation for the mufti to respond. Hajj Amin allowed a counterdemonstration the next day, and for a week agitation against the Jews rippled through the countryside. Militant Palestinian Arabs incited country peasants around this religious issue of high emotion. The challenge at the Wall drew them into the larger struggle, political and national, between the Arabs and the Jews.

On Friday, August 23, Arabs converged on Jerusalem as usual for the Moslem prayer day. But the crowds around the Old City were larger and their mood nasty. By the time noon prayers ended, the congregation at the mosque was so convulsed that mobs abandoned the holy site and swept into Jerusalem's nearby Orthodox Jewish quarters, looting shops and houses and attacking Jews who got in the way. Some of them responded; among the first deaths recorded were two Arabs blown up when a hand grenade was launched from a crowd of angry Jews. Hajj Amin, who had circulated among the people earlier in an apparent effort to calm them, was unable to contain the furious mobs armed with guns and clubs. They set out to punish what they viewed as Jewish interlopers grabbing for sacred Moslem ground. It did not end in Jerusalem. The next day bands of incited Arabs circulated through Palestine, releasing the tensions fueled by real fears and by weeks of manipulation by the mufti's followers and by even more radical Arab nationalists. It had gone too far. All Hajj Amin could do was warn the British authorities that trouble was on the move.

News of the afternoon's bloody turn in Jerusalem jolted the Sorek Valley. Just days before, these poor farmers had been out reaping grain, singing in the fields they worked, and wondering whether this harvest would see them through the winter. The religious fervor inspired by the nearly year-long dispute in Jerusalem may have touched some local Arabs, but the agitation didn't make sense to most fellaheen simply trying to get through the rigors of daily life, like their Jewish neighbors. Local Arabs returning from Friday prayers in Jerusalem warned the Hartuvians about the agitated scene. That night thieves tried to relieve the Hartuv Jews of their sheep, but a few shots from inside the settlement scared them off, as usual. But when Arab elders heard of the violence radiating out from Jerusalem the next day, they moved at once to save their friends in Hartuv. They went to the Jewish colony to tell them gangs were advancing and to offer to hide the Jews in their own homes till this new fury was spent.

The Jews, numbering around 120, anxiously gathered in the house of their own mukhtar, Itzhak Levy, to debate their chances. Some said to go with the neighbors. Yehuda Appel, the Goldberg farm manager, who often denigrated Arabs, rebelled. "Fellows, what are we doing? We will turn ourselves over to the Arabs with our own hands. No, it won't be that way," he said. They should defend themselves, he urged. After all, didn't they have men with Haganah training? They agreed to defend the colony together, from this one house.

Not that they had the makings of much defenses. "They only

had five weapons and were trying to make a plan. My father was among the five that would hold a gun," said Yoshko Levy, who was the nephew of Mukhtar Levy and only five years old at the time. "Then we received a message from the Arabs on Saturday night that we were about to be attacked." The men with guns were assigned positions, and the rest tried to keep out of the line of fire. "In that period the Arabs would attack with a lot of people, yelling and beating drums, just to make a lot of noise. Women and children too, but they would be behind. It would be a mass coming at us." Close in and retreat, in and retreat. Ululating cries of the Arab women, children clacking sticks, men with clubs and, of course, some with guns. It went on for hours. The hunkering Jews began to see flashes of fire eating into the sheds and houses around them.

"I was a child and I remember it by my father's stories. The policy was not to shoot them, as much as possible, so as not to raise a blood revenge," Levy said. "That was the situation until five in the morning. It was decided to send my father to the railroad station because there was a phone there." It was quieter then, perhaps because the marauders were exhausted. Gavriel Levy dressed up as an Arab—kaffiyeh and sandals and long cloak—and slipped out in the predawn to sneak down the hill to the station, less than a mile away. He called Jerusalem to report that Hartuv was under attack and to ask the British for help. Captain P.H.L. Playfair got the plea, at five in the morning. He took it seriously.

When Gavriel Levy returned to the moshava, the elders were making ready to escape. The train would come at around six o'clock, and it would be the Jews' last chance to get out if the British were unable to evacuate them. They had no illusions that the angry Arabs were finished with them. The men with rifles would stay in the house to divert any more assaults, while the rest would make a run for the train. They set off. In the midst of their flight, an armored car of the South Wales Borderers rumbled down the road. Captain Playfair had come through. Yoshko Levy remembers the car fired all around, scaring off returning attackers and enabling all the Hartuv Jews to escape with no casualties or injury. One Arab was killed. As the train pulled out of the station for Tel Aviv, the anguished Bulgarian settlers looked out the windows and watched their few possessions being jammed into looters' sacks, their houses ripped apart for salvage. Homes already scoured by thieves were going up in flames.

The Arabs of the Sorek Valley villages don't like to recall the riots that drove out their neighbors and seldom will discuss it today. "We had good relations with them," said Hajj Diab Abu Latifah, who grew up across the valley from Hartuv in the hilltop town of Saraa. He denied any local Arabs were involved, blaming outsiders caught up in the troubles of the times. Mahmoud Hamdan of Ishwa wasn't even born yet in 1929, but said he knows from stories of the elders that there were just some fires in Hartuv, nothing very bad. In one open moment his mother, Alia, admitted that people from the villages did join the assault. "They attacked to steal things. The Jews all left," she said. "The Arabs who attacked said Hartuv was for them, not for the Jews."

Local Arab lore may diminish the severity of the attack, but it is true the people of Hartuv fared better than some others. Earlier, Arab bands had chosen the old community of Orthodox Jews twenty miles to the south in Hebron as a target, and they hit it in a bloody frenzy. Sixty defenseless Jews, among them at least twelve American rabbinical students, were butchered in an assault that has not been forgotten today. Some in the mob that descended on Hartuv had come from the direction of Hebron, but something held the crowd back from the ultimate destruction that had come so swiftly in that city. Avraham Behor, one of the Jewish settlers, believed that Arab elders from the valley attempted to calm the agitated *shebab*—the Arab boys and young men—by urging them to turn their rage to looting. Perhaps the knowledge that the Jews had some guns also helped deter a worse attack until the settlers had time to leave. Something held them back. Other sites of Jewish settlement also fared less well than Hartuv. Jews in Jaffa on the coast, in Safed up near the northern border, and in other rural communities like Hartuv were attacked over several days. In all, 133 Jews were killed and 339 were wounded. Arabs died, too, mostly at the guns of police and British troops rushed up from Egypt. Over the days of rioting, 116 Arabs were killed and 232 were wounded.

The Hartuvians survived the riots with their lives, but not much else. For days the ransacking of the colony continued. American archaeologist C.S. Fisher, excavating at the original site of Beth Shemesh, a hill overlooking these valley towns from the west, wrote that his Arab laborers returned for work on Monday tired from the weekend of looting. Most of the workers came from Deir Aban, the larger town some two miles down the road toward Hebron, which always had been less friendly to the Jews than the closer neighboring villages. New fires broke out in the Jewish colony that Monday night, Fisher recorded, and the British tightened their control with martial law over much of Palestine. They began airplane patrols that lasted more than a week and restricted movement on the ground. Deir Aban was under nighttime curfew.

The 1929 riots set a new course in relations between Arabs and Jews that was never to be reversed. Hostility was an undercurrent to Palestinian life that sometimes subsided, but never vanished. The immediate Jewish response was a boycott of Arab goods, followed by an even more complete Arab blacklisting of Jewish products and services. Both sides were pinched tighter than ever by economic hardship. It took months to renew anything approaching normal commerce.

The events of that August also further soured relations between the British and each of the two groups they were trying to make coexist on one small bit of territory. Arab leaders already faulted Great Britain for opening Palestine's doors to Jewish immigration and land purchase. It was after the riots that the British made new enemies among the common people through wide use of a tactic that Israeli governments still would be employing some sixty years later. They tried to teach the Arabs a lesson through collective punishment. Towns were put under twenty-four-hour curfew or levied heavy fines if it was found that local people had joined in the disturbances. The aim was to create social pressure on troublemakers from within the community by making everyone suffer for the actions of a few. The British hoped that law-abiding friends and neighbors would stop future agitators before they stirred new displays of violence.

The tactic may have made some Arabs more obedient, but it also served to anger many Arabs who till then had tried to keep detached from the three-way dispute among British, Arabs, and Jews. If the British were going to make them suffer anyway, they might as well join the struggle to get the foreigners out of their land. It was one more spur to Arab nationalism already on the rise.

The British fed Jewish antagonism, too. British security forces did move quickly to save Jewish lives when they could— as in the case of Hartuv. But the Jewish community still felt betrayed that the authorities hadn't acted sooner to arrest the tide of Arab sentiment growing toward violence in the days preceding the attacks. The Jews also chafed when the acting high commissioner submitted to Arab demands and disarmed Jewish constables organized by the British as a supplemental security force.

The worst blow to the Jews, however, was the conclusion reached at the end of a formal inquiry into the causes of the 1929 riots. The British royal commission, headed by Sir Walter Shaw, reported the following March that the outbreak was embedded in "the Arab feeling of animosity and hostility towards the Jews consequent upon the disappointment of their political and national aspirations and fear for their economic future." The Shaw Commission found the Arabs responsible for the violence, apportioning a share of blame directly to the mufti and other leaders for creating the atmosphere of belligerence, but said the assaults had not been premeditated. Palestine's poor Arab farmers, it said, had their backs to the wall and had been crowded there by the sale of land to Jews. "Their position is now acute," the commission said of the fellaheen. "There is no alternative land to which persons evicted can move. In consequence a landless and discontented class is being created." The report's key recommendations were that the government (1) put limits on the flow of Jews into Palestine to prevent "a repetition of the excessive immigration of 1925 and 1926," and (2) find ways to protect Arab tenants from eviction by Jewish land purchasers. Land, the commission said, should be transferred only to Arabs.

The riots and their aftermath slapped the Jews of Palestine into a new consciousness of their vulnerability. It forced them to turn inward to develop their defensive shell. They began planning how to expand and toughen their community, which till now had grown haphazardly. Land-purchasing efforts would begin concentrating on geographically contiguous land areas to minimize the isolation of settlers. And there would be new focus on discipline, self-reliance, and self-defense.

· 7 ·

SHARING THE
DROUGHT

*T*he Jewish refugees of Hartuv endured for up to a year in the rented rooms or run-down flats in Tel Aviv to which they had fled from the chaos of August. Some valley Arabs, sympathetic villagers like those who had warned Hartuv an assault was coming, were worried enough to travel to Tel Aviv to tell the Jews they would be welcome back home. "Arab neighbors from Hartuv came to visit us to ask how we were," Avraham Behor later wrote. "Yes, there were among our neighbors true friends, and there were no shortages of flickerings of light in the darkness of those days. There was a story about an Arab from Artuf who when he passed down the street in Tel Aviv, a Jew jumped on him and started to hug and kiss him."

Testimonials of friendship from a few Arabs were not sufficient to lure back all the 120 or so Hartuv exiles. Some were too frightened by the Arabs' venomous display of temper that night in August to resume life on a tiny Jewish island, surrounded by more than three thousand Arabs with no bridge to safety. The murder of a Hartuvian walking late one night on the beach between Tel Aviv and Jaffa—his friends assumed at the hands

of an Arab—must have hardened sentiments that return to the
valley would be folly. Others were too old or too poor or too fed
up with the unending work to go back to the colony. "In Tel
Aviv people suddenly understood what a dry hole was Hartuv,"
said Chaim Levy, Yoshko's brother. "Many of them decided not
to return. The constant argument between the people who were
for remaining in Hartuv and those who said it had no chance
whatsoever tore them apart." Bitter divisions sometimes even
vexed families. Gavriel Levy, the father of Chaim and Yoshko,
was the leading exponent of return and rebuild, while their
mother was reluctant ever again to step on that rocky soil. It was
an argument that Gavriel won.

The Jews found that Arab farmers who had been swept into
frenzied attacks on Hartuv made no move to renew hostilities
as the settlers trickled back to their devastated colony. "The men
and boys came back with no trouble to rebuild the moshava,"
said Yoshko Levy, who remembered those childhood days
reconstructing his own home. "We would come Sunday to Friday and stay here." They slept under the sky or in the shells of
buildings not fully destroyed in the riots, and returned to Tel
Aviv on weekends. Slowly they put their settlement back together. Their homes. The mill across the road. The oil-pressing
plant. Sometimes, he said, they hired local Arabs to help them.

It was exactly that easygoing relationship with the Arabs that
was to bring the Hartuvians trouble, this time with their fellow
Jews of Palestine. Political leaders of the Jewish community
now were more wary than ever of the Arab population and
more than ever dedicated to promoting Zionist ideals of self-
sufficiency through physical labor. Even before the 1929 violence, the Jewish National Fund (JNF) followed a policy requir-
ing that only Jews be allowed to settle and to work the land it
bought in Palestine. JNF deeds stipulated that its land never
could be transferred out of Jewish hands. Nor were Arabs to be
employed in any capacity. There had been agitation among
labor leaders, too, with David Ben-Gurion in the forefront of
the powerful movement to get all Jewish landowners and employers to hire only Jews. Especially on the big citrus planta-

tions owned by non-Zionist Jews, the use of cheap Arab labor had been common and increasingly controversial, provoking boycotts and strikes by Ben-Gurion's union forces. These assaults on Arab employment had fueled the political agitation that led to the disturbances.

After 1929 the tendency toward separatism strengthened. It also got a new organizational base in 1930, when Ben-Gurion oversaw the birth of Mapai, the Israel Workers' Party. This new amalgam of several smaller political parties became the dominant political force in the World Zionist Organization, in the Palestinian Jewish community, and later in the state of Israel, eventually evolving into the Labor Party. Its goal was to reestablish the Jewish people in Palestine "as a free nation of workers," and to do that it was essential to create more jobs to bring in more Jewish immigrants to build the nation. It made no sense to hire Arabs.

Such sentiments made jagged cuts over the grain of daily survival in Hartuv. It was much like other older colonies of Jews, who settled in Palestine in days when there were no Jewish institutions advising how to farm or negotiating labor contracts or supplying emergency welfare to the sick and aging. There hardly were any other Jews back then. Other than absorbing the lessons of an early Jewish agricultural school, the settlers learned from and relied upon their neighbors, as rural people do everywhere. But they were innovative, too, and soon contrived new forms of agricultural development. They conceived small industries and some became businessmen-farmers. Why not lease some land to Arab neighbors? Their attitude was like that of Jewish plantation owners around Petah Tikvah, who were able to develop big citrus farms only because Arab labor was there to work them. These longtime settlers did not want everything they had built to crumble under straining relations between the larger communities of Arabs and Jews. But they still were Zionists. That is why their parents or grandparents had come here from Central Europe and Russia decades earlier. As they were drawn into the growing conflict and wounded by it again and again, they knew which side was theirs.

Authorities of the Jewish Agency and the new Emergency
Fund for Palestine, an agency set up to funnel contributions to
Jews displaced by the August riots, were unsettled when they
stepped in to help Hartuv rebuild and saw what had been the
way of life there. The first shock was that the Hartuv Jews had
been leasing more than half their cultivable land to the Arabs.
At a meeting in January 1930, leaders of the settlement were
asked to detail the land and building ownership, the income and
debts, and all the works of Hartuv, from the number of chickens
raised to the bags of seed planted each year. The farmers were
open in admitting that of some five hundred acres of cultivated
land, normally three hundred acres or more were sharecropped
by the neighboring Arabs in return for half the harvest. The
Arab farmers had kept at it even while the Hartuvians brooded
in Tel Aviv. Photos in the files of an American archaeological
dig in the area show the fields around Ishwa in April 1930 filled
with arching stalks of grain. It was a booming spring harvest,
undisturbed by the autumn pillage of Hartuv and the flight of
some Jewish landlords. The caption described the area as a "lush
valley covered with wheat."

One of the first questions the representative of the Jewish
Agency asked was whether the Hartuv colonists would be willing to give up the land they could not themselves farm. The
excess could be sold or leased to new settlers, whose presence
would add to the strength and safety of the moshava. Some
might refuse, replied the Hartuv farmers, but most probably
would do it. They badly wanted more families to join them.

The second disturbing discovery of the Jewish Agency was
the proximity of Hartuv and its Arab neighbor, Artuf. They
were scarcely separated by a cow path. The two peoples had
mingled here for three generations, their children playing together, neighbor visiting neighbor, working, celebrating,
mourning losses. But an architect advising the Jewish Agency
on the rebuilding warned that the Jewish settlement always
would be endangered as long as the top of the hill was in Arab
hands. He recommended that the Jews simply buy out Artuf
and shift the Arabs off to somewhere else, perhaps to some
excess land farther away owned by another Jewish moshava.

A letter from the Emergency Fund for Palestine said the reality of the times would not allow such a solution. Unquestionably, it is "very undesirable for sanitary and security reasons to have the Arab village within the vicinity of the Jewish settlement," the letter said. "In our present situation, we cannot overlook the fact that an Arab village does exist there, and even if it was possible to persuade them to remove the village to another place (against compensation), it will take a few years before that could be accomplished, particularly in the present political atmosphere."

Besides, by this time nearly a year had passed since the colony was burned out, and some settlers already had repaired their homes and returned. The answer, the letter said, was to abandon the remnants of buildings closest to the Arab village and to raise ten new homes farther away. They still would be adjacent to the renovated houses. Perhaps the Arab village could be acquired sometime in the future, the letter suggested, and a public building planted there for security.

The Hartuv Jews got their money for houses, cowsheds, chicken coops, cows, mules, tools, and vines. The British mandatory government helped out with small cash payments, giving victims of the August riots about 10 percent of the worth of what they had lost. The establishment of a British police post inside the colony was a greater help. The Jewish Agency and its Emergency Fund granted the Hartuv settlers a total of about 10,000 Palestinian pounds (about $40,000) in loans, but along with the funds the agency handed them a plan for what it deemed to be the best cycle of farm work. The cycle had no phase for Arabs to farm Jewish-owned land. These Jewish colonists acquired something else, too: a new border one hundred yards wide between their homes and those of the Arabs of Artuf, giving them a margin of safety and one of separatism.

There was plenty of use for the money. Raphael Levy convinced the Jewish Agency that he didn't need the chickens they wanted him to buy, but would be better off reprovisioning the store he used to run. The family of his uncle, Gavriel Levy, was luckier than some. Their four-room house with a kitchen, bathroom, and broad terrace sat atop a cellar-floor cowshed and

chicken coop amid a group of isolated buildings on the hill. It
had some damage that would require carpentry and plastering
repairs, but generally it was in good condition by the time the
Jewish Agency inspector came to assess damages in March 1930.
Other buildings had suffered worse. One house had completely
lost its wood-and-tin balcony to the fire. Fixing the roof, ceiling,
balcony, and bathroom would cost the equivalent of at least
$420. There had been what the colonists called the "common
building," an apartment house that held seven families. It was
severely damaged and would cost nearly $4,000 to repair.

By the end of 1930, Jewish Agency field inspectors found some
crops had been planted. But they also discovered the "cycle of
farm work" the agency plotted for Hartuv was not in full swing.
Some settlers resisted buying work animals. They had gone
beyond the Arabs' primitive farming methods in their decades
at Hartuv and were now used to plowing with tractors, not
behind mules. Even worse, the agency was told, several people
refused to buy work animals because they didn't have land to
work. Many who owned land had turned it over to Arab sharecroppers to farm the previous year and had not yet reclaimed it.
One agent still was able to strike a positive tone after his visit,
finding that "everything is getting rebuilt and the attitude of the
farmers is serious and decent." Perhaps he decided it was too
soon to expect the Hartuvians to make full withdrawal from old
dependencies, while they still were trying to pull their colony
back together.

But a year later, in December 1931, an extension agent found
the old habits had endured. "Their land does not supply the
needs of the animals. A primary part of the land has been given
by loan to neighbors, and they in sowing of the land obviously
do not concern themselves with the needs of the landowners,"
wrote agent Shlomo Tzemach in his report to the Jewish
Agency. These Jews still were leasing land to the Arabs, who
were not about to waste their time growing fodder. If the Hartuvians had more land to farm themselves, perhaps they could
meet the needs of their cowsheds, Tzemach said. "But I am
under the impression it will be difficult to shake the settlers out

of their inert state," he warned, observing they must find another source of feed soon or their valuable cows would be lost.

The returning Hartuvians made peace with some Arabs of the neighborhood, but the underlay of tensions at first sat close to the surface. In an impassioned letter to the Emergency Fund, Yehuda Behor told how one of the fund's contractors from Tel Aviv had reneged on his word to employ Hartuv men, who were desperate for money that summer of 1930. The job was right there in the valley, digging sand and gravel for construction repairs to be done at their own colony. After signing an agreement, the contractor came back to say wages must be lower than promised because he had found Tel Aviv laborers who would do the work for less. The Hartuvians refused to take the lower wages. The contractor brought the Tel Aviv diggers, but not for long. "In the first day they worked about two to three meters and immediately in the second day they went to the village and they invited Arabs to work in the wadi," Behor wrote. "And they just got the most brash troublemakers who were laughing at us, since those destroyers will be the first ones to get the moneys that were meant for rebuilding what they themselves destroyed." Behor, outraged, said the gravel would not be permitted on the grounds of Hartuv. A repeat of such action "can really make trouble between us and the Arabs in the area and can cause the delay of work," he warned. The Jewish Agency put a stop to this Arab labor immediately. But it may have been too much for Yehuda Behor, who records show left the colony to resettle farther north in the coastal plain at Evan Yehuda, a moshava with rich land and Jewish neighbors.

For those who remained, the next few years in the valley ground into a routine of work and survival for Arab and Jew alike. Hostility diminished throughout Palestine, and in pockets like this valley it could be as forgotten as a teakettle simmering without a whistle. Relations repaired to a working level between the Jewish settlement, which now had been reduced to 107 inhabitants, and the villages immediately surrounding it. After all, they faced a common enemy. The war in those years was the daily battle to draw life from fields in the valley floor, to coax

olives and almonds and grapes from the groves and vineyards
terraced across parching hillsides. "The way of life in Hartuv
of those days wasn't very much different from that of the Arabs
around," said Raphael Ben-Aroya, a grandson of original Bulgarian settlers. "Perhaps it was the friendship of the people
thirsty for water. Perhaps it was being cut off from Jerusalem
and the rest of the Jewish issue. Whether it was this or that,
between the Arabs and Hartuvians relationships of strange
friendship have been created. There were periods when we
were closer to the Arabs than to the Jews."

One of those periods must have been 1933, when the country
suffered a drought that hit especially hard in the hill villages
around Jerusalem. From the late 1920s the mandatory government had been toying with ways to get the valley more water.
Technical experts had come up with a scheme for a series of
dams that would create a reservoir with a capacity to irrigate 125
acres of land. Once the Jewish Agency got interested in Hartuv,
it tried to reactivate the plan. A geologist who had studied the
area for the British mandatory government was encouraged at
this new inquiry. He described the proposal as "an important
experiment" of "wider technical and economic significance"
than for this one settlement. But just a provisional dam would
cost $6,000 to $8,000, and the final version would require some
$16,000. The cost apparently had dampened British enthusiasm
for the plan, and now the price tag seemed to close correspondence on the topic from the Jewish Agency. The British in
charge, however, were spurred by the drought to try drilling a
new well at Jewish Hartuv. They bored 985 feet but never penetrated the bituminous limestone to find groundwater. So they
dropped the project and moved on to other towns where water
had failed entirely. The decision was a blow to all the thirsty
villages there.

Moslem, Jewish, and Christian mukhtars and religious leaders
from the valley—and some from beyond—joined in imploring
the British high commissioner to pursue the hunt for water at
the place they called Artuff, referring to the two adjoining settlements, Arab and Jewish. They wrote on behalf of the villages

whose population "amounts to about 5,000 souls, and whose sufferings are great as a result of the drought, especially during the last year," their petition said. "We thought that after this experiment all other villages would follow this example so that the benefit would be general. However, we now hear that the Government intends abandoning this scheme in Artuff before achieving any results and all our great hopes are doomed to disappointment," they said. "We therefore beg to bring this petition before Your Excellency hoping that Your Excellency will see to it that the boring activities in Artuff are brought to a successful conclusion with the blessings of God." The mukhtars of Artuf, Hartuv, Ishwa, Islin, Deir Aban, and Beit Mahsir, a priest from Beit Jimal, the Latin patriarch at Rafat, and the director of a Greek Orthodox convent joined to make the plea in September of 1933. Religion, race, nationality—all such divisions fell before a common threat to survival. British documents of the time said the work merely was temporarily suspended, but they never did get the well.

Besides being joined by their adversity, the Arabs and Jews in this valley restored relations because the Jews ignored the advice of their politicians and institutions. They continued to deal with the fellaheen as before, even increasing their economic connections. The work they offered would begin to carry greater consequence for the Arabs, as they saw the pattern of life changing throughout Palestine. A rural, land-based economy, in which agriculture was supreme and bartering common, was shifting to a more formal and Westernized structure in which industry was developing, modern foreign goods were appearing in the cities, and hard cash was the medium of trade. Cheap grain, imported largely from Syria, was driving down prices of local products. At the same time the costs of seed and supplies were rising. Small farmers were becoming increasingly dependent upon loans, which were becoming increasingly costly to obtain. The British rulers and the Jewish immigrants were bringing change. It was a time for Hartuv and its Arab neighbors to draw from each other.

"The people in the village used to go and work in the lands

of Hartuv. They used to work together and share half-half," said
Alia Mohammed Daher, the mother of Mahmoud Hamdan. She
walked across the hillside from Ishwa as a young woman to farm
on the land of the Hartuv Jews. "They became like the Arabs.
We were good to each other." They did not work side by side,
Alia recalled, but would farm in adjacent fields, planting and
digging through the rocky land. Arab farmers ground their
grain in the Levy brothers' mill that sat in the valley bottom not
far from the land owned by Ishwa, across the fields from the
stone elementary school where Arab village boys were taught.
Some Arabs worked in the mill, too. Awad Ibrahim Awad was
one of them, and he became close enough to the Jewish neighbors to invite them to his wedding in Ishwa in 1935. "We used
to live together with the Jews from there. When I got married
they brought some sheep to us," Awad said.

Occasionally Arab women got paid to work in the homes of
Hartuv, and villagers from all around sold goat's milk that the
Jews made into a popular cheese and marketed as far as the cities
of Jerusalem and Tel Aviv. Sabiha Abu Latifah was assigned the
childhood chore of carting tins of milk down the hill from Saraa
to sell in Hartuv. "My father had goats. I used to take milk to
them every morning and evening. There was lots of trust between us," she recalled. "I would measure it there and they'd
pay every day. . . . It was secure and calm. We used to get along.
There was no war then."

Most Sorek Valley Arabs were luckier than other fellaheen,
having land of their own to farm or nearby fields to sharecrop.
In 1931 the villagers of Ishwa, in common and individually, held
nearly fourteen hundred acres, centered by the cluster of 126
homes laid out in the shape of a star. Saraa had just sixty-five
houses, and much of its nearly one thousand acres was consumed by the barren mountaintop that supported little more
than olive groves. Arab Artuf had been reduced by its ancestors'
land sale to fewer than one hundred acres for the 250 people who
lived there by 1931. Peasants without land of their own had the
neighboring tracts owned by the Hartuvians and the Christian
monastery to farm. Yet even those holding land were finding it

harder to exist just by farming. They took advantage of employment in the small industries run by the Hartuvians and of the land the Jews were willing to lease them, but they also looked elsewhere for income. Half the Artuf Arabs had stopped farming in favor of outside employment such as the railway. Women routinely drove carts of vegetables and other farm products to sell in Ramle to the north or Jerusalem to the east. Men began quarrying rock from the Jerusalem Hills or digging in the nearby pits of sand and gravel, which came under growing demand for urban construction.

In this time of change, traditions were the foundation stones of the old life. Today fellaheen still recall the elaborate festivities of weddings as high points of those years. Alia Mohammed Daher became wistful when recounting her own marriage to Asad Hamdan Asad, celebrated with uncommon gusto because it was a double wedding. She described it as an "exchange" of daughters and sons between families already related, an arrangement considered most desirous by generations of fellaheen. Asad was the cousin of Alia's father, and the other couple marrying were Alia's brother and Asad's sister. The two girls simply switched homes.

"It used to be like a fantasy," Alia recounted. The celebrating started from the engagement, at least for men, when the prospective husband would invite his friends over to announce the betrothal. "When I got married the festivities lasted five or six days. All the villagers came and sang and danced. There's a special dance for the men. . . . We used to have big courts for the dancing. And they would take the bridegroom around the village on a horse that was decorated." Guests came from all around and brought sheep and goats as gifts. "The bride, she would be very well dressed," Alia went on. "There's a special dress they call the queen's dress, embroidered with shiny gold threads. I was dressed in this dress. And a special hat with gold and a veil with gold coins on it. I had lots of gold bracelets." In the afterglow of time, she remembers her new home as "a palace," a seven-room house of stones cut from the mountain, where Asad and his two brothers each had two rooms for their young families. These were families of some substance, to afford the long celebration and the coveted "queen's dress" that brought fame to dressmakers of Bethlehem.

Landownership and their own enterprise saved valley Arabs from falling into the destitution that struck thousands of Palestinian fellaheen in these same years. The less fortunate were overwhelmed in the late 1920s and early 1930s by a combination of adversities—drought, locusts, escalating interest rates, the changing face of the economy, and, increasingly, the sale of land they had farmed as tenants. Displaced Arabs were being forced to the cities in search of low-paying day-labor jobs. They competed for work with Arab immigrants from outside Palestine, who were attracted by the relative order and new commerce brought by the British administration. One study showed that by 1935 more than eleven thousand Arab workers lived in shantytowns on the outskirts of Haifa, in shelters made of petrol tins and lacking water and toilets. In Jaffa, almost exclusively an Arab city, the population grew from 27,400 in 1922 to 47,500 in 1931.

When they could find jobs, Arab workers usually did not earn as much as Jewish laborers. Even in government jobs, Arabs doing unskilled labor made one-half or one-third the wage paid to Jewish unskilled workers. Arabs drawn to Palestine by stories that Jewish capital was being invested at an accelerating rate found less opportunity than they might have expected. Now Arabs more frequently were prevented from working for Jewish employers. Zionist labor organizers would raise pickets at firms using Arab labor, or the workers might be scared off by threats. The awarding of colonial government contracts to Jewish companies to provide supplies and construct roads and buildings compounded problems for Arab workers.

The Shaw Commission inquiry into the 1929 riots had outlined growing hardships, but the Permanent Mandates Commission of the League of Nations, which had granted Britain the mandate over Palestine, declared dissatisfaction with both British administration and the Shaw Commission report. It was followed by a more detailed study by Sir John Hope-Simpson, who reported in October of 1930 that conditions were even worse than brought to light so far. He described as alarming the policies of the Jewish institutions—the Jewish Agency, the Jewish National Fund, and others—which purchased land and prohibited Arabs from ever regaining or even working on it. Hope-Simpson, a longtime British civil servant, accused the Zionists of following policies incompatible with their public expressions of friendship and desire to improve the lot of the Arabs. He concluded that 29 percent of the rural Arab families were landless already, and that there was no more land available for new Jewish immigrants. He said newcomers should be permitted only on unsettled land already in the hands of the various Jewish agencies. More space might become available, he suggested, if some state-held lands were developed and if irrigation and better methods of Arab cultivation were introduced. Hope-Simpson was more positive on prospects of Jewish immigration for industrial work, reasoning that Jewish capital creating new industrial jobs for Jews might not directly help the Arab population, but would not hurt it as land purchases were doing.

Zionist leaders were stunned, not only by Hope-Simpson's report but by the British government's Statement of Policy in the White Paper of 1930, which was released at the same time under the aegis of Colonial Secretary Lord Passfield. It clearly had been based on Hope-Simpson's report, which the Jews declared to be inaccurate in its statistics and wrong in blaming Arab poverty on Zionist settlement. The Passfield White Paper adopted the conclusion that there was no margin of land available for new agricultural settlement, except the land already held by Jews. It called for immigration restrictions, at least as long as overall unemployment persisted, and said further land sales to Jews would have to be limited. What the policy statement did not pick up from Hope-Simpson's report was any suggestion that future development might open more land for Jewish settlers. Nor did it adopt Hope-Simpson's soft stand on continued Jewish industrial immigration. It was clearly a policy favoring the interest of Palestinian Arabs.

The outcry by Jews, not only in Palestine but in Britain and

America, too, was immediate, sharp, and effective. Chaim Weizmann resigned as president of the World Zionist Organization and Jewish Agency, and David Ben-Gurion threatened that if the British choked Zionist genius "then our destructive force will be unleashed and we will blast away this bloodstained empire." Their protest was aided by timing: Britain's Labour government was facing a by-election in a constituency where the Jewish vote could be critical. Prime Minister J. Ramsay MacDonald was influenced, as well, by complaints from non-Zionist Jews that the Hope-Simpson report had overestimated the Arabs' land losses. Within months he invited Zionist leaders to confer with the British government because of "misunderstanding" over the White Paper and questions raised over its compatibility with articles of the Palestine mandate. Out of these meetings came MacDonald's letter to Weizmann on February 13, 1931, which recast the Passfield White Paper and rendered its critical passages meaningless. MacDonald wrote that the "obligation to facilitate Jewish immigration and to encourage close settlement by Jews on the land remains a positive obligation of the mandate," and assured that Jews would be stopped neither from acquiring more land nor from entering Palestine. This letter, MacDonald said, was the authoritative British position.

The Arabs quickly tagged it the "black letter" and returned to their old habit of refusing to cooperate with the British masters of Palestine. They had no means to compete with this flexing of Jewish political and financial power in the west, which seemed to the Arabs to be driving Britain's Palestine policy more than ever. Earlier, the Arabs had testified before the Shaw Commission and then sent a delegation to London in the spring of 1930 to reiterate their contention that only a democratic government and an end to Jewish immigration would bring peace. Even though those demands again were rejected, the Arab leadership was consoled at seeing the Hope-Simpson and Passfield documents. The Arab Executive Committee submitted detailed reports responding to both. In a show of good faith, it canceled the normal day of mourning on Balfour Day.

Then came Britain's repudiation of the Passfield paper. It

quickly iced what had been softening Arab attitudes. Musa Kasem al-Husseini, the aging president of the Arab Executive, wrote to the British high commissioner that MacDonald's action "has ruined hope of a policy of cooperation between Arabs and Jews, if there existed such a hope, and has rendered the possibility of understanding between the two parties absolutely impossible." What was viewed as a British betrayal helped stir a new round of Arab political mobilization—unions, militant youth groups, political parties. They proved to be sometimes viciously competitive, but all were galvanized by anti-Zionism. Within a few years the passions of the Arabs would be uncontrollable.

REBELLION

*M*errymaking filled the narrow pathways separating the houses in Saraa, the ancient hilltop village on the northern lip of the Sorek Valley. Weddings were the most memorable events in Palestinian village life, and this one was a double spectacle—two sets of cousins getting married the same day. It was a special day, too, because there had been little to celebrate in these waning years of the 1930s. The countryside was in chaos, rent by a long and violent rebellion. Saraa's poor villagers were savoring a respite from present troubles, rejoicing that two families were building strong new ties into the future.

Suddenly a villager saw horsemen climbing toward the town. An alarm was raised. Sabiha Abu Latifah, who was a girl then, remembered how the festivities were snapped off and the celebrants disappeared: "Someone said the mujahideen were coming, so everyone went to hide in the houses and locked the doors." The mujahideen were rebels engaged in the serious pursuit of dislodging the British rulers who had been changing the face of Palestine. They hadn't come to attack Saraa, but to chasten the revelers for indulging in frivolity. "They said we weren't supposed to be singing and celebrating," Sabiha said.

From 1936 to 1939, life in Palestine was upended by such disruptions, but for many people the consequences were far more
wrenching than a ruined wedding. British, Arab, and Jew all
would be targets during the years of unrest. Hundreds of people
would die. The Arab rebellion also would seed longer-term
results surely not expected and not even understood once they
began to evolve. The Jews would be propelled to new militancy,
backed by new stocks of arms smuggled in to underground
defense forces which would grow steadily into an army. Palestine's Arabs, too, would acquire more weapons, but they would
lose an entire layer of leadership, killed or deported or forced
into exile under Great Britain's formidable assault on the resistance. By the time Arab and Jew would get down to real war a
decade later, the legacies of this rebellion would help shape the
victory.

The Arab unrest was induced in large part by a new current
of Jewish immigration, which unsettled the Arabs and also
brought potential recruits for the Zionist struggle. Even the
Jewish colonists of Hartuv, who described themselves as apoliti-
cal, grew optimistic as they saw the new rush of immigrants in
the 1930s. Some, they thought, might be replacements for the
settlers who had given up on the place after the 1929 attacks.
Many among the newcomers were groping for a safe haven from
the latest anti-Semitic tyranny in Europe, a regime that in only
a few years would bring horrific new meaning to the concept of
evil. The reaction to the establishment of the Nazi government
in Germany in 1933 had been dramatic. Jewish immigration to
Palestine, less than 5,000 in 1931, reached 37,000 in 1933 and 66,000
in the year 1935. From 1932 to 1935 the population of the Yishuv,
the Jewish community of Palestine, doubled, rising to 375,000.
Maybe some from this pool of new settlers, the Hartuvians
thought, would be channeled to their isolated roost in the hills
by the Jewish institutions guiding settlement.

But it was not to be. All the new migrants would land elsewhere. The Zionist agencies already had reason to question the
way this shaky, unsocialist moshava ran itself. And the colony

was a crude, rural place that hardly would catch the eye of Europeans shopping around Palestine for a settlement. Perhaps a more critical deterrence to these escapees from Nazi brutality was the fear of settling into another set of potent dangers—the Arabs who had overwhelmed Hartuv in 1929. Indeed, as the Hartuvians puzzled over how to enliven their colony with new settlers from the wave of immigrants in the mid-1930s, another deep surge of discontent already was rumbling through Palestine's Arabs. Once it broke into the open, the Arab rebellion would ruin hopes of growth at Hartuv. It also would make the Hartuv Jews prisoners in their own homestead.

The colony sat in the wrong place to be a target for expansion. Settlement patterns were now being molded consciously by Jewish leaders in Palestine, who were moving to concentrate their forces and create contiguous Jewish areas, especially in the coastal regions where Jews already had their biggest landholdings. The 1929 riots had taught that isolation could be fatal. Besides settling Jews along a rational scheme, institutions such as the Jewish National Fund tried to clear Arabs out of lands between or abutting Jewish areas. When the JNF bought a plot of land holding Arab tenants—and now it was buying more land than ever—it made sure the Arabs got relocated as far from Jews as possible. In 1935 alone, more than eighteen thousand acres of Arab land passed into Jewish ownership. These settlement patterns started an unofficial partitioning of Palestine into Arab and Jewish spheres. British administrators likewise nudged along the tendency toward separation. A 1931 directive that landless Arabs should be resettled in the inland hill country meant they were directed to a swatch of land running from Hebron in the south up past Nablus, one edged by the Sorek Valley.

Hartuv's elders may not have been aware that the preferred Jewish settlement pattern excluded their small colony, but they did understand that their rock-studded land offered little attraction. They knew immigrants surely would view Hartuv as a harsh place to begin a new life farming, so in 1935 the Hartuvians conceived a scheme that might persuade more Jews to join the colony. They would industrialize. Abundant land lay behind their cluster of houses, mountainside land rich in limestone and sand that would crush perfectly for cement. "We needed more people. So the idea was to build some industry," said Yoshko Levy, in 1935 a boy of eleven whose father and uncles were the colony's leading businessmen. The elders, acting much as development-hungry town fathers in America would do decades later, went hunting for investors with economic bait. They offered the site for quarrying free of charge, and land to build a factory at a cheap price. Investors snapped at the lure. They would call the factory Shimshon—the Hebrew version of Samson—in honor of the strongman who roamed the same hills three thousand years earlier.

But Shimshon inherited the legacy of conflict that surrounded Samson, rather than his legacy of strength. A long and sour dispute with neighboring Arabs soon broke out over the land the Hartuv Jews decided was theirs to give away. And the factory never would bring the expansion the colony so badly needed. "The Hartuvians gave all this land to Shimshon so they would set up the factory. We gave the mountain away for free and the other land we almost gave for free," said Levy, bemoaning that even such a good deal failed to bring much result. Preliminary work at the site did give jobs to a few Jews already living in Hartuv, but before Shimshon even could build its plant, new trouble broke over the countryside.

The radicalization of Palestine's Arabs suddenly blew like steam from a geyser in the 1930s. The influx of immigrants that led the Hartuv Jews to dream of expansion only intensified discontent among the Arabs. Where there had been no formal political parties, by early 1935 six of them were competing for followers from the frustrated population. But it was the perennial rivalry of the Husseinis and Nashashibis, a competition honed by British divide-and-rule tactics, that would become the crucial cleavage in Palestinian politics. Raghib Nashashibi started the first party in 1934, when he failed to win reelection as mayor of Jerusalem and sought another forum to compete against Hajj Amin al-Husseini, who emerged as the most popular Palestinian political figure thanks to his reputation as the

man who blocked Jewish acquisition of the Wall. The Nashashibis and their National Defense Party were accessible to the
British and had ties to neighboring Transjordan's Amir Abdullah, a grasping British tool who had visions of subsuming Palestine into his domain. Hajj Amin's cousin Jamal al-Husseini soon
founded the Arab Party of Palestine, which preached a radical
nationalist message appealing to angry Arabs. Its broad support
partly stemmed from Hajj Amin's leadership of the Moslem
hierarchy, through which he could tap funds from religious
endowments and manipulate a network of patronage jobs.

Whether moderate or radical, Husseini or Nashashibi, the
Arab parties at this formative time shared one characteristic:
strident anti-Zionism. Expanding Jewish immigration stimulated vitriolic comment in the press and at public meetings. So
did land purchases, forming a more visible pattern and coming
at a time of economic distress that made more Arabs willing to
sell. The mood grew so hostile against the increasing Jewish
presence that the competing Arab political parties managed to
unite in November of 1935 to press their case: an end to Jewish
immigration and land purchase and establishment of a democratic government in Palestine with democratic elections. It was
the first time such a unified group of Arabs had appeared before
the commissioner. Britain responded with a plan that evoked
Arab interest: a new legislative council and the promise of a
bureau of statistics to gauge whether Jewish immigration was
threatening the economy. Jewish allies of the Yishuv quickly
mobilized in Britain, getting the legislative scheme killed in
Parliament just three months after it had been proposed. This
added another layer to Arab anger.

It was not political agitation from an elite stratum of Palestinian Arab leaders that brought about a general strike in 1936
and three years of subsequent disturbances. All over Palestine,
discontent percolated up from the mass of Arab people increasingly squeezed under economic hardships they linked to the
presence of British rulers and Jewish immigrants. Added to
dissatisfaction over official British policies were isolated incidents that rolled one after another into an unstoppable momen-

tum for action. In early 1935 a group of Arabs threw stones at police who were evicting them from land purchased by Jews. Police responded with gunfire, and an Arab was killed. Another Arab died in August, when a group attacked Jews farming a plot that the Arabs claimed was rightfully theirs. In October, Arab dock workers went on strike in Jaffa and saw their jobs immediately snatched up by Jewish immigrants. In the Sorek Valley, Arabs were agitated when they watched mountain land that had been common grazing ground for centuries suddenly designated for the Shimshon cement machines. The greatest alarm spread through Arab communities after a cache of smuggled arms and ammunition was discovered hidden in a shipment of cement from Belgium, destined for the Jewish center of Tel Aviv. Rumors grew that the Jews all over were taking up arms.

The first sign of revolt was an armed band out of the north, from the hills of Galilee, led by Sheikh Izzed Din al-Kassam. A charismatic religious leader who appealed both to discontented, educated youth and dispossessed peasants in teeming shanty-towns near Haifa, Kassam long had counseled that disciplined guerrilla action would spur political change. In 1935, Kassam carried a fighting cadre into war against the British masters of Palestine, whose forces quickly overpowered his band. The sheikh was among those killed in a British ambush that November, but his influence would survive. Kassamite bands, copying his style, quickly formed. The next April one of these bands killed two Jewish travelers on the Tulkarm-Nablus road, leading to a retaliatory murder of two Arabs in a hut near the earliest Zionist settlement of Petah Tikvah. Riots persuaded the British to set a curfew and proclaim emergency regulations governing all of Palestine. So began three years of rebellion.

Palestine buckled under the Arab revolt. Local Arab "national committees," the first formed in Nablus, issued calls to strike in protest of British governance. Five of the Arab political parties responded to the grass-roots initiatives by declaring a general strike that halted business and transport, and on April 25 they created a new Arab Higher Committee to be the master coordinator. Hajj Amin al-Husseini, already the preeminent re-

ligious leader as the mufti of Jerusalem, became the undisputed
Arab political leader in Palestine when he was elected president.
The Higher Committee vowed to continue the strike until the
British changed their policies, beginning with the halting of
Jewish immigration. It was questionable, however, whether the
Palestinian Arab leaders could have stopped the protest even
had they been so disposed. Arabs eagerly joined the strike, and
some pushed for more radical action such as nonpayment of
taxes. Volunteers on local committees tried to assure that people
got food and basic care.

The disorder almost immediately skipped southward to the
Jerusalem Hills, putting Hartuv directly on the line of combat.
Arabs attacked public property, sabotaged the railway, and cut
telegraph and telephone lines. Soon after British defense patrols
got underway, they confronted barricades and ambushes on the
roadsides. The strikers mounted assaults, as well, against Jewish
property and even against Arab villagers who disregarded the
strike by carrying produce to the towns to sell. Sniping incidents in Hartuv and other Jewish settlements increased over the
summer, as did sabotage against the Jerusalem-Jaffa railway that
cut through the Sorek Valley. Twice in June of 1936 saboteurs
managed to wreck trains, causing railroad authorities to intro-
duce armored railcars and foot patrols along the tracks. After
London set an immigration quota of 4,500 for the last six months
of the year, violence accelerated, prompting the British to reinforce their troops with forces from Egypt and Malta.

Neighboring Arab leaders, some running newly independent
nations and others still aspiring to throw off colonial rule, were
aroused to sympathy for the Palestinians and antipathy toward
Zionism. They took the first steps toward what would become
disastrous embroilment in the battle for an Arab Palestine. The
Arab regimes sent some weapons, and volunteers from Syria
and Iraq swelled the bands of fighting Arabs in the hills. Guerrilla leader Fauzi al-Kaukji, a veteran of the Ottoman army in
Syria, arrived in Palestine in August to begin training these
Arab irregulars, as he would do on a bigger scale in 1948. By
autumn, the British had called up another division of troops to
Palestine and announced the military would begin hunting

down the Arab attackers who called themselves mujahideen and called their fight a holy war.

With the roads haunted by "revolutionaries," as the roving fighters were known, as well as by common robbers exploiting the chaos, Hartuv and similar Jewish outposts survived through combined protection from the British and the expanding Jewish militia, the Haganah. Itzhak "Levitza" Levi was a Haganah commander who ran the twice-weekly convoys to Hartuv that became a supply lifeline from Jerusalem. The convoy guards and drivers were Jews who served in the Jewish Settlement Police, an organization cooked up by the British army and the Jewish Agency. The police were trained, paid, and supervised by the British, but most of them secretly doubled as Haganah militiamen. "Our gravest problem was to defend Hartuv, because Hartuv had about twenty families, and we had to supply them, defend them against odds. There were bands of hundreds of Arabs who attacked Jewish settlements," Levi said. Besides running convoys, Levi got a cadre of settlement police from Jerusalem stationed inside the colony itself. More than that, he relied on an unofficial, unsanctioned squad of protectors for Hartuv—Haganah members from outside and others from among the Hartuv settlers themselves whom he was able to arm and to pay a stipend for their services. About thirty armed men from Jerusalem came to help defend the Hartuvians.

The unofficial network of supplemental defenders was armed through an underground Jewish arms industry which was growing because the Haganah felt the British sanctioned neither enough men nor enough weapons to protect their community. "We had machine guns issued to the force, legal. And we had our own weapons, Haganah weapons, hidden in the legal [convoy] car, because they were better and because there were people for whom the British did not provide," Levi said. Their own weapons already included machine guns, hand grenades, and light mortars. The training and the accumulation of weapons stocks, which continued after the Arab rebellion ended, would become the nucleus of a Jewish army that finally wrested a homeland out of Palestine little more than a decade later.

Dreams of expanding the colony with strong new families

dissipated under the reality of life under siege. The Hartuvians vowed that they would not abandon their homes again, in a replay of the 1929 riots, but the decision to stay meant they were sometimes captives inside the newly fortified moshava. The Hartuvians never wandered far from home except in the safety of an armed convoy, said Yoshko Levy. "We worked in the fields a little with the Arabs," he recalled, "but not too much." They concentrated more on defense. One of the Haganah field commanders who came to train the Hartuvians was Itzhak Sadeh. He was the former Russian Red Army officer who developed the first Jewish preemptive military tactics, starting with guerrilla ambush attacks and leading to a disciplined strike force. Hartuv was one of the first places Sadeh tried out his notion of aggressive defense—patrolling outside the perimeters of the moshava to ward off interlopers before they got close enough to strike. Raphael Ben-Aroya, a Haganah member, called his employment in the Jewish Settlement Police a "cover" to fool the British. It meant he could carry a gun.

As the local commander, Ben-Aroya ascribed the sniper attacks and assaults on local convoys to Arabs from Hebron, whom he saw as more highly politicized than those in the valley. And Levi, the Haganah convoy leader from Jerusalem, said it was clear that Hartuv's strong ties with some of the Arabs here remained intact, so his forces did not worry about marauding Arab forays onto Hartuv's farmlands. The colonists liked to think it was because of friendship, while outsider Levi attributed the reticence of local Arabs to Jewish guns. "Arab Artuf was in fear that we will retaliate on them. And they tried to talk to the bands and tell them to keep away," he said.

Turmoil throughout Palestine receded in the fall of 1936, but it soon was followed by a new round of protest sending even more Arab rebels into battle and driving the Jews back behind their barbed-wire fences. The lull came after the Arab Higher Committee called off the strike on October 11, in response to an appeal by neighboring Arab kings who feared the spread of instability. After their gesture of compromise, Palestine's Arab leaders were rewarded with a shocking blueprint for their future. The British royal commission investigating the unrest said Palestine must be divided into two states, because the Arabs and the Jews could not live together in peace. The same day this Peel Commission report was issued in July of 1937, the government published a policy statement agreeing that the two peoples are locked in "irreconcilable conflict" that could best be solved by breaking up Palestine. It endorsed the plan for a Jewish state along the coast and in the north of Palestine, an Arab state composed of Transjordan and the rest of Palestine, and a permanent British-controlled enclave containing the holy places in the strip from Jerusalem to Bethlehem. The farmers in the Sorek Valley must have been bewildered: they would live in neither the Arab nor the Jewish state under this plan, but would sit in the limbo of never-ending British control.

The Palestinian Arabs rejected the plan, although Raghib Nashashibi—who envisioned himself as a future prime minister of the partitioned Arab state—indicated he would accept the division if the boundary lines could be juggled more favorably for the Arabs. Hajj Amin and the leaders of other Arab factions, however, were appalled at the notion of losing the coast as well as the Galilee, which then had only a meager Jewish population. Not only would these areas fall under Jewish control, but under the British partition plan the Arabs living there would be forcibly "transferred" out of their homes and into the Arab part of Palestine. Jewish leader Chaim Weizmann had campaigned for the plan during private meetings with a member of the Peel Commission and had discussed with British leaders ways to make the proposed boundaries more beneficial to residents of the proposed Jewish state. The leaders of the Yishuv again had outmaneuvered the Arabs in a forum that was supposed to be impartial. Amin, who had been making public calls for nonviolence, began preparing to restoke the fires of rebellion.

Among the Jews in and out of Palestine, reaction to partition built toward approval. Only Jabotinsky's radical Revisionists stood flatly against it. Weizmann, who had helped bring about the plan, was ecstatic at the prospect of a Jewish state of any size. Agricultural experts said even the small nation contemplated would be large enough to absorb 100,000 Jewish immigrants a year for the next twenty years. David Ben-Gurion, Weizmann's aggressive young rival for leadership, had encouraged Weizmann's pursuit of partition and repeatedly assured doubters that this small zone would be merely the first stage of statehood. "I do not doubt that our army will be among the world's finest, and then it will not be beyond us to settle in the rest of the country, either by mutual agreement and understanding with our Arab neighbors, or by some other way," Ben-Gurion wrote in a letter to his son.

Arab Palestinians struck back with a resumption of sporadic attacks, primarily against the symbols of British rule. When a British district commissioner was murdered in Nazareth in September 1937, the colonial power sprang into action. In an unprecedented offensive, the British outlawed the Arab Higher Committee and the national committees, ordered six leading nationalist figures arrested and deported to the Seychelles Islands in the Indian Ocean, and stripped Hajj Amin of his positions as president of the Supreme Moslem Council and chairman of the religious lands committee. He fled to Lebanon. About two hundred lesser leaders were arrested and many others bolted from the country, fearing imprisonment. Britain's actions stunned the Palestinians, then propelled them into violent reaction. Perhaps more important, the British sweep left angry masses without any leaders able to cool them and contain the protests as they grew increasingly destructive.

The Sorek Valley got sucked into the political whirlwind. Guerrilla groups—some of them political revolutionaries, others simply criminal bands—materialized all over the map under diverse, often rival local commanders. In the valley, chief of the mujahideen was a Palestinian known as Abu Walid. He was associated with the guerrilla leader Abdul Khader al-Husseini, who carried the reputation among Arabs of a heroic revolutionary fighter. Abdul Khader was a nationalist, not a brigand. He was the son of the late Musa Kasem al-Husseini—the same Musa Kasem who as a young Turkish bureaucrat back in the 1890s was credited with temporarily stopping Arab harassment of Hartuv. Abdul Khader also was the nephew of Hajj Amin.

Abu Walid's improvised, fluctuating force of villagers occasionally attacked the Haganah convoys to Hartuv, the rail line, and other targets from the valley to the main Jerusalem–Tel Aviv road. Hamed Odeh Faraj of Deir Aban was among the peasants who would join the roving bands of horsemen when they had a slack afternoon or a few days free from their fields. "In 1936 we were fighting against the British. They were the ones who were handing the country to the Jews," Faraj said. "I was one of the ones who didn't have a gun to fire, so I used a stick."

If they didn't join the fray, Arabs were expected at least to house and feed the peasant soldiers as they slipped from town to town, trying to avoid detection by British patrols. Diab Abu Latifah remembered the men coming through Saraa, his village overlooking the valley. "They would come to have food and to sleep. Someone from the village would stand guard outside. Then when you would come back, they would be gone," he said. Sabiha Abu Latifah, who was a girl back during the rebellion, said the revolutionaries often would sneak into town at night to consult her uncle about tactics. He was considered a wise man, she said, and supported the movement. Commander Abu Walid rode a horse given by her uncle.

The roaming cadres of fighters were belligerent but not always terribly effective, according to the Haganah's Levitza Levi. His defense force of the Jewish Settlement Police traveled extensively around the Jerusalem district, so he knew the roads and the colonies and which Arab villages routinely harbored rebels, which tended toward friendliness. "There were bands in the district of Jerusalem everywhere, and they just wandered from place to place to organize a mass attack on a certain settlement," he explained. "And in these attacks about four hundred to five hundred Arabs participated. Their weakness was they had no organization. They were emotional. They were a very great force. But that's all. And so they rarely succeeded. Nevertheless if four hundred people shoot at you and you have twenty or thirty, the situation was very bad."

It was the Jewish militiamen riding convoy duty who encountered the most danger. In 1939 a premonition saved Levi's con-

voy just a few miles from Hartuv. His force of thirty people,
armed with rifles and three machine guns, had made a short stop
to deliver supplies to Hartuv. It was no longer than fifteen
minutes, he said, before the cars were heading back down the
small road toward the Bab al-Wad junction and the major Jerusalem–Tel Aviv route that would carry them back home. They
reached the descent just past Ishwa, little more than a mile to
the east of Hartuv, when Levi was struck with an uncomfortable
feeling. "I stopped the convoy and I sent my deputy with one
man and said, 'You go up the next hill and have a look.'" The
envoys signaled back with their rifles—plenty of enemy ahead.
About seven hundred yards farther, beyond a curve, the road
was fully barricaded. Only forty minutes earlier the convoy had
passed the spot with no trouble, no sign of rebel activity. "It
means that they waited for us with cars, and they dragged these
stones from the cars and they blocked the road and they are now
in the mountains waiting for us," he said. "So I decided that
there are hundreds of them and we can't pass to Jerusalem, that
it would be foolish to go ahead." Levi took his troops—and a
pregnant woman they were escorting to Jerusalem—back to
Hartuv to call for British aid. It took the British two hours to
clear the road.

The Jewish settlers of Hartuv continued to get supplies from
convoys and seldom wandered beyond their fortified perimeter,
but the colonists said they suffered no serious assault in the
renewed round of violence that continued intermittently into
1939. Avraham Behor, the mukhtar of the moshava during the
riot years, wrote in a memoir that the British commander of the
Jerusalem police district expressed bewilderment at Hartuv's
good fortune in the midst of virtual anarchy. "He told me, 'I am
surprised until today nothing happened to you, since there is no
Jewish settlement that wasn't hurt. And you, a small settlement
surrounded by Arabs, were just unharmed up until now.' He
asked me to explain to him what is the secret of our relationship
with the Arabs." Behor wrote that the commander's comments
made him afraid the British officer was about to withdraw the
special police unit assigned to help guard Hartuv. "But he

calmed me and scattered my fears about it," Behor said. The commander pulled out neither the police protection nor the arms—two mortars, bombs, and rifles with ammunition—that the British had given to the Hartuv Jews.

What may have vexed the Hartuv settlers most during the rebellion was the scarcity of water. The colony still depended on the well a mile to the east in the town of Ishwa, a place where friendly Arabs had declared Allah made the water for everyone to enjoy. In these times, a mile had become a walk that no one wanted to risk. The British police at the station farther down the road also were inconvenienced by the lack of water. Behor said he arranged a meeting with the British sergeant and the mukhtars of Ishwa and proposed running water through a pipe down the slope from Ishwa's well to the dry settlers and police. "The mukhtars agreed on condition the water will be supplied only to the police station, but not to the Jewish farmers of Hartuv," Behor wrote. "Because if so, the terrorists would explode the machinery." They feared rebel retaliation if they helped their Jewish neighbors. Behor made the agreement, but as his memoirs recounted, the Hartuv settlers did not keep it. Once the pipe was fixed, guards stationed on the hill by the Ishwa mukhtars saw Jewish colonists drawing from the waterline. "The mukhtars came to the police and notified them that they stopped having the water put in the pipe, after the person from the moshava broke the agreement," Behor wrote. "And so it stopped, and the mukhtars were obligated to bring water on donkeys for the police station. At night we would go to the police station and would get a very small amount of water, just for drinking."

The hardship soon was alleviated, however, after a British army officer in charge of the railway station visited Hartuv and felt the problem firsthand. He asked Behor for a drink of water. "I said beer and cognac I can give you as much as you want, but no water," the leader of the colony recalled. The British officer told Behor he could help. Every family should prepare four empty cans by the next morning, he said, and he would arrange for water to be delivered to the railroad station and for a military vehicle to get it to the colony. That kind of cooperation was what convinced rebels like Hamed Odeh Faraj that the British were handing Palestine to the Jews.

The knot of Arab towns around the colony escaped most of the bloody infighting that scarred the rebellion in other places. "It wasn't dangerous for people like us on the roads—not Arabs," said Diab Abu Latifah. "Only those discovered to be traitors were killed. There was no war among Arabs." Elsewhere in Palestine, collaborators, those who informed to the British or cut quiet deals with Jewish businesses, met a bloody end. Many moderate middle- and upper-class Palestinian Arabs simply left, rather than feel compelled to participate in the violence and expose themselves to Jewish reprisals. Rebel courts tried and executed both Arabs and Jews who offended the revolutionary zealots. And the bruising political feud between the followers of Hajj Amin al-Husseini and the Nashashibi clan played itself out in political assassinations. Principals of the Nashashibi family, considered traitors by many for their soft approach to the British, their repudiation of the mufti, and their increasing dealings with Jewish leaders, fled from Palestine during the height of rebel activity.

The superior British forces made it possible for the Jews to withstand the years of conflict and keep their foothold in Palestine. Although Jewish leaders complained about British treatment under the mandate, the Jews and the British did lock hands in the face of the Arab rebellion. Under the circumstances, the British often winked at clandestine arms funneling through the Haganah network. British commanders also taught strategy and trained the Jews under them in the Jewish Settlement Police. Hartuv exemplified the cooperation. Levitza Levi said the British sergeant supervising defense in the area confronted him once with the knowledge that he was in the Haganah and had a cache of illegal weapons. Rather than warn him or arrest him, Levi said, the sergeant proposed that they work out a common defense plan for Hartuv that would take into account the Haganah's contraband weapons. "They attack us as well as you," the sergeant said in explanation.

Avraham Behor wrote of another joint venture. The British sergeant came from the police station to warn of rumors that a mass of Arabs was advancing toward Hartuv. The sergeant said he didn't have enough weapons to defend the place, but he knew the Hartuvians had some. "I know that you have illegal weapons, and it would be good if you bring them to the railway station so we can clean them and make them fit for action," the sergeant told Behor. "I promise you as an English gentleman that nothing will happen to you if you bring these illegal weapons to make them good. If an officer appears, I will tell him that we found them in one of the caves." Despite his fears, Behor said, he decided he had to trust that the Briton meant well and would not arrest the Jews for keeping prohibited arms. The police checked and cleaned the six English rifles and several pistols the Hartuvians had been hiding. They immediately returned a stock of thirty Haganah-supplied hand grenades to the settlers. Behor had given the sergeant a sofa in which to hide the guns and had made him promise to sleep on it himself so he would be responsible in case anyone told the secret. The big attack did not happen, but the sergeant did keep his word a month later when he returned the weapons because he was transferred to another station.

The English colonialists never would have reason to wish they had confiscated these few weapons from the Hartuv Jews. But as the Arab rebellion finally was crushed in 1939, and the political scenario was rewritten in London, the British administrators of Palestine found themselves with a new set of enemies whom they had permitted to build a deadly fighting machine.

ECHOES FROM ABROAD

*S*nuggled at the base of the hill, the old stone school-
house and its lone teacher drew Arab boys from Artuf,
Ishwa, Islin, and Saraa when farm chores didn't keep
them in the fields. As usual, Ismail Abdul Fattah Rahhal strolled across the valley after classes and then climbed up
past the Jewish settlement that sat just below his village, Artuf.
He got home just in time to learn a most peculiar lesson that
didn't appear in his textbooks. He was ten or twelve, so the year
had to be about 1940, some time after the Arab rebellion had
cooled. It was a time when Arabs and Jews and British administrators of Palestine were getting back to more normal pursuits,
though rough edges from the conflict still caught snags.

As he got to Artuf, he saw several strange men scurrying
away from the mountainside behind his village, outdistancing
by not too many paces a gaggle of angry village women shaking
their fists and shrieking. As Rahhal recalled the scene nearly
fifty years later, a British policeman in town was just as awed
as the boy to see women—Arab women at that—instigate such
a bold encounter.

The British police and the Jewish settlers of Hartuv had anticipated a belligerent Arab performance that day, and so had collected all the men of Artuf and ordered them to wait in the mosque. The strangers had come to survey the mountain land in order to untangle a hydra-headed dispute in which land was claimed by the Arabs, the Hartuv settlers, the Shimshon cement factory, and the Jewish National Fund. The Arab rebellion had stopped preparations for the factory and now the Jews were anxious to get Shimshon moving. They were talking about expanding Jewish settlement in the valley, too. First they needed the survey. But the plan to contain Arab objection to it was foiled by a canny villager, an old man let out of the mosque when he claimed he was sick. The elder did go home as promised, but once there he told his wife to gather all the women to drive off the intruders and uphold the rights of the village. The dispute would go on for years.

The account of the mountainside confrontation epitomizes the distrust and animosity separating Palestinian Arabs and the Jewish minority in the final years of mandatory Palestine. The end of the Arab rebellion did not bring a truly peaceful condition. Just in this one small valley, the 1940s yielded four land conflicts that were nasty enough to require outside arbitration. As elsewhere, the Arabs and Jews here were beginning nearly a decade of tension that would accumulate and stretch under outside events and carry Palestine to the threshold of war. The story told by Rahhal, the son of the last Arab mukhtar of Artuf, embodies the Arabs' feelings of resentment and fear that they would be denied their land—their connection to history and identity—and reflects the frustration of the Jews trying to make a place for themselves in Palestine.

Such intense sentiments prevailed across the quieting countryside, partly because of the way the rebellion had been contained. The British imposed calm through a combination of punitive, security, and political measures beginning in the autumn of 1938. The entire country was put under curfew, and travel by car and train outside the cities required a military pass. With more troops rushed in from Egypt and from England, large-scale military operations dislodged revolutionary gangs from the hills. The British conducted constant searches of villages, demolished houses where they believed rebels or weapons had been hidden, and sent hundreds of suspects to concentration camps without benefit of trial. The Arabs were beaten down, but their wrath was not subdued. "They were giving the Jews arms, while any Arab found with a knife or an empty cartridge was put in prison," said Diab Abu Latifah, whose anger at the British scarcely had dissipated fifty years later. "If they stopped me with this cane," he said, raising his wooden walking stick to show the sharp, metal-tipped end, "I would have been put in jail because I could kill someone with this if they attacked me."

A British political decision weighted in the Arabs' favor did as much as bullets and prison bars to stem unrest. The Woodhead Partition Commission, created at the start of 1938 to find the best way to partition Palestine, declared in November that it found division into Arab and Jewish states was not technically and economically feasible. The British cabinet quickly concurred that partition was impracticable and called a round-table conference of Arabs and Jews in London to talk about alternatives. British officials had indicated to the Woodhead Commission that they wanted such a finding, less than a year after they had adopted partition as official policy. Anomic strife in Palestine pushed the British into this bow to the Arabs, but they also were pulled to it from another direction. Nazi Germany and Fascist Italy had been courting Arab states, throwing out a web of cultural and political ties and directing radio broadcasts into the Middle East denouncing British and French imperialism. With the scent of war blowing across Europe, Britain could not risk losing its hold on the eastern Mediterranean. The British had to keep the Arabs.

Hajj Amin al-Husseini, who had been banned from the round-table meeting, took a negative course that would haunt the Arabs till today. Hajj Amin rejected the British White Paper issued in 1939 after the London talks. Its terms: a single, independent state after ten years and a five-year maximum immigration of 75,000 Jews, after which any further Jewish immigration would be subject to the approval of the Arab majority. Palestinian leaders allowed to return from exile in the Seychelles were frustrated at Hajj Amin's intransigence as they tried to convince him at meetings in Beirut to accept the deal. They saw at last an answer to their prayers for an independent Arab state, albeit a decade away. But Hajj Amin's was the key opinion and the man could not be dissuaded. Leaders of the Yishuv deplored the changed British policy that would limit their numbers and keep them a minority. But after sporadic violent protests, they would turn their energy against a broader danger and join the British in fighting Hitler. The deep impact of the White Paper and of Arab and Jewish responses to it would not be apparent until World War II ended. For now, Britain's political machinations, coming on top of its heavy show of force, were enough to bring relative quiet to Palestine.

Neither Arab nor Jew forgot their grievances, not in Palestine and not in the cluster of villages in the Sorek Valley. The conflict moved from the fields and highways to the offices of judges and bureaucrats, and it brought a new round of problems to the detached Jews of Hartuv. By spring of 1939 times had calmed enough that the Haganah told the Hartuvians it was pulling out its special protectors. Worse yet, it was stopping the stipends paid to eight local colonists who had aided in the defense of their homestead. The local recruits had earned only 4 Palestine pounds (about $16) a month, barely enough for subsistence. But for families kept from working their fields for three years by the disturbances, the payment made the difference between little food and no food. So what if the roads were safer and assaults fewer? These people still didn't have a crop.

The colonists led by Mukhtar Avraham Behor wrote an anguished letter to the overseers of the Haganah special defense force, issuing a threat that cannot have been taken lightly by political leaders of the Yishuv, who were anxious not merely to keep but to expand their presence in Palestine: the settlers would abandon Hartuv if the monthly stipends were indeed cut off. "However, before we take that dangerous step, which has an element of shame for the entire Yishuv," they wrote, "we refer to all our institutions and beg them please don't let an old moshava be destroyed in one day for such a small appeal that we require. . . . Don't let our haters be glad for our humiliation, because this is what they are waiting for!"

The settlers raised another disquieting thought, an early stirring of what would become a hurtful internal dispute during the later history of Israel. The Hartuvians implied that the leaders of the Jewish institutions, primarily Eastern European Ashkenazim, were neglecting Hartuv because its people were Sephardim. "Don't let the rumor expand," Behor wrote, "that only because Hartuv is a Sephardic moshava did the national institutions let it be destroyed, while at the same time they go and establish other moshavot in other places." Such threats and accusations surely did not win Hartuv champions among the leaders of the Yishuv, who must have felt they had bigger problems to tend, such as the British immigration cap that was frustrating their efforts to rescue Jews from Hitler. Relations between the Hartuvians and the Jewish institutions remained strained through the mid-1940s, and the bitterness would last beyond the creation of the state of Israel. For now, however, the Jewish Agency sent Hartuv indignant denials of discrimination. And soon it granted the settlers a $600 loan to help them crank up farm production again.

So the Hartuvians rebounded from the stressed, unpredictable years of Arab unrest, as did the rest of the Yishuv. In some ways the Jews in Palestine felt stronger and surely closer for having survived the uprising, ready to move on and out to other horizons. Not only did the Jews in Hartuv stay, but they made a stretch to get use of lands in the estate of the recently deceased Itzhak Goldberg. The executor of his estate decided the more than three hundred acres of land should be sold to the Jewish National Fund to assure that more Jewish settlers would land in the valley. Only thirteen Jewish families now remained. But even before the JNF could get possession of the Goldberg land, eleven of the Hartuv families formed a cooperative and started farming part of it, apparently with permission from his heirs. They set in motion a request that the JNF award them the land, but around this time the Jewish institutions learned to their distress that the Hartuv farmers were not managing both their land and Goldberg's farm by themselves. They continued using their old backstop, the Arabs.

To some leaders of the Yishuv, continuing such relations with the Arabs was a greater offense in the post-rebellion days than it ever had been before. "I hear today that in Hartuv they started to work with the Arabs," L. Pinnar of the Jewish Agency wrote in February 1940 to Yosef Weitz, a high official of the Jewish National Fund. "If this is correct it is very saddening, especially since this particular moshava received from us only a few months ago loans for emergency in the sum of 150 pounds [$600] for the sake of renewing the cultivation. This is on the basis of their promise to cultivate the areas by pure self-work." Weitz quickly responded that the JNF had no intention of compounding the offense by giving the Goldberg land to the Hartuv farmers. This kind of Arab-Jewish interdependence was especially galling to Weitz, who by now was convinced that the future of Palestine must not include Arabs. He wrote in his diary in June 1941:

> Among ourselves it must be clear that there is no room for both peoples in this small country. If the Arabs leave the country, it will be wide open for us. And if the Arabs stay, the country will remain narrow and miserable. . . . [T]here is no way besides transferring the Arabs from here to the neighboring countries, to transfer them all. Except perhaps for Bethlehem, Nazareth, and Old Jerusalem we must not leave a single village, not a single tribe.

The Weitz view of Palestine emptied of Arabs reflected a strong current of Zionist thought in the Yishuv, but it was by no means universal. It certainly was not held by the Jewish farmers of Hartuv. The result was conflict between those espousing full segregation till the Arabs could be removed, and those who wanted to try living and working together. The disagreement extended far beyond the Sorek Valley, and would grow into a much more painful cleavage.

The Hartuvians, already working new crops on Goldberg's

land, felt justified in having their own land farmed by Arab neighbors. A Jewish Agency inspector sent to see how the Jewish farmers were using the $600 agency loan felt they should have a chance. It was not that they suddenly imported Arab labor after the rebellion, found agent Shimon Meckler. The colonists had been so strapped during the disturbances that they devised a sort of land-use mortgage, in which the Arabs would make loans to the Jews and in return get to farm their land without sharing the crops. Under such loan arrangements, the neighboring peasants held a third of Hartuv's property. No wonder the colonists were so anxious to work Goldberg's estate. Meckler cited the troubled history of Hartuv and recommended compassion. "With all the farming problems that you have in this moshava you have to treat kindly these people that are sitting isolated in this place. They are worth not being neglected until a better time would come for a wider action to save the place," Meckler said.

So they continued. And so began the caustic disputes that would eat into the residue of good relations in the valley. Avraham Behor, the Hartuv mukhtar who became the JNF agent on the site, quickly learned that working the Goldberg land was agitating the Arabs next door in Artuf. "After working for four days they threw stones at us and drove us off," Behor said. The Jews were plowing areas listed on Goldberg's deed, but it happened his deed included land the Arabs had used as common farm or grazing land for decades.

Unexpected cultivation of their grazing land is what brought out the young stone throwers, and it is what caused their parents to file a case in the British-run courts. "This land in dispute . . . is in our undisputed possession since hundreds of years. We used to graze our cattle and cut our wood from it through all these years," said the January 20, 1941, complaint by six "mukhtars and notables" of Artuf. "Fifteen years ago by agreement between the villagers we partitioned part of this land and allotted a parcel to each villager. Some of the owners of these parcels are sowing them with barley, wheat and beans, others after sowing their parcels like the others for some years, they planted them with fruitful trees."

The villagers denied the Jews' counterclaim that the Arab farmers had occupied the land only during the rebellion, when lawlessness overruled the boundaries of deeds. Avraham Behor earlier had taken to court fellaheen from up the road in Ishwa, after they boldly tilled and planted some six acres of idle Jewish land during the days of the uprising. A judge ordered them to get off the land, according to Behor's memoirs. The Artuf Arabs said this was a different story. Just look at the fruit trees on the soil in dispute, they said. They are five or six or ten years old, so they were planted long before the rebellion. "It is not true that we took possession of this land during the disturbances. The trees can prove the righteousness of this statement."

The Artufis contended that Goldberg's deed for at least this part of the land must have been illegal, since village common land could not be sold under the prevailing law of the Ottoman Empire. Indeed, testified Artuf Mukhtar Ismail Abdul Fattah, everyone grazed his animals here through the years, even the Jewish farmers of Hartuv. Elder 'Eissa Hassan Ahmad suggested Goldberg must have known the land belonged to the Arabs, because he never chased them away. "We have had grazing there for more than fifty years," said the elder, who spoke of the time in his own memory. "Nobody has challenged us."

The March 14 order signed by W. R. McGeagh in the office of the Jerusalem district commissioner found for the Arabs. Part of the disputed land had remained all along in the hands of the Arabs of Artuf, the order said, but agents of the JNF—the Jewish farmers of Hartuv—had plowed and planted some of the land that winter. "I find the Arab inhabitants were forcibly dispossessed of this land," the British official ruled. The Artuf Arabs, he said, were entitled to possession of all the land in question.

The Goldberg land got the JNF in another argument, one that showed the grudge many of the Yishuv's leaders held toward the British after the White Paper of 1939. This time the disagreement was over a fortified police station the British wanted to build under a new security plan. They chose a flat spot between Jewish Hartuv and the train station, the two most likely targets of assault. The site happened to belong to the Jewish National

Fund, and the JNF was not about to surrender nearly twenty-eight acres of arable land without a fuss—even if the Hartuvians would become the prime beneficiaries of the project.

Just a few months earlier, the government had provoked a Jewish strike and a week of disorderly demonstrations when it published the new Land Transfers Regulations under the White Paper policy limiting the sale of Arab land to Jews. The regulations prohibited sales in some areas of Palestine. This valley was a restricted area. The Jews were being told to give up land they would not legally be able to replace. Besides, the condemnation panel offered the JNF only the equivalent of $48 per acre, which was the average per-acre price the JNF had just paid to acquire it in a friendly deal with the Goldberg estate.

In June 1940 the JNF appealed to the director of land registration that the bureaucrats consider the small, isolated colony of Hartuv, so badly in need of the strength new settlers would bring. "For this very reason, every piece of land which is fit for agricultural cultivation is so valuable to us, especially in this place which is in Zone A, where sale of land to Jews is restricted," the JNF said in a letter. Expropriating their "scanty" land would deprive at least two families from settling there. Why not take the land from the Arabs? the JNF asked. Or if not that, grant an exception to the land regulations and let the Jews buy replacement land in the valley? If the government wouldn't buy those schemes, the JNF said it at least should pay a better price, more like $120 an acre, since all the land in question was good farmland.

Understanding the speed with which the wheels of justice turn, the British went ahead and built their police station before getting a final decision on the land challenge. The station was dedicated the next year, 1941, and Mukhtar Avraham Behor was not deterred from participating by the enduring litigation. Behor proudly noted that all the mukhtars and elders from all the Arab villages in the area attended, but it was to the Jewish mukhtar that the district governor gave the honor of cutting the ribbon. "It made me more important in the eyes of the participants," Behor wrote. "They shook my hand and said, 'Ya Mukhtar, today is your day.'"

The government's price finally was judged to be fair in July 1942, but the JNF kept up a string of appeals for two more years trying to increase the condemnation price. The efforts finally ended with no success in 1944. But the energy the JNF threw into this one twenty-eight-acre parcel taken for a police station was evidence of how determined the JNF was to grind down anyone obstructing its job of getting and keeping as much land as possible for Jews to settle in Palestine.

These land disputes and, more important, the involvement of outsiders—the JNF with the Goldberg land, the Jewish Agency prodding Hartuvians to break their ties with the Arabs—complicated already frayed relations in the valley. "We continued working for them. My uncle used to work their fields after he finished his own land," said Diab Abu Latifah of Saraa. "But then later some newcomers came to Hartuv and they tried to divide the people. They didn't want the Arabs to work with them. Then the confidence was lost between the people." The Jews claimed their neighbors moved boundary markers in the fields. The Arabs complained their neighbors demanded cash payment to return a stray sheep. Less often, these days, did neighbors settle problems over a cup of coffee.

Yet throughout the arguments, hearings, and judgments, the people of the valley were able to resume a life certainly more normal than they had lived during the rebellion's years of anarchy. Schools, farms, small industries, and stores did their business much as before. With bus service restored, Arab villagers could ride up to Ramle, a small city that offered more stores and odd supplies than could be found in the valley. Once again the fellaheen could take the ten-piaster ride to Jerusalem every Friday to pray in the sacred walled compound inside the Old City, the men at the cavernous al-Aqsa Mosque and the women at the smaller Dome of the Rock under a glitter of mosaics. It was a day to catch up on the news and to shop from dozens of vendors who plied the Friday crowds, spreading a marketplace across the broad steps fronting the Damascus Gate and along the walkways outside the Old City walls.

Routine returned at home. Young mother Alia Mohammed Daher of Ishwa could walk any evening among the olive trees across the road, as she always had been fond of doing, without fear that a robber band might swing through the valley. Her husband, Asad Hamdan Asad, a tall fair man with a striking angular face, sometimes would join the men who gathered to sit and talk in the courtyard of Ishwa's guest house, even when there was no visiting sheikh or British bureaucrat putting up there. Or they might stroll down to Artuf to listen to the radio Mukhtar Ismail Abdul Fattah had bought from the British and ran on a car battery. But those were pursuits of leisure, and the routine more often was just hard work harvesting olives or fruits or tending fields of wheat, corn, and barley. Mahmoud, the son of Alia and Asad, had the job of herding goats and cows by the time he was ten. And when the family fields were done, Mahmoud joined his father and uncle on the four-mile walk to reach the lands of the Christian monastery in Deir Rafat, where the monks took one-third of the crop the Arab peasants planted and reaped.

Life opened up too for the Jews at Hartuv. It was safe for them to appear in the fields again, but the times had bypassed the Levy family's grain mill and oil press. The generator for the mill, idle for several years during the rebellion, never cranked into full speed, and the Arabs by now had gone back to traditional ways of pressing olives at home with rocks. Yoshko Levy remembered the colonists still took precautions, ordering the children not to go out alone. "The political problem between the Arabs and the Jews existed. It was in the background," he said. "Here in daily life, in day-to-day existence, it didn't bother us." He was a teenager in the post-rebellion years, lucky to have a bicycle and bold enough to ride off by himself even as far as Zekariya, the Arab town ten miles southwest where he earned spending money by measuring water levels for the Jewish National Fund. Levy said Arab kids might throw stones now and then as he pedaled past, but they didn't really try to hit him.

Hartuv never got to be a rich settlement, but at least the families who lived there had fresh air and space and the vineyards and fig and palm trees that tinged the place an exotic hue. The poorest of the Hartuvians lived in concrete boxes uglier

than the rock-and-mud homes of poor Arabs, while others had
done well enough to match the big stone houses with red-tiled
roofs that neighboring Arab mukhtars enjoyed. For all the mis-
fortunes Hartuv suffered, the place became a country retreat in
the 1940s for young Jews itching to get out of Jerusalem. Scout
troops would take the train or hike to the countryside and sleep
out under the stars at this moshava, one of the few places close
and safe enough to spend the night. And it wasn't totally primitive, not since the mayor of Tel Aviv had sent the Hartuvians
a generator to help them through the disturbances. Now they
had electricity. Hartuv was inviting enough for Tel Aviv welfare and court officials to choose it in 1944 as the site for an
institution for abandoned and delinquent Jewish boys, a home
for "the kids who just roll around the city streets."

The colony, however, never did get the expansion its people
said they so badly wanted. The Goldberg farm that the JNF took
over in 1941 wasn't big enough to support an entire new settlement, and the Jewish institutions were reluctant to add more
settlers to Hartuv, a colony with a poor record of farming which
adhered to private-enterprise principles instead of collective
economics. One company bringing new Jewish settlers to colonize did want to settle forty new families from the Balkan countries alongside the Hartuvians. It had plans to build the long-
awaited dam and even had a promise of JNF financial help to
do it. But the project hinged upon the Hartuvians' selling sub-
stantial blocks of their privately owned land to the JNF, to be
incorporated into the new settlement. At one meeting in 1944
they did agree to sell. Somehow under the strained relations
between Hartuv and the JNF, most of the settlers did not sell
off their land, and the new dam and settlement never materialized. What did finally materialize was the Shimshon cement
plant. After years spent unraveling property disputes, it finally
got its land title in 1946 and soon started hauling in machinery
to eat away the mountain behind Hartuv.

As the commonplace prevailed, the valley was touched by
changes invoked by war carried out on other stages by other
actors. There was an economic boomlet. It came primarily from

the British army's demand for everything from produce to tank treads. Throughout Palestine, Jewish and Arab farmers got higher prices for their crops, laborers higher wages. Merchants were awarded government contracts and entrepreneurs started factories that made uniforms and vaccines and antitank mines.

There were jobs at new factories like the British munitions plant built in Wadi Sarar, eight miles west of the police station. Diab Abu Latifah came down from his hilltop village of Saraa in 1941 to work as a carpenter in the munitions factory for three years, letting the rest of his family tend to farming. He earned enough to get married by the time the job was through. He knew little except that the workers made underwater mines. "There were a lot of things we were not allowed to see," he said. Some farmers were able to branch out in other directions. In Ishwa several fellaheen went into truck transportation, making their village the place to go to get crops and goods moved to the market. Among the new businessmen was Asad Hamdan Asad, who took a loan to buy a truck. "Life was good. But we didn't have lots of money," said his son Mahmoud. "As for grain and goats and food, we had plenty." There was even spare change to be made by kids like Mahmoud, who did odd jobs for British soldiers who sometimes bivouacked in the area.

Broader events in and out of Palestine touched the valley indirectly. People were more mobile and communications more widespread, so news of the world outside filtered in to Arab peasants and poor Jewish farmers now. They heard about the war approaching from North Africa and the European front, and they knew Hajj Amin al-Husseini had gone from exile in Lebanon to Iraq and then to Nazi Germany. The desperate efforts of the Jews to sneak illegal immigrants into Palestine and save them from European horrors were also known by anyone who read newspapers or listened to the couple of shortwave radios that had made their way into the valley. Despite the publicized failures, a good many of the illegal immigrants were getting into Palestine. The Jewish population in Palestine had grown by 1946 to almost 600,000, nearly one-third of the total population.

Everyone knew, too, about the Jewish terrorism exploding in the cities, the delayed response to the White Paper of 1939 that withdrew the prospect of Jewish self-rule and tried to stymie Jewish growth in numbers and in land. The robberies and murders, the bombings of police stations and government offices, the assassination of Minister of State Lord Moyne in Cairo by Jewish terrorists unsettled the Arab population. But there were no attacks on this cluster of small, unimportant villages. Diab Abu Latifah had joined an Arab company of the British armed forces after he left the munitions plant in 1944, but he saw no assaults by Jewish terrorist squads during his four years guarding British installations. He heard, though, that the Jews, including his neighbors at Hartuv, were getting secret military training at night at their settlements.

For the British the new Jewish aggression was a dilemma. They had to fight terrorists and increasing mob violence, but they also had to react with care now that the world was appalled by evidence of the Nazi extermination of Jews in Europe. Great Britain was being pressed by President Truman to allow entry into Palestine of 100,000 displaced Jews, even though America was refusing to significantly relax its immigration quotas. The British response was an attempt to engage the United States— with its vast resources and space—in helping to solve the problem. It proposed a joint Anglo-American committee to investigate the plight of European Jewry and the situation in Palestine in light of its findings. The result, delivered in a report on May 1, 1946, was no solution. It proposed admitting the 100,000 Jewish refugees to Palestine, but offered no answer to how Palestine should be governed. The report was a formula for continuing conflict, agitation, and stalemate. It said the Arabs should not be allowed to control Jewish immigration, but the Jews should not be allowed to outnumber the Arabs. The British mandate, it said, should continue.

· 10 ·

"WE THOUGHT WE'D BE PROTECTED"

*I*n the summer of 1946, the Arab kings, sheikhs, generals, and diplomats who held the proxies for the Sorek Valley fellaheen were certain the Arab cause in Palestine was just.

Why, they asked, should Hitler's Holocaust force the Arabs to give up land to the Jews? The Arab states "were second to none in regretting the woes inflicted upon the Jews of Europe by European dictatorial states," as one resolution at a meeting of Arab leaders put it. But the Holocaust was a massacre carried out by one group of Europeans against another. Why shouldn't the victims of Nazism be compensated with land and houses in Germany? If the Jews didn't want to stay in Europe, then why didn't their American friends waive U.S. immigration quotas so that Jews could go to New York?

That was the frame of mind of the one-year-old Arab League in May 1946 when it met for the first Arab summit meeting at King Farouk's farm at Anshass, Egypt. Instead of signaling a readiness to concede anything on Palestine, the Arab League declared that all Jewish immigration to Palestine must be stopped, that sales of Arab land to the Zionists must be prevented, and that all of Palestine must be given its independence as an Arab state. When a few days later President Truman repeated his call for the entry of 100,000 Jewish displaced persons into Palestine, the Arab League convened an emergency foreign ministers' meeting in Bludan, Syria. After much anger and bickering, the ministers passed "secret resolutions" which they leaked to Western diplomats. The resolutions declared that the Arab states would refrain from granting any new oil concessions and would "consider" canceling Western concessions already in force if the proposed surge of Jewish immigration came about.

In this atmosphere of self-righteousness, rage, and quibbling at Bludan, the Arab League foreign ministers made a disastrous mistake from which the Arabs of the Sorek Valley and the rest of Palestine have yet to recover. During one secret session in June 1946, the assembled Arab ministers held what amounted to an election to choose the postwar political leadership of the Palestinian Arab community. There were no local councils or other structures inside Palestine by which fellaheen like Asad Hamdan Asad or Diab Abu Latifah could choose a national leader. They had to count on neighboring Arab politicians who, they trusted, had the requisite will and money and arms to act on their behalf.

The ministers at Bludan could have decided to cobble together a Palestinian united front representing the remnants of the dozen Palestinian political parties. Instead, they gave their blessing to the most inflexible and bigoted faction to the exclusion of all the rest. They gave the Arab League's blessing to the Palestine Arab Party, dominated by the exiled mufti of Jerusalem, Hajj Amin al-Husseini, who still retained much of his aura of popularity from the early 1930s. His hatred of the British colonialists had taken him to Berlin in World War II to work as a Nazi propagandist and guerrilla organizer. While in Berlin, his hatred of Jews seems to have metastasized until it took over his whole thinking.

When the Arab League settled on Hajj Amin as chairman of the Arab Higher Committee of Palestine, he was hiding in

Egypt, having just slipped out of France to avoid the attempts
of world Zionist leaders to have him tried as a Nazi war criminal. After his selection he surfaced at Abdin Palace in Cairo and
asked King Farouk for refuge. King Farouk honored an old
desert custom of granting hospitality to travelers, and at the
same time placed Egypt's bet on the future direction of Palestinian politics. The king accepted Hajj Amin with elaborate
courtesy and arranged a villa for his life in exile.

Hajj Amin's return to the Middle East touched the Sorek
Valley's future in two ways. Not only did this event put the
political leadership of the Palestinian Arabs into the hands of an
absentee Jew-hating fanatic. It also served to nudge Hajj Amin's
enemy King Abdullah of Transjordan into pursuing a deal behind his back with the Zionist leaders of the Yishuv. If the deal
came to fruition, it would mean that the Jews would finally win
the right to create an independent Jewish nation in the rich
coastal plain of Palestine. Simultaneously, King Abdullah
would gain the opportunity to expand his kingdom into the
mountain region of central Palestine. For the Sorek Valley's mix
of Arab villages and one Jewish settlement, it would mean a
future under the sovereignty of King Abdullah and his Hashemite dynasty.

This would, of course, have been a detour from Zionist goals.
Ever since Rabbi Pines tried to buy the village of Artuf in 1883,
the Zionist movement had considered the Sorek Valley as part
of the Land of Israel that rightfully belonged to the Jews. As
recently as the Biltmore Conference of 1942, the mainstream
Zionist leadership under Ben-Gurion had demanded a "Jewish
commonwealth" covering all the British-administered territory
of Palestine, including the Sorek Valley. The right-wing Revisionists, whose young stalwarts already included future Israeli
prime ministers Menachem Begin and Yitzhak Shamir, went
even further, claiming that the Jewish state must also take in
King Abdullah's entire kingdom east of the Jordan River. Except for a small Jewish leftist fringe that favored a single "binational" state for Jews and Arabs, the entire Zionist movement
was advancing demands for all of Palestine. They were, that is,

until late June 1946, when Ben-Gurion and the other leaders of the Jewish Agency Executive decided it was time for a pragmatic retreat to the idea of partitioning Palestine between Jews and Arabs. Their biggest worry was not that Hajj Amin had resurfaced but rather that they had to thwart the trend of British and American statesmen toward making Palestine a "binational state." To Ben-Gurion and his cohorts, a combined Arab-Jewish state would mean the frustration of the Zionist ambition. They decided to ask the allies for a Jewish sovereign state on an "adequate" portion of Palestine, a place of their own that could take in several million Jewish refugees regardless of Arab objections. As Ben-Gurion saw the future, Palestine would be divided between a state for Jews to which he gave the biblical name "Judaea" and a state for Arabs which he personalized as "Abdallia."

Two representatives of the Jewish Agency gave the U.S. State Department a preview of the evolving Zionist strategy even before they broached the idea to King Abdullah. In late June, Eliahu Epstein and Leo Kohn informed the department's Near East bureau that they hoped to lure Abdullah into defecting from the six other nations in the Arab League—Syria, Egypt, Saudi Arabia, Iraq, Lebanon, and Yemen. This they would achieve by offering Abdullah a share of Palestine, which included the Sorek Valley. Kohn said that conceding the Arab town of Jaffa and "the Arab mountain district of central Palestine" to Abdullah's Transjordan would split the Arab opposition to the formation of a Jewish state. Abdullah's Hashemite dynasty "would immediately favor such a plan," Kohn predicted.

Two weeks later, the Jewish Agency's American branch sent the State Department a memorandum on how the Jewish Agency thought Palestine should be partitioned. The boundaries of its proposed Jewish state were similar to the outline of present-day Israel. The Jewish state was to receive about three-quarters of the land within the British Palestine mandate under the Jewish plan. Left for King Abdullah was a potato-shaped piece of inland Palestine with somewhat more land and economic potential than the present-day West Bank. For instance, the plan proposed putting three big Arab population centers that are now inside Israel—Jaffa, Ramle, and Lydda—into Abdullah's kingdom. There was an even more striking difference between the Jewish state then envisioned by its proponents and the Israel that has since evolved. Back in 1946 the Jewish Agency proposed to make Jerusalem and its suburbs into a permanent international enclave, not part of the Jewish state. Since Jerusalem was to be internationalized, the Jewish Agency did not even suggest any corridor of Jewish land linking Jerusalem and Tel Aviv. That is why the Valley of Sorek—including the Jewish settlement of Hartuv—sat squarely in the middle of Abdullah's zone on the maps outlined by the Jewish Agency.

For the next two critical years, the Palestinian nationalist movement was centered not in Palestine, where it might have turned in a more pragmatic direction, but in Hajj Amin's villa in the Egyptian port of Alexandria. As the Arab League foreign ministers must have anticipated, the British refused to allow him to return to Palestine. His 1941 meeting with Hitler and his letters in 1943–44 to other Nazi officials, in which he tried to block efforts of Jews to leave Germany for Palestine, made the mufti *persona non grata* in every Western country. His involvement in the botched pro-Nazi coup in Iraq in 1941 also made him unwelcome in Iraq, Transjordan, Saudi Arabia, and Lebanon—more than half the membership of the Arab League.

In choosing Hajj Amin despite these impediments, the Arab League ministers probably envisioned him in a role something like that of the Tibetan Dalai Lama in the 1980s—a religious stalwart who would exhort the faithful from a distant exile. They apparently intended to use him as a propagandist to oil up the rusty Palestinian nationalist movement and make it a more effective counterweight to the increasingly violent Jewish nationalist movement. They didn't realize that by putting Hajj Amin in office, they were giving up all flexibility on the Palestine question just at the time when the world's leaders were about to get down to the nitty-gritty details of decolonizing Palestine.

Hajj Amin's return to the Middle East scared King Abdullah and reawakened his interest in making a deal with the Zionists. Ever since the British brought up the idea of partition in 1937, Abdullah had entertained designs on a slice of Palestine which included most importantly Jerusalem, but also its Arab environs stretching out beyond the the Sorek Valley. From time to time he had imagined it as part of a vastly expanded Hashemite kingdom of "Greater Syria" that would start somewhere south of Jerusalem and stretch northward through Syria, maybe even into Lebanon. In the process, the Jews would get a piece of Palestine for their own state, but Hajj Amin's ambitions to create an independent Palestinian nation also would be destroyed. All the better from Abdullah's viewpoint. Hajj Amin had been in the way of his ambitions to be king of Palestine ever since the 1920s.

In August 1946, Abdullah met for an hour and a half with Elias Sasson, a suave Arabic-speaking agent from the Jewish Agency. This meeting at his summer palace was to be a foundation stone of the future state of Israel's recurring preference for dealing with Abdullah and his grandson King Hussein rather than with indigenous Palestinian Arab leadership. When Sasson asked Abdullah why the Zionists should be interested in dealing with Transjordan, the king listed several advantages. Most compelling among them was the avoidance of a new hostile Palestinian state which would be "headed by your archenemies the Husseinis." By preventing its creation, Abdullah said, the Zionists could avoid "shut[ting] the gates of the Arab sector completely before them and los[ing] the possibility of expansion." Abdullah was initially dubious about whether the Jewish portion of Palestine should be fully independent, as the Zionists wanted, or should become an autonomous canton under his monarchy. When Sasson pressed for a commitment to full Jewish independence, Abdullah replied that if the Zionists could get partition approved by England, the United States, and the United Nations, he would support it. Abdullah claimed that Iraq—then ruled by his Hashemite relatives—could probably be persuaded to go along as well. Thereupon the king asked Sasson for £40,000 ($120,000) in secret payments to finance his own political designs. He needed money, Abdullah explained, to enable him to recruit some supporters in a forthcoming Syrian election and also to finance a new pro-Hashemite political organization inside Palestine. A week later, Sasson brought Abdullah a £5,000 down payment. The ample baksheesh sealed a bargain for back-channel cooperation that was supposed to lead toward the partition of Palestine between Jews and Hashemites.

All this maneuvering in the summer of 1946 would have left no permanent footprints on the map of Palestine, except for one startling development. The following winter, Britain's weary Labour cabinet decided to give up trying to police Palestine in the face of rising Jewish terrorism and Hajj Amin's haughty refusal to accept any compromise which didn't recognize his supremacy as the Palestinian leader. Just as American will to remain in the Middle East would be smashed in the 1980s by the truck bombing of the U.S. Marine compound in Beirut, so British will to hold Palestine was undermined by the bombing of the British government offices in Jerusalem. On July 22, 1946, Irgun saboteurs under the command of Menachem Begin detonated a load of gelignite in the basement of the offices at the King David Hotel, killing ninety-one people, mostly Britishers. Her treasury drained by the war and her people at home standing in breadlines, Britain was forced to contract the empire. By early 1947, India was now all but lost. Egypt was slipping away and British troops were about to withdraw from Greece. Although the British chiefs of staff wanted to cling to Palestine as a hub for future Middle East military operations, the cabinet decided it could no longer afford to keep eighty thousand British troops pinned down in the bootless task of policing Jews and Arabs. Foreign Secretary Ernest Bevin told the House of Commons on February 18, 1947: "We have decided that we are unable to accept the scheme put forward either by the Arabs or by the Jews, or to impose ourselves a solution of our own. We have, therefore, reached the conclusion that the only course now open to us is to submit the problem to the judgment of the United Nations."

Thus it fell to a delegation of diplomats from eleven "neutral" countries to visit Palestine in June 1947 and recommend what would become the UN's solution to the Palestine question. Representatives of Palestine's 600,000 Jews rose brilliantly to the challenge of presenting their case to the panel of Dutch, Iranian, Latin American, and other delegates who made up the United Nations Special Committee on Palestine (UNSCOP). From the Galilee in the north to the Negev in the south, Jewish settlers turned out to welcome the UNSCOP delegates and tell of their accomplishments in the inhospitable terrain. Though no one from UNSCOP reached the Sorek Valley, several delegates did spend an evening at Kiryat Anavim, a kibbutz seven miles northeast of the valley. Jorge García-Grenados, the Guatemalan delegate, has described how he and three other delegation members were caught up in the spirit:

> After dinner, one of the old settlers made a moving speech. It was followed by others equally moving. Then there were songs, with a beating of hands and a swelling chorus; and the celebration finished with the Hora, danced first by a few of the young people, then by more and more until even elderly grandparents pushed aside chairs, took their places in the whirling circles and danced vigorously until exhausted. We ourselves could not withstand the gaiety, the spirit, the sparkle of that dance, danced by these simple and wholesome people, and so we, too, found ourselves in the circle, arms linked with arms, yielding ourselves to the exultant joy of that communal moment. This was my first Hora, but not my last. I was to take part in many another in Palestine.

Later, in hearings in Jerusalem, David Ben-Gurion and his Jewish Agency colleagues gave UNSCOP a fervent description of the Jews' historical attachment to Palestine and of their humanistic desire to live with the Arabs without trying to displace them. When the Czechoslovak delegate asked his position on partition, Ben-Gurion gave a supple reply. He said that while the Jews "are entitled to Palestine as a whole," they were prepared to consider a UN offer "of a Jewish state in an adequate area of Palestine."

Partition was the last thing the Arab Higher Committee meant to encourage during the UNSCOP visit. But its arrogance and contempt for Palestine's 33 percent Jewish minority achieved precisely that effect. In establishing UNSCOP, the United Nations had recognized the Arab Higher Committee as the body authorized to testify on behalf of the 1.2 million Palestinian Arabs. Rather than seizing the opportunity to present a Palestinian case on the same footing as that of the Jewish Agency, the Arab Higher Committee decided to boycott UNSCOP. The Arab Higher Committee did present two witnesses to a UN preparatory session in New York. But once Hajj Amin learned that the UNSCOP delegation might visit Jewish refugees at displaced persons' camps in Germany, he ended all Palestinian contacts with UNSCOP. Figuring that any inquiry which included the DP issue was bound to yield a pro-Jewish conclusion, Hajj Amin decided it would be better to give UNSCOP no answers at all during its month-long visit to Palestine. An Arab Higher Committee communiqué even warned Palestinians not to read "the Jewish press in English for fear of false news" during the UNSCOP visit.

Hajj Amin's boycott not only kept all Palestinian Arabs from testifying at the UNSCOP hearings in Jerusalem. It also led to scattered episodes of Arabs discriminating against reporters from Palestine's Jewish press who attempted to cover the UNSCOP investigation. Among those who barred these Jewish journalists from accompanying the UNSCOP delegates were the owner of an Arab tobacco factory, the town clerk of the Arab town of Ramle, and the Arab custodian of Abraham's Tomb in Hebron. At one stop, UNSCOP delegates were affronted to hear that an Arab café owner said he would serve coffee only to UNSCOP's thirteen Arab drivers and not to its thirteen Jewish drivers. More than any of Ben-Gurion's words, these petty episodes served to convince the UN delegates that the Jews needed a state of their own. The Guatemalan delegate would write in his memoirs: "We had come to Palestine ready to extend a hand of friendship to the Arab leaders. . . . I think the Arab Higher Committee's uncompromising attitude, its refusal to consider the possibility of any conciliatory gesture, was to prove a convincing argument for partition.''

Hajj Amin wasn't alone in failing to grasp the moment to bring a Palestinian state into existence during that deceptively peaceful summer of 1947. His archrival King Abdullah flubbed a historic chance of his own, and it is perhaps in consequence that the towns in the Sorek Valley fly an Israeli rather than a Jordanian or a Palestinian flag today. Abdullah missed his opportunity in late July. After the UNSCOP delegates had finished in Jerusalem and gone on to Beirut to hear testimony from an Arab League delegation, several members of the delegation detoured to Amman to see Abdullah. With part of his mind, Abdullah wished that the world community would impose a division of Palestine between his kingdom and the Zionists. But when the UNSCOP delegates pressed him to express his real views, King Abdullah didn't. Rather, he echoed the Arab League's uncompromising testimony in Beirut against partition, telling UNSCOP that Palestine had already taken more than its share of Jews. Pressed about partition, the king seemed to oppose it, saying: "It will be very difficult for Arabs to accept a Jewish state in even a part of Palestine."

A few days later, Abdullah sent a message to British Foreign Secretary Bevin saying that he really was in favor of partition after all. Although he had felt unable to tell this to UNSCOP for "political and tactical" reasons, he wished London to know that he saw partition as the only solution. One diplomat wrote that if the world community opted for partition, Abdullah would be perfectly willing "to take over all the Arab areas of Palestine, or as much of them as were offered to him, and to withstand the abuse and criticism to which this action might expose him from other Arab states." Abdullah's equivocation during the UNSCOP inquiry would cost him in more ways than one. First, he failed to give the UN any reason to believe that Transjordan was the best umbrella for the Arab parts of Palestine. Second and more important, his Jewish Agency contacts believed he had broken what they interpreted as a binding commitment to support partition. His chief Jewish Agency handler, Elias Sasson, was so indignant that he suggested to his colleagues that they should pay no more subsidies to Abdullah until he committed himself in writing to partition. After that the money stopped and they never quite concluded a partition deal.

The Arab mishandling of the UN inquiry was founded on the belief that nothing was going to change. After decades of watching one British royal commission after another devise contradictory plans for Palestine, hardly anyone expected that eleven neophytes from the United Nations could concoct a solution that would stick. While UNSCOP was still in Palestine in July, a correspondent quoted the expectation of one Arab source in London: "The [UN General] Assembly would not be able to agree on any course of action arising from this. There would be an inconclusive debate . . . and about October the Assembly would adjourn the question with Britain still in control." Even in late August when the UNSCOP delegates voted 8–3 in favor of a plan to partition Palestine, neither the Jews nor the Arabs foresaw that the British mandate was actually about to end. The most obtuse of all were the Palestinians of the Arab Higher Committee, who clung to Hajj Amin's vision of one Arab-dominated state of Palestine as though they couldn't imagine the world denying their claim. A few days after the UNSCOP report was published, a British official reported from Jerusalem that "Arab opinion here still finds it difficult to regard the plan as a serious proposal at all. The absence of any immediate violent reaction by the Arabs can be attributed to this incredulity, and many Arabs regard it rather as a joke."

As proposed in the UNSCOP majority plan, the Jewish state was surprisingly spacious, though it wasn't as big as the state envisioned in the Jewish Agency's 1946 secret proposals to the State Department. From the Jewish Agency's perspective, it was much more generous than any proposed solution put forward by any of the British royal commissions that had gnashed their teeth over the Palestine problem. Most important, the UNSCOP majority plan gave the Jews clear sovereignty over their portion of Palestine. The plan assigned the Jewish state three times as much territory as did the partition plan put forward in 1937 by Britain's Peel Commission, owing mainly to the inclusion of the large bedouin territory of the Negev desert in the Jewish boundaries. About nine-tenths of the prime farmland near the coast was included in the proposed Jewish boundaries, including large tracts of Arab-owned orange groves. Since the Zionist movement had accepted the Peel plan ten years earlier, it could scarcely balk at this improvement. After internal discussions the Jewish Agency said it accepted the UNSCOP majority plan as an "indispensable minimum." Some of its officials, including the future prime minister, Golda Meir, lamented that UNSCOP had made Jerusalem an internationalized zone and not part of the Jewish state. But for the time being, the Jewish Agency muted its demand for Jerusalem. Even the Jewish Agency's own partition plan had called in 1946 for internationalizing the Holy City.

The biggest loser in the UNSCOP plan was King Abdullah. In the Peel Plan, he had been designated to absorb the Arab share of Palestine into his kingdom. But after meeting him in Amman, the UN committee came out cleanly in favor of leaving the non-Jewish portion of Palestine to an "independent" Palestinian Arab state. UNSCOP said it should cover the mountainous midlands of Palestine, a southern strip around Gaza, and the western half of the Galilee. The majority report said that the Arab Palestinian state should participate in an "Economic Union" with Palestine's Jewish state and that each should be considered for membership in the United Nations.

The fall of 1947 was a blur of surprises. On September 26, Britain told the United Nations it was planning to abandon the mandate and withdraw its military forces from Palestine, except in the unlikely event that Jews and Arabs should settle their differences. In a three-day period in mid-October, the United States and the Soviet Union came out on the same side of the Palestine question. Neither government was ideologically committed to Zionism. Yet despite their Cold War antagonisms over Germany, Korea, Greece, and almost every other sore spot in the world, both wound up favoring the UNSCOP partition plan. It was a case of unrelated forces pushing the superpowers in the same direction. By coincidence, the Truman administration's desire to find a home for the Jewish displaced persons in the American zone of Germany coincided with Stalin's anticolonialist desire to push the British out of the Middle East.

The next shock was that despite the convergence of Cold War adversaries, partition came within an inch of failing to win the necessary two-thirds majority of the General Assembly. But finally on November 29, 1947, the General Assembly passed Resolution 181, which recommended the partition of Palestine into a Jewish state, an Arab state, and an international zone of Jerusalem. The critical votes were won in a final three-day frenzy of lobbying by Zionist representatives, aided at the last moment by the Truman White House. Three American client states—the Philippines, Liberia, and Haiti—fell into line on the final day after they had been threatened by various go-betweens with deprival of U.S. aid or investment. Michael Comay, a Zionist representative at the UN, reported a few days later that the refusal of the Palestinian Arab spokesmen to speak in conciliatory terms gave the Zionists one of their strongest weapons. "But for this," Comay wrote, "we may have had an even more difficult time, as many delegations supported the partition scheme with the greatest reluctance, and were willing to grasp at any possibility of rapprochement." The UN plan assigned the independent Jewish state 55 percent of the total land of Palestine. By then less than 8 percent of Palestine's land had actually been purchased by Jews. If both the Jews and the Arabs remained in their home towns as the UN plan anticipated, the Jewish state would consist of 538,000 Jews and 397,000 Arabs. Alongside it would exist an independent Arab state on 45 percent of the land with 804,000 Arabs and a minuscule minority of 10,000 Jews—among them the settlers at Hartuv.

Abdullah, ever the slippery pragmatist, had already responded to the UN's snub by sending his prime minister to Lebanon to press the Arab League's political committee to reject all forms of partition. Since the rest of the Arab League was already dead set against partition, the rejection was quickly adopted. Then, in another layer of intrigue, Abdullah resumed his secret contacts with intermediaries close to the Jewish Agency. The contacts culminated in a meeting before the UN vote between the king and a high-ranking official of the Jewish Agency, Golda Meir (who then went by the name Goldy Meyerson). After expressing amazement that the Jewish Agency would send a woman on such an important mission, the king delivered a monologue in which he committed himself to partition so long as it "will not shame me before the Arab world." How, he asked, would the Jews react if he attempted to capture the Arab part of Palestine? Mrs. Meir replied that this would be fine with the Jews—especially if it avoided a military encounter between their respective armies, and if Abdullah assured her his sole purpose was to establish order until the UN could set up a government. Abdullah answered acerbically: "But I want this part for me, in order to annex it to my state, and I do not wish to create a new Arab state which will interfere with my plans, and allow the Arabs to 'ride on my back.' I want to be the rider, not the horse." Serving as translator at the clandestine talks on November 17 was Elias Sasson, the Jewish Agency agent. Although nothing was finally agreed, Sasson reported glowingly that Abdullah "will not allow his forces to collide with us nor cooperate with other forces against us. . . . In case he will decide [to] invade Palestine [he] will concentrate [on] Arab areas with a view to prevent bloodshed, keep law and order, [and] forestall [the] mufti."

Unbending till the end, Hajj Amin not only rejected partition but also attacked a plan put forward by the three pro-Arab UNSCOP members to cantonize Palestine in the manner of Switzerland. Neither Hajj Amin nor any other Palestinian leader was wise enough to foresee that the UN majority and minority plans were the best deals the rest of the world would ever offer the Palestinians in their lifetimes—and perhaps for centuries. Though the majority plan would have meant sacrificing their claim to sovereignty over 55 percent of Palestine, they could at least have founded an independent Palestinian state on the remaining 45 percent of the land. Why didn't they accept?

Because in 1947 they thought, with considerable reason, that their cause in Palestine was just. Still full of righteous rage long after the partition vote, the distinguished Palestinian historian Walid Khalidi pressed the same point in 1971: "What were the Zionists conceding? You can only really concede what you possess."

At the Jewish moshava of Hartuv, Raphael Ben-Aroya was elated as he heard the news on the radio on November 29, 1947, that the United Nations had approved the partition plan. "About six or eight of us danced the Hora in the courtyard by the school," Ben-Aroya would remember. It wasn't until two or three days later that he and the other Hartuv settlers learned that Hartuv was now smack in the middle of the UN-approved Arab state. "We didn't know what to think," Ben-Aroya said long afterward. "We felt bad. We had been born in the place and we wanted to keep it."

At the Palestinian village of Ishwa just a mile away, Mahmoud Hamdan's family never did get an accurate account of what the United Nations decided in 1947. Responding to the Arab Higher Committee's disapproval of what happened, Arabic language newspapers in Palestine gave only sketchy coverage of the details of the United Nations decision. He understood that the UN delegates had decided that Ishwa was part of the international zone of Jerusalem.

Still, that was reassuring news. "We thought we would be protected," he would remember. "We were not very anxious."

• 11 •

SHADOW OF PLAN D

Once the United Nations voted, the Hartuvians immediately began transforming their settlement into a military outpost. First to take charge was third-generation settler Raphael Ben-Aroya, a thirty-three-year-old bus driver who had been a sergeant in the Jewish Settlement Police. "We made a wire fence around the moshava," he would remember. "We built firing positions, especially on the roofs of the houses." His cousin Chaim Levy, who had learned about electrical wiring at school, rigged up beacons that could be cranked by hand to revolve like searchlights. From the secret stockpile of the moshava they parceled out weapons. When Ben-Aroya took inventory, he found five Sten submachine guns, five Canadian-made rifles, and five Italian rifles, as well as one hundred hand grenades that had to be lit with matches. Ben-Aroya, who had been trained in the British course for the Jewish Settlement Police, was already the Haganah commander of Hartuv. Another five men also had been in the police. They, along with fifteen other Hartuvians, had received enough training from the Haganah to consider themselves members of the Jewish underground army. Counting these twenty, there were 120 Jewish men, women, and children at the Hartuv settlement. Fifty of these were teenagers in the new reform school on the grounds of Hartuv, which had been built by the Tel Aviv Juvenile Court in 1946.

Ben-Aroya didn't view Hartuv as a marker in some grand strategy, or even think the valley would get caught up in any real fighting. At first, the toughening of his perimeter looked to him like an insurance policy that would never be needed. Ben-Aroya could hear occasional gunshots from the direction of Ishwa, but Hartuv's Arab workers seemed friendly. What he did not know was that the Hartuv defenders would play a dangerous role in the enlargement of the Jewish state beyond its UN-proposed boundaries. They had begun acting it out already—by staying put. Hartuv lay deep inside the territory allocated to the Arab state by the UN. Rather than pulling the Hartuvians and other isolated settlers back inside the perimeter of the proposed Jewish state, David Ben-Gurion and the top commanders of the Haganah had reached a fundamental decision: they would try to hold every inch of Jewish land, even land inside the UN-proposed Palestinian Arab state. They were gambling that despite the finality of the vote, the UN hadn't really settled the borders. "The military planning," said Itzhak "Levitza" Levi, then the Haganah intelligence chief in Jerusalem, "was based on the presumption that the Arabs would not agree to the partition and that the frontiers would ultimately be decided on the battlefield."

Thus by December 1947, Haganah leaders had already decided to cling to Hartuv and the roughly twenty-five other settlements which stood in the UN's projected Arab state. The decision was based, according to Levi, on a fundamental Haganah doctrine: "Once you have put your foot in a place, you do not pull back." That Haganah doctrine traces back, Levi said, to one of the legends on which Haganah was founded. After World War I, about twenty Jewish pioneers held out for months in the surrounded settlement of Tel Hai, which was part of a no-man's-land between Palestine and Lebanon. The pioneers were determined to cause French and British diplomats to place this strip under British jurisdiction because of Lord Balfour's promise of a Jewish national home in Palestine. Concurrently, Arab nationalists were demanding the same no-man's-land as part of "Greater Syria." Two months before the 1920 conference to draw the boundary lines, attacking Arabs killed six of Tel Hai's Jewish defenders. The diplomats at San Remo rewarded their last stand by redrawing the borders between Lebanon and Palestine to place Tel Hai within Britain's Palestine mandate. Tel Hai had shown that even an indefensible settlement can impress international boundary makers. After such a precedent, how could Hartuv be abandoned?

Israel's War of Independence evolved almost imperceptibly out of the rioting and street fighting that swept through Palestine's cities in the fortnight after the UN partition vote. Only one day after the vote, an Arab flipped a hand grenade into a Jewish bus near Jaffa, killing six Jews. Over the next week, thirty-six more Jews were killed in riots, sniper attacks, and street murders. The British government, instead of cracking down as it had in 1929 and 1936, stirred both Arab and Jewish violence with its unexpected announcement that it would pull out of Palestine the following spring without any agreement for a peacekeeping force or a replacement government. Menachem Begin's right-wing Irgun organization, committed to seizing all of Palestine by force for the Jewish state, started a campaign of retribution. On the night of December 11, Irgun began by blowing up six houses and killing thirteen Arabs in a village called Tireh. Within forty-eight hours another six Arabs died when Irgun raiders rolled a barrel bomb—an oil drum loaded with nails and explosives—into an outdoor café in Jaffa. In Jerusalem, six more Arabs died from an Irgun bomb tossed into a bus station. At first, the establishment Jews of the Jewish Agency denounced Irgun's reprisal killings. But as Arab murders of Jews continued, Haganah launched its first retaliatory raid on the village of Khissas in northern Palestine. The future Israeli defense minister Moshe Dayan led this assault, in which ten Arabs were killed. By the end of 1947, tit-for-tat sectarian violence emerged on a scale that wouldn't be matched in the Middle East until Lebanon's civil war a generation later.

What did the most to elevate sporadic rioting into civil war was the December 30 carnage at the Iraq Petroleum Company's refinery in Haifa, one of the few institutions in Palestine with a mixed Arab-Jewish work force. In spite of a cease-fire in Haifa between Haganah and the Arab forces, an Irgun squad set off a car bomb near a crowd of Arabs waiting at the plant's employment office. When word spread inside the plant that six Arabs had been killed, Arab workers went on a rampage. Forty Jewish workers were killed, and Haganah ordered a retaliation strike at the Arab village of Balad ash-Sheikh, where many of the refinery workers lived. Haganah officers were told in a pre-battle briefing to kill a hundred males, according to one participant's recollection. The operation order called for a selective slaughter: "To attack the village with a force of 120 men, divided into six units, to kill maximum number of men, to destroy furniture . . . to avoid as much as possible injury to women and children, and to avoid arson."

No one could quite believe that Britain meant to let the Jews and Arabs fight until they reached a stalemate. But that was precisely what Britain intended to do. Sir Iltyd Clayton, the adviser on Arab affairs in the British Middle East Office in Cairo, outlined the cold-blooded scenario to an American diplomat:

> There is a sporting chance that if left undisturbed by direct foreign intervention, the Palestinian Arabs and Palestinian Jews will tire sooner or later of the conflict. . . . In the early fighting the zealots of both sides would probably be killed off. . . . From the fighting would emerge the outline of a defensible Jewish state—i.e., the area which the Jews prove they can defend. In the course of the fighting, a great part of the Arab population in the Jewish state would probably make its way through the lines to the safety of the Arab area. . . . If and when this stalemate occurs, there is a good prospect that the moderates on both sides will be ready to negotiate with each other. . . . If they should come to an agreement, it will fulfill the 20 year hope of His Majesty's Government and represent the only practical long-term solution of the Palestinian problem.

Clayton left no doubt about what the fighting would do to isolated settlements like Hartuv. As he put it, "the more exposed

Jewish settlements would be abandoned." For their part, the Hartuvians knew they couldn't hold their fenced-in moshava if their neighbors turned on them. The Hartuvians were outnumbered by nearly fifty to one by the 5,500 Arabs living in a three-mile radius. After a few weeks of tranquillity in the valley, they began to see the violence closing in. The first warning came on December 24, the day someone snuck up within a mile of their compound and blew up a pump on the old Goldberg farm. Two days later, their Haganah supply convoy was ambushed by Arab guerrillas just four miles north of them.

That attack put them on the flank of the most important early battlefield of the war, the struggle for the road between Tel Aviv and Jerusalem. Haganah used the road not only to push arms and food convoys from the coast to the 100,000 Jews in Jerusalem, but also to send convoys in the opposite direction to supply Hartuv. To reach Hartuv a convoy from Jerusalem would have to snake down through the Jerusalem Hills past Kastel, Deir Yassin, and several other Arab villages. Then, after half an hour's drive, the road curved down through a mile-long ravine called Bab al-Wad, whose slopes had been planted in evergreens by British foresters. Bab al-Wad—in English, Gate of the Valley—ended at a major road junction just north of the Sorek Valley. Most traffic kept going straight ahead for Tel Aviv across the treeless coastal plain. Other cars swung left into the narrow road through the Sorek Valley, past the Arab villages of Ishwa, Islin, and Artuf, past Jewish Hartuv, and on south toward the Negev desert.

The December 26 convoy had driven almost all the way through the Bab al-Wad ravine when the Haganah driver found the main road blocked with boulders. The moment the convoy slowed down, Arab guerrillas opened fire from the tree-covered hillsides. About a dozen Haganah guards leaped out of the armored cars and began firing back with their submachine guns. When a British unit rescued the convoy four hours later, Haganah counted three of its men killed and six wounded. Three Arabs were also killed and four wounded. Fearing that Hartuv could be attacked any moment, Ben-Aroya arranged to evacuate more than half the inhabitants—twenty children and old people from the settlement and the fifty teenagers from the Hartuv reform school. Now the Hartuvians were down to twenty armed defenders and about forty unarmed women, children, and old men.

Hartuv's defenders got the news in January that Kfar Etzion, another isolated Jewish settlement south of Jerusalem, was surrounded and being attacked by Arab irregulars. In Jerusalem, the Haganah command decided to use Hartuv as a staging base for a counterattack. On the night of January 11, a unit of the Palmach—Haganah's mobile strike force—stopped at Hartuv on the way to Kfar Etzion. Local commander Ben-Aroya was not as forceful as Dani Mack, the university-educated Palmach commander. But Ben-Aroya had an instinct about when it was safe to travel. He begged, even ordered, the twenty-three-year-old Mack not to leave Hartuv that night. Ben-Aroya said it was too late to reach Kfar Etzion before daylight. Mack brushed him aside and led the thirty-eight Palmach and Haganah troopers out the gate. The unit crept past the British police station and hiked six miles south of the valley before turning east. After two hours of marching, one Palmachnik sprained an ankle, and he had to hobble back toward Hartuv with two companions. Just at daybreak the remaining thirty-five commandos were spotted by an Arab shepherd, who warned the elders of the nearby villages that armed Jews were penetrating. The villagers took to arms. In the resulting day-long battle near the village of Surif, all thirty-five Palmach and Haganah troops were killed, along with fifty-seven Arabs. Like the rest of the Yishuv, Ben-Aroya was devastated. "I was mad at myself, and I was angry at Dani Mack," he would say. "It hurt me more than anybody that I didn't, that I couldn't stop them."

Three days later, while the Hartuvians were still shaken, they heard gunfire near the police station. Half a dozen young settlers grabbed their rifles and ran to investigate. When they returned, they gathered on a porch. Ben-Aroya would remember one of the young settlers slapping the bolt of his Sten to engage the safety. He forgot that there was a bullet in the chamber. The Sten fired and the bullet hit the ground. The slug ricocheted into Shmuel Ben-Besset, who fell bleeding. Ben-Besset, a twenty-year-old Haganah recruit, was a descendant of one of the twelve founding Bulgarian families. During the three hours it took for the British army to send an ambulance, he died. It was the first time since their grandfathers arrived from Bulgaria that a Hartuvian had been killed defending the settlement.

The picture got even gloomier. Three days later, a column of seventy more Haganah troops arrived at Hartuv and set off south across the railroad tracks, hoping to recover the bodies of the missing thirty-five. Three miles south of the valley, they, too, were startled by Arab gunfire from the slopes. Panic spread among the untrained Haganah draftees. One commander reported seeing Haganah troops throwing away their weapons. Demoralized, the troops straggled back to Hartuv while their commander stayed behind to collect their guns. They soon departed for Jerusalem.

Talking by wireless radio to Haganah headquarters in Jerusalem, Ben-Aroya cycled between bravado and despair. He pleaded for more troops. He also pleaded to go on the attack. One day he asked for permission to lead a few of the Hartuvians out to Bab al-Wad so they could ambush the enemy commander, Abdul Khader al-Husseini. "I wanted to finish him," he would complain long afterward. It wouldn't be hard to kill him as he rode by like a king in his white jeep, he had insisted to Jerusalem. One hand grenade would do it. By Ben-Aroya's recollection, Jerusalem refused him permission on grounds that "there are thousands of Arabs in the area, and this could make them angry."

In February, Haganah's Jerusalem command decided that the defense of Hartuv was too important to leave just in the hands of the colonists who had grown up there. As Ben-Aroya would tell the story, he made it to Jerusalem in a British armored car and confronted his Haganah superior with a demand for ten more men. "Send me anywhere else, but I won't stay here as commander of this place with so little ammunition and men," Ben-Aroya remembered saying. The answer he recalled from his commander was "Okay, go." Ben-Aroya was drafted into a unit in Tel Aviv. In the next convoy to Hartuv, headquarters sent a few dozen Haganah troops and a new commander, Ariyeh Shepach. From then on Hartuv began to exemplify the advantages in experience and weapons that would gradually help the Jews of the Yishuv to overcome the more numerous Palestinian Arabs. Shepach, who had been a British machine gunner in World War II, ordered all the defenders to begin digging trenches and bunkers. Within two weeks the garrison increased to about seventy soldiers and there was enough firepower inside to hold out against the lightly armed villagers around them. By February the armory included thirty-nine rifles, twenty-seven Sten submachine guns, and four medium machine guns.

The Sorek Valley was emerging in the minds of operational planners in Haganah's general headquarters as an important military objective. Their war plan, Plan D, spelled out in meticulous detail how Haganah forces were to take control of all the territory allotted by the UN to the Jewish state. When the plan was approved by Haganah headquarters on March 10, it was a bold advance beyond Haganah's traditional defensive doctrine. Now for the first time, Haganah approved a strategy of preemptive strikes. Plan D envisioned seizing a network of forward bases throughout the UN-proposed Arab state before any foreign Arab armies could occupy the high ground. As spelled out by the war planners, the goal was not "usually" to take permanent control of territory outside the Jewish state. However, there was an exception. As the plan bluntly put it, "Some bases of the enemy that are located close to the [Jewish state's] borders and that might be used as stepping-stones for invasion of important sections of the state will be occupied temporarily and will be cleaned out."

One of the most far-reaching assumptions of Plan D was that Jewish forces must try to seal off the UN's international zone in Jerusalem. The Haganah planning for Jerusalem proceeded just as if the United Nations had allocated the Holy City to the Jewish state. A supplement to Plan D listed the nearby police stations, Arab villages, and road junctions that Haganah should seize in order to protect Jerusalem from nearby Arab towns.

These included the Hartuv police fortress, which was half a mile west of the Hartuv settlement. The Wilson Brown Police Post, as the British called it, had been built by the British in 1941 to replace their small police station inside the settlement. It was important to the Haganah war planners because it dominated one of the roads the Arabs might use to reach Jerusalem from the south. The 1929 attack on the settlement had brought the police station to the valley. The 1936–39 Arab revolt had influenced the British to fortify it. Now, because the police fort existed, the Sorek Valley was doubly important to defense of the nascent Jewish state.

The Sorek Valley had been set aside by the United Nations to become part of an Arab nation. However, the 5,500 fellaheen who lived in and around the valley had no David Ben-Gurion and no war plans division to confirm their nationhood. Their future was in the hands of blustering, backstabbing leaders who lived outside Palestine and rejected the UN plan. Of the Arab political leaders who mattered in 1947, only one was a Palestinian. He was Hajj Amin al-Husseini, the exiled mufti of Jerusalem and chairman of the Arab Higher Committee, who now lived in Cairo. The others who counted as decision-makers were the kings, princes, and ministers of the Arab League nations. To them, Palestine was not a homeland to be defended inch by inch. Rather it was a distant prize to be claimed, cleansed of infidels, and perhaps plundered—preferably with someone else doing the fighting.

Even Hajj Amin, who was obsessed with opposing every Zionist advance, had been curiously passive about preparing to fight for Arab interests in Palestine following his appointment as head of the Arab Higher Committee. As was typical throughout the countryside, Hajj Amin and his agents had not begun to organize an underground fighting force in the Sorek Valley analogous to the Haganah's. By the end of the 1936–39 Arab revolt, the British had exiled the vanguard of the Arab resistance, and Hajj Amin had done little to have them return or replaced after World War II. Within a few Palestinian cities, he had taken some feeble steps to form an armed Arab youth orga-

nization. But by the time the United Nations voted for partition, Hajj Amin's organization counted its strength in the whole
Jerusalem area as only twenty-five rifles. While Mahmoud Hamdan was a schoolboy in 1947, he used to hear about Hajj Amin
as an indomitable freedom fighter struggling for the Palestinian
cause somewhere far away. "We all used to know that he existed," said Mahmoud. "But nobody was there in Ishwa for him.
We didn't know what he did."

Why had Hajj Amin done so little except fulminate against
partition? Apparently because his ideas about fighting had
coagulated back during the 1936–39 spontaneous peasant revolt.
So confident was Hajj Amin of another geyser of rage that he
insisted to the Arab League that there would be no need to send
Arab armies to defend Palestine. His guerrillas could take care
of Haganah with the help of a few outside Arab volunteers. He
was so sure the Palestinians would rise up against partition that
he didn't trouble himself with reestablishing the network of
local "Arab national committees" which had served as rallying
points for resistance in 1936. This time, Hajj Amin and his followers were thinking on a much grander scale. Instead of working to form village militias, they occupied themselves debating
over questions of high policy, such as whether they would make
Palestine a monarchy or a republic after the Jews had been
defeated. Emile Ghoury, one of Hajj Amin's confidants, told an
American diplomat late in 1947 that Hajj Amin would probably
head the future Arab state of Palestine only temporarily. In
Ghoury's opinion, Hajj Amin wouldn't remain as the permanent leader because "Palestine was too small for the talents of
the mufti." Ghoury was apparently visualizing Hajj Amin as the
leader of a much wider anticolonialist revolt throughout the
Arab world.

The kings and princes who ruled the Arab League nations
feared Hajj Amin, recognizing that the broad masses throughout the Arab world were behind his anti-Zionist nationalism.
They saw eye to eye with him about only one thing: it was a bad
idea to send Arab regular troops into Palestine. As a group, they
were not as blind about Haganah's potential strength as was

Hajj Amin. Iraqi General Ismael Safwat, the ranking Palestine expert among the Arab League's military men, had given the Arab League Council a chilling and accurate diagnosis. In October 1947 the former Iraqi chief of staff had warned that the Zionists could field twenty thousand well-trained troops immediately and could count on twice as many trained reservists. They already had commandos, a covert arms industry, and a source of volunteers in Europe and the United States. Although there were twice as many Palestinian Arabs as Jews, the Arabs could not compare militarily to the Jews in "manpower, organization, armaments, or ammunition," he warned. He recommended that the Arab League nations deploy large numbers of regular troops close to the frontiers of Palestine as a deterrent. He called also for a single Arab military commander and for an immediate campaign to recruit, train, and arm Arab volunteers.

Safwat's call for combined military preparation exposed the fecklessness of the Arab coalition. The Arab states of the 1940s were backward clients of the Western powers which didn't possess oil wealth or skyscrapers or strong armies. Egypt's King Farouk, ensconced in negotiations for his country's independence from Britain, opted out of any military intervention. King Abdullah of Transjordan, whose 7,400-man Arab Legion was the only modern army of any Arab country, shied away as well. About this time King Ibn Saud of Saudi Arabia received accurate intelligence that King Abdullah was receiving bribes from the Jewish Agency as part of a deal to extend Transjordanian sovereignty over the UN-designated Arab part of Palestine. Much as Ibn Saud hated the idea, he refused to join in Arab League military or economic sanctions to prevent it. Saudi oil royalties that year came to only $14 million; Ibn Saud wasn't about to jeopardize that paltry cash flow. When Iraq tried pushing the Arab League states to cancel oil concessions to pressure Britain and the United States on Palestine, the Saudi minister refused.

Syria and Iraq were left as the only Arab League members ready to join in a fight against Haganah. In late 1947 even they were not willing to commit their regular troops. Instead, they set up training camps near Damascus and began to raise a volunteer expeditionary force called the Arab Liberation Army. Syrian Defense Minister Ahmad Sharabati, after drinking three old-fashioneds with an American diplomat in Damascus, let it slip that the Syrian and Iraqi armies would join the fighting only by occupying the territory assigned by the UN to the Arab state. Further, he said the Arab armies would enter Palestine only after the British had withdrawn. Sharabati appeared to be convinced that when the time came, the Haganah would be shown up as "the biggest bluff in history" without any need for regular troops.

Like a good many Arab military men, Sharabati had a view of warfare that was both cynical and romantic. He truly thought that Palestine could be saved by fortune-hunting bedouins and guerrillas who would sweep in off the desert, just the way Colonel T. E. Lawrence's irregulars captured Damascus in 1918. Sharabati told the American diplomat that as the Syrian and Iraqi troops advanced to occupy the Arab part of Palestine, they would be buttressed by "100,000 loot-seeking bedouins" who would serve as "mine fodder." He wasn't the only Arab leader with antique ideas of how to raise a force to defend Palestine. Even the Arab League's urbane secretary-general, Abdul Rahman Azzam, said in November 1947 that he expected that "with proper coaching" tribesmen from all over the Middle East would migrate to fight in Palestine. They would come, he said, for two main motives. First there was the religious motive of cleansing Palestine of the infidels. Second, and "perhaps most important," was what he called "the prospect of doing some looting, especially among Jews."

They were a mixed gang of patriots, cutthroats, bandits, these 6,500 Arab irregulars who finally did take up arms against the Haganah. They belonged to two Arab forces that operated independently of each other. The larger, with about four thousand men, was the Arab Liberation Army under the command of the swashbuckling guerrilla fighter Fauzi al-Kaukji, who was in the pay of the Syrian government. The Arab League, suspicious of Hajj Amin's motives, had decided to put Kaukji in command because he was not a Hajj Amin loyalist. After calling for a *jihad* to save the Moslem holy places, Kaukji pompously vowed in October 1947 to "inflict crushing defeats upon our enemies"— even upon the British and Americans if necessary. Over the next few months he used a training camp near Damascus to gather and arm his volunteer fighters, mostly Syrians, Iraqis, and exiled Palestinians. In January 1948 they began infiltrating into northern Palestine, divided into eight "battalions" and led for the most part by officers loaned from the Syrian and Iraqi armies.

Hajj Amin's Arab Higher Committee finally had started to organize a militia force of its own called the Holy Struggle. Its commander in chief, Abdul Khader al-Husseini, was the picture of a guerrilla fighter, a strapping man with two bandoliers across his chest and a white headdress. He crossed into the present-day West Bank from Transjordan in late December 1947 and began recruiting anyone who would fight. Abdul Khader was the son of the late Musa Kasem al-Husseini—the supposed protector of Hartuv in the 1890s, the mayor of Jerusalem from 1918 to 1920, and finally a Palestinian nationalist leader until his death in 1934. Presently, Abdul Khader's most notable relative was his uncle, the exiled mufti. Beyond his connection with the Husseini clan, Abdul Khader had a personal aura among the villagers because of his exploits against the British during the 1936–39 revolt. The British still considered him a wanted man.

Abdul Khader started his recruiting where his roots were strongest, in the hills around Jerusalem. One place he had friends was the village of Beit Susin, where the Husseinis owned farmland. Beit Susin was only two miles over a ridge from the Sorek Valley. In early 1948, Abdul Khader would occasionally hike on that ridge and stop in Saraa. Diab Abu Latifah, then a twenty-nine-year-old Saraa farmer, would remember the Palestinian commander turning up from time to time in Saraa with a small entourage, usually at night. "The villagers would make a big meal for his men," Abu Latifah said. "He would come just for an hour or so to eat with the people and to talk. Then he would be gone." Saraa was not considered safe enough to stay overnight, since it was just a mile from the Hartuv police fortress and the Jewish garrison. However, Abdul Khader and his men did maintain a secure base camp in the mountains five miles southwest of Hartuv, at an abandoned village called Khirbet al-Tantura. "You couldn't reach it by car or even by horse," remembered Diab Abu Latifah. "He used to stay up there sometimes with half the leadership."

During the cold, rainy days of March 1948, the Palestinian farmers who lived in the Sorek Valley joined the war. It happened almost overnight when a grizzled, black-eyed sheikh appeared in the valley with his band of twenty-five to fifty of his bedouin tribesmen from southern Transjordan. They were members of the Howeitat clan, a bedouin tribe with a tradition of fighting and plundering. Now they had come to join Abdul Khader. Their sheikh, Haroun Ibn Jazzi, was a first cousin of Abou Taya, the Howeitat chieftain who fought in the Arab uprising of 1916–18 beside Lawrence of Arabia. During the 1930s the Howeitats had settled into an encampment in the badlands not far from Aqaba, the city Abou Taya and T. E. Lawrence captured. When the fighting started in Palestine in 1947, old urges stirred the Howeitats. Ibn Jazzi gathered his men and made his way one hundred miles north to the headquarters of Abdul Khader. The Palestinian commander in chief accepted the bedouin sheikh into his inner councils. At first, Abdul Khader put Ibn Jazzi in charge of attacking Jewish convoys in the Bab al-Wad gorge. By one account, Haroun Ibn Jazzi borrowed a flock of sheep and wandered for days up and down the ridges, masquerading as a shepherd while reconnoitering for the best firing positions. No one knows how many Jewish armored cars trying to supply bullets and food to Jerusalem under Plan D were turned into rusting hulks by Ibn Jazzi's bullets. It was more than a few.

In early March, Ibn Jazzi and his men set up a temporary camp in the Sorek Valley. The villagers of Ishwa put up Ibn Jazzi in their stone guest house and found space around the village for the other bedouins. Within a few days, Ibn Jazzi expanded his band to include about two hundred part-time fighters from Ishwa and nearby villages, most of them farmers who joined in raids when there was no work to be done in the fields. Mahmoud Hamdan's father was among the Ishwa villagers who joined Ibn Jazzi. His son Mahmoud was only thirteen, too young to be a full-fledged guerrilla. But sometimes he was sent out at night to guard the road and look for Jewish convoys.

Just after noon on March 18, 1948, Ibn Jazzi and his followers found a target of opportunity. On this rainy, muddy day, four Haganah armored cars and four supply trucks rumbled southwest from the Bab al-Wad junction toward Hartuv. The Haganah operations staff had designated this caravan as Convoy Tova. Inside the armored cars were fifty Haganah troops armed with submachine guns, a smaller complement than Haganah sent on some of its convoys. The convoy had fallen behind schedule that morning because the fan belt in one armored car had broken. The convoy had to stop for four hours near Abu Ghosh, an Arab village outside Jerusalem. Word of the approaching convoy probably reached Ibn Jazzi, for when the convoy finally turned into the Sorek Valley, the Howeitat was ready.

The sheikh had his bedouins and local Arab fighters deployed in the hills along the four-mile road to Hartuv. They let Convoy Tova pass to Hartuv untouched. When the convoy turned back for the return trip, the drivers found the road blocked with boulders. One armored car hit a boulder and veered off the road, sinking into a muddy ditch. Ibn Jazzi's men opened fire, puncturing two tires and the radiator. When several other armored cars rushed to help, Arab fighters in a green farm truck pulled up from the rear and began firing. The Haganah car hit back with the German machine gun atop one of the armored cars, but they had come too late: Sheikh Ibn Jazzi's fighters rushed the trapped armored car and tossed grenades and possibly Molotov cocktails. They set it ablaze, forcing the soldiers out onto the road. The pilot of a Haganah Piper Cub, ordered to make a surveillance, radioed a report to Tel Aviv: "Two cars at halfway point from the road to Hartuv. One is burnt. And next to them two bodies. A group of Arabs was near it, one that shot at the airplane. Afterwards, four of our armored vehicles appeared and entered, so it seems, into battle with the Arabs and returned in the direction to Jerusalem." Before the shooting stopped, eleven Haganah soldiers had been killed. Seven others ended up stranded but alive in the Hartuv garrison. The other thirty-odd soldiers fought their way through nine more roadblocks to reach Jerusalem. A Haganah report said the Arab fighters made off with a machine gun, two radio transmitters, various small arms, and some ammunition. The Arabs paid a price. One Hebrew-language newspaper claimed at the time that twenty-two Arabs were killed and thirty-seven wounded, though in retrospect that was clearly an exaggeration.

· 12 ·

UNDER SIEGE

round the middle of March, an Arab "teller" who worked for one of the Hartuvians warned that Haroun Ibn Jazzi's men had pitched camp up the road in Ishwa. The Haganah intelligence branch took this message from its paid informant seriously and advised Chief of Operations Yigael Yadin to hold up Hartuv's convoys until Ibn Jazzi's men moved on. Somehow the warning was disregarded, and Convoy Tova was decimated.

After that, one attack seemed to stimulate another. On March 20, dozens of Arabs from Deir Aban broke into the Shimshon cement plant and began carting off chains, metal parts, even pieces of wood from the doorframes. The Shimshon factory stood half a mile beyond the perimeter fence that separated the 120 Jews inside the Hartuv garrison from the rest of the valley. A dozen Haganah troops rushed the gates and tried to save Shimshon, shooting off two rounds from a mortar and some bursts of submachine-gun fire. When they pulled back after a few hours to save ammunition, the looting resumed.

Now it was dusk on March 21 and the Hartuv garrison commander, ex-British gunner Ariyeh Shepach, was sure that the

Hartuv garrison would be hit next. His sentries spotted "many foreign Arabs" entering the village of Artuf, one hundred yards up the hill. Shepach rushed off a radio message to his Haganah superiors calling for reinforcements. "The situation is serious and urgent," Shepach radioed. "The people are tired from guarding and working on fortifications. They are not trained at all and it could have a bad ending."

Just after midnight, the defenders heard the first shots. One bullet shattered the searchlight that faced up the hill toward Artuf. The nine young defenders in the nearest Jewish position—seven men and two women—were thrown into a panic. They were green troops from Hulon, a town near Tel Aviv, who knew nothing of the valley. They were also low on ammunition. Their squad leader called Shepach's headquarters bunker and asked permission to retreat from their machine-gun nest on top of one of the moshava's rooftops. "The Arabs are crossing the fence and sneaking into the yard," he called into his field telephone. "We can see them and hear them."

Fifty yards away, someone in Shepach's headquarters bunker ordered them to stay put while he sent reinforcements. As the attack intensified, Yoshko Levy's local squad and Mati Peled's half-dozen Palmach commandos were sent as backups. When Peled reached Position Seven, he found the squad leader's "teeth shaking." Peled asked him where the enemy was. "Here he is," the squad leader said. "There. Everywhere. All around." Peled could see Arabs crouching in the ruins of an abandoned building fifty or a hundred yards away. Describing the scene on the rooftop, Peled would later write in the official journal of the Israeli army: "All the people of the position are stuck in one hole. They don't see anything. They instill fear into each other."

Yoshko Levy, now twenty-four, ran twice to Position Seven— first to carry ammunition to the Hulon squad and then when he had been sent back to take command. "The commander was shaking all over," Levy said much later. He remembered telling them to hold on, "or otherwise we'll all go to hell." He sent two men with Stens down to guard a window on the ground floor. At another point, Levy sent the Palmachniks down to find a position in the ruins from which they could get the Arabs in a crossfire. Meanwhile he stayed on the roof with the Hulon squad, firing their machine gun while the two women soldiers fed ammunition.

Levy watched as the Arabs "would shoot and advance, shoot and advance." At one point they snuck up behind an old wall within ten meters of his outpost. After a pause, he heard a huge thump, and the wall crumpled. A TNT explosion, Levy figured. Immediately came the crackling of Arab rifles, accompanied by a chorus of warbling shrieks. "The Arab women from the village were trying to frighten us," said Levy, a third-generation Hartuvian. "The men were shouting, and there was shooting from all over." Levy saw the Arabs were making a run on his position. "I threw the rest of the hand grenades we had in Position Seven," said Levy. "There were about ten."

Everything seemed to happen within a few moments, though the shooting stretched out over several hours. Peled heard the same big explosion, some shouts in Arabic, and a crescendo of rifle fire. Then came something totally unexpected. He heard a voice shouting "Withdraw" in Arabic. Suddenly the shooting tapered off. It was only after dawn that the defenders figured out what had probably saved them. A Haganah patrol found blood blotches spotting the ground near where Yoshko Levy had aimed his grenades. It was over before anyone could really figure out what had happened. "The attack was serious, but it could have been much rougher considering the number of Arabs in the area," the garrison radioed shortly after dawn on March 22. "I assess that there were one hundred Arabs there."

But in Jerusalem, rumors circulated that the assault was more significant. A *New York Times* dispatch, quoting unnamed Jewish sources in Jerusalem, said that Abdul Khader al-Husseini himself was believed to have commanded the attack. The *Times* also reported that six hundred Arabs had attacked and fifty of them had been killed or wounded—exaggerations that no one bothered to correct.

The next day British headquarters in Jerusalem, fearing that the colony would be annihilated, sent steel-helmeted troops of the Warwickshire Regiment in an armored convoy. It is unclear what stimulated the British commander to depart from the normal policy of letting the two sides go at each other with minimal British interference. Whatever the explanation was that day, the Arabs in Ishwa mistook the British armored cars for Haganah reinforcements and opened fire from above the road. The British blasted out of the ambush, firing four twenty-five-pound high-explosive shells and sixteen smoke shells into the middle of Ishwa. In the melee, as many as twenty Ishwa residents were killed or wounded and two British soldiers were killed. Three other Warwickshire soldiers were rescued with wounds. It would turn out much later that a lanky farmer named Asad Hamdan Asad, Mahmoud Hamdan's father, was among the Ishwa mujahideen who shot at the British convoy. Asad used to hunt deer and he had excellent vision. It was he, according to his son, who shot two British soldiers—"one in the eye and one in the mouth." When the shooting died down, Mahmoud's father rushed out and made off with a British mortar.

One day later, a British colonel led six hundred troops into the valley on a punitive expedition, one of the last British shows of strength in Palestine. British officers were incensed by the two killings, and all the more so because of rumors that the two Warwickshire soldiers had been stripped, beaten, and stoned to death in Ishwa. The British expedition marched into Artuf, Ishwa, and Beit Mahsir, driving out the few villagers who had not fled into the hills already. After Artuf had been emptied, a British armored car rolled up to the Jewish settlement. Out stepped a British colonel. He said this was the last British convoy to Hartuv and it would be advisable for everyone to evacuate. Garrison commander Shepach served him wine and cakes but replied that no one from the garrison would leave. The Hartuv defenders had been warned by their Haganah superiors that a British relief column would visit the settlement. The message from Haganah, as Peled remembered it, was that "we had to resist being evacuated."

Why was the Hartuv garrison ordered to hold such an exposed position deep inside the UN-delineated Arab state? From

the outset, Ben-Gurion and the twelve other leaders of the Yishuv's national council were determined to avoid any sign of
military weakness. Just now, this factor was more compelling
than ever because of a stunning turn of events at the United
Nations. On March 19, the United States called on the UN
Security Council to suspend its efforts to partition Palestine.
Rather than risk the peace of the entire world, as U.S. Ambassador Warren Austin put it, the UN should place all of Palestine
under a UN trusteeship. A banner headline in the *Palestine Post*
conveyed the sense of alarm reverberating throughout the Yishuv: "U.S. ABANDONS JEWISH STATE; SUGGEST TEMPORARY
TRUSTEE." Trusteeship would mean local autonomy for the Jews
and Arabs, probably under an extended British colonial administration. To Ben-Gurion, who was bent on obtaining full Jewish statehood, mere "autonomy" was unacceptable—just as it
was unacceptable to most Palestinians four decades later. As he
put it in his diary, "We shall not accept any trusteeship, not a
short, transitional one, not even for the shortest period."

Over the next ten days, some of the Hartuv defenders rued
their decision to stay. A dozen Haganah enlisted men went on
a hunger strike, claiming they had been promised that they
would have to serve only two weeks in Hartuv. The radio messages from Shepach sounded increasingly despairing. "In our
opinion the Arabs will attempt soon to attack the place and this
time with enormous forces," the garrison radioed. "Our people
are untrained and dead tired from building fortifications and
constant guard duty at night. It is six nights that we sleep with
our clothes and shoes. I demand this time in all seriousness to
do something about it. . . . In my opinion the people in the place
should be replaced by others." Two days later, Shepach radioed:

It is impossible to build bunkers. The land is rocky and I don't
have cement or gravel for construction. In addition, there are no
explosives and detonators to destroy houses. . . . Our people are
mostly a bunch without any understanding and no training.
There is no possibility of training. The platoon commanders are
not experienced. The squad commanders are from the last

courses. There is a sum total of only seventy weapons, including six pistols without any bullets . . . [and] thirteen Italian rifles that misfired 80 percent of the time when we were attacked. . . . I have done the maximum but it is zero.

For the moment, Shepach's anxiety was wasted. After the British raid, the Arabs returned to their villages and made no move against Hartuv. Having shot up much of their ammunition, they were content with a temporary stalemate. For his part, Asad Hamdan Asad went to an arms dealer in Jerusalem and traded the mortar for a World War II Canadian rifle.

The military standoff in the valley seemed to reflect pretty well what was going on throughout Palestine. Communal strife had hardened into a civil war. The carnage had kept up at the same appalling pace, claiming roughly equal casualties on both sides. By the end of March, 851 Jews and 944 Arabs were recorded as killed. Yet the appearance of a stalemate was deceptive. The truth was that the war was proceeding on two levels, with the Arabs winning on one and the Jews on the other. Arab guerrillas were demonstrating that from their hilltop sanctuaries they could destroy enough Jewish armored convoys to make supply lines to isolated Jewish communities unreliable. March 27 was the zenith of Arab success in the convoy war. Along the Hebron-to-Jerusalem road, Abdul Khader's fighters trapped a convoy returning from the fortified kibbutz Kfar Etzion south of Jerusalem. The attackers killed twenty Haganah troops and made off with 170 guns. On the same day in northern Palestine, forty-two Haganah troops died trying to defend a supply caravan. Meanwhile, the Tel Aviv–Jerusalem highway remained impassable, and in Jerusalem, the Jews' supply of food and ammunition was running low.

But while the Arabs were winning the convoy war, the Jews were winning an equally important war for territory. Every few weeks, Arab forces tried and failed to dislodge Jews from their fortified settlements, even settlements like Kfar Etzion and Hartuv, which were deep inside the boundaries of the UN's Arab partition zone. On the other hand, Jewish forces were finding most Arab villages had no fortifications and could be cleared out

with little difficulty. Haganah had begun its raids on Arab villages in December, under a policy of retaliation for all Arab
attacks on Jews. The raids seemed to be restricted at first to Arab
villages within the Jewish zone outlined in the UN partition
plan. In March, the raids within the UN's Jewish zone continued, and the Arabs were coming to expect them. After an
unsuccessful attack by Fauzi al-Kaukji's forces on a northern
kibbutz, a Haganah unit punished the nearby village of Dhubiya, destroying ten homes after its residents had fled. In the
Negev, a Haganah squad took over an Arab village, summoned
the inhabitants, and announced that the village well was being
blown up because local Arabs had attacked a Jewish car. In one
village, Haganah intelligence officer Yehuda Burstein induced
the 140 tenant farmers to abandon their homes by giving what
he would call "friendly advice" that a Jewish attack was coming.

Inside the Hartuv garrison, the Jewish defenders kept waiting
for an Arab blow to fall upon them. Radio messages, preserved
in the Israeli army archives, convey their feeling of helplessness:

> March 30, 0130: Send by plane mines and electrically detonated
> explosives for a minefield near the gate. . . . In addition there is
> an urgent necessity for the Stens and rifles that are requested.
> . . . The road is good and safe now. Without reinforcements the
> settlement is weak, I repeat, very weak. I need additional explo-
> sives.

> March 31, 1200: Hartuv should get an air drop of vitamins, a firing
> pin for the German machine gun, three firing tubes for two-inch
> mortars, four hundred hand grenades, twenty magazines of Bren
> ammunition, the shoe mines and shrapnel mines and English,
> Italian, German rifle ammunition.

> April 1, 1200: What about the equipment I requested that would
> be dropped by a plane? . . . We live here under terrible stress.
> . . . In our vicinity the Arab gangs are equipped with a three-inch
> mortar. What are you waiting for? We can't hold on in case of a
> serious attack. . . .

Though the commander at Hartuv was intending to convey
the flimsiness of his position, his radio messages contained clues

suggesting the Jews' overall situation was improving. For in fact, the military forces of the Yishuv were gaining three crucial advantages over the Arab forces.

The Jews held a decisive edge in modern weaponry. The messages from the Hartuv garrison demonstrated that Haganah's arsenal for defending this one settlement included light airplanes, wireless radios, hand grenades, submachine guns, machine guns, and armored cars. Some were scarce and others didn't function very well. But as long as the conflict was limited to the Jews and the Palestinian Arabs, the Jews were far ahead in the arms race. A case in point was the Piper Cubs that airdropped ammunition to the Hartuv defenders. In the first five months of 1948, Jewish agents in Britain delivered about twenty-five war-surplus Piper Cubs, which Haganah used for surveillance, supply missions, and bombing. The Arab irregulars had no planes at all. As for infantry weapons, whereas by February the Hartuv settlement itself had sixty-six rifles and Sten submachine guns, it would be April before Abdul Khader's Holy Struggle could count 250 rifles throughout the whole rural belt around Jerusalem.

The Jews were gaining a second crucial advantage in trained man and womanpower. Shepach was a combat veteran, and his young platoon leaders had gone through Haganah officers' courses. The core of Haganah's officers and noncommissioned officers derived from a pool of 27,000 Palestinian Jews who fought in World War II in British or American uniforms. And there were always recruits to fill the ranks—even if Shepach complained that his lacked training. On the day after the partition vote, leaders of the Jewish Agency ordered every male Jew between seventeen and fifty to report for the draft. Women weren't drafted, but they volunteered in large numbers. No such mobilization occurred among Palestinian Arabs, because the leaders of the Arab League countries feared that a Palestinian army would make Hajj Amin too powerful. The two Arab volunteer forces that did take shape were short of both officers and recruits. Since neither the British nor the German side had recruited Arabs for World War II combat units, only a handful on the Arab side had true battle experience. For all these reasons, the Jews had between three and ten times as many armed troops and militiamen fighting in Palestine as did the Arabs by early May 1948.

Along with the disparity in weapons and military manpower came an even wider gap in financial backing. Jews from abroad—mainly from the United States but also from Europe, South America, and South Africa—threw tens of millions of dollars into the civil war in Palestine. Immediately after the 1947 partition vote, the New York–based United Jewish Appeal increased its annual fund-raising target to $250 million, of which $114 million was designated for the Jewish institutions in Palestine. To stimulate contributions, the Jewish Agency dispatched Golda Meir on a fund-raising drive in the United States that brought in $50 million. Of this, $16.1 million was secretly spent to buy weapons from the Czechoslovak Ministry of Defense and Supply. On March 31, a chartered American DC-4 brought the first load of Czech weapons to a hidden airfield in Palestine— two hundred rifles and forty machine guns plus ammunition. A few days later, a ship slipped through the British blockade to bring Haganah another two hundred machine guns and 5.5 million rounds of ammunition.

The Yishuv's war chest wasn't enormous by the standards of modern guerrilla warfare, but it vastly exceeded that of the local Arab fighters during the crucial six months leading up to Israel's declaration of independence. Judging from available records, Arabs devoted less than one-sixth as much money and arms to the war effort in this period as did Jews. In the fall of 1947, Arab League delegates agreed to contribute $3 million and ten thousand rifles to support "volunteer" forces in Palestine. Almost all of this went to field Fauzi al-Kaukji's hapless army of "volunteers" in northern Palestine. Meanwhile, Abdul Khader al-Husseini's smaller force of Palestinian mujahideen had to depend almost entirely on what the Arab Higher Committee could raise in taxes and contributions from Palestinian merchants, orange growers, and others. The committee raised only about $700,000 in the year leading up to April 1948, judging from the memoirs of the Committee's treasurer. Of this, only part filtered down to support the Holy Struggle. Some of the mujahideen, including Sheikh Haroun Ibn Jazzi, derived their main compensation from looting.

As the Hartuv garrison was holding out, the Yishuv's overall advantages in weapons, manpower, and money were meshing. Late in March, Haganah Chief of Operations Yigael Yadin came to Ben-Gurion with a plan of attack called Operation Nachshon. The plan aimed to carve a Jewish corridor straight through the UN's Arab partition zone from Jerusalem to the coast. The operation was proposed as the opening stage of Plan D, the Haganah war plan to consolidate the Jewish state—and, if possible, to seize a corridor to Jerusalem—before Arab regular armies could join the war. Ben-Gurion, the *de facto* defense minister in the Yishuv's National Council, became enthusiastic about Nachshon and took the idea before the rest of the council on the night of March 31–April 1. After three hours of discussion, these *de facto* cabinet members of the Yishuv's unofficial government voted the war plan into motion. In so doing, they were deciding to put aside the tenuous, tentative plans to split Palestine with King Abdullah along the UN partition boundaries. For the first time, Haganah was about to kick off "operations of conquest and occupation," as Israel Galili, head of the Haganah National Command Staff, put it at the time.

The most critical target was to be the village of Kastel, one of a ribbon of Arab villages along the Tel Aviv–Jerusalem road. Kastel was just five miles north of the Sorek Valley. Because of its proximity, the high command thought Hartuv might play a supporting role by helping to choke the flow of Arab supplies. On April 2 a Haganah plane dropped the largest load of ammunition the garrison had received since the end of the road convoys: thirteen hundred rifle rounds, fifteen hundred submachine-gun rounds, nine hundred machine-gun rounds, sixty hand grenades. On April 3 the commander of Operation Nachshon sent an operational order to various battalion headquarters units directing that "all the Arab villages" along the axis between Jerusalem and the Jewish settlement of Hulda "were to

be treated as enemy assembly or jumping-off bases." That axis
went straight across the Sorek Valley. As Plan D had already
spelled out, Arab "jumping-off bases" were to be "destroyed"
and their inhabitants "cleaned out" if they put up resistance.

Exactly what the Hartuv garrison was ordered to seize is
unclear. Documents surviving in Haganah archives do say that
Hartuv received some kind of order to support Nachshon,
though its text has not been found. In all likelihood it was a
radioed instruction to capture the Hartuv police fortress, for
that was already one of the key objectives listed for capture
under Plan D. One thing is clear: garrison commander Shepach
was sure the proposed action would provoke wrath among the
Arabs. In fact, he replied by radio that the garrison was too
exposed to take the risk of carrying out the order. The message
said: "My reasoning about your order from today is: I can't
execute it efficiently because of a lack of mining materials and
fighting people. I am not certain we can stand the results of the
action since we can't protect our water machinery. And the
place cannot stand in front of a strong attack." While his reply
from Hartuv did not win him medals for daring, it probably
saved his garrison from retribution.

As it turned out, Operation Nachshon worked without any
help from Hartuv. Nachshon's success was far more sweeping
than anyone had anticipated—so much so that it was responsible
for clearing tens of thousands of refugees out of Palestine. As it
happened, on April 3, Haganah troops seized Kastel and expelled its inhabitants—the first time Arabs had been expelled
from a village inside the Arab partition zone. Haganah had now
deprived the Palestinian irregulars of one of their main staging
bases for convoy attacks along the road to Jerusalem. At that
moment Abdul Khader was in Damascus trying to persuade the
Arab League military committee to send him more rifles and
cash. Learning that Kastel had fallen, the Palestinian commander in chief drove back to Jerusalem and pulled together
about three hundred men for a counterattack. Around 3:30 A.M.
on April 8, he led a small party up the hill toward Kastel, not
knowing exactly where his forces were deployed. "Who is

there?" one of the Haganah soldiers demanded in English from a balcony of one of Kastel's houses. "Hi, boys," came Abdul Khader's reply in Arabic.

A seventeen-year-old named Yoram Kaniuk was one of five Jewish soldiers who saw him coming about twenty-five yards away. "We five young men had seen a majestic figure wearing crossed bandoliers. I was startled, my hand trembled, and I missed. But the fellow next to me did not." A burst from his companion's Sten dropped Abdul Khader in his tracks. Around daybreak, Kaniuk's commander went through the pockets of the dead Arab and found a driver's license in the name of Abdul Khader Suleiman, but failed to grasp exactly who it was his men had killed.

That afternoon, one of the phone tappers in Haganah's intelligence headquarters on Ben Yehuda Street in Jerusalem heard an Arab official dejectedly saying, "Abdul Khader is dead." Realizing what had happened, Haganah intelligence seized an opportunity. Its psychological warfare unit disclosed Abdul Khader's death by means of a somber bulletin on its impostor Arab radio station. No matter how the news was announced, his death would have been devastating to the Palestinians. It was even more catastrophic to morale because it was announced before the Arab Higher Committee could figure out how to react.

Abdul Khader's funeral the following day drew Palestinians by the thousands to the Dome of the Rock in Jerusalem. Among the mourners were the mujahideen who by now had recaptured Kastel. When they returned from the funeral procession, they found that the Haganah had once again captured the village. The Arabs fought for two more days in an attempt to take back the hilltop stronghold, but the Jews held fast. It would be weeks before the Arab Higher Committee designated a new commander. The man finally chosen was a Husseini family member with no military talent. For Palestinians, Abdul Khader's death was the beginning of the end.

The day after the funeral, Palestinians were bludgeoned by another psychological shock. Three miles from Kastel, a Jewish commando force attacked a village called Deir Yassin. These 120 right-wing raiders from the Irgun and the Stern Gang were determined to drive out the four hundred Arab residents, one way or another. This time, Palestinians didn't run from an attack. Some of Deir Yassin's youngsters, along with an Iraqi volunteer soldier, holed up in a school and shot back. In the early going, several Jews were killed and wounded. On the spot, the Irgun and Stern Gang battlefield commanders held a debate. "The commanders were divided over what to do in Deir Yassin," as one of the commanders, Ben-Zion Cohen, would later write. "A majority were in favor of destroying all the males or whoever would resist, including women and children."

The majority won. Before nightfall, more than a hundred Palestinian men, women, and children were shot, blown up by grenades or stabbed to death by the Irgun and Stern Gang commandos. One of the commanders quickly announced on the Irgun radio station that "254 Arabs" had been killed in the battle. It was an exaggeration, he later insisted, to frighten Arabs in other places. To heighten the effect, his men loaded some of the terrified survivors on a truck and drove them to Jerusalem, where they were let go near the Old City. There the survivors told amazed spectators of mass killings and of Arab girls being raped by the Jewish attackers. A British policeman assigned to investigate the report of rapes judged at the time that the allegation was true. After interviewing surviving Deir Yassin women in a hospital, the British officer wrote to his superiors: "Many young schoolgirls were raped and later slaughtered."

The Haganah and the Jewish Agency tried to distance themselves from Deir Yassin. They were successful, but only temporarily. Israeli inquiries would disclose that the Irgun and Stern Gang commanders had notified Haganah in advance of their plans to take Deir Yassin. Haganah's Jerusalem commander, David Shaltiel, had approved the attack—though not the mass killings—because it was one of the villages marked for capture under Operation Nachshon. It would also come out that Haganah's Jerusalem commander supplied the Irgun force with four thousand bullets before the attack, and that both Palmach and Haganah fighters were present in Deir Yassin during the raid as backups for the raiding party.

On the radio, Arabs heard about the attack in gruesome detail

from a broadcast by Hussein Khalidi, secretary of the Arab
Higher Committee. Khalidi's emotional descriptions probably
did achieve his purpose of pushing the Arab kings and other
potentates closer toward sending their armies into Palestine.
But in the process, the broadcast had an unintended side effect.
News of Deir Yassin spread defeatism among Palestinians, who
up to then had been exposed to an upbeat account of Arab
"victories" in the civil war. Deir Yassin didn't set off a mass
panic flight, as has sometimes been assumed. But the episode did
make unarmed Palestinians more ready to leave their villages
when Jewish forces attacked.

Chance played a part in Deir Yassin, just as it had in Abdul
Khader's death. But the Jews' spring offensive of 1948 did not
succeed through mere happenstance. The men and women of
the Yishuv prevailed because they had mobilized faster and
fought harder than the local Arabs. As soon as their leaders
knew they had a sure military edge, they struck up and down
Palestine with the ferocity of a people who believed destiny was
on its side.

In mid-April, the Haganah and Irgun moved from capturing
villages to capturing whole cities. The first to fall was Tiberias,
a big half-Arab town up north in the Galilee. Within twenty-
four hours of Haganah's attack on Tiberias, nearby roads to
Transjordan were chockablock with six thousand refugees.
Three days later, Haganah descended on the Arab quarters of
the northern seaport of Haifa. It was the first battle in which
Haganah unleashed the Davidka mortar, whose horrifying explosions caused some Arabs to think atomic bombs had fallen.
The Davidka's effect was magnified when loudspeaker cars
broadcast in Arabic: "The Haganah is in control of all roads to
the city and no help is going to come for you." Within two days,
forty thousand Arabs abandoned Haifa by sea for Egypt and
Lebanon. Next came the fall of Jaffa, part of the Arab partition
zone. Jaffa was overcome by Irgun commandos and artillerymen
in a two-week battle. When the fighting ended on May 9, what
had been the largest Arab city between Cairo and Beirut was
now Jewish. In Tiberias, Haifa, and Jaffa, the flight of the popu-

lation was accelerated by the precipitate departures of local Arab municipal and military leaders soon after the shooting started. In Haifa, the Jewish mayor did try to convince Arab residents to stay on after Haganah took control of the city. Until today, Israel cites this special case as proof that caring Jews pleaded with Arabs not to flee.

In the Sorek Valley, none of the Arab villagers had yet abandoned their homes. The grain harvest was coming, and that was the local imperative. But the events in Deir Yassin, which was only twelve miles away, did bring an overlay of fear. Teenaged Ismail Rahhal of Artuf would remember: "People thought, 'Today they've done this in Deir Yassin, tomorrow it will be in our village.'" Up on the ridge in Saraa, Diab Abu Latifah was getting apprehensive about his pregnant wife, Sabiha. "We were scared about the massacres and about the raping of the women," he remembered. "For the fighters it was okay. But if they start coming to the houses . . ."

· 13 ·

"THEY'LL NEVER GET A ROAD THROUGH THERE"

*T*here had been something odd about this siege. For nearly two months the Hartuv garrison had been cut off from all road convoys. By all reasonable calculations, the food should long since have run out. The war between the Haganah and the Arab irregulars was going on all around them. Every few days, a truck carried the Palestinian mujahideen past the settlement. Gunfire could be heard almost every night from the direction of Bab al-Wad. Yet in the Sorek Valley, the war seemed to have gone into remission in early May 1948.

A dozen of King Abdullah's Arab Legionnaires, outfitted in crisp uniforms and red kaffiyehs, occupied the former British police fortress a half mile down the hill from the settlement. They had moved in when the last British policeman left the valley more than a month earlier. The Arab Legion platoon leader held several clandestine meetings in the woods with Aharon Levy, a Hartuvian who was the Haganah deputy commander. Together they arranged an unofficial local truce—one of at least half a dozen local Jewish-Arab truces that prevailed in villages around Jerusalem. "We had good relations with the

Arab Legion," said Aharon's cousin Chaim Levy. "People thought that very soon the Legion would capture Jerusalem, and we will be able to go and cut our wheat." Another young Haganah volunteer heard the Jordanian officer remarking that "the tipping of the scales" between Jews and Arabs would be determined somewhere else.

Besides being protected by the truce, the cadre of Jews was able to hold out inside Hartuv because enterprising Arabs set up a market outside the garrison fence. Each afternoon the Jews behind the barricades could gauge what was going on beyond the horizon by what they found at the market. Sometimes they found Hebrew writing on the packages of biscuits and margarine, proof that the food had been "liberated" from a Jewish convoy on the Tel Aviv–Jerusalem highway. If some unit of Holy Struggle—the Palestinian irregulars loyal to Hajj Amin—had camped in a nearby village, the market would disappear for a few days. "The villagers feared anything that broke the quiet," Palmach platoon leader Mati Peled said. "They understood in their simple way that it's better to wait for what's next, and to live peacefully, and to see how things will turn out."

There came times, too, when the Hartuvians would share their resources with their Arab neighbors. One day, Ismail Rahhal's sister-in-law went into labor. The birth was difficult. In peacetime, the Arab women in the valley had depended on a Jewish doctor who lived right at Hartuv to deliver their babies. With the woman's life in danger, Ismail's father, who was the mukhtar of Artuf, approached the barbed wire and asked the Haganah soldiers if the doctor could deliver a baby. The doctor, a woman, and the Haganah men agreed that she would accompany the mukhtar to the woman's bedside. "Now she is your responsibility," one of the soldiers told Rahhal's father. "If anything happens to the doctor, we will destroy your village." Heeding the warning, the mukhtar summoned armed relatives to guard the blessed event. After half an hour, an Arab boy was born and the doctor was escorted unharmed back into the besieged moshava. "She wouldn't take money, so my father gave her a basket of eggs and chocolates and other things from his store," Ismail said.

In early May the garrison's martial spirit was pumped up by the sight of a stream of Arab refugees straggling through the valley. Hartuv defender Yoshko Levy wrote: "On the road from Bab al-Wad I saw thousands of Arab refugees escaping in convoys of vehicles toward Hebron. These were the Arabs of Jaffa and other places. . . . I started to think about a plan to conquer the Hartuv police station. We knew the layout because we had worked on it when it was being built. We went on night patrols to plan our attack on the station." The sight of so many refugees affected Palestinian morale as well. Few, if any, of the valley villagers left their homes, but several took the precaution of coming to the garrison fence and asking the old Hartuvians for letters attesting their past loyalty.

On May 10 and 11, the Jews in the garrison saw explosions flashing on the north rim of the valley. Commandos of the Palmach had seized another mountaintop Arab village in a follow-up to Operation Nachshon. From his vantage inside the garrison, platoon leader Peled saw "a lot of Arabs running away"—Arabs who had clambered down a steep shepherd's track from the village to the valley road. They were leaving their homes in Beit Mahsir, a village of eighteen hundred Arab residents. Though Beit Mahsir was only three miles from them, the quirks of mountain geography left the village almost cut off from the Sorek Valley. Its only decent road led northward toward the Tel Aviv–Jerusalem highway. Because of its perch two thousand feet above sea level overlooking the main highway, Beit Mahsir had become a prime objective of Operation Maccabi, an extension of Operation Nachshon. Its capture was another bite out of the territory the UN had assigned to the Palestinian Arab state. When the Palmach took over Beit Mahsir, the commandos blasted its limestone houses to rubble in order to keep its Arab residents from returning. Peled's reaction illustrates the feeling of deliverance that much of the Yishuv felt while the Arabs were being put to flight. Peled wrote in the official Israeli military journal in 1950:

After a short while, explosions started that were seen and
heard to the enjoyment of every viewer. Such joy and happiness
absorbed the moshava and also the defenders who had shared its
grief of loneliness and isolation and despair for many days. Immediately we felt a renewed capacity to act and the will to do
anything possible. Everyone guessed that now was the time for
Hartuv to act. Here comes the day of repaying all that it had gone
through. This was the day for which the defenders and the settlers suffered together.

On May 12 that moment of elation was pierced. Fifteen miles
over the hills toward Bethlehem, an Arab Legion unit launched
an artillery bombardment against a block of four kibbutzim. It
was the first assault on a Jewish position by an Arab regular
army unit. The throaty rumbles of artillery signaled the end of
six weeks of passivity by the Arab League in the face of the Jews'
brilliantly executed Plan D blitzkrieg, and the beginning of
full-scale war for Palestine.

The shock of successive Jewish triumphs, the collapse of the
Arab irregular forces, the sudden appearance of 300,000 Palestinian refugees, the imminence of British total withdrawal, the
failure of the UN to provide peacekeeping forces—all these
developments had wrapped themselves so tightly together that
an attack by the Arab regular armies was now inevitable. Arab
leaders can be faulted for their failure to grasp for peaceful
compromise during the 1947 UN inquiry into Palestine. But by
May 1948 no Arab ruler, not even the pliant King Abdullah,
could have acquiesced to the Jewish capture of Haifa, Jaffa, and
other Palestinian population centers. Patriotic anger was rushing through the Arab masses, fed by rumors of atrocities and by
cries for vengeance by Moslem clerics. From the perspective of
the Arab kings and presidents, there was only one honorable
solution, and that was war.

The event which began to tie together the Arab war coalition
was the Haganah's capture of the Arab quarters of Haifa on
April 21–22. As the Haifa refugees began flooding by boat into
Lebanon and Egypt, Lebanese Prime Minister Riyad al-Solh
took the initiative. Solh convinced Prince Abdulilah, the Hashe-

mite regent of Iraq, to visit King Farouk in Egypt. There the Iraqi ruler begged his rival Farouk to allow the Egyptian army to participate in an invasion of Palestine. In reply Farouk talked of the sorry condition of his army, but agreed in principle after hearing that Transjordan's King Abdullah was going to march into Palestine in any case. With the two strongest Arab armies tentatively committed, the Iraqi regent had no trouble enlisting Syria. However, the chiefs of staff of the Arab League armies warned that it would take six divisions and six aircraft squadrons to win—about twice as much as they had. The Arab League Political Committee ordered the generals to press on with "such forces as are available."

In hopes of keeping Transjordanian troops on the sidelines, the Jewish Agency reactivated its secret talks with King Abdullah even as the Jewish offensive was blazing across Palestine. But after the succession of Arab humiliations, the king said he wasn't in a position to go through with the plan they had discussed to partition Palestine between a Jewish state and Transjordan. Now he was merely one among five Arab leaders, Abdullah told Golda Meir at their secret meeting on May 10. Abdullah said there was only one way to avoid war: if the Jews would postpone declaration of an independent state and accept his offer of autonomy inside his kingdom. Meir replied with an ultimatum: accept a sovereign Jewish state within the exact UN partition boundaries. While there was peace, she said, the Jews would respect the UN partition borders. But if war came, they would fight everywhere and with all their might. When Ben-Gurion heard Mrs. Meir's account of the meeting, he concluded there was no hope of keeping Transjordan out of the war.

On the morning of May 12, Abdullah's Arab Legion attacked south of Jerusalem, hitting Kfar Etzion and its three satellite settlements making up the Etzion block. About one hundred of the five hundred defenders of the Etzion block would be killed during the two-day attack, including about fifteen who were machine-gunned after they had surrendered. After overrunning the stronghold, the Arab Legion took 389 Jews captive and trucked them off to a military prison in Transjordan. Before the end, nearby villagers burned and looted Kfar Etzion while some chanted "Deir Yassin, Deir Yassin." A Jewish woman Palmachnik was dragged into the trees by two Arab men who ripped at her clothes. She was saved from rape when an Arab Legion officer shot them.

The news of the first Jewish settlement being overrun traumatized Hartuv. On the afternoon of May 13, Yoshko Levy stood on the roof of the garrison headquarters and tuned the bulky Model 300 shortwave radio to one of Haganah's aircraft frequencies. "One of our Piper Cubs was flying above the Etzion block," Yoshko Levy would remember. "I heard him reporting to the high command in Tel Aviv. The pilot was saying, 'Kfar Etzion has fallen.' " Kfar Etzion was among the best-protected of the Jewish settlements that remained inside the United Nations' boundaries for the future Arab state. "When the terrible disaster was known, the despair ate everything," Peled said. "Nobody deluded themselves enough to believe that Hartuv could stand after the Etzion block fell."

In Tel Aviv, the Haganah general staff reached the same conclusion: Hartuv would have to be abandoned. Of the roughly twenty-five Jewish settlements inside the UN's proposed Arab state, the military leaders of the Yishuv decided to evacuate five, including Hartuv, while continuing to hold the other twenty. On May 14, Haganah's chief of operations, Yigael Yadin, sent a message to Haganah's Jerusalem headquarters: "It was decided on evacuating Hartuv. It will be accomplished by [the] Givati [Brigade]. You have to instruct them [at Hartuv] to evacuate, and that Givati will be coming tonight and will arrange it. Confirm immediately."

Never had Hartuv seen a more macabre day. The Haganah troops in the garrison were already beginning to pack when a voice sounded on the radio. It was the voice of David Ben-Gurion, the short, stocky dynamo who had goaded and inspired and beseeched his people into statehood over the forty-two years since he first set foot in Palestine. At four o'clock that afternoon, he pronounced the words for which Jews had been waiting for two thousand years: "We hereby proclaim the establishment of the Jewish State in Palestine, to be called the State of Israel."

There was a curious omission in the declaration of independence. Nowhere was there any mention of the UN partition plan that brought Israel into existence, or any delineation of the borders of the new state. The final lines, Ben-Gurion believed, would be settled on the battlefield. And he was prepared to fight.

Throughout Jewish Palestine, it was a moment for exuberance. Not at Hartuv. "We didn't know if this thing would last," said Yoshko Levy. "Of course we were happy, but we couldn't celebrate. We were under siege." At three o'clock the following morning, six rescuers from the Givati Brigade, led by twenty-one-year-old Shlomo "Cheech" Lahat, slipped over the ridge near Saraa. Approaching the Hartuv fence, Lahat gave a password and was led to Ariyeh Shepach, the commander of the Haganah soldiers in the garrison.

"Where are the armored cars?" Shepach demanded. "We were notified you were coming with armored cars."

"Which armored cars?" Lahat replied. "The armored cars will never come. We will walk."

Now their problem was the forty unarmed settlers who had stuck it out inside the garrison along with the troops. They included twenty old people, women and children, even a few babies. If all forty civilians tried to leave along with the ninety soldiers, there would be a greater risk of ambush. But if the civilians stayed at Hartuv, what would the Arabs do to them? After daybreak, an argument broke out between Shepach and Gavriel Levy, the ranking elder among the settlers. Shepach said he had decided the Haganah troops would break out as fast as possible that night, leaving the unarmed Hartuvians behind to surrender to the Arab Legion.

No, said Gavriel Levy. The settlers would depart along with the fighters. As a further complication, the defenders learned that Lahat's team had been spotted by Arab villagers the night before. An Arab Legion soldier summoned Gavriel Levy's nephew Aharon to the police station to say that Jewish "reinforcements" had been observed sneaking toward Hartuv. Could the Jews assure him that the police station wouldn't be attacked? There would be no attack, Aharon Levy promised. Once back inside the garrison, he and his cousin Yoshko brusquely told Shepach that the Hartuvians would manage their own evacuation. Finally Shepach agreed to take all 130 men, women, and children out in a single column that night.

The soldiers and settlers spent May 15—the first day of Israel's independence—packing and destroying everything they were not able to carry. It happened to be the Sabbath, but there was no time to wait. "A complex system of machines in the Shimshon factory was made useless by using hammers," said an eyewitness two weeks later. "Clothes and materials were cut by knives. We didn't want the enemy to be joyful with the pillage." Someone went down into the granary and cut open the remaining sacks of wheat, pouring diesel fuel on some of them. "There was no time to think," another defender said. "We had to pack our things and destroy whatever was left. I remember throwing my movie projector down the well so that the Arabs would not enjoy it."

A moon brightened the valley that night as the Jews began their retreat. Around ten o'clock the first Haganah soldiers moved out and set up a firing point on a hill. One by one, the soldiers and civilians followed, some wearing socks over their shoes to muffle the noise. Several children were carried in backpacks. Chaim Levy and six other Haganah troops stayed behind for several hours. Their job was to make everything look normal by keeping the spotlights shining. Chaim Levy went out to the fields and killed the settlement's remaining animals. Then he, too, slipped out of Hartuv to join the evacuation column. As the night dragged on, clouds darkened the moon. The escaping band made its way westward across the ridges toward the next Jewish settlement at Kfar Uriah. Ordinarily it was a two-hour walk, but they had to carry a soldier with a broken leg and a settler suffering from paralysis.

A baby cried as the column passed a half mile below the Arab village of Saraa. "It may be that you will have to strangle him," commander Lahat remembered telling a soldier near him. "Otherwise we will all be killed." It was a moment of terrible tension. "I saw somebody there putting his hand over the baby's mouth,"

Chaim Levy said later. "The baby was wiggling in his hands. Without thinking at all, I snatched the baby away and held him and kissed him and he calmed down pretty fast." About this time, a medic gave the baby a morphine injection to assure that there would be no more crying. Just before dawn on May 16 the column arrived at Kfar Uriah.

The escaping Jews never knew that they instilled as much terror in some of their old neighbors as they felt themselves. Sabiha Abu Latifah, a young mother with one infant and another on the way, was sleeping outside that night along with some other Saraa villagers. They were worried that their houses might be attacked, just as those in Beit Mahsir had been attacked only a week before. Sabiha was immobilized with fear when she saw a column of armed people passing the village in the middle of the night. "They didn't take anything with them, just some clothes they carried on their back," said Sabiha.

In the morning, some villagers in Artuf wondered why the searchlights were still burning. They shouted for the Haganah sentries. When they got no answer, someone ran to the police station to tell an Arab Legion officer that the Jews were nowhere to be seen. Within an hour the abandoned moshava was looted. According to the recollection of villagers, the bedouin sheikh Haroun Ibn Jazzi helped himself to the remaining equipment from the cement plant and then left Artuf for good. Everyone took a share, as Ismail Rahhal would remember long afterward. "At that time the people were very hungry," he said. "We didn't have our crops yet. So whatever we found, we took it."

Shepach wrote the only contemporary epitaph for Hartuv. He said in a message to Haganah headquarters:

> We left by foot to Kfar Uriah. The convoy had ninety troops and forty civilians, among them twenty elderly persons, sick persons, children, and women. The journey took us seven hours. We reached Kfar Uriah at 5:00 A.M. One unit was held back in Hartuv and put explosives in the buildings and the defense lines. Sixteen people were killed in defense of Hartuv. Only one was killed inside the defensive perimeter. The rest were killed on way to Hartuv. Twelve people were wounded.

Now it was time to see how much of its newly conquered
territory the state of Israel could defend against the regular
Arab armies. On the night of May 14–15, the first contingents of
Arab regulars crossed the borders of Palestine. The attack came
from three directions at once. From the north, Syrian armored
cars and a token Lebanese force struck at Jewish settlements in
the Galilee. From the east, Transjordan's Arab Legion moved
across the Jordan River to occupy positions around Jerusalem.
Also advancing from the east, an Iraqi brigade took up positions
in the hills of the West Bank's central "Triangle," threatening
to pinch off Israel's six-mile-wide "waistline" north of Tel Aviv.
Meanwhile, from the south, two Egyptian brigades lumbered
northward through Egypt's Sinai desert aiming for Gaza and
Tel Aviv.

From the Israeli side of the lines, the May 15 attack looked like
a "massive" coordinated invasion that reached deep inside Israeli territory. This is the picture of the 1948 war that persists
in many history books, but it is misleading in several respects.
For one thing, the Arab regulars carrying out the "massive"
invasion were heavily outnumbered. The Arab expeditionary
forces numbered as few as fourteen thousand troops, compared
to the forty thousand troops the Haganah already had mobilized. The Arab generals had no unified command, no war plan,
and no forewarning about what their brother Arab forces intended to do. Abdullah's Arab Legion was commanded by sympathetic British officers, a remnant from Transjordan's years as
a colony, but even these clipped Anglo professionals were in the
dark. "Not one word regarding the Egyptian operations was
ever made available to us," the British general who commanded
Abdullah's Arab Legion complained. That is not the only reason
why almost all of the fighting in the next month took place
either on the soil of the UN's projected Palestinian Arab state
or in the international zone of Jerusalem. The Haganah's earlier
preemptive strikes had done their work. By May 15, the Haganah
had taken control of most of the UN's Jewish zone and could
therefore fight the Arabs beyond the UN-established frontiers.
Perhaps most important of all, King Abdullah refrained from

attacking targets inside the Jewish partition zone, in keeping with an assurance he had sent a few months earlier to his ally and arms supplier Britain.

In the first confused week of combat, the converging armies shared the Sorek Valley as a no-man's-land. The Arab Legion continued to occupy the Hartuv police fortress. "We used to cooperate among ourselves to give them food," Mahmoud Hamdan recalled. The fifty-odd Arab Legion troops in the valley were commanded from the police fort by Transjordanian Lieutenant Issa Mafudi. His problem was that his unit had no wireless radio, so he was temporarily cut off from his superior officers. On the night of May 19, an Arab Legion patrol did reach the valley from the north and asked Mafudi what was happening. Mafudi reported that a band of Palestinians from Ishwa, Artuf, and Islin had tried earlier that day to take Beit Mahsir back from the Palmach. His Arab Legion troops had not joined in the attack, or so he led the patrol to believe. In any case, the machine guns clattering in the distance gave proof that the Palestinians had run into heavy resistance, and before long the local fighters were driven back down the hill.

A week or so later, Mafudi's Legionnaires were joined in the valley by a detachment of about fifty Egyptians. It was a volunteer force that seems to have been made up of Moslem Brotherhood members given leave to fight in Palestine by their Egyptian army commander. They and other small Egyptian volunteer forces had moved across the Egyptian border into Palestine a few days before May 15. One of these other volunteers was a nineteen-year-old engineering student, living in Cairo, named Yasser Arafat. Arafat tells of taking part in an unsuccessful attempt by Egyptian volunteers to capture the Jewish settlement of Kfar Darome south of Gaza City. When that failed, he and his companions made their way back to Cairo, while other Egyptian units continued north.

Though nothing had happened so far, the Sorek Valley was doomed to become a battleground in the inevitable fight for Jerusalem. When the last Britishers lowered the Union Jack on May 14, the cease-fire collapsed. Within minutes Jerusalem convulsed into street fighting, as the Haganah and Irgun battled groups of Arab irregulars in an ugly struggle to possess each other's neighborhoods. The early skirmishes favored the Israelis, who executed a Haganah contingency plan called Operation Pitchfork to clear out pockets of Arabs between Jewish neighborhoods. The tide changed in the Arabs' favor on May 18 when Abdullah's Arab Legion occupied Latrun. A onetime crusader fortress, Latrun was halfway between Jerusalem and the coast, and only four miles from the Sorek Valley. By dominating the main highway with its cannons, the Legionnaires could now prevent food and ammunition convoys from reaching Jerusalem. The city's 100,000 Jews were trapped, their water lines cut and their ammunition dwindling. After taking Latrun, Abdullah strengthened his grip on Jerusalem by sending Arab Legion troops down the road past the Mount of Olives and into the Arab quarters of eastern Jerusalem. The Jews would have to find another way to reach Jerusalem with supplies, and the Sorek Valley fit into the plan.

To David Ben-Gurion, the Jerusalemites' predicament was more than a humanitarian issue. Now that the Arab armies had invaded Palestine, he no longer felt bound by the 1947 resolution making Jerusalem an international city. Now, like his right-wing critics Menachem Begin and Yitzhak Shamir, he talked of Jerusalem as the future capital of Israel. "At last we had a state," he wrote at the time, "but we were about to lose our capital." Ben-Gurion summoned Haganah's chief of operations, Yigael Yadin, and told him, "I want you to occupy Latrun and open the road to Jerusalem." Yadin objected, saying it was more important to defend Tel Aviv and the Galilee, which he saw as gravely threatened. Ben-Gurion gave an order: "Take Latrun." Twice—on May 23 and May 30—the Haganah flailed at Latrun with infantry, armored cars, even flamethrowers. Twice the Arab Legion repelled the attacks, imposing high casualties and leaving the highway to Jerusalem blockaded.

Was there another way? Colonel Shlomo Shamir, the Haganah brigade commander in the Latrun sector, figured there was. Perhaps it would be possible to build a detour—one that would

slice just north of the Sorek Valley. On May 28, his men had
captured Beit Susin, a Palestinian village south of Latrun. Later
that night, Colonel Shamir's patrols clambered from Beit Susin
down a goat path and accidentally encountered a Palmach patrol
hiking from the direction of Jerusalem. Now they knew that it
was possible to circumvent Latrun on foot. Could Haganah's
engineers bulldoze a three-mile detour through these hills? Colonel Shamir thought it would work. It would be their "Burma
Road"—just like the supply route that U.S. Army engineers
punched across the mountains between eastern India and
Burma in World War II. Four Haganah officers—among them
Colonel Vivian (Chaim) Herzog, the future president of Israel—
reconnoitered the route for the Burma Road in a bucking jeep.
Once Ben-Gurion learned of the plan, he gave immediate orders
to send every available bulldozer as well as civilians with pick-
axes to widen the rocky track. The secret route ran from Beit
Susin across the hills to the Sorek Valley road, skirting a mile
and a half north of Islin and Ishwa. After reaching the valley
road, the new route jogged north for half a mile before rejoining
the main highway to Jerusalem. On the night of May 31–June 1,
the first convoy of Jewish jeeps to Jerusalem broke through after
Haganah crews had portaged the cargo of ammunition up the
steepest inclines. The next night, Itzhak "Levitza" Levi, the
Jerusalem Haganah intelligence chief, rode the next convoy
back toward Tel Aviv. "Every now and then we were forced to
push the jeeps and lift them over boulders," Levi remembered.
The following morning when the convoy reached Rehovot, the
first Jewish town in Israel, Levi stopped at Café Kapulski. The
overjoyed staff treated him to strawberries with cream—both of
which had run out weeks earlier in Jerusalem. Levi led another
jeep convoy back to Jerusalem that night. It was loaded not with
food but with Czech submachine guns.

Recounted from the viewpoint of the Israelis, the Burma
Road is a story of ingenuity, valor, and gumption. Yet like so
much to do with the founding of Israel, the story has a different
ring from the viewpoint of Palestinians. Those touched most
directly by the Burma Road were the roughly one hundred

Palestinians who had lived in Beit Susin. A clinical account of what happened to their village has come from Zeev Eytan, then an eighteen-year-old Palmach commando:

> We attacked with about seventy men. By that time we had heavy mortars, 120-millimeter I think. Or maybe 81-millimeters, but even the 81s made a tremendous amount of noise. We deployed around the village and started firing. Our shells fell on target in the village. Then we assaulted the village and when we got there we found not a single soul. What we found instead were hot stoves with food ready to eat. The people had just left in front of us.

The British officer in charge of the nearest Arab Legion brigade was slow to react to his intelligence reports that the Jews were bulldozing a secret road. One of his Arab officers did believe the reports and gave a preliminary order to blast the Jewish road-builders with his cannons. His British superior, Colonel T. L. Ashton, refused to draw down his dwindling ammunition stocks. "The terrain is too tough," Ashton said. "They'll never get a road through there." Ashton put the order in writing: "Under no condition are you to waste your 25-pounder ammunition in the sector Beit Jiz–Beit Susin."

By now, all the main combatants were not only pinched for ammunition but ready for a time out. When the UN mediator Folke Bernadotte proposed a thirty-day cease fire, King Abdullah was only too eager to accept, since he hadn't wanted to fight in the first place. The Egyptians were also driven to accept the truce, because their army was dangerously overextended. Despite Cairo's roseate battle communiqués, which suggested that Tel Aviv was tottering, the Egyptian army was short of food, water, and ammunition after its reckless advance through the Sinai. Even the Israelis, who started the fighting with twice as many troops as the Arab armies, were ready for a breather. Their gamble to add Jerusalem to the state of Israel seemed all but lost. The Old City, including the Wailing Wall, was now in the hands of the Arab Legion. The western two-thirds of the city was solidly Jewish, but food was running low. How long could the Burma Road sustain its 100,000 inhabitants? Supplies "were running out everywhere," Ben-Gurion would remember. "We were at the end of our rope."

Only once was there an attempt by the Arabs to cut the Burma Road. That came not from the Arab Legion but from a band of Palestinian irregulars trying to retake some of their destroyed villages. On June 9 they attacked in the vicinity of Beit Susin, killing eight Israelis and wounding twenty. This obscure engagement was among the costlier battles the Haganah ever had to fight against Palestinian irregular units during the 1948 war. After being driven back, the Palestinians retreated toward the Sorek Valley, regrouped, and struck again the next morning. As before, the attack was driven back and the Palestinians were seen retreating toward the valley.

If the UN partition maps meant anything, the territory around Beit Susin was going to be Arab territory. But with the cease-fire approaching, Ben-Gurion decided the time was ripe to extend Israel's defense lines beyond Beit Susin and into the Sorek Valley. "We have checked out an alternative action: expanding the road of Beit Jiz–Beit Susin, and for that reason conquering Saraa and Islin," he wrote in his diary on June 10. Early that day he gave his commanders an order to conquer Saraa and Islin, the two villages overlooking the valley. It was too late: the cease-fire was due to come into effect the following night. Neither brigade commander Yitzhak Rabin nor operations chief Yigael Yadin had time to pull together enough troops to attack the ridgeline above the valley.

But there was time for a punitive air raid. And so only hours before the UN cease-fire was to come into effect, Haganah airplanes took to the skies above the valley. What Ben-Gurion recorded in his diary was simply: "Our air force bombed Saraa. In addition our planes shot at Ishwa, Artuf, and Islin."

· 14 ·

OPERATION
DANI

*T*he bombs fell out of the sky in midafternoon. Sabiha Abu Latifah kept remarkably cool for a nineteen-year-old pregnant mother. "When the planes attacked, my husband said, 'Let's take the baby and run.' I said no, I have to bake the bread and put the potatoes on to cook first. While her husband paced in agitation, Sabiha collected food and blankets, and only then did the family trek down from Saraa with their year-and-a-half-old baby to the security of the Arab-occupied Artuf railway station. The Abu Latifahs and other families camped around the station for days, returning home in the morning to tend to the fields, the animals, and the cooking.

But there were no more attacks, not then. On June 11, 1948, the day after the valley was bombarded, the United Nations Security Council cease-fire order came into force. The ground held by each side was somewhat different from the UN partition scheme, primarily because Egyptian forces, not Israeli, occupied the Negev. But so far each controlled a share of Palestine. The cease-fire period would prove critical. Politically, the Israelis would have time to make decisions about their territory and about the nature of their nation that would carry momentous consequences for the Palestinians. Militarily, the Israelis and the Arabs would use the month-long respite in radically different ways. At the end of it they would resume hostilities from radically different postures.

For the Arabs of the Sorek Valley, the cease-fire became a peaceful deception. The air raid had rattled them, especially the villagers in Saraa. But now even the rumbling of artillery heard from over the hills in Latrun had quieted. Most all the valley tried to get back to daily business. The harvest was about to begin, and they had to plan for getting in the crop. Whatever time they could snag from work the men spent down at the police post, talking to the soldiers and listening to the radio tell the Arab version of news. Ismail Abdul Fattah, the mukhtar of Artuf, had handed over his prized radio, the one he had bought from the British and operated on a car battery, to the Jordanian in command. The commander had requisitioned it, saying his soldiers needed to keep up with events. But he said the mukhtar could come down to the police station to listen to the radio all day, if he wanted, and he often did just that, sitting outside with the soldiers for hours. As soldiers wandered in and out of villages, they gave the people confidence. Awad Ibrahim Awad of Ishwa, who had worked at the Levys' mill before the Hartuvians left, described how: "The Jordanians came and told us to stay in the village, that they would defend everybody. The Arab Legion will drive the Israelis out of here."

These assurances were more hollow than the Sorek Valley fellaheen had any way of knowing in those calm June days. The Arab regimes which had been fighting on behalf of the Palestinians faced a dilemma: could they afford to resume the fight at the end of the cease-fire? The Arab armies, short of firepower and trained soldiers before the truce, got no significant resupplies during the UN-ordered cease-fire. Since the cease-fire terms prohibited either side from enhancing its arms, troop strength, or fortifications, Britain refused to fulfill weapons contracts it had with Egypt and Transjordan. The Arab countries had only marginal contacts with the Eastern Bloc, which the Israelis would find to be a valuable supplier. Nor had the still parochial

Arabs ever dreamed of building a sophisticated international arms smuggling network parallel to one their Israeli enemies had created.

By the closing days of the cease-fire, Syria was reduced to commandeering ninety-two private trucks and fifty-one buses for its military, which had suffered almost total devastation of its tank force during the first round of fighting. The Transjordanians would be told to conserve ammunition by not shooting until the enemy fired first. Yet somehow the lack of arms would pale beside political motivations driving the Arabs back toward the battlefield.

In Transjordan, King Abdullah's regime wanted to extend the truce. Sir John Bagot Glubb, the British officer in charge of the king's troops, tried to convince the Transjordanian prime minister to authorize the drafting of more men and purchase of ammunition during the cease-fire. He couldn't. "There won't be any more fighting," Glubb quoted the prime minister as responding. "No more fighting! I and Nokrashy Pasha [the Egyptian premier] are agreed to that, and if we two are agreed, we can sway the rest." The decision not to reinforce the Arab Legion would have repercussions in the Sorek Valley within weeks.

Abdullah himself did not want to fight one more day. He knew the Israelis were stronger. After a meeting at which the Arab League Political Committee overruled his counsel against hostilities, Abdullah told Glubb: "If I were to drive into the desert and accost the first goatherd I saw, and consult him on whether to make war on my enemies or not, he would say to me, 'How many have you got and how many have they?' Yet here are these learned politicians, all of them with university degrees, and when I say to them, 'The Jews are too strong, it is a mistake to make war,' they cannot understand the point. They make long speeches about rights." The king happily would have accepted the settlement proposed during the truce by Count Folke Bernadotte, the UN mediator, who called for approximately what Abdullah wanted all along: a union of Palestine and Transjordan comprising an Arab state and a separate Jewish state, with each state controlling its own affairs and with a Jewish-Arab council coordinating economic ties, foreign policy, and defense. Under Bernadotte's scheme, Transjordan would be enlarged by the addition of the Negev, Jerusalem, and parts of what the UN had proposed as the Arab Palestinian state, including the Sorek Valley.

The plan was so favorable to King Abdullah that it gave the other Arab leaders a powerful new motive to take up arms again. The prospect of Abdullah splitting Palestine with the Zionists repelled most of the Arab leaders, who viewed him as a doormat for both the British and the Zionists. U.S. diplomats tracking Arab sentiment found the Syrian prime minister worrying that Transjordan would become "a Jewish colony" under the mediator's plan. But he and others also opposed it because it aggrandized Abdullah. Beyond that, they still refused to accept any form of partition that accommodated an Israeli state. "The Arabs are living in a dream world where the political fact of the existence of Israel [supported by the USSR and the U.S.] is denied, and where it is imagined that even the ghost of this fact may be laid [to rest] by resort to arms," said one assessment made for the State Department that summer. The fact remained that these Arab rulers truly believed that the Arabs who had roots in Palestine for centuries had a right to live and govern there, and the Jewish immigrants did not. And so they refused to compromise.

By now the Arab leaders also were afraid of a backlash snarling their own ability to stay in power at home. The notion of peace without an Arab victory seemed outrageous to the Arab press and public. The Egyptians, the Syrians, the Lebanese, and the others had been so taken in by propagandistic stories of valiant battlefield progress that they were unshakable in their conviction that their armies could have beaten the Jews, had they just kept on fighting. By the time the cease-fire ended, there was a rare and genuine clamor in the Arab world for their governments to finish the job. The American chargé in Cairo cabled Washington on June 25 that several Arab governments risked overthrow "by resentful masses" if they agreed to a partition scheme including a Jewish state. In the end, even Abdullah's government could not publicly endorse the mediator's plan and vote to continue the truce.

While the Arab leaders felt pressed to continue, they did little to bolster their chances in battle. After meetings that had leaders crisscrossing the Arab world, the Arab League nations finally refused to extend the cease-fire. In the meantime, some of the Arab armies had actually managed to recruit more troops, but they had not even discussed a joint strategy to use them. They did not trust each other enough to share battle plans. Glubb, commander of Transjordan's Arab Legion, said the politicians had come to the "fantastic decision" to resume fighting with their weakened armies arrayed in a passive defense. There would be no possibility of making battlefield gains, Glubb said in his memoirs, and only the hope of not incurring loss. "Presumably the politicians hoped that they would regain their reputations for patriotism by refusing to renew the truce, and that the Security Council would then insist more forcibly [on another truce]," Glubb wrote.

There was one other gnawing problem that soon would grow into a disaster for the Arabs. It explains why the Jordanian soldiers in the Sorek Valley were telling the fellaheen to stick to their homes. By the start of the cease-fire in June, nearly 400,000 Palestinians had become refugees from more than 250 towns and villages, mostly in areas under Jewish control. Arab leaders outside Palestine now were urging the Palestinians to stay—sometimes even threatening them. These refugees were burdening the Arab nations fighting on behalf of the Palestinians. Thousands had fled across the borders into surrounding Arab countries, and tens of thousands had crammed into the eastern portions of Palestine not under Israeli control. The Arab League feared that setting up some new administration to manage the incipient chaos there would imply acceptance of partition.

The Palestinians who held fast during the truce, including most of the farmers of the Sorek Valley, did so with trepidation. Families took precautions out of fear that fighting would resume and sweep into their villages. In Islin, some worried fathers carried sacks of grain to store with relatives in a town several miles east, a place where they would flee with their families if the Israelis invaded. In Saraa, Diab Abu Latifah took his sick, aging parents to a cave farther away from Israeli lines, where they could be picked up en route out of town, if it came to that. But few, if any, abandoned the valley. The war's economic dislocation already had eaten away small gains some had made in the last few years. Asad Hamdan Asad, who had tried to supplement farming with a truck transport business in Ishwa, found the roads too dangerous, the times too uncertain to seek work. That July he had to sell the truck when he fell behind in loan payments. Unlike many of the Jerusalem and Jaffa merchants, he wasn't wealthy enough to take his family to safer grounds. Besides, the Palestinians still were counting on the Arab leaders to be their protectors, not knowing how divided and weak-willed those leaders had become.

Unlike the Arabs, the Israelis used the cease-fire with extraordinary efficacy, filling the month with decisions and actions that would be critical not only to future battles but to the definition of the Jewish state. One of the most important developments was the growth of a consensus that the Palestinian refugees should not be allowed to go home. Angry settlers agitating to harvest Arab land were allowed to do so. More than a dozen Arab villages were razed. Homeless Jewish immigrants started filling up Arab homes in cities like Jaffa. By mid-June, Prime Minister Ben-Gurion was clear about his attitude. "As for the return of the Arabs, not only can I not accept the opinion of encouraging their return . . . but I think that one should prevent their return," Ben-Gurion said at a June 16 cabinet meeting. It was the Arabs who had declared war, he said, and they would have to bear the consequences.

The military, now called the Israel Defence Forces (IDF), was about to become as instrumental in keeping the Palestinians out as the Haganah had been in pushing them out in the first place. An analysis by IDF intelligence in June 1948 was a telling indication of how the first 400,000 Palestinians had come to flee. It attributed "at least 55 percent of the total exodus" to operations by the IDF and by its forerunner the Haganah. Radical Jewish paramilitary groups caused another 15 percent of the refugees to flee, the report said. "The factor of surprise, prolonged [artillery] barrages making loud explosive sounds, [use of] loudspeakers in Arabic [to spread frightening 'black propaganda' messages], proved their great efficacy when used properly," the report said in explaining the role of the military.

During the cease-fire, military strategists saw a danger in the return of destitute Arabs who started filtering back to harvest their crops once the shooting stopped. Yigael Yadin, the chief of military operations, ordered all his brigades to "prevent completely" any Arab reaping in areas the Jews controlled. "Every enemy field in the area of our complete control we must harvest," he said on June 19. "Every field we are unable to reap must be destroyed. In any event, the Arabs must be prevented from reaping these fields." If they came back to reap, they might stay. In several cases refugees returning to their land were shot. Elsewhere refugees stumbled into land mines planted in their fields by Jewish settlers, who were as anxious to claim possession of this land as the army was to keep the Arabs out. Before the cease-fire ended in July the young state managed to add six to seven thousand tons of grain to its economy by taking over Arab fields.

Israeli attention focused less on Palestinian refugees during the cease-fire than on winning a war. The Israelis proceeded as though the UN requirement to hold the military status quo simply did not exist. With the British out of the way and fighting no longer a hazard, Israel was able to import the crucial stocks of arms bought by its agents around the world. One ship delivered ten 75-millimeter cannon, ten Hotchkiss tanks, nineteen 65-millimeter cannon, four antiaircraft guns and 45,000 shells. A second brought 110 tons of TNT, ten tons of cordite, and 200,000 detonators. From the United States, Mexico, France, Italy, and Czechoslovakia came everything from Messerschmitt fighter planes to Sherman tanks.

That crude little "Burma Road" that Israeli soldiers had

forced through the hills just north of the Sorek Valley made an indispensable link with Jerusalem during the cease-fire and thereafter. The UN mediator had agreed to let the Israelis send provisions over the main Jerusalem–Tel Aviv road, but the trucks could carry only enough food and necessities to keep the Jews in Jerusalem supplied for the duration of the truce. They were not to haul any weapons or extra food to stockpile, and the trucks were inspected by both Arab Legion and UN teams before entering the city. "But we were not satisfied with that and so we made illegal convoys on the Burma Road," said Itzhak "Levitza" Levi, by now a ranking Israeli commander. "We wanted to create a reserve and we could not create one with those limitations." The road, constantly being smoothed and straightened till one-and-a-half-ton trucks could rumble across it, saved Jewish Jerusalem. Israeli warehouses had been practically licked clean six weeks earlier. By the end of the cease-fire, they were loaded with 2,200 tons of flour, 260 tons of sugar, and 150 tons of beans. Weapons stocks burgeoned, too. The supply of machine-gun ammunition that stood at 33,000 rounds on June 1 was up to 760,000 by the end of the cease-fire. Three-inch mortar shells had increased from seventeen to 4,452. Jewish Jerusalem was ready for war.

At the same time that weapons were rolling into Israel, the ranks of soldiers were growing and getting primed for return to battle. To swell the ranks of native Israelis, thousands were recruited from abroad during the one-month cease-fire, both veterans of Allied forces and European Jews in displaced-persons camps. By mid-July, an analysis by the U.S. Central Intelligence Agency found that the Israelis had built a decisive edge in fighting potential. The CIA estimated that Israel had 97,800 men and women under arms, and the Arabs had a total of 46,800 ready to fight. Of the latter, only 27,000 Arabs actually were in Palestine, and the rest were near the borders. The agency also reported that Israel had vastly improved both its fortifications and its weapons stocks during the month-long truce, while the Arab gains had been "insignificant" in comparison. If the 1948 war had a climactic turning point, it was the June 1948 cease-fire.

Israeli training at Sarafand, a former British army camp near the coast south of Tel Aviv, would have direct and permanent relevance to the Sorek Valley. "There we became soldiers," said Avizohar Nachshon. "All of us got a uniform, ID cards, and we were paid for the first time. I remember I was very rich. I got two and a half pounds." Nachshon was an eighteen-year-old squad leader in the Harel Brigade, part of the Palmach shock troops formed as a full-time Jewish defense corps during World War II. Palmach was under Haganah command but held distinct, more socialist political ties and an esprit growing from the youth of its members and their base in kibbutzim. The original members were mostly Sabras, Jews who had been born in Palestine. But by this time Nachshon's brigade, like others in the elite Palmach, had become a hybrid of trained, experienced young soldiers alongside new recruits who not only didn't know anything about fighting, but often didn't speak the same language. Dead and wounded often had been replaced with new immigrants, some just out of DP camps.

At Sarafand, Avi Nachshon's company got a new commander, another Sabra and Palmach veteran of three years, Ariyeh "Ikki" Nir. A Jerusalem native, Nir had progressed from boy scout to kibbutznik and finally to the Palmach, a route that infused many young Jews with the spirit of political Zionism and toughened them for the battles they would face. By the time he reached Sarafand, Nir was twenty-one and wartime commander of his own platoon. He oversaw dispersal of the new equipment and training in how to use it. Each squad got a Czech Spandau machine gun, and every soldier was handed either an Israeli-made Sten submachine gun or a Czech rifle. The platoon got a couple 52-millimeter British-made mortars, while every company was assigned at least one truck, a jeep, and a water tank. Nir was lucky. Not many of the soldiers he was teaching to handle new weapons had just stepped off a boat. "Most of them were new immigrants who came during the past four, five, or six months. Some of them had already engaged in battles," he said. Regardless of their proficiency in Hebrew, one more duty assigned the polyglot collection of soldiers was to swear allegiance, for the first time, to what was for all of them a new country. In a few days they would be out fighting for it.

The Israelis actually would have been happy to postpone the fighting longer, and they told the UN mediator they were willing to extend the cease-fire. It was the Arab League that refused. The day before the truce expired, the Arab leaders, propelled by fear of angry populations, by mistrust of Abdullah, and by blindness to Israel's military strength, wrote to the mediator that they would not continue the cease-fire.

The Israeli soldiers were prepared to return to battle on the offensive and perform a series of swift strikes designed to enlarge their territory—north, south, and center. The soldiers from Sarafand were among those assigned to carry out Ben-Gurion's desire to broaden the Jerusalem Corridor, the goal stopped short by the month-long truce. Ben-Gurion described his targets: "We have not succeeded in Latrun. And there remain the two thorns: Lod [Lydda] and Ramle. It is a hard wound in our present position." The second problem, he wrote, was Jerusalem and the corridor without which it could not exist. "It is not enough having a road between Tel Aviv and Jerusalem in order to get ahold of Jerusalem. One needs consecutive territory," he said. Winning the corridor and taking its villages— villages like Ishwa, Islin, Saraa, and Artuf—was the way to secure Jerusalem.

The plan to open the corridor was called Operation Dani, .named after the head of the Jewish squad of thirty-five soldiers wiped out in January not far from Hartuv. The operation's first assault was a spectacularly successful offensive at Lydda, the Palestinian town directly on the diagonal between Tel Aviv and Jerusalem. Palestine's main airport was located there. The aim was driving out Jordan's Arab Legion troops from the midsection of Palestine, an area that the UN partition plan designated Arab, not Israeli. In fact, most of the Arab Legion troops already were gone from Lydda and nearby Ramle by the time Israeli forces began pounding the towns. Glubb had pulled them out as soon as he realized the Israelis were making an offensive. He knew the Legionnaires there could not repel the newly fortified

Israeli troops without reinforcements, and Glubb was unwilling to jeopardize Latrun and thereby Jerusalem by sending them.

When the Israelis attacked Lydda, they swept into a city defended by untrained locals bearing rifles. The townspeople quickly surrendered, but when they saw an Arab Legion vehicle on reconnaissance, they mistakenly thought the Legion had returned to rescue them. A knot of Arab irregulars resumed firing from a mosque. Once the Israeli forces snuffed out the opposition, they gave the population three hours to start evacuating. Prodded by blaring loudspeakers and soldiers firing behind them, the Arabs set out eastward on a deadly trek. Heat stroke was too much for some of the elderly and the youngest to survive. " 'Driving out' is a term with a harsh ring," brigade commander Yitzhak Rabin wrote. "Psychologically, this was one of the most difficult actions we undertook. The population of Lod [Lydda] did not leave willingly. There was no way of avoiding the use of force and warning shots in order to make the inhabitants march the ten or fifteen miles to the point where they met up with the Arab Legion."

At Ramle the victory was as fast and as complete, but there the Israelis offered buses to take the Arabs across the frontier to a point where the Arab Legion could claim them. At least fifty thousand people were forced to flee, and both towns were sacked by the victorious soldiers. It was Ben-Gurion who ordered the depopulation. Just after the attack began on Lydda, Rabin and the operation commander Yigal Allon were discussing with Ben-Gurion what to do with the Arab inhabitants. One Israeli chronicler of the period has described the scene: "Ben-Gurion made a dismissive, energetic gesture with this hand and said: 'Expel them.' "

Palestinians still sticking to their homes began to get the drift of events. When some Ramle refugees arrived at the Sorek Valley with their stories of the assaults and evictions, a few local families left. Most remained. They had no trouble believing angry accusations that cowardly Arab Legion troops had retreated before the fighting started, because the villagers suddenly saw exactly the same thing happening in their own valley. A few days after the end of the cease-fire, the unit of fifty Transjordanian soldiers occupying the police station pulled out. It must have been part of Glubb's effort to marshal his forces. The Arab Legion didn't even give a few days' warning to their Egyptian allies holding down the police station, but pulled out immediately upon receiving a telegram from Amman.

The fellaheen had been stunned to see the Jordanian soldiers go. Now their only protection was the fifty Egyptian soldiers, in whom they had little faith. Ismail Rahhal said that during the cease-fire an Egyptian officer had warned his father, the Artuf mukhtar, that times were darkening. The officer predicted the Jews would take over all of Palestine, and said he believed the Egyptian soldiers would be gone soon. If the mukhtar wanted to leave, too, he said, he could take his family to an Arab country and be safe. "My father came back and told us about this," Rahhal said. "He told us we will stay. And he said, 'I think these Egyptians are cowards and they will leave.'"

Not only had the Jordanians promised to defend the valley towns, but one day the Jordanian commander even pledged to the mukhtar that if they were forced to leave, they would take the people with them. A week later, however, the Jordanians pulled out. "Around 4:00 P.M., we saw the cars coming from Hebron to the police station. They [the Jordanians] started taking the furniture from the police station, taking everything with them," Rahhal said. His father went down to see what was happening and asked the Jordanian officer about the promise to take the villagers with them. These were his orders, the officer responded. The Jordanian drove away, taking the mukhtar's radio with him.

The fellaheen tried to hold on after the Jordanian soldiers left. It was still the harvest season, and they had put too much work into the crop just to let it stand and rot. Even when they heard the booming of artillery from Latrun, the whispers of horrors that befell the Arabs in Lydda and Ramle, the firing from the direction of villages just over the shoulders of the hills to their north, still they didn't go. More families now from Saraa and

Ishwa and Islin had taken bedrolls down to the police station in the valley bottom where the Ramle refugees had camped, knowing the Egyptians still were there, figuring it was an easier springboard for escape than the confines of their homes and villages. They slept there at night and came back to their fields and houses by day. But they didn't leave their valley.

The Israelis' success at Lydda and Ramle did not spill over to their efforts at Latrun. Part of the new offensive focused on cutting Latrun from its supply line in the east and from supportive Arab artillery positions to its north. Company B, 4th Battalion of the Harel Brigade, the company of Ikki Nir and Avi Nachshon, had been sent to reinforce a company pinned down under Arab Legion artillery fire at the town of Yalu, on one of the fortified hills to the north. "Another unit of the Arab Legion came through the wadi to stop us," Nachshon said. "We thought they were Israeli army—they had the same uniform. Then they took positions and started firing." The Israeli soldiers were thrust into retreat, some in panic. "One Yugoslav soldier [a recent immigrant] went hysterical here. . . . We had a deputy commander killed."

Theirs was not the only failure in those days after the cease-fire, and it became clear the Jews could not widen their tenuous corridor to Jerusalem by cutting down Arab Legion defenses holding territory to the north. Pressure on the Israeli military command was growing. Already there was talk in the UN Security Council about another cease-fire. The Israelis would have to move fast if they wanted to expand the corridor, a feat critical not only to support their claims on Jerusalem, but also to strengthen their presence between Jordan's Arab Legion and the Egyptian forces that had moved up from the south. The obvious choice left to the Israelis was concentrating more forces on the soft belt of Arab villages sitting below the road to Jerusalem. The villages sprinkled over the Sorek Valley would be part of Operation Dani as it moved south. Company A would begin at Saraa.

• 15 •

"A LITTLE PUSH
AND
THEY WILL DESERT"

*I*t was the fifth day of Ramadan. We were sleeping at the Hartuv railroad station," said Sabiha Abu Latifah. "The Egyptian guards were still at Saraa, and some of the villagers who had guns also were guarding the village." Most of the families at their improvised camp by the station already were awakening and beginning to move, even though the sun's rays hadn't begun breaking the darkness. In their holy month of Ramadan, Moslems fast all day, eating and drinking only after the sun has set or before it reappears. Sabiha, the young mother who one month earlier had refused to flee an air raid till she cooked some bread and potatoes, was among the sleepy women fixing breakfast before 4:00 A.M. The men and children were stirring, some already eating, others just rising from their stuffed mats or beds of blankets on the earth.

Suddenly they were startled full awake by shuddering blasts coming from their hill. Looking up toward their homes in the dark, they could see glowing explosions of light. They didn't need to see any more to know the Israelis were attacking. Defenders were there, but not many more than a dozen. Nobody down in the valley bottom could gauge the strength of the assault force and certainly not its intentions for the Palestinian people whose village was being menaced. They could guess. The houses of Beit Mahsir had been blown up across the valley only two months earlier. Only three days ago they had heard stories of townspeople driven out of Lydda at gunpoint. And after that Ramle. They remembered what they had heard about Deir Yassin and the slaughter of Palestinian villagers.

The Abu Latifahs made their decision quickly. "We wanted to flee before the Jews would recognize us. We were afraid they would shoot us," said Sabiha. "People were pushing each other to leave because they were talking about the massacres at other villages," said her husband, Diab Abu Latifah. The young couple, he twenty-nine, she nineteen and four months pregnant, had heard stories of bayonets piercing the stomachs of pregnant women at Deir Yassin. Other Saraa families joined them, gathering up children and cook pots and blankets in the dark, the few possessions they hadn't left in their houses on the hill. "We left the wheat and barley and corn," Sabiha said. "We only took a few clothes and mattresses and blankets. We didn't think we'd go forever. We had very nice china plates. I didn't want to take them because I was afraid they would break." They would return, they said, in a few days.

And so the first of the fellaheen of the Sorek Valley lost grip of their land and homes and became awash in the anonymous flow of more than 400,000 Palestinian refugees, a number that would nearly double by the time the fighting ended.

They say today that the Israelis drove them out and kept them out and meant to do it from the start, had to do it to fulfill their dream of the Jewish homeland. Hundreds of thousands of other Palestinian refugees carry similar views about Israeli designs on Arab land. Israelis then said and still say there never existed a coherent plan to push the Palestinians out of their homes, though the once-prevalent Israeli argument that Arab leaders exhorted their people to leave to clear the way for invading Arab armies has been discredited. Some explain the widespread phenomenon of flight as a simple by-product of battle, a not uncommon result of war. The most exhaustive Israeli study on the

cause of this exodus takes a middle ground, saying once the
Israelis saw the Palestinian enemy fleeing, they encouraged
them. Still it is a controversy, as the principals of that war and
their descendants yet today try to assess responsibility and cal-
culate what, if any, obligation remains to be paid. The ledger is
complicated not only because of subsequent wars and terrorism
and occupation, but because the refugee problem in the beginning was created under circumstances that differed at different
times and in different places. What happened in the Sorek Valley over a few days in July is as telling a case as any that some
Palestinians were indeed intentionally driven out of their homeland. The stories of events told by the dispossessors fit almost
exactly with the recollections of the dispossessed.

The Abu Latifahs were gone before the fighting stopped at
Saraa that morning of July 13 with the defending villagers surprisingly still in control. Several had been killed in the hard
fighting, others wounded. The Egyptian soldiers with the defending villagers had had enough of battling for a tier of Palestinian hamlets, and they withdrew. Surely they sensed the
fighting wasn't finished yet. It wasn't. That night the Israeli
troops renewed their assault, now with the aid of at least one
65-millimeter French artillery gun. Even the additional firepower didn't immediately clear out the resistance. When the
Israeli soldiers got close enough to be seen, it was their turn to
be the targets. Some were hit. But their artillery and hand grenades and submachine guns did the job. Finally the remaining
Palestinian fighters and the few families that had held out in
their village till the end realized they were about to be overwhelmed, and they slipped away. Saraa was conquered that
morning of July 14, 1948.

At the same time Saraa was under fire, another Israeli battalion was on the offensive farther to the east, attacking the small
towns lining an old, rutted road that wound over the mountains
to Jerusalem. It was a narrow track that started in the Sorek
Valley across from Ishwa, then ran parallel to the Jerusalem–
Tel Aviv highway. Taking over the valley and this road would
give the Israelis a ready-made route to Jerusalem. Suba, the

easternmost town on the small road, a town sitting eight rugged miles from the valley, had been captured the night of the first, unsuccessful attack on Saraa. Six miles away from the valley Deir al-Amar was targeted for attack, as was Kasla, no more than five miles east. The sounds of assault rang out in the night. Dozens of families in chaotic flight from the nightmares in their towns passed into the valley, some stopping at Ishwa or Islin or the train station in hopes the Israeli soldiers soon would leave and they could return, others continuing to more secure territory further away from Jerusalem.

Ikki Nir's 2nd Platoon of Company B, rested after the debacle at Yalu, was dispatched to Saraa to reinforce the battered Company A attackers. Saraa was securely in their hands, but the soldiers made a house-to-house hunt to flush out any hiding Palestinians. There were none. They discovered Saraa was a dominating position to hold, seven hundred feet above the valley floor. The Israelis could look down directly at the police station across the valley, where intelligence told them Egyptian soldiers were based. The invading force set up machine guns to shoot down at the station, even though they scarcely could shoot that far with accuracy. "They could cause some trouble, you know, firing from time to time," Nir said of the gunners. "And they were worried there. We saw movements. Kind of nervous." Some flares were set off down at the station, but there was no return shooting.

When the Awad family heard shots fired down toward them from Saraa, they knew their time had come to go. The Awads, one of the Ishwa families that had made the railway station their nighttime refuge, had not left with the Abu Latifahs a couple of nights earlier when Saraa first came under attack. As Amira Shahin remembered it, they held out until the seventh day of Ramadan, the early-morning hours of July 15, out of some vain hope the Israelis would desist. Their camp beneath trees at the railway station was less than half a mile down the road from the police post, and they didn't wait to learn exactly which of the two was under the gunners' sites. They knew enough about attacks from the refugees who had already passed down their road. "The people were fleeing because they were afraid. They were hearing the shooting," said Awad Ibrahim Awad, who was thirty years old. "There was nobody to defend us," said his wife, Amira. "It was for everyone to take their sons and flee." Awad and his brothers piled their families into their one truck and headed southeast, in the direction of the town of Deir Aban. "There was not a person there, just the dogs. The road was blocked," Awad said. "We had to go back. We thought the Israelis would see the lights and shoot at us. So we turned off the lights and my two brothers got out and led the way." They walked through the darkness stalking turns in the road as though they were hunting some living prey, whispering back to Awad to go right or left or to watch the pothole ahead, hurrying to get away before daylight so they would not become the quarry. They got back to the valley road and veered south toward Hebron.

After its stay at Saraa, the 2nd Platoon was sent back about five miles northwest to the Palestinian village of Beit Jiz—now empty of villagers—where the company had set up a temporary headquarters. There Ikki Nir got a new assignment. "My orders were to take Ishwa and Islin as an independent operation of my platoon," Nir would say forty years later. "I only had attached to me a scout to show me the way. And the information said these villages are already abandoned or are on the verge of being abandoned. And they only need a little push and they will desert." Scouts already had made a reconnaissance of the valley and had seen that sandwiching these villages with assaults to their east and west had been effective. Those who had not left, they figured, must be on the edge of flight. Clearing the villages would not be hard, not like fighting against the soldiers who were trained and equipped and holding forth at Latrun and Yalu. Had there been any hint they would encounter resistance, Nir said, his platoon of thirty to forty people would not have been sent out alone.

They may have been only three dozen soldiers, but they were well enough armed when they set out the night of July 17. Nir recounted: "We had three or four medium machine guns, German types G-34. We had Sten guns and light machine guns, you know, submachine guns, Israeli-made, we had a few rifles, which were the Czech Mauser. We had hand grenades. I had a medic with me, a girl." There was at least one two-inch mortar that made plenty of noise and could reach 450 yards. Avi Nachshon, a squad leader under Nir, said the platoon and its arms may have been driven in trucks part of the way from Beit Jiz, but they walked the last couple of miles over the hilly terrain. "It was very dark," he said. "We could see nothing."

They reached the top of the hill above Islin. Its four dozen houses sprawled across the higher ground of the slope, about two hundred yards above the larger presence of Ishwa, which covered the lower half of the hill with a population of more than six hundred. By now it was the middle of the moonless night, around one or two in the morning, and the Israeli soldiers scarcely could define the houses of Islin. They knew they were close enough, though. They could hear the people. "There was still movement in the village," Nir said. "We heard some movement. We heard people who were maybe still collecting their belongings. I don't know exactly what they did there. However, we opened fire. . . ." They fired on the village with machine guns and lobbed in mortar shells with their frightful, crashing sound. "You really couldn't spot a target. There was nobody firing at us, so it was just creating noise, making people who were there even more afraid so as to encourage them to move out. So that we could come in." There was no resistance, just as expected, no answering fire. "We were not in a hurry to rush in. It would have meant maybe to cause them to resist, which was useless for them. As far as I was concerned, better give them more time to evacuate and go in without any casualties, rather than start chasing after them to catch them." So they waited. When Nir decided it must be safe, his troops advanced into Islin. He was right. The Palestinians had gone.

From there they fired down on Ishwa. "Here again," Nir said, "there were some people there. But no resistance. Nobody answered [with firing]." Avi Nachshon led the assault squad, positioning the mortar and a machine gun to fire on the village.

"The first thing we did, we shot into the village with the 52-millimeter [mortar]. And nobody answered," he said. Then he ordered his machine-gun operator, a recent refugee from Czechoslovakia, to let it rip. Then they waited again.

Ishwa was in pandemonium. Some villagers had left in previous days, but not all had. Now they heard the attack on Islin, saw their neighbors fleeing. Those who didn't have an emergency pack fixed—after listening to five nights of gunfire echo around them—quickly made ready and got out. Some probably were bolting for safer terrain by the time the Jewish soldiers actually opened assault on their village. "The people had to leave," said Asad Hamdan Asad. "When they started shooting at us, the villagers, we decided to leave. We took only some blankets." There was no more time to brood about what to take or where to go. How could Asad, thirty-eight, and his wife, Alia, thirty-three, worry about the newly harvested stores of grain or the kerosene stove or her gold wedding bracelets when they had to organize a family of seven children, one a newborn? The sisters-in-law helped. "We put the blankets on the camel. And an old woman who was with us, we put her on top of that," Alia said. "We were forced to go. They were shooting behind us. Everybody left. How could we stay? They would kill us inside our houses." Like so many others, they never dreamed it would matter too much, what they took and what they didn't. "When we left we said we will be back in two or three days. That's why we left everything behind," said Asad.

The Asads had the foresight to herd some cows and goats ahead of them as they made their way down the hill out of town and across the valley. They would need the animals when they returned and couldn't leave them to the whims of invaders. Mahmoud, only thirteen when they left, knew well the route his family followed as they climbed on foot through their olive grove across the road, up the slopes that formed the southeastern wall of their valley. This was where he normally drove the goats to graze. On this trip, though, they soon realized they couldn't take the easy way and follow the small road up the hill to the place where it swung sharply east to Jerusalem. Through the

darkness Mahmoud saw enemy jeeps up the road. They probably belonged to troops that had cleared out those villages farther
east. The Asads and other villagers of Ishwa and Islin had no
choice but escape through the trees and the brush and the slippery rocks of the hillside.

As the 2nd Platoon entered first Islin and then Ishwa, the
soldiers walked into twilight zones of living towns with no
people. There was no one either to wave a white flag or shoot
at them. "By the morning, comfortably, it was taken. I had no
feeling I was in battle at all," Nir said. Still he demanded his
troops take care, just in case an ambush or booby trap lay waiting in the villages. He had already made the rules clear: no
groping through houses or grabbing up loot, even a chicken for
lunch. Other units had lost people when they ran into a well-
placed grenade or a Palestinian in hiding. Here there were neither grenades nor Palestinians. "There were chickens. There
might have been sheep or goats, or a donkey. It was definitely
a place where you will say you might find hot mattresses," said
Nir. His medic, Penina Yariv, also heard movement from the
villages as the troops stole up to them in the darkness. By the
time they entered, though, the villages had been emptied. "All
the houses were like the people were still living there," she said.

Avi Nachshon was unsure whether he actually drove villagers
out of their homes. "We didn't see anyone. I think the village
was simply empty. Maybe not. It's very difficult for me to say."
Nachshon did not recall getting much instruction on what to do
if villagers didn't evacuate. "I was told to open fire on the village, then to be sure that nobody is in the village, to pass through
it, and then just to report that it is an empty place. This I have
done. . . . As far as I remember, if we met people, they were
supposed to answer fire. If not, at least to wave with the white
flag. But how can you see white flags at night?"

A correspondent from an Israeli newspaper was up on the
hilltop of Saraa with Israeli troops that night and watched the
villagers flee. "With the break of dawn I stood over the hilltop
of Saraa and I saw from the east the smoke coming up from Islin
and from Ishwa. The villages were conquered by storm and the

last of the enemy people escaped to the nearby mountains," he wrote.

The platoon sent out to capture Islin and Ishwa not only accomplished its mission but also made a bonus hit that night. It seems to have contributed to the evacuation of Artuf, the Palestinian village sharing a hillside with the now empty Jewish colony, a hillside where Jews and Arabs had passed three generations in relations more often friendly than stormy. Artuf was on the assault list of a different platoon that wouldn't come plowing through the valley for hours. Ismail Rahhal, then the nineteen-year-old son of the Artuf mukhtar, said that after days of offensives around the area the people of his hamlet suddenly discovered themselves under direct fire that night. Rahhal said there was more shooting from the Israelis perched up in Saraa, probably aimed at keeping occupied the Egyptian soldiers they believed still were holed up at the police station less than half a mile west of Artuf. The war correspondent's account confirms that the troops on the hilltop did indeed lob mortars down on the station and on Artuf. That, combined with the mortars and stream of machine-gun fire trained first on Islin and then on Ishwa, a mile to the northeast of Artuf, produced the sense that the Artufis were surrounded. "No one knew what direction they fired from," Rahhal said. "No one cared about the others. No one knew what to do. I took some blankets and mattresses on a donkey, and I left with the sheep and cows. And the rest of my family came behind." The mukhtar and some elders stayed in Artuf past daylight, discussing a plan to carry a white flag up to the Israelis in Saraa and plead with them to spare a peaceful village. But no one, Rahhal said, could summon the courage to walk up the hill where the Israelis were shooting.

The Artufis in flight headed the same direction as the fellaheen from Ishwa—south and east over the rising hills, up to the town of Deir al-Hawa, about a three-mile trip from the valley bottom. Rahhal had a frightening, frustrating walk as he tried to herd the family's one hundred sheep and twenty cows up the steep slope behind Artuf. Halfway into the climb something exploded up ahead of him, blinding him with a spray of dirt so he lost all the animals except the donkey. The explosion shook him, and so did the prospect of facing his father without the livestock. After a moment to compose himself he hurried ahead, Rahhal said, and farther up the mountain ran into the spooked cows. He collected them and drove them on up the slope. When Rahhal met some townspeople on the same route to safety, he got them to take the animals so he could retrace his steps in search of the sheep. Rahhal skidded back down the dry hillside through the trees and brush under a lightening dawn sky. He found the sheep standing at almost exactly the place he had left them. It was already daytime when he resumed the trek to Deir al-Hawa, rushing the sheep as quickly as sheep can be rushed, scared and hoping that Israeli soldiers would not be on the lookout for laggard Palestinians in flight. Rahhal and the cows and the sheep all made it. He knew the animals were important to the family, but neither Rahhal nor his fellow exiles realized then how crucial any possessions of value soon would become to them as Palestinian refugees.

The villagers no longer had military support after the last defenders in the police station—either the Egyptians or irregulars from Deir Aban—were observed moving out by the Israelis hitting on them from up on Saraa. The few Palestinians remaining in Artuf until sunrise with Ismail Rahhal's father occasionally fired their shotguns out toward the unseen enemy. But they hardly could ward off mortars and machine guns. Around dawn, an advance unit of Israeli forces did run into one strong pocket of resistance as it started moving out from Ishwa. "Twenty rebels concentrated and poured fire from a hand machine gun on our guys," the Israeli war correspondent reported. "One mortar that was activated against them made them withdraw, leaving ammunition behind them." Sporadic firing at the Israelis would continue, but from unidentifiable positions in the distance.

The departure of all the 350 Artuf Palestinians was a break the next morning for Rafael "Raful" Eytan, the nineteen-year-old commander of 1st Platoon, Company A. His company had gotten an unusual assignment for the Israeli forces. In his memory, it was the first daytime attack in the course of the war. His job was to start out with the lead platoon from Bab al-Wad, the junction on the main Jerusalem–Tel Aviv highway where the road to the valley began, and advance southwest along that road through the valley, removing any resistance along the way. Artuf was one of his targets. The fact that Saraa, Ishwa, and Islin also had been cleared of potential enemies the previous night was another plus for Eytan, who thought he was walking straight into enemy territory in broad daylight. He did not know about the night raids that preceded him.

"The topographic features of the area consisted of low hills with vegetation," Eytan said. "We started in the morning at ten o'clock. We advanced from hill to hill with the system of advance and fire. . . . You put a fire base on a hill and advance in front. When you seize the next hill you pull the fire base and establish it on that hill and advance. That was it. This is the system of daylight fighting." His platoon had the same two-inch mortar that Nir's had, but Eytan said he relied mostly on machine-gun and submachine-gun fire for cover. They needed it, he recalled, because they met resistance on every hill. "And we found some enemy killed and blood signs," he said. The towns down the road may have been emptied, but Palestinian irregulars, the gun-wielding villagers, hadn't given up fighting for their homes. If they couldn't drive away the invaders, they would trouble them with sniping harassment.

Eytan's platoon made it the four miles to Artuf, walked in, and took it over. As they approached they shot at the place to scare off any villagers, and Eytan believed that the firing from his soldiers cleared the whole valley. "Just when we started [the attack], they vanished," he said. "The Arab village [Artuf] had been populated, but they escaped when we arrived." The last Palestinians to leave Artuf, the mukhtar and old men of the village, actually had taken off three or four hours before Eytan's troops breezed into town around noon, and the rest of the valley had fled under fire before dawn. His one salient memory of Artuf was a letter that Eytan found attached to the doorway of a house. It may have been one of the testimonials which the

Hartuvians wrote for their Artuf neighbors a few months before. "The letter was written in Hebrew: 'I am Mohammed, such and such'—some Arab name—'and I was a laborer of Mr. Friedman in the Hebrew settlement, the Hebrew village. And I ask you not to damage my house.' We took the letter. I took it and put it in my pocket. We continued the attack."

Nir's 2nd Platoon of B Company had remained on the Ishwa hill through morning. By the time he saw Eytan's platoon approaching, Nir had new orders: retake Jewish Hartuv. Nir does not recall exactly who gave him the mission, but he remembers getting revved up for it by the company's political instructor, a position the leftist Palmach borrowed from the Soviet system it admired. Benny Marshak, an ebullient father-figure working to recharge the morale of fatigued soldiers, told Nir how lucky he was to be reclaiming an old Jewish settlement that had been evacuated and under Arab control. It was, Marshak said, a historic moment, the first such redemption of a Jewish place.

"He was pumping in all this, which was good," Nir said. "It's not exact that it was the first place, but it was the first place that the Arabs kept a long time. There were during previous battle a few places that were abandoned and retaken the next day or a few days later." But it was enough to be reclaiming a place that had been Jewish and had been out of Jewish hands for a couple of months. It was enough to make Nir feel he was indeed playing a historic role. Besides, he knew this place. Nir had visited Hartuv as a kid growing up in Jerusalem, when his scout troop would take excursions out of the city and hike or ride the train to a country haven where they could sleep out under the trees and breathe air fresh and tangy with smells of ripening grain and wildflowers. "So Hartuv said something to me and I was very happy that I was lucky enough to go into Hartuv," he said.

Nir staged not quite a ceremony but a brief moment to honor the moshava they were about to recover. "I gathered my people around and I said, more or less taking the line he [Marshak] had given me, I said, 'We are carrying out a historical moment.' They never heard of this Hartuv. I was lucky, because to me it was something. I said, 'Look, we are now going to recapture this settlement that was abandoned and this is a big moment. And so here are my instructions to the different squads, and so let's go.' "

Nir took his platoon off the Ishwa hill and across the road and down it a mile west. They walked up the slope before reaching Hartuv, practically to the evacuated Palestinian neighbor Artuf that Eytan was reconnoitering, then entered the old colony from above, passing by shells of ruined houses. "It was broad daylight," Nir recalled. "It must have been twelve, one o'clock, something like that, and we had to be very careful because there was shooting. But the shooting was not from inside Hartuv. There was no resistance from inside. It was from all kinds of people we couldn't see. From around. Shooting at us as we advanced." But they got into Hartuv, and it was theirs. "It was completely in our hands. What was Hartuv? It was fifteen houses. We went past the whole thing. We went through the whole thing. And we were under fire, but there was nobody to shoot at." Palestinians from some distance, perhaps somewhere beyond the police station, were training rifle fire at the soldiers. Some were good shots, Nir said, but they were too far to damage much more than the buildings that already were falling down. Little remained to impress those soldiers who were first-time visitors. Most of the red tile roofs were gone, and in some places the floors. Scavengers had taken anything of possible use once the Jewish colonists abandoned the place, Nir said. "It was really a complete ruin. You could not even live in a house, not even us. We stayed overnight outside."

In the meantime Eytan's unit had finished the capture of Artuf and climbed down through Nir's troops en route to his next objective, the police station. Eytan said there was some fighting at the police station, but it may have been just sniper fire from villagers hiding in the hillside brush to take potshots at enemy soldiers. "There were Egyptians," Eytan said, "but after a blast of fire they escaped. There was no fighting there from room to room. They collapsed very quickly." The Israeli troops up on Saraa had seen the station emptied by the light of dawn. And Nir said his recollection is that nobody was inside the police station at all. "But I think they had to blow up the door to get in. I think it was locked." No matter. However it was taken, the police station too became Jewish property, as would all the land and houses and possessions the Palestinians left behind when they escaped under attack.

By now all that remained for the Israelis was to radiate their presence into the countryside to create a widening band of territory to claim as their own at the end of the day. For this was the day the second United Nations cease-fire was to begin, at 5:00 P.M. Wherever they could dig in, they could say they had won the spot in the course of battle. Some odds and ends had to be finished. "I had to do two things, and I was given a jeep," Nir said. "That jeep took fourteen people to get ahold of the railway station. We knew that it was empty. We had to show our presence there to show that, when the freezing [cease-fire] was in, we were there. We took fourteen people in a jeep. The driver could hardly see." They took over the railway station, then, Nir said, he split off a few soldiers and a demolitions expert from the battalion headquarters and went to blow up a pillbox on the railway a mile or so toward Jerusalem. It, too, was empty, but Nir showed a presence.

Then it was quiet. The medic Penina Yariv found those two days in the valley a genial respite from battle. "It was so beautiful. It was so nice, this area, because you could see all around," she said, recalling the jeep rides around the valley. "It was summer and you could see the fruit and everything on the trees. You couldn't believe it was wartime. Maybe in one or two places there were a few Arabs [shooting] but in most places they had gone."

They had not always gone far. Three miles away from the Israeli-occupied valley sat scores of the Palestinians who had fled it, now stopped to regroup in the hill town of Deir al-Hawa, where they could look down from fifteen hundred feet above the valley floor and pick out not only their villages but their own houses that sat silent amid the fruits ripening in the midsummer sun. Most of the Israelis were leaving, and that was a hopeful sign. It was safe enough that Ismail Rahhal and the men of his family could sneak almost back home in the dark of the night to perform a sacred job. His cousin had died giving birth, a day after the frightful, tiring escape from Artuf. The Moslem faith demands immediate burial, so the men made a stretcher with a blanket and tree branches and slipped back to the village cemetery to put her to proper rest that night. She was the last Palestinian who would be laid there.

Then the quiet and the hope suddenly were lost. It was a few days after the Palestinian Arabs of Ishwa and Islin and Artuf had left when they began to hear explosions down in their villages. The platoons of Ikki Nir and Rafael Eytan had finished roving the valley and had been dispatched elsewhere for the cease-fire. Now other Israeli soldiers came to the valley planting dynamite. "It was during the day," Mahmoud said. "It took five hours to destroy it. People of the village were together there." They sat up in Deir al-Hawa and watched the stones hewn from the mountainsides crack and crumble and the red tile roofs slowly cave in on top of the furniture and clothes and life's accumulation left behind. In just five hours Ishwa as they had known it was dismantled. Not every home and every cow barn and every grain shed was hit, not then, but the biggest houses were blown. By the time Rafael Eytan came through the valley a few weeks later, he said, none of the villages was intact. Mahmoud's mother, Alia, told what happened to the seven-room stone house that sat up front in the bottom right leg of the star-shaped village of Ishwa. "When they came, they put explosives in every corner and destroyed it," she said. They set them off all at once, Mahmoud added. One big blast and it was done. "We felt sad about it, but what could we do? It was all the villages." Also up at Deir al-Hawa that day was Abed Ahmad Salameh, the Palestinian who had left a note in Hebrew tacked to his door pleading that the house of this employee of the Jews be spared. Ismail Rahhal was with Salameh as they watched the demolition proceed through Artuf. One house and then another they watched fall, and all the time Salameh must have been praying that someone would see his message and have pity. But of course it was gone, so no one did. His house, too, crashed in a dust-clouded heap. "He started weeping," Rahhal said.

• 16 •

ODYSSEY

*T*he Sorek Valley farmers melded into a new wave of refugees that had no place to go but away, fellaheen spreading eastward, numbly wandering under the shock of violent uprooting. They moved at whatever pace their entourage of babies and elders and, if they were lucky, cows or goats or camels could be organized to move. Deir al-Hawa was not a place to stay. It had been the perfect way station for valley families escaping the shots of Israeli soldiers in the night. But the hamlet of eleven houses propped on a hilltop fifteen hundred feet above the valley seemed little more than momentarily safe. Enemy troops still were in sight below them. And it wasn't a big enough town to provide food for long. There would be no odd jobs here, if it came to that. And although it didn't enter their thinking then, Deir al-Hawa certainly had no market for the few possessions the fellaheen packed along. It was a place to stay only long enough to figure out where to go.

In fleeing, the refugees' first rule was stopping out of range of Israeli bullets and bombs. A second condition, at least for the majority of Palestinians plodding across miserably hot, dry countryside, was that they not go so far from home as to make returning difficult. Even the valley refugees who had seen their homes shudder and cave in to the power of Israeli explosives were already thinking about returning, about how they would puzzle back together the pieces of their lives once the fighting was done. What they did not know was that the Israelis were laying plans to keep them from doing exactly that.

The family of thirteen-year-old Mahmoud Asad Hamdan spent perhaps a week in Deir al-Hawa, while the adults tried to organize a better refuge. All the immediate family lived in Ishwa and had been driven out together, so there were no relatives to gather them in. Their one hope for shelter was the teacher from the Ishwa school, a man who came from a nearby village. He had stayed in their houses when it was the season for classes, so now maybe he would return the favor. They were rightly pessimistic. At his house, they found no room. Mahmoud's family had no choice but to move with the stream of refugees, herding along their two dozen cattle, thirty goats, and one camel. They found a cluster of valley families camped around Allar, a town of about five hundred people, where they settled themselves under the trees to wait. It was only six miles from Ishwa, but lay on the other side of the mountain from the valley and felt protected from the Israeli soldiers occupying it. They would wait for the war to be over and the Israelis to leave.

Those first months were not so bad. The night air still was warm. Food was plentiful as crops came into harvest and fruits began to ripen. During these months of the second cease-fire, there were few Israeli troops left to hold down the valley that was their new front line, and those who stayed weren't always vigilant. Mahmoud joined his father and uncles in sneaking back to Ishwa, back to their own house and their own land, to steal away the grain they had stored in a cellar bin and the honey produced in their hives on the outskirts of the village. "I'd carry as much on my shoulders as possible," Mahmoud remembered, describing several clandestine trips to pull from the rubble of his house some of the basic supplies his family had left behind. Over the weeks the infiltrators got careless on their trips back home. Or maybe they got desperate and took more chances as the stores of food dwindled. Before long one of the men got caught by Israeli guards he could not outrun. Mahmoud never saw his uncle Abdullah again.

Some refugees were luckier than Mahmoud's family. Artuf Mukhtar Ismail Abdul Fattah had enough cash to put his family up in a rented house in Beersheba, forty miles south in the Negev where a son was clerking for the Egyptian army. After the mukhtar and his two sons got up to Deir al-Hawa with their cows and sheep the night of the July attack, they drove the animals a few days further to leave in the care of a brother near Bethlehem. Then they joined the rest of his family sent on ahead by car to Beersheba. Putting up in Beersheba was a bothersome but temporary expense, they figured. They would wait, like the rest of the valley refugees, till they could go back home. It was not an irrational plan, given that the Sorek Valley still was supposed to become part of an Arab country under the United Nations partition scheme.

Diab Abu Latifah of Saraa had friends from his days in an Arab company of the British army. His family spent a few weeks with one, whose village remained in Arab hands, then moved on with fellow exiles from Saraa to the town of Beit Aula, some twenty miles southeast of the valley near Hebron. The strain of the flight was too much for Diab Abu Latifah's father, who died fifteen days after they set out. In Beit Aula they crowded with three other Saraa families into the home of another army friend, whose family slept out in their vineyards during the long grape harvest. They could not stay for the winter, but the friend's hospitality kept them sheltered until Sabiha Abu Latifah delivered the child she had carried through the bombing of their town and the first stages of an odyssey that would carry her farther and farther from home in dimensions she did not imagine—in time, in distance, and in spirit.

Surely none of them, not the families from Ishwa or Saraa or Artuf, realized how lucky they were in those days, luckier than hundreds of thousands of other refugees, luckier than they themselves would be in a few months. Part of their luck was that their flight took them south of the great masses of refugees elsewhere in Palestine, jammed especially into the West Bank cities of Nablus and Ramallah. There were concentrations, too, farther north across the borders in Lebanon and Syria, farther east around Amman in Jordan, and farther southwest in Egyptian-controlled Gaza—all areas solidly in Arab hands and less vulnerable to Israeli guns should hostilities resume. By the time fighting would trail off the following year, there would be at least 750,000 Palestinian refugees from cities and villages which came under Israeli control. About one-third of them had lived in territory—like the Sorek Valley—that they had every reason to believe was safe, because the UN had designated it for the Arab state or for an international zone.

By August 1948, the world was beginning to take note. The American consul-general in Jerusalem described the Ramallah area as breeding disaster. More than 100,000 refugees had filled every available room, school, and stable and were overflowing into makeshift campsites everywhere. Most were impoverished. Many had little to eat beyond a skimpy portion of bread that Transjordan was trying to supply. "Sanitation practically non-existent. Latrines unknown; and no attempt has been made to instruct in their construction or use," he noted in a cable back to Washington. "No water available for bathing or laundry. Sick not isolated. Complete lack of organization apparent. Local authorities overwhelmed by magnitude problem and admit own inability to cope with situation." Medics without hospital beds or medicine already had sent twenty suspected typhoid victims back to sleep under the trees.

The mayor of Nablus appealed to neighboring Arab kings and leaders for help. Refugees in the hundreds were arriving daily in his city. "There is no food, no clothing, and no shelter, and they are living under the trees and have insufficient water," he said. "The situation is very dangerous, and horrible political, social, and moral results are expected if no immediate help is forthcoming." But the Arab governments were scarcely better prepared to meet this crisis than were the local Palestinian mayors. The Syrian government was spending 1.2 million Syrian pounds a month—one-eighth its total annual budget every month—to keep the refugees alive. Lebanon, much smaller in land and population, was spending even more. It had exhausted $500,000 collected in donations from the Lebanese people and by early 1949 had spent more than $3.5 million in government funds on the refugees. With Transjordan putting out well over $4 million, the three governments alone by the beginning of 1949 had spent on Palestinian refugee aid nearly triple the amount that the entire Arab League had been able to muster "for the defense of Palestine" in the flush of war fever in 1947. The British grew fearful that the fragile Arab governments—mostly friendly to the West—would capsize under the economic and social pressures carried by Palestinian exiles who had poured across their borders.

Some international pressure began bearing on Israel to take back the Palestinian refugees, but it was not heavy and the Israelis were in no mood to bend to it. The foremost proponent of an Arab return was Count Folke Bernadotte, the United Nations mediator who was trying to turn the cease-fire of July 18 into a permanent peace. A week after the cease-fire took effect, Bernadotte asked the Israeli government to let the refugees come home as a prelude to full settlement of the hostilities. Ben-Gurion's provisional government refused. Secretary of State George Marshall became increasingly alarmed that Israel was moving to make the predicament of the Palestinian refugees permanent by moving thousands of new Jewish immigrants into the homes the Palestinians had vacated. Marshall signed a cable to his ambassador at the UN saying it would be "unfortunate" for Israel "to create the impression that assimilation of Jewish immigrants was taking place at expense [of] former Arab inhabitants." Reports from Bernadotte and from American envoys in the area detailed how Arab property was being either destroyed or confiscated, often for use of new Jewish immigrants. But 1948 was an election year, and the White House of President Harry Truman would not authorize the political pressures Secretary Marshall wanted to apply to gain Israeli cooperation on the refugees.

At the June 16, 1948, cabinet meeting, Israeli leaders had reached a consensus that the refugees should be kept out, although they had not taken an official vote. By July 22, the *Times* of London was reporting that the Israeli government had decided on principle not to allow the general return of refugees to their homes even after the sides declared a final close to the war. Only approved groups would be permitted to return, the paper said, and these groups would be negotiated in peace settlements with the enemy Arab states. Pronouncements of Israeli leaders were not so explicit. Moshe Shertok, the foreign minister of the Provisional Government of Israel (PGI), had told mediator Bernadotte merely that the Palestinian refugees would not be permitted back during the cease-fire, calling them "a politically explosive and economically destitute element" that would only detract from Israel's war effort. The fate of the Arab exiles would be negotiated along with other peace terms and tied to the counterclaims of Jews who had lost life or property as a result of hostilities, he said. In his speech to the PGI State Council on July 29, Shertok underscored the leadership view that the truce period was simply another phase of war. Letting in the Arab refugees now, he said, would be inviting "a large and well-organized fifth column" whose aim would be furthering the Arab cause of victory, and solution of the Palestinian refugee problem could only be part of a broader peace settlement with the Arab nations that had attacked Israel.

Security was one reason for the Israelis to prohibit the Palestinians from returning, but the desire to colonize the land of Israel was an even more powerful motive for many Israeli leaders. The flight of the Arabs had given Israel an unbreachable Jewish majority and opened to Jewish settlement what was considered immense new space. "It was a miraculous clearing of the land, the miraculous simplification of Israel's task," said Chaim Weizmann, the elder statesman of Zionism and the first president of Israel. Some of the gravest problems of the new state were solved by the Arab exodus, and the Israelis had begun thinking immediately how to take fullest advantage of it.

The Jerusalem Corridor—the Sorek Valley included—was priority territory. Just weeks after the fellaheen stood atop Deir al-Hawa and watched dynamite pop out the walls of their

homes, a very different party of observers appeared in the Jerusalem Hills to survey the captured valley. It was a small caravan
of Israelis, two cars and a jeep, carrying a band of determined
men who were literally mapping the future of Israel. Their
vision did not stop at the partition boundaries which Ben-Gurion had accepted during the UN inquiry a year ago. Yosef
Weitz looked carefully at every field and potential homesite.
Thoughts percolated about dozens of Jewish settlements
stretching in a belt from the plains to Jerusalem. For months
this land guru of the Jewish National Fund had been Israel's
foremost proponent of destroy-and-rebuild, so to him the destruction spotting the countryside was timely. It closed the most
recent chapter in the story that had been written through millennia, and his mind focused on the new chapter. "We went up
the hill of Saraa. The village is empty," Weitz wrote in his diary
that August 12, 1948. "The mud houses stand next to each other
and they look as gray as the earth of the hill." He looked down
at what had been Jewish Hartuv and saw the ruin, but he also
saw a future with Jewish settlements everywhere. "We found it
possible to set up a [settlement] point here, too, in order to
complement the inhabiting of the plain. The plain of Samson."

Already Israeli leaders were laying plans for the land they had
occupied and were determined to keep. Finance Minister Elie-
zar Kaplan was talking about confiscating these Arab fields and
villages and selling them to private Zionist institutions such as
the Jewish National Fund. The JNF Land Division then would
have ample new space to create more settlements, as it had been
straining to do under Weitz's direction since the 1930s. With the
money the JNF paid the government for the land, the new state
of Israel in theory would compensate the Arabs whose property
it took, but some of the proceeds could finance the immigration
of hundreds of thousands of Jews. They would populate the new
settlements. Weitz and his compatriots would create not simply
communities, but the strong, almost exclusively Jewish nation
he had contemplated at least seven years earlier. It was the
ultimate Zionist dream, to which Weitz had devoted his life and
to which he had lost a son in 1946, when Arabs shot back at

Palmach raiders trying to buttress a wobbly Jewish foothold in the Western Galilee. But this grand blueprint for expanses of land kept by vigorous new immigrants was merely a plan, and Weitz alluded in his diary that August 12 to troubling thoughts that it might not work.

Weitz already had discovered this was a sticky business, and the Israelis would spend months figuring out how to make the confiscation of Palestinian property legally acceptable to themselves, if not condoned in international circles. Little more than a month earlier Weitz had been stymied when he rushed with his typical efficiency and enthusiasm into converting newly evacuated Arab property into Jewish homesteads. Ben-Gurion refused to explicitly endorse Weitz's proposals for consolidating Israel's gains, a wish list that included destroying Arab villages, resettling the sites with Jewish Israelis, and enacting legislation that would make it difficult for Arabs to come back. But the prime minister did not utter a definitive no, so Weitz began making his wish list a work list. He managed to get more than a dozen abandoned Arab villages destroyed, but then Israeli left-wingers in Mapam, the United Workers' Party, complained. The government never had adopted a policy that Arabs should be expelled or banned from returning home—a policy of population transfer that violated Mapam's notion of living peaceably alongside the Arabs. Continuing criticism temporarily stopped Weitz's bulldozing drive to rid Israel of its Palestinian identity.

But sentiment was moving in Weitz's direction, and the transformation of the countryside continued under other auspices. Statements such as Ben-Gurion's mid-June pronouncement that repatriation of refugees must be prevented soon were matched by equally strong views by other cabinet members. Foreign Minister Shertok, for example, asked the cabinet quite simply, "Can we afford a return to the *status quo ante?*" He answered the question himself. "They are not returning," Shertok said. A new, cabinet-level Ministerial Committee for Abandoned Property was created by July to take charge of what the Arabs had left behind. It was more powerful than a previous caretaker committee, but it was frustrated repeatedly by the army. The

IDF not only blew up homes when it chose but also confiscated Arab possessions from household furniture to industrial equipment. Bechar Shitritt, the minister for minorities, who was considered by some to be rather soft on the Arab question, complained that at least eighteen hundred truckloads of Arab goods had been carted away by the army. Sometimes soldiers barred agents of the committee even from entering abandoned property. If the direction taken by the army continued, there would be no homes or possessions to which an Arab refugee could return, should he get the notion to come back.

Ultimately the same direction was chosen by the politicians, under strong lobbying by Weitz. His most persuasive arguments must have been on behalf of Jerusalem, the historic city that the Jews above all else wanted in their state. By now, most Israeli leaders felt that the war and their military successes had freed them from the Jewish Agency's acceptance in 1947 of the UN partition boundaries, which had given Jerusalem to the world as an international city. The Israelis held more than half of Jerusalem. Nearly as important was their occupation of the corridor five miles deep and thirty miles long, including the Sorek Valley, that tied the city to the UN-approved Jewish state along the coast. Weitz now was designing ways to strengthen Israel's hold on the city. "Jerusalem will be established if the corridor that connects her with the state of Israel in the plains will be settled," he wrote in an August 14 letter. "And I am dealing now with all my might to make that plan come true: To have as many Jewish settlements [as possible] in the route between Hulda and Jerusalem." A primary concern, which Weitz expressed in a letter just the next day, was the Palestinians who so recently and for so long had lived there. "I worked all day on numbers. I am occupied now with the problem of the Arabs that ran away: how not to bring them back. Never to return them," Weitz wrote. "I speak and preach to everyone. I want all of the nation of Israel here to know and feel and recognize that their leaving is for us as a miracle that should not be dismissed."

Similar sentiment was widespread among the leadership by August 18, when Prime Minister Ben-Gurion called a meeting to review policies on the Arabs, their villages, and their lands. "The view of the participants was unanimous, and the will to do everything possible to prevent the return of the refugees was shared by all," one of the participants, Ya'acov Shimoni of the Foreign Ministry, said in a letter describing the session. The Arabs would be barred and their property would be resettled, cultivated, bought, or expropriated. The next day all units of the Israeli army got renewed orders to do whatever was necessary to prevent the return of refugees. The new ministers rounded another crucial policy corner two days later, when they sat as the Ministerial Committee for Abandoned Property and approved a proposal for thirty-two new Jewish settlements. All but five were in land that was occupied by the Israeli army, but that the United Nations had allotted to the Arab state. One settlement approved was a Kibbutz Tsora, to be built on the site of the Arab village of Saraa, from which the fellaheen had been driven one month earlier.

By now even Minorities Minister Shitritt had been convinced the plan was just. "As for the Arabs, if they are left enough land for their needs and you formally expropriate the land and pay for it, there is no wrongdoing towards them," he said. He apparently had been persuaded by the reasoning of Mapam, made up primarily of socialist kibbutzniks who as farmers saw the value of additional land, but had to square its confiscation with their political idealism. They developed a "surplus-lands" formula, under which a portion of land at each site the Israelis took over would be left for the Arabs, should they be allowed to return at some undetermined time. Using the Israelis' modern agricultural methods, the Arab fellaheen would need less land to farm the same amount of product. Thus it would be "surplus land" that the Israelis settled, and everyone could be made happy.

Still, the ministers worried from the start that the plan for extraterritorial settlements would violate international law. At the meeting they discussed both security reasons—this was border territory—and agricultural reasons—so the land would not lie fallow—that might hold up to international scrutiny. Some nonetheless thought it a risky expense to raise fully twenty-

seven settlements on land that technically was outside the
bounds of the state. Most of the settlements were planned for
areas particularly desirable to the Israelis, in the Jerusalem Corridor and the fertile Western Galilee. Ya'acov Shimoni, the acting director of the Middle East Department in the Foreign
Ministry, said that simply having settlements there would
strengthen Israel's later claim to keep this territory. In a pro-
phetic statement which would guide Israel's territorial policies
for the next forty years, he said it did not seem realistic that the
Jewish settlers would be forced to leave. "In his opinion," the
minutes said, "there is nobody that will remove them after we
refuse to do it."

The lone voice favoring a significant return of Palestinian
refugees was that of Shimoni's boss, Elias Sasson, the accomplished Arabist who had been the main conduit to the Jewish
Agency's former collaborator King Abdullah. As government
policy on the refugees was solidifying, however, Sasson was
sitting in Paris casting out scores of feelers to Arab politicians
and intellectuals in hopes of starting a dialogue. The Israelis did
not trust the United Nations mediator to serve their interests in
the new peace plan, so they were maneuvering to open direct
communications with Arabs. Abdullah, who earlier had agreed
to divvy up Palestine with the Jews, responded in August.
Through envoys he said he would make peace with the Israelis
on terms similar to those discussed before the fighting had
started—but Israel would have to take back at least some of the
Palestinians who had fled from Lydda and Ramle. Such a move
would soften Arab criticism directed toward Israel and toward
him for making a deal. But it was not just to win over Abdullah
that Sasson lobbied long-distance for leniency on the refugees.
He thought his nation's long-term future tied to their fate, and
to the way Israel dealt with its Arab neighbors now. Israel could
take a hard line. It even could conquer more land and make more
refugees, but Sasson questioned what that would accomplish.
"The tension will not subside. Tranquillity will not prevail and
the peace will not come any nearer," he wrote to his deputy. No
other serious responses emerged from the Arab world, but Is-

raeli leaders dallied with Abdullah in hopes of ultimately striking a deal in which they would not repatriate any refugees.

Events outpaced their negotiations. When Bernadotte di-
vulged his new prescription for peace on September 16, the
Israelis' fears were confirmed. Bernadotte's plan, which largely
represented the views of the United States and Britain on how
to forge a permanent peace, would have made Israel give up
some of the territory it had captured, including the Jerusalem
Corridor and the Sorek Valley. He proposed a juggling of
boundaries to give Israel all the Galilee, including the western
sector, which was supposed to be Arab under the partition plan
but had been occupied by the Jews during battle. In return,
Israel would give up the Negev, which the partition plan allotted to Israel but which Egyptian forces were occupying. Jerusalem would be under UN control with the Arab and Jewish
communities running their own local affairs. The corridor to
Jerusalem would go back into Arab hands. The hands, however,
would belong to Abdullah, since Bernadotte favored giving the
Arab portion of Palestine to Transjordan, not to an independent
Palestinian Arab state. Another key element to his proposal was
the right of refugees "uprooted from their homes by the present
terror and ravages of war" to be repatriated, or to be compensated for their property if they chose not to go back home.

Both sides rejected Bernadotte's plan out of hand, but it was
radical right-wing Jews who made the most rabid protest. The
day after it was issued, a group of them assassinated Bernadotte
as he rode down a Jerusalem street. The Israeli government
condemned the murder but never found the murderers, who
were known to be members of the terrorist Stern Gang. The
slaying of the mediator transformed Bernadotte into a martyr
and drew international support behind his plan, which had
minimal attraction for the Israelis. They wanted to keep the
Galilee, but, as Prime Minister Ben-Gurion had told an American envoy just a week earlier, they also wanted the Negev and
Jerusalem and to keep out the Arabs who used to live inside the
lands Israel now occupied. As for the Jerusalem Corridor, he
said, it was absolutely vital to the Jewish state. International

diplomacy was not working in Israel's favor, so Ben-Gurion very soon began thinking about getting what he wanted through the force of arms. He would resume the war.

Most of the Arab governments were no better pleased by Bernadotte's peace plan. Not only were they still unwilling to recognize Israel, they were just as loath to see Arab Palestine ceded to King Abdullah. To prevent this the Arab League made a belated attempt to perform its own political fait accompli, as the Israelis had done when they declared their government in May. On September 22 the league established what it called the All-Palestine Government. It was headquartered in Egypt-occupied Gaza, reflecting Egypt's leading role in organizing and then controlling the government. By October a select group of Palestinian notables had met and formally declared a new Arab state to exist in all the territory of Palestine, from the Mediterranean to Transjordan. And they had selected Hajj Amin al-Husseini, the mufti of Jerusalem and the nemesis of King Abdullah, to be its president. Abdullah did not sit idly before this challenge, even though the Gaza government attracted almost no support outside the Arab bloc. On the same day the new nation declared itself into being in Gaza, he called a First Palestinian Congress in his capital of Amman. Thousands of Palestinian delegates came to denounce the Gaza government and declare allegiance to Abdullah. The Arabs, divided as ever, were prey too vulnerable for the Israelis to resist.

The new offensive started October 15, after Ben-Gurion secured cabinet and military approval of a battle plan. He was determined to draw Israel's borders in the battlefield rather than accede to the scheme of the late UN mediator. The cabinet had turned down his first plan—yet another assault on Latrun to finally knock out the Arab Legion, then a march eastward that would put under the Israeli flag the whole of Jerusalem, followed by capture of the remaining major cities of Bethlehem and Hebron to the south. He wanted all the territory up to the Jordan River, all of the West Bank. Such an offensive without provocation unsettled other leaders, who worried about international censure. Military planners simply doubted they could carry it out. The prime minister did win cabinet consent to try for the Negev. Israeli forces, with their armor, artillery, and air force reinvigorated during the second cease-fire, smashed into Egyptian positions in what they called Operation Yoav. A spin-off operation set out to strengthen and expand southward the Jerusalem Corridor.

In the third week of October, Mahmoud Hamdan's family was still living under the trees in Allar when they heard the sounds of battle. There had been talk for a week of the Israeli assault on Egyptian forces to their west and south. Now fighting was closing in on them from the north. The panic of people already refugees once, people detached from their land and home and livelihood, welled up in the families scattered through the groves with their blankets and cook pots. Caravans began moving out. Fellaheen from the Sorek Valley and other corridor villages were joined by new refugees from newly taken towns like Allar, which was captured on October 22. They walked southeast toward Bethlehem, ten miles away, heading farther from home and they hoped toward safety, but realizing it was motion toward uncertainty. "When we left [Ishwa], we said we will be back in two or three days," recalled Mahmoud's father, Asad Hamdan Asad, who would age to acid memories of this odyssey. "That's why we left everything behind. Every time we would go further, we would say we will be back later. Then we thought maybe one week or two. And we never went back."

Bethlehem became a new magnet for the autumn wave of refugees. Ismail Abdul Fattah, the mukhtar of Artuf, also was driven out by Ben-Gurion's October offensive. His family still was sitting in Beersheba, the capital of the Negev, when the Israelis sprang their dawn assault on the city. Beersheba was captured by 9:00 A.M. on October 21, but the mukhtar's family got out in the middle of the shelling. Like the family of Mahmoud Hamdan, they headed for Bethlehem, where the Palestinians hoped the Arab Legion would protect them. They were losing faith in the Egyptians, whose forces were fighting hard, but were outnumbered and outgunned. The Israelis had

counted on inter-Arab feuding to keep Transjordan from rein-
forcing the Egyptians, and they had been right.

Around the same time, the Saraa families who had gathered
in Beit Aula also moved toward Bethlehem. The fighting had
not reached them, but it was approaching. Besides, Diab Abu
Latifah and his family could not continue to tax the hospitality
a friend had offered them. His wife, Sabiha, had given birth by
now, so they could leave with other Saraa families who had been
sleeping only under shelter of trees there. The weather was
compelling them to seek a better haven, just as the chilling air
and ground would have sent Mahmoud Hamdan's family from
Allar had the Israelis not gotten to them first.

Around Bethlehem it took wealth and connections to find
housing. Even the Artuf mukhtar had barely enough money left
to rent a house in the outlying town of Beit Sahour. He would
have to sell off some of the animals, but he saw only a buyer's
market in the West Bank cities where thousands of refugees
already had resorted to dumping the cows and goats and sheep
they no longer could afford to feed. Some friends had gone to
Amman, and he heard the prices were better in Transjordan. It
was not always easy getting livestock across the bridges into
Abdullah's neighboring kingdom, but they would try. The boys
and young men of the family, his nephews and his son Ismail
Rahhal, got the job of walking the herd all the way to Madaba,
more than fifty miles distant. The boys weren't fully prepared
for the trip—for Transjordanian demands for veterinary cer-
tificates at the Allenby Bridge and for their own hunger once
they finally got across. A bedouin woman helped them make
bread from the flour they carried, not out of pity but in a deal
to keep half the bread for her children. Ultimately the journey
paid off, for the family made the equivalent of $1,000 by selling
the twenty cattle. The sheep they left in the care of a shepherd
till they would need more money, when perhaps the prices
would be higher.

Most of the Sorek Valley peasants had neither the connections
nor the wealth of the Artuf mukhtar. Like him, others ended up
in Beit Sahour, but not in houses. As the winter rains threat-

ened, the Abu Latifahs and other Saraa families felt lucky to
collect themselves in the dank caves of Beit Sahour. It was
hardly warm or dry, but it met the key prerequisite of being
free. Diab Abu Latifah looked for work, but there was little to
be found with so many refugees crammed into the Arab sectors
of Palestine. "I couldn't even get a cup of tea," said his wife, who
was nursing her newborn. "Just some bread and lentils."

Mahmoud Hamdan said his family took shelter once or twice
in run-down barns or feed sheds, but they too finally settled into
a cave at Beit Sahour. They had earned a few coins in Allar by
smoldering wood into charcoal that they sold to other families,
but now it was hard enough finding wood to burn for their own
cook fire at the mouth of the cave. Not that there was much
cooking to do. Sometimes they still had chick-peas or lentils
from earlier raids on their Ishwa storage bins, but often dinner
was bread fried on a round pan over the open fire, with a dot
of precious honey. For a while the camel was their meal ticket.
They rented its service as a hauler often enough to pay for feed
with a little left over. As the weeks passed into months, that
wasn't sufficient. They sold Mahmoud's father's gun and they
sold the cows and goats and even the camel in Bethlehem, where
everyone seemed to be selling something. They weren't starv-
ing, but now there was nothing left to sell, no house, no work.
"We put our rags on the ground and sat there," Mahmoud said.
"What else could we do?"

· 17 ·

IN-GATHERING
A NATION

*T*he day was gray, but not so cold for the winter rainy season. Luckily no rain showered down that December 7, 1948, and hadn't for days, or the terrain would have sunk into impossible sogginess for the couple hundred young Palmachniks working on a remote ridgetop. To them, it was an empty, barren place, a perch above a stark valley devoid of people and trees and life. They had come to build the beginning of change. Only eighty of them, all young people eighteen, nineteen, and twenty years old, would stay to be Jewish farmer-soldiers on the border land they felt was theirs now to defend and to renew. The other workers had been mobilized in Jerusalem to help their friends throw up the kernel of a new settlement, seven prefabricated buildings that would become home to the young kibbutzniks. When the helpers left at the end of the day, with the heavy construction done, the new settlers bedded down in one of the remaining old stone houses of people unknown to them, people like the Abu Latifahs who had lived on the site only five months earlier and who now lived in caves on the West Bank. The stone house on the edge of the hilltop gave a view that swept the whole valley. Aliza Tibon remembered standing out in front of that house that had been an anchor of the village of Saraa and looking out into overwhelming darkness. "There were no lights all around except for the police station," she said. "It really was an empty country."

The Israelis had midwifed into being the Zionist dream of a land without people. And now, quickly, they had begun acting on the second half of the vision that had moved Jews since the nineteenth century: filling this space with a people without a land. An extraordinary in-gathering of Jews already had started. Tens of thousands of Europeans had reached the new state and more would come, the survivors of death-camp terrors as well as others displaced by war. And Israel's leaders were searching the world for other pockets of Jews ready to be immigrated. They needed to come to be saved from pogroms and threats of violence, especially in the Arab nations of the Middle East, or they wanted to come to fulfill the Jews' ages-old spiritual longing. These were the reasons Israel had been created. Some of the people brought to the new state would be worlds removed from those who founded it, but now was not the time to worry about culture gaps. Now that the process had begun, there were practical reasons to speed it. Here in the Sorek Valley, as in much of the rest of Israel, the Palestinians had left so much land that the Israelis did not have enough hands to work it. They did not have enough people to fill the spaces they needed to fill if they were to create an irrevocable presence on the land they had claimed for their state. There would be years—starting right now, before the war was even finished—of clearing, plowing, planting and more planting, building, irrigating, transforming. Even with multimillions of dollars flowing into Israel from Jews worldwide, there would be years of sacrifice and hard living for many, especially for those new immigrants who came with little more than the clothes they wore. But they were ready. It was time to gather their people to build their nation.

The Palmach fighters from the Yiftah Brigade were the first Israeli settlers in the Sorek Valley. Ultimately they would be joined by thousands, but they were an isolated crew when they founded Kibbutz Tsora in the winter of 1948. They were mostly

kids who knew each other from high school in Jerusalem and
had fought together in the Galilee. They had committed themselves to the socialist spirit of kibbutz life, but there had been
no time for the normal training most kibbutzniks received
before striking out to make a new settlement. The new government had decided in August to settle—and to settle fast—
throughout the Jerusalem Corridor in order to secure the link
between the Jewish-occupied portion of the Holy City and the
Israeli heartland along the coast. The army had expanded the
corridor southward in Operation Yoav that fall. But this band
of territory now held by Israel still was a frontier in places not
ten miles wide, with enemy just over the hills both to the north
and to the south. When Prime Minister Ben-Gurion decided
that fall to dissolve the Palmach, which was led by his left-wing
rivals, it was logical to send the brigades' young farmer-soldiers
to hold down new border positions like this one in the Sorek
Valley. They would be demobilized from active military service,
but would form a *kibbutz michlat,* a stronghold established for
strategic reasons.

It was a spare life on the brush-covered hilltop. "We didn't
have water, we didn't have electricity, we didn't have a road,"
said Yoav Tibon, a founder of Kibbutz Tsora. "During the winter it was so muddy a car couldn't go to the top of the hill." They
lived in prefabs, four or five to a room, and nobody had much
more than the bed where he or she slept. For months they got
water from an army truck, till a two-inch pipe connected them
to the spring at the devastated Palestinian village of Ishwa. Aliza
Tibon, who married Yoav three years after their group founded
Tsora, was struck by what she found to be the desolation of the
place that only a year earlier had been alive with Palestinian
villages and a single Jewish settlement. "There was one tree by
the stream. We called it the lonely tree," she said. Yet the land
was not fully barren, for centuries-old olive trees still remained
at the site of old Saraa years later, along with seven kinds of fruit
trees an Israeli forester identified as ones planted by the Arabs.
Nevertheless, the expanses of rock-laden hillsides left the new
settlers with an empty feeling. The whitish dirt wore only a

sparse covering of weeds and low bushes of oak or pistachio, always low because the Arabs' goats had munched them down for decades. It was terrain the Israelis would change.

The settlers had no sense that they were replacing a population recently gone, even though the first crops they harvested in spring were barley and hay that the Palestinians had planted. The Palestinian village Saraa had been so cleaned out by the army that the kibbutzniks felt no lingering identity of the Arabs, Aliza Tibon said. It had been different during the war when she entered a city in the Galilee just after the Palestinian population had left under attack. There she felt a moral stricture against even touching the possessions left behind. "But when we came here, there was not a sign anyone had lived here before. It was completely empty. You didn't have the personal feeling that somebody had left it."

They knew, however, that the Palestinians sometimes returned to what had been their homes and land, whenever they found signs of surreptitious picking in the fields. "This land was a no-man's-land," said Aliza Tibon. "The Arabs fled. They didn't understand that it was a war and they had lost their land. They thought they would just be able to come back. So what you had was the Arabs were still coming and going, still coming back to find things they had buried." Sometimes it caused trouble in those early years. A Tsora night watcher shot into the darkness at a noise once, and the next day a wounded Arab wandered out of the ruins of Saraa to be turned over to the army. Another incident followed the arrival of a herd of goats, given to the kibbutz by soldiers after the animals had strayed from Arab to Israeli-controlled territory. One night they were stolen—or perhaps just retrieved by their owner, Aliza said—and the kibbutznik guarding them was killed. Mostly the infiltrators wanted only to sneak to their homes or fields or vineyards for food and to sneak back out, Yoav said. But they were a potential danger. To discourage them, the army blew up those Arab homes of Saraa that had not been destroyed in the war.

Even an armistice signed by the spring of 1949 did not stop infiltration. But the agreement between Israel and Jordan (the new name for Transjordan) answered the lingering question of who would possess this no-man's-land. The valley and the Jerusalem Corridor were Arab territory on the UN partition map, but the might of the Jews on the battlefield had been enough to convince King Abdullah that the land was Israel's. The armistice signed that April became a *de facto* borderline of the new state. There was no Palestinian entity, certainly not Hajj Amin's floundering "All-Palestine Government" based in Cairo, with the strength to undo it. What the armistice did not settle was the fate of the 750,000 Palestinians who had lived throughout the Israeli territory and now were homeless. While months and then years of negotiations continued, Israel methodically filled the places the refugees used to live.

Kibbutz Tsora spent one year as a lonely outpost, but in the second year development sprouted like the wild red poppies that startle the Jerusalem Hills each spring. In December of 1949 the first of a new group of settlers began working the valley, fresh from their remarkable mass transfer to Israel. They were Yemenites and they were part of Operation Magic Carpet, a feat of Jewish Agency logistics and politics that in less than a year carried nearly 45,000 Jews out of medieval existence in the most primitive Arabic kingdom. For reasons he never explained, the king of Yemen reversed the policy followed by his father for decades and permitted the Jews to leave. His decree in April 1949 was a signal that sent a floodtide of poor Yemenites walking the length of their country, across its mountainous border, to exit to the British protectorate of Aden. Some were propelled by anti-Jewish riots a year earlier in the capital of San'a and other towns, but the mystical Yemenites also were swept up by a calling, by a compelling sense that now was the time to "return" to Zion. Great Britain had been persuaded to reverse its own policy and let the Jews transit through a camp in Aden. Even so, the British requirements that they be moved out rapidly challenged Israelis and Americans organizing the exodus. They did get the thousands of Yemenites into Aden, fed and vaccinated them, and usually within weeks of their arrival got them out on one of the seven or eight daily flights they had managed to charter. They flew round-the-clock except Saturday, for the Yemenites refused to fly on the Sabbath, even on the magic carpet.

Once they got to Israel, the Yemenites were crowded into tents or huts in transit camps, sometimes for months, in a winter of heavy rain and, that year, snow. "The conditions here weren't so good. The state was in its diapers. Nothing was ready," remembered Ovediah Aqwa, one of the Yemenites. "But we were very glad in heart." It was time, he said, to be in Zion. Ovediah Aqwa was among a group of about a hundred men taken to stay in Jerusalem and do manual labor in the corridor, while their families remained in a transit camp. "There was nothing there, no trees, no nothing. We came to plant trees all over these places," he said. "These places" included the Sorek Valley, and it was here that Ovediah Aqwa and other Yemenites were settled first into wooden huts on a hillside, then into tin shacks that finally gave way to real houses. They planted trees everywhere, and they planted themselves in a place the Jewish Agency called Eshtaol, on top of the remnants of another place the Palestinians had called Ishwa. More arrived in the valley and its outskirts in 1950, mostly Yemenites, to populate more than half a dozen work settlements that would become permanent Jewish farm communities where each family would have its house and garden. One named Nahum grew on the site where Arabs had lived for centuries in the village of Artuf. By 1961, Eshtaol would grow to 307 people and Nahum 410, almost all of them Yemenites.

As the new valley residents tried to settle down, frictions sometimes arose among them and at times between them and the Israeli Sabras who were running things. The Yemenites themselves were divided by clanlike loyalties which were strong enough at Eshtaol to break out in mass fistfights when one group felt another got preferred housing or work. Farm work itself was alien to the men, who had spent their lives as peddlers or craftsmen, and the women, who had been cloistered inside their homes in ghettos in northern Yemen. They did not understand forestry and farming, much less the notions of community obligation that attached to settlement in Israel. The Jewish National

Fund, which under Yosef Weitz's inspiration was spending tens of millions of dollars to settle the new immigrants, counted on them to harvest the fields and fruit groves left by Palestinians and turn over the proceeds to the JNF. In those early years JNF agents repeatedly were frustrated upon learning the Yemenites at Eshtaol had picked the valley's almonds and plums too early, or finding them stashing carobs to sell in Jerusalem rather than collecting them for the common pot.

They should not have been surprised at such confusion, given the cultural milieu out of which the Yemenites had walked so they could enter this unexpectedly foreign promised land. Many Yemenites were not used to sleeping on beds—some began sleeping under them—or eating with knives and forks. Their women had never gone to school or worked outside their homes. Their men kept several wives, sometimes girls not yet in puberty, for whom they paid a dowry and over whom they expected to rule. It was not so uncommon for a Yemenite to consult a witch doctor. These newcomers so strange to the Sabras were clustered in the harshest and most dangerous border areas, such as the Sorek Valley, partly because settlement executives decided they were better able than new European immigrants to withstand hardship conditions. Yet their isolation and concentration would make more difficult their cultural assimilation into the rest of Israeli society.

A different sort of settlement was raised in the valley, spread behind the railroad station and given the name of the colony that had been the first Jewish outpost there in modern times. It was a *ma'abara*, or transit camp, and the Jewish Agency called it Hartuv-B. It was different because it was bigger and because everyone knew it was only the provisional quarters for new immigrants who eventually would live in a city that was planned for the hillside behind it, a hill that a few years before had been pastureland for the Palestinian village of Deir Aban. Although considered temporary, the ma'abara would last more than a decade and grow to hold 650 families at its peak. At first the people there worked in public works, clearing brush and crunching rocks so they could fill the Jerusalem Hills with trees.

They also prepared the site for the city that would be named Beth Shemesh after the Israelites' precursor city of three thousand years earlier. In the grand scheme, the city was to feed thousands of workers to an industrial complex to be developed in and around it. Already when the first families arrived at Hartuv-B a revival was underway at Shimshon, the cement factory destroyed by Palestinian irregular attacks in the spring of 1948, the factory that the original Hartuvians had hoped would draw new Jewish settlers to their valley. It finally did.

Hartuv-B was different, too, because its earliest settlers were Europeans. A Polish Jew, Ester Shulim, came to the valley as a ten-year-old with the first three families that arrived at the ma'abara in December of 1950. The previous years had been laden with fear and shock, yet her family was luckier than millions of European Jews. They had escaped the death camps because her father had taken them to Russia early in the war, but when they returned to their village in Poland in 1946 they found no relatives left alive. The Nazis had killed seven of her father's brothers and sisters in Treblinka and Auschwitz. And Jews were no longer welcome. One uncle who had fought with communist partisans in the war had returned to their Polish village only to find his house occupied and his old neighbors treacherous. With no place to stay, he had gone to a neighbor's house and was taken in and offered food, but as he sat at the table the neighbor and his son jumped and murdered him. "When my father heard the story, he decided to leave Poland," Ester Shulim remembered. They joined the masses of Jews seeking a safe and free life in their own state—340,000 new Israelis by the time her family finally arranged passage to Israel in 1950. That was a few months after the government adopted the Law of Return, codifying the fact that this was one place all Jews were welcome.

Her father, long an active Zionist, was picked by the Jewish Agency to open and lead the settlement of Hartuv-B. As soon as they saw the rugged place, they realized they would be pioneers. In one way, Hartuv-B was no different from the other collections of new Jewish immigrants in the valley: the living conditions were no better. It started with fifty tin shacks, twelve feet by sixteen feet, where occupants could not possibly get warm that winter, then sweated all summer long. "We didn't have water inside. Water was outside. We had a door and one window and that's all," Ester Shulim said.

After a few days, more and more immigrants came to join the three families. They were from Poland, Russia, and Rumania, and soon from Iraq, where the Jewish Agency had run a second massive airlift, this time for Iraqi Jews who had been subjected to increasing persecution since the outbreak of war between Arabs and Jews in Palestine. Hartuv-B expanded under new waves of migrants in 1951 and 1952, who came from all over the world, and then it burgeoned with an influx of Moroccans. They began leaving North Africa in 1955 under the uncertainties of rising Arab nationalism and the movement toward independence. There was no universal language in this cultural stewpot, so people talked through improvised hand signals. The children learned Hebrew first and were so in demand as translators that some even helped their parents through job interviews. There were other things they all learned in the early years: cooking with the American-furnished powdered milk and powdered eggs, washing dishes outside, bathing in water heated over the fire, reading at night by a lantern rigged from a candle and tin can.

The new immigrants were not left to flounder, but helped by teachers and guides and work advisers to figure out the new way of life. One of these instructors was an old hand at life in the valley: the Hartuvian Yoshko Levy. The Levy men—Yoshko, his brother, Chaim, and their father, Gavriel—had come back to try once more to reestablish themselves on their land at old Hartuv. Only Ben-Zion Gueron, Yehuda Ben-Besset, and Itzhak Arditi were game enough to join them, to face again the rocky slopes and the memories of siege and isolation. The rest of the Hartuvians opted for better land or city jobs or simply places that felt safer than a moshava that was still frontier. Little remained to return to, except the fickle land that still flooded in the winter only to dry like ancient bones by summer. When the Hartuvians came back in the waning days of 1949, after the

young men had been released from active military duty, Hartuv
was a ruin. They fixed one house at a time and scraped by
financially by quarrying rock and crushing it to sell for construction and by planting vegetables to feed themselves. The old
settlers got small help from the Jewish Agency, no more than
materials to fix their houses, but they plodded along and
watched in wonder as their valley filled up with new settlers.
When Yoshko Levy brought a bride to Hartuv nearly two years
later, he had to replace the uncertain income of rock crushing.
The Jewish Agency quickly hired him to be the deputy at its
regional office in Eshtaol. Who else was more qualified to teach
the newcomers how to live and farm in the valley? In some ways
they were like Yoshko Levy's ancestors, who had been clerks
and shopkeepers when they made their aliyah more than fifty
years earlier. "The big difference is that when our families came
from Bulgaria we didn't have any help," he said. "We were a
single settlement alone."

That "big difference" transformed the valley and much of the
rest of Israel that had belonged to Arabs. Early government
decisions to take over property left by Palestinians were crucial
to the state's ability to resettle Jewish immigrants, many of
whom scarcely could afford to rent a room, much less finance a
farm. At least 140,000 immigrants were placed in abandoned
Arab homes in cities from Haifa to Ramle. And in the five years
following declaration of the state, 350 of 370 new settlements
were raised on abandoned Arab property. The legal cover
which made this possible was the regulation adopted in 1948 by
the cabinet, which gave the government custody of all property
if the owner was absent after May 15, 1948. This applied even to
Palestinian Arab owners who were still inside Israel, such as
those who had left their homes for a safer city within the borders
and were Israeli citizens. In 1951 the government took the further
step of transferring the "abandoned" land from merely Jewish
custody to Jewish ownership. A new law enabled a freshly created Development Authority to sell "abandoned property" to
the state or to the Jewish National Fund, but not to individuals.
More than half a million acres of abandoned land already had

been put into the hands of the JNF, which now was able to buy the property and gain title to it. The JNF then leased plots of land, usually to people it already had settled on them. So it was that in 1953 the JNF bought the entire village of Ishwa, including the land of Mahmoud Hamdan's family, for a price that ranged from $31 to $142 an acre. It already had been the home of the Yemenites for three years, and that would not change. The refugees from Ishwa were not consulted about the sale of their village and never received any money for it.

Transactions like this one were recorded with full formality in the land records offices the British had maintained during the days of the mandate. The objective was to give some legal basis to the confiscation of Palestinian land. In a further effort to make the acquisitions palatable to outsiders who might wonder, government and JNF officials made repeated public pledges that the proceeds from land sales would be reserved for the Palestinian refugees. The Israeli rationale was expressed in a fundraising speech in New York by JNF World President Dr. Abraham Granovsky as early as 1949, long before details of the land sales had been arranged. "This point must be made perfectly clear: as long as property rights continue to be respected in Israel—and there are none who wish to abrogate this right—the Arabs remain the legal owners of the land to which they have title," Granovsky said. "If we wish to transfer the land to our ownership, we must pay the price, in one form or another, for every dunam [quarter acre] we take." The money was not expected to be parceled out to individual Arab landowners but perhaps used as part of a resettlement scheme in some Arab country. The JNF did pay a price, but the money was recirculated into Israeli development rather than ever finding its way to Palestinian landowners.

It was the JNF and the Jewish Agency, both tightly plugged into the government leadership, that drew the features on the face of the new country. This was especially true in the Sorek Valley, part of a vision of reforesting thousands of acres of the Jerusalem Corridor. Weitz and the others in the nongovernmental "institutions" decided what would be forest and what farmland and what places would be peopled. They persuaded the young settlers of Tsora to move their kibbutz from the mountaintop farther down toward the valley bottom, where there was more room for expansion. They brought chickens to the Yemenites at Eshtaol and told them they would be chicken farmers, then steered them to apricots and avocados. People such as Yoshko Levy were ground-level guides to development, teaching the new arrivals how to terrace the land and clear it of stones and tend their trees and gardens. But they could not have made it happen without loans and contributions that came from the United States in greater abundance than anywhere else. The jackhammers that Yemenites used to break up rocks in Sorek Valley hillsides and the bulldozers they maneuvered to clear the rubble were made in the U.S.A. and came to Israel courtesy of a U.S. government loan of $100 million from the Export-Import Bank. The JNF, which contributed to settlement costs beyond just the price of the land, relied heavily on the goodwill of American Jews. From 1947 to 1951, the JNF received no less than $105 million of its worldwide income of $133 million from donations from the United States, according to JNF internal documents. It was this money that made possible its acquisition from the state of Israel of the "abandoned" Palestinian land for the new Jewish forests and some of the settlements of the Sorek Valley.

The most stunningly visible JNF achievement was the trees. In 1950–51 the JNF set almost two million saplings in the Jerusalem Corridor alone. Its subsequent five-year plan called for planting another fifty million trees. Financing small forests around the Sorek Valley and elsewhere became projects of youth groups and women's groups and wealthy individuals living in Jewish communities all over the world. The Baltimore chapter of the Independent Order of Brit Shalom raised money, for example, to reclaim a forty-acre tract around Eshtaol. The Jerusalem Hills were a prime candidate for afforestation, since the hillsides were too rugged for intensive agriculture. All around the Sorek Valley new immigrants cleared and dug and planted, filling the slopes with Jerusalem pines and cypress trees, yellow-blooming acacia and carobs dripping clusters of long pods. To the north the President's Forest grew up, placed in honor of the state's first president, Chaim Weizmann. To the south were planted six million trees in the Martyrs' Forest, memorializing the deaths of the Holocaust. Afforestation was surely the most fitting public work that could have been devised, giving new citizens not merely occupation and income, but an opportunity to build their nation, by building monuments to the past that would bring pleasure far into the future. It meant something else as well: every sprig was living evidence of Israel's determination to retain sovereignty over all of the land it occupied.

The state brought other improvements for which the old Hartuvians had pined in prewar years. The first installment of housing at the new city Beth Shemesh, in planning by mid-1951, was a block of three hundred apartments that gave the immigrants jobs as well as hope of escaping their tin shanties in Hartuv-B. There was new machinery for Shimshon, including a crusher that would pulverize 150 tons of stone an hour. The plant even was getting its own factory to make bags to hold tons of cement for export. In May of 1955 the valley held a "feast of light" to celebrate completion of the electricity network in the heart of the Jerusalem Corridor. It was part of the modern world now, no longer limited by reliance on undependable generators or kerosene lamps or candlelight.

And the state brought one very precious commodity to the valley: water. Within a couple of years the state water company Mekorot was piping water to much of the valley, enough so that photographs as early as 1952 showed sprinklers irrigating the lands of Eshtaol. Water was a boon to Kibbutz Tsora, which was plunging into intensive agriculture in the broad fields it acquired from the "abandoned property" rolls and from the land it purchased from the Latin Patriarchate that still kept its church and small convent on the hills behind old Saraa. The young Tsora farmers, their ranks expanded by the arrival of new English-speaking émigrés from South Africa, were experimenting with the land and with their own agricultural capabilities in the early years after they moved the kibbutz down from the hilltop. They had problems with the first, labor-intensive crops such as plums and apples, because one guiding principle of kibbutz life is that the members do the work themselves rather than hire it out. They tried cotton in 1954, and found the climate and land congenial, as long as there was irrigation. Cotton—something that had grown for centuries in Egypt but had never grown in the Sorek Valley—became a major crop, once the kibbutzniks could afford picking machines.

Even with all the new conveniences, life didn't go well for the old Hartuvians. There was water, but they had to pay more than most of the new settlers, who were charged a lower agricultural rate. The few Hartuvians who returned scarcely were considered a settlement, with only small-scale gardening that placed them in the higher rate bracket for drinking and household water. In their scattered houses they also felt more vulnerable to the dangers that still peppered valley life. Even a relatively small settlement such as Eshtaol had plenty of people available to stand night guard duty. Ovediah Aqwa said guarding was routine in the early years when infiltration by Palestinians was a constant threat. "There were lots of troubles," he said. "There were thefts, we were shot at. Pretty much every night they tried to steal the mules. They tried to steal everything, and to kill us." The Hartuvians did not have the luxury of people to spare for night guarding, and the young men who were there got called up periodically from reserves for active military service. Yoshko Levy did not like leaving his elderly father and his wife and soon their baby alone in this frontier. The family liked it even less after a Yemenite from Nahum, the settlement on the hill just above them, was killed in a night raid by a trio of Arabs in the spring of 1956. The settler was shot when he went to a window to check out a noise outside. The leader of the band, armed with a Tommy gun and called by the press "the most notorious hired killer in the Middle East," was himself killed by a pursuing patrol. But the death of one terrorist, even a known assailant charged in the Israeli press with killing twenty-one Jews, did not end the fears of frontier settlers. "To give you an idea of how serious the anxiety was," said Yoshko Levy's wife, Gita, "we even filled the windows with stones because they used to fire in the houses."

But the gravest problem for the Hartuvians, for the families trying now to raise a new generation on their land, was schooling. The predicament grew out of the differing cultures and political philosophies of the conglomeration of people suddenly all become Israelis. By the mid-1950s, several of the Hartuvian children were ready for nursery school, but there were not enough Hartuvians to start their own. Gita Levy remembered being reluctant to send her daughter to a school dominated by Yemenite children who had to be taught Hebrew and even how to brush their teeth. When would they get to reading and math? The only other school was operated across the valley at the kibbutz, which the Levys and other old Hartuv families thought was the logical solution. However, the kibbutzniks thought otherwise. "They didn't accept my daughter Miriam in the nursery school at Tsora," Gita Levy said, still with an edge of bitterness years later. It may have been partly a reluctance to let in outsiders, but the rejection also stemmed from ideology that the Levys would not accept. Children in the kibbutz not only went to classes together but, to foster equality and communal values, slept together in a children's dormitory. "I wanted my child in my house," said Gita Levy. The Levys thus refused to follow the rules that governed children at the Tsora school, and Tsora refused to bend its rules. It would end up a predicament that the Hartuvians could not solve.

There were other occasional sparks, when the flint of one culture smacked up on the steel of another. In one 1951 flare-up, the Tsora kibbutzniks warned the JNF that they would "expel" any Yemenite found inside the property of the kibbutz because of what their secretary described as "cases of stealing that are too numerous to count." At the same time, the Moroccans and Yemenites and other Middle Eastern Jews who were in the vast majority at Beth Shemesh would for years resentfully compare their crowded apartments with the verdant, irrigated fields and landscaped grounds that the kibbutzniks labored to keep up at Tsora.

But in one way all the new settlers were and still today remain alike. Just as Aliza Tibon remarked upon the emptiness of the valley when she arrived, at the absence of any Palestinian identity, so did settlers like Ovediah Aqwa and Ester Shulim feel they had moved into a space that was empty and unpossessed until they came. Ovediah Aqwa knew that a nearby Arab village named Islin had been destroyed in the war, but he resisted acknowledging that another Arab village called Ishwa had existed in the very spot his house was built. "Perhaps this was Ishwa," he finally admitted, but very little was left of it when he arrived. Ester Shulim also saw the valley as empty when her family came to the ma'abara, and she was very quick to insist that no Arab houses stood exactly on the site where Beth Shemesh has come to sprawl. That three thousand Palestinians were driven out of their valley homes is a discomforting fact of which she is aware, but to which Ester Shulim does have an answer. "The state of Israel is a fact," she said, "and we need a state. There is no other place for us. There is no other place for us."

FROM TENTS
TO HUTS

*I*t was the ride from Beit Sahour to Jericho that Labiba Suleiman remembered best. "The road was so narrow and twisted and went up and down steep hills so that we were praying all the time in the cars," she said. "It was so dangerous." While ten-year-old Labiba was transfixed by the cliffside road, her parents had to be worrying about what awaited their family at the end of the journey. Their placid life as farmers in Islin got further removed by the day. Their harvest was lost, their home demolished. Worst of all, their son had been caught by enemy soldiers when he sneaked back to their Sorek Valley village to reclaim some food. He hid in a haystack instead of fleeing with his companions when an Israeli patrol appeared, and some Ishwa men who later dared to make another trip home said they had found his body. Now the families from Islin and Ishwa who had tried to stick together since they escaped the July Israeli attack, who had traveled from trees to sheds to caves with only each other for comfort, were headed to yet another uncertain destination. This time they were not alone. The Red Cross was taking them.

It fell to the International Committee of the Red Cross to feed

refugees in the West Bank in the last months of 1948, while other
international agencies focused their help on Palestinian exiles
who had fled to the neighboring Arab countries. It was time to
move decisively now that night air penetrated the blankets and
clothes of refugees as winter arrived wet and cold. The big
concentrations of refugees, living in the streets of the Old City
or camped out around Ramallah to the north, were the easiest
to reach. Word got to them by the end of October that the Red
Cross was making winter camps over in Jericho, a city only
twenty miles east of Jerusalem but normally warmer and drier.
They needed little persuading beyond the promise of medicine,
regular food, and two gallons of free kerosene. It took months
longer to channel the odd rivulets of refugees not moving with
the main streams, like the people hunkered in the caves of Beit
Sahour, but finally they, too, learned there was a place for help.
Mahmoud Hamdan and the families from Ishwa, Sabiha Abu
Latifah and the families of Saraa, and Labiba Suleiman with the
families from Islin all finally gathered in Jericho around the
turn of the new year. There they received food and fuel and the
tents that would be their mobile homes for coming years.

International concern was expressed in other venues as well.
The United Nations decided in November of 1948 that $32 mil-
lion was needed for immediate relief, and President Truman
asked Congress to supply half of it. But the refugees' future was
not the foremost topic addressed in the United Nations Middle
East debates, where the big powers were wrangling for their
own strategic reasons over how the whole region should be
divided. They barely discussed the right of Palestinian refugees
to return to the homes they had vacated in wartime, but their
actions said it was a given, that this was a right the refugees were
due. When the UN General Assembly adopted a resolution on
December 11, 1948, establishing a three-member Palestine Conciliation Commission to bring a peaceful solution to the conflict,
the return of peaceable refugees was the only specific action the
UN mandated. The resolution said that refugees "wishing to
return to their homes and live at peace with their neighbors
should be permitted to do so at the earliest practicable date." It

also said those choosing not to return should be compensated by the government that was responsible for any loss or damage to refugees' property. Every other point of contention was left to negotiation, including the exact means of UN control over Jerusalem.

If any of the Sorek Valley refugees heard of the resolution and took solace from it, they were only to be disappointed as weeks added up to months and then years, and they never were allowed to return. The Palestinians got caught between inflexible positions taken and held by both the Israelis and the Arab nations. The Israelis would refuse to give any bit of land—in fact they would continue demanding expanded boundaries at the expense of their adversaries—and the Arabs would refuse to give peace. The Israelis would refuse to allow more than a token number of Palestinians to return to their homes, and the Arab countries would refuse to allow resettlement projects designed to integrate large blocs of Palestinians into their local populations. The failure of both sides to compromise would have fatal consequences, producing a state of non-peace and sometimes a state of active war taking the lives of thousands more Arabs and Jews. As for the Palestinians, some of them would become party to the hostilities themselves. But hundreds of thousands would trudge along from one campsite to another, finally staking their tents in a camp where they ultimately would trade them for huts, and they would work to put back together their lives. For decades the substance of their cause would be lost in its symbolism.

In the winter of 1948–49, Jericho grew a massive tent suburb. Refugees gathered in similar temporary camps in Lebanon, Syria, Transjordan, and the Egyptian-controlled Gaza Strip. There was food, but little more. "They gave every family a tent and ten kilos of flour. They gave us identity cards, one for each married man," said Mahmoud Hamdan. "It was the worst period of all. There was no work to do. Anyone who had ten dinars [$30] was very very happy." Some refugees were resourceful. Mahmoud Hamdan's family built an oven out of stone at Jericho, where they charged two piasters (six cents) to bake a loaf of bread. To keep it fueled the family had to walk the country-side searching for wood, which was becoming scarcer as thousands of refugees tried to maintain fires for cooking and warmth. Labiba Suleiman made small change by collecting branches to sell around the camp. Mahmoud's father earned money working in the orange groves of Jericho—about thirty cents a day.

Even the normally mild weather turned on the refugees that year, as if they didn't already feel sufficiently betrayed. As one Jerusalem resident described it: "Jericho in 1948 was a very bad place. The people were freezing and angry. It was cold. It even snowed in Jericho that winter." They were indeed angry and had few outlets to vent anger in the dense camp population. Sometimes the frustration spilled out. In early 1949, a mob of refugees turned on a group of Transjordanian and Iraqi soldiers who were having a party at a hotel in Jericho. They physically attacked the soldiers, whom they accused of squandering money, and several people were injured. The whole place was put under curfew. Yet even in the midst of these bleak days, a point of happiness occasionally broke. One day Labiba Suleiman's family joined a family celebrating the release of their son from Israeli prison, and the day became a celebration for the Suleimans, too. The boy said he had been imprisoned with Hassan Ahmad Suleiman of Islin, who was due to be released soon. They made their way to the Jerusalem prison, and it was true. Labiba's brother, the boy believed killed by Israeli soldiers, came back to his family.

With the masses of refugees despondent, jobless and homeless, and with the wealthy Palestinians scattered about the world, the Palestinian people had neither the financial nor the emotional strength to organize themselves into a political entity in what was left of Arab Palestine. The leaders had been divided for years and remained so, each aligning himself now with whichever Arab power he believed most likely to stand for the Palestinian people, or to advance his own career. The All-Palestine Government led by Hajj Amin al-Husseini in Gaza never had a chance of success, constrained by a lack of international recognition and by the very short leash on which Egypt held it. It had small support among the bulk of Palestinians, who by now had lost faith in the fulminations of Hajj Amin. Month by month his government became a paler shadow until finally it faded away. Most of the Arab governments were occupied with keeping themselves in power in the storm of disaffection that was sweeping the Arab people, who had seen their armies humbled by the Jews. Riots, coups, and assassinations disrupted the Arab countries throughout the 1950s.

Free rein in Arab Palestine was left to the Transjordanian King Abdullah. And that is how Palestine disappeared. Not that Abdullah snatched it in a coup or by military force. After all, from whom could it be snatched? His troops already occupied much of the Arab rump of Palestine that the Israelis had not overrun, and Abdullah's military administrators were in place overseeing at least a skeletal bureaucracy. Then the king sprinkled his favors among West Bank and refugee notables who maintained their own small power circles. He made royal visits to Hebron and later Nablus and granted sympathetic audiences to men who used to be mayors of cities or mukhtars of villages now in Israeli hands. His attentions were reciprocated. After his successful Palestinian National Congress in Amman in September of 1948, Abdullah arranged a Second Palestinian Arab Congress in Jericho in December. Hundreds of Palestinian delegates, some rounded up by the king's minions, pledged their allegiance to Abdullah and declared him to be the monarch of both Transjordan and Palestine. They also resolved that the king should formally join Arab Palestine and Transjordan into one united kingdom. Soon after, Abdullah declared himself monarch over what he called the "Hashemite Kingdom of Jordan," signifying his rule now covered the land extending down both banks of the Jordan River.

The annexation could not be accomplished right away, for Abdullah found the other Arab governments virulently opposing the move and both the Americans and the British cautioning him to go slowly. So he pursued what has been described as a policy of "creeping annexation." In February of 1949 he offered

Jordanian citizenship to the Palestinians, in March he moved from military to civil administration in the West Bank, and in May he named three Palestinians to his cabinet. Parliamentary elections were held in April 1950, in both the West Bank and the East Bank (the original Transjordan). When the new parliamentarians met in Amman later that month they enacted the unification of the two banks into one country. Only the governments of Great Britain and Pakistan formally recognized the annexation, but the series of moves by which Abdullah intruded his control throughout Arab Palestine effaced it as a separate entity. Palestine was off the map.

What determined the borders of the land Abdullah annexed was the armistice agreement he signed with the Israelis in April 1949. It was one of a series of deals that Israel made with most of the Arab governments that had fought it. These negotiations, in which the Palestinian people had no voice, froze them out of decision-making for the coming years by defining the conflict as a struggle between Israel and the surrounding Arab countries. The armistice agreements, which were considered preliminaries to full peace settlements, generally recognized military lines as temporary, *de facto* boundaries. Egypt signed the first armistice that February, after buckling under a string of attacks in which Israeli troops not only won much of the Negev, but invaded Egypt itself and occupied a deep strip of the Sinai desert. Only Britain's threats to intervene convinced the Israelis to back out of Egypt. That added the Negev to the whole of Galilee, half of Jerusalem, and a connecting corridor through the midsection of what was to have been Arab territory—giving Israel by armed conflict what it could not get under peaceful international auspices. A notable case of Israel willingly withdrawing from territory it occupied was in Lebanon, where it agreed to remove its troops from a narrow zone back to the international border.

In retrospect, Israel missed a singular opportunity when it delayed making a true peace with Syria in order to reclaim a sliver of land in the northern Galilee held by Syrian troops just inside what the UN had outlined for the Jewish state. General

Husni Zaim, who had headed a Syrian coup in March 1949, proposed skipping armistice talks and moving directly toward a peace agreement with full recognition of Israel, an exchange of ambassadors, and open borders between the two countries. However, Zaim wanted to keep the narrow strip where Syrian troops were lodged and to alter the border to give Syria half the Sea of Galilee. Besides formal peace, he offered to settle permanently 300,000 Palestinian refugees, nearly half the total number scattered around the region. Israel refused even to discuss the plan. It demanded the Syrian soldiers be withdrawn and the old international border—not the battle line—be the basis of the armistice. Zaim's position in Syria was fatally weakened during the four months of negotiations, at the close of which Israel had won its demands. Three weeks later Zaim was overthrown, and the deal he was willing to offer Israel was never repeated. Syria, the only Arab country to offer a quick peace, would become Israel's most implacable enemy.

Likewise, the Israelis were able to expand their borders at the expense of Jordan, whose negotiators were refusing to give up the southeastern sector of the Negev held by their troops. With armistice talks already in progress in March 1949, and with a cease-fire in effect, the Israelis went on the attack again. They sent troops down through the southeastern Negev all the way to the Gulf of Akaba, easily clearing out small Jordanian patrols and taking the territory. Israel got itself a port with access to the Red Sea, at the same time it spoiled Abdullah's dream of access through the Negev to a Mediterranean port at Gaza. After this show of force, the Israelis threatened during direct, secret talks with Abdullah to resume war if the king refused to cede a strip of West Bank land forty miles long and three miles deep, containing sixteen villages, prime farmland, and some 35,000 Arab Palestinians. The king got no success out of direct appeals to President Truman and to the British government for assurance that they would intervene if Israel attacked. And Abdullah's military advisers warned that in renewed fighting, lacking outside help, he could lose much more to Israel than this one strip of land. And so he agreed. Under these pressures Abdullah scarcely thought about demanding anything from the Israelis. A few points that remained important to him—getting access to the sea was the most vital—would wait for peace negotiations. He had no need for most of the chunks that Israel had taken out of the UN's Arab zone, areas like the Sorek Valley, and he gave no thought to liberating them. The armistice was signed in April 1949.

Palestinian refugees cared for nothing except survival in those months and knew little about the borders being drawn across their land at UN conference tables or at secret meetings in King Abdullah's palace chambers. Only later would Abdullah's role in the cession of so much territory become public. For now, most of the West Bank refugees had little objection to the king's effort to join them to his domain, seeing it as an anchor in their still unstable, mobile existence. Sorek Valley families that wintered at Jericho moved their tents to the cooler environs of Neve Yacoub in the hills just north of Jerusalem in the summer of 1949, and some went back again to Jericho the next winter. There was little to keep them in one tent camp over another, except the weather. At least Abdullah's overtures held promise. "People were very hungry and wanted more jobs. It [the annexation] seemed like a good thing," Mahmoud Hamdan said years later. "It was the only government we had." The Jericho meetings and parliamentary sessions were not events for common people, but for the heads of leading families, the men who always had run Palestinian affairs. That was comforting, too. Such traditions and old allegiances for years patched together what fabric remained of Palestinian society. In the 1950 parliamentary elections, which the candidates vigorously contested during campaign visits to camps and towns across the West Bank, it was perfectly accepted that Mahmoud Hamdan's family voted for the man the old Ishwa mukhtar told them was best.

One time they restaked their tents in a new place, for a different reason. It was called Kalandia, and part of it had been the land of a pre-1948 Jewish settlement. It, like Hartuv, was one of the few that didn't survive the war. Unlike Hartuv, its land became home to Palestinians. Mahmoud's father, Asad Hamdan Asad, probably had learned about Kalandia when his family went up to Neve Yacoub to escape the desert heat. This new place was farther north, about five miles above Jerusalem. What attracted Asad Hamdan Asad was not the remnants of some Jewish colony, but the Kalandia rock quarries. He had done some quarrying in the Sorek Valley hills, and here was a chance to use his experience. He took his sons to work with him to learn the craft, cutting slabs of whitish-gray rock into building blocks and chiseling their surface with the dappled patterns in demand for years in Palestinian construction.

When they got to Kalandia there were some refugees in tents, and there was the road to the quarry. Nothing more. It was not a camp like Jericho where refugees could find water and rations and medical care. But there was work, and that was more important. The site attracted more and more families. Palestinian refugees everywhere—in the West Bank, in Lebanon, in Gaza— seemed to collect in their old geographical affinities. The lands of Kalandia filled up mostly with families from the villages that had sat among the limestone rocks of the Jerusalem Hills. The Abu Latifahs and Labiba Suleiman were among them. They did not repay the Jews, who lost their land and won a nation.

In 1950 the United Nations Relief and Works Agency for Palestine Refugees in the Near East (UNRWA) got rolling. Created by the UN to provide not only relief but work that would make refugees self-sustaining, UNRWA quickly adopted a policy of taking its services to places refugees already had gathered. At Kalandia, UNRWA made a plan to organize a camp out of the haphazard jumble of tents, then made level sites. Mahmoud Hamdan's family moved onto a bulldozed patch, carried heavy stones to it, and tied their tent to the stones. "We had more than twenty people from our family in it," he said. "It was three meters by four meters." More tents and slowly a few amenities arrived. The UNRWA target was providing ten liters of water per person per day, but it had to be delivered by truck. On each street UNRWA put two or three outhouses under a formula calling for one latrine hole for every fifty people. It was a formula for frustration, so refugees soon began digging their own latrines. It took years to get piped water, and even when it finally arrived it came in the form of one five-tap standpipe per street. Sometimes there were setbacks worse than the water truck blowing a tire and missing a visit. There was the stormy winter of 1951–52. "We had twelve to fifteen thousand people shelterless over night," said Antranig Bakerjian, a longtime UNRWA official. "We'd go in the middle of the night and find small children all tangled up in the mud and the water. The tents would be torn down by gale winds."

UNRWA tried to trade work for rations when possible, giving able-bodied refugees jobs building roads, terracing the land, or planting trees. Mahmoud Hamdan and his father sometimes worked as day laborers constructing streets and buildings, and Diab Abu Latifah learned finer points of the construction trade when he got a job with the contractor building a vocational center. Nothing was permanent at first. The girl's school, for example, started out as a tent. UNRWA encouraged the refugees to build walls around it, and when the walls got high enough the agency supplied a roof. UNRWA's main objective was moving into longer-term rehabilitation projects, ranging from public works to supplying tools for a refugee to open his own business. But as rehabilitation efforts progressed they became more suspect in the eyes of the refugees, who fully understood the aim was to make the refugee camps their new homes, not just a way station on the route back to prewar life.

Persuading the Palestinians to build houses was a long and painful process. "The first ten years were years of desperation. They didn't want to cooperate in any manner. They wanted to go home," Bakerjian said. Houses were symbolic. "They thought it was an indication that we wanted them to forget their homeland. As long as they were in tents they thought they might go back." Diab Abu Latifah, who was elected to the camp committee that conveyed refugee concerns to UNRWA, said people at first were glad to get aid, but began fearing it was part of a plot to keep them away from their real homes. "Later the people didn't want any help from the UN, because everyone thought they would be going back the next week or the next month," he said. "They felt they had everything they needed in their own villages, so why should they have to be given ten kilos of flour?" Even when the refugees did want UNRWA help, when they petitioned for rations or jobs or more latrines, they would include in the petition a demand that they be allowed to go home. Finally the successive bad winters, the repeating illnesses among children, and the failure of Arab-Israeli peace talks to produce any hint that a return was imminent combined to wear down the Palestinians' resistance. By the mid-1950s some of them began to accept the building materials that UNRWA offered for raising one- or two-room tin-roofed huts that were more protective than tents.

Not all the refugees ended up in camps. Ismail Abdul Fattah, the Artuf mukhtar, is one example of a Palestinian lucky enough to escape with some small assets and resourceful enough to multiply them to keep his family's life more normal. This is a family that integrated with the new reality. One son who had finished high school got a job with UNRWA, then a scholarship to college in Damascus and later a job in an Amman veterinary lab. The second son, Ismail Rahhal, followed a tougher course, beginning with manual labor on UNRWA roads. But then he crossed back over the river to Madaba on the East Bank, where he had left the family's sheep. With the profits from selling them he bought a horse and plow and leased some land to farm. It was a good crop that his parents came to help him harvest, and they took it back home to Bethlehem to sell. This was the beginning of a new occupation. "I started working in trade. We brought all the things from Jordan and sold them to the merchants here," said Ismail Rahhal, who was doing much the same thing, with considerable financial success, more than thirty years later. A few years after his stint as a farmer, Ismail Rahhal opened a store in the central souk of Bethlehem, got married, and started his own family. His is not a unique story among the Palestinians, who had their share of city lawyers and physicians and entrepreneurs with skills they could market even as refugees. There were other families like his, headed by sheikhs and mukh-

tars who had managed to accumulate the edge of wealth that
kept them out of the camps. But Ismail Rahhal's story was not
often the kind told by the fellaheen or day laborers who had fled
with almost nothing and who wanted nothing more than to go
back home.

Taking them back was something the Israelis continued to
resist, as strenuously as the Arab nations pressed for their return. The fate of the refugees became the tightest of the multiple
knots which never were unraveled by the Palestine Conciliation
Commission, the three-member body charged by the UN with
bringing peace to the Middle East beyond simple armistice
pacts. Newspaper editor Mark Ethridge, the American member
of the PCC, repeatedly tried to extract from Israel one conciliatory gesture—an expression of willingness to take in a fraction
of the refugees—which his talks with Arab leaders led him to
believe would open the way for negotiations on the range of
peace issues. Ethridge, the State Department, and finally even
Israel's great friend President Truman pressed the Israelis in
the latter half of 1949 to accept not all the Palestinians, but fewer
than one-third of the approximately 700,000 Arabs who fled
Israeli-occupied lands. By the time Israeli attitudes began troubling the White House, however, Israel already had gained two
of the most important items it wanted from the West—approval
of the $100 million loan from the U.S. Export-Import Bank and
admission to the UN. Potential pressure points were fast disappearing. Less than two weeks after the UN membership vote on
May 11, 1949, Israeli Prime Minister David Ben-Gurion felt bold
enough to brush off angrily a personal warning from Truman.
Israel did make a conditional offer to let 100,000 refugees return,
a figure that included 25,000, mostly women and children, who
already had been accepted back in a family reunification pro-
gram. Israel said the return would come only as part of a general
peace settlement, and even then Israel would determine exactly
which refugees were allowed back and where they would be
allowed to live. The PCC found the proposed figure so low and
the conditions so onerous that it never officially transmitted the
offer to the Arabs.

The Arab delegates, who never met formally face to face with the Israelis at the PCC conference in Switzerland, refused to entertain formal peace talks until Israel began bending on refugee repatriation. The Arabs' public posture on territory, however, was almost as stiff as the Israelis' stand on refugees. The Arabs rejected the boundaries delimited in the armistice agreements, which they had said from the beginning they regarded as temporary lines separating hostile troops. Ironically, they demanded instead to go back to the November 29, 1947, partition boundaries, which they had fought a war to avoid. The Israelis refused even to consider retreating to the UN partition lines, which among other things would have meant abandoning their first settlements in the Sorek Valley and elsewhere around Jerusalem. That was history, and Israel's present reality had been forged by its army. It was a stalemate that the PCC never was able to crack. But Israel's claims, still being repeated today, that the Arabs refused to recognize it or to talk peace did not reflect the entire picture. While the Arabs refused to engage the Israelis in public negotiations, individual Arab regimes tried to make deals in a series of private talks. Egypt and Jordan, similar to Syria earlier, offered peaceful coexistence and backed off the public insistence on the old partition boundaries. But they demanded some concession from Israel in return, in the form of territorial adjustments or the repatriation of a portion of the Palestinian refugees. Israel refused to give.

Neither side had a lock on intransigence. Despite the United Nations decision to internationalize Jerusalem, Israel had moved most of its government to the Holy City by early 1950, and in January of 1953 the Knesset declared the city had always been the capital of Israel. Meanwhile, Jordan, having occupied the eastern half of Jerusalem, refused to accept any plan that would diminish its sovereignty there. The Arabs kept up a full economic blockade of Israel, which meant it had to import from considerable distance all the food it could not grow and all the oil it needed. In a less-known but increasingly sensitive point of contention, both sides claimed rights to the headwaters of the Jordan River. The Israelis began using the water first, however, with a monumental project diverting between 50 and 75 percent of the river's flow all the way from the Sea of Galilee in the north down to the sands of the Negev. That diversion project, known as the Israel Water Carrier, was how the Israelis made the Negev desert, and even the Sorek Valley, bloom. The Arabs say it happened at their expense.

If the Israelis sealed one route to the future for the Palestinian refugees—return—the Arab countries closed down another. They refused resettlement and development plans that would have been financed and technologically guided primarily by the West, which wanted to see as many refugees as possible integrated into normal Arab society. This was Israel's vision of the future for all the refugees. It is not that the Arab nations were unwilling to help their Palestinian brothers. The Arab states had contributed more than $11 million in refugee aid by early 1949, a sum that was peeled off their slender budgets with great difficulty. A principal factor in the resistance was the Palestinians themselves, who did not want to be resettled and integrated into another Arab country. That, after all, was why they refused for years even to give up their tents for houses. The Arab governments, already in precarious standing with their own populations, also saw "resettlement" as one more Israeli victory they could not afford. And if they assimilated and dispersed the identifiable mass of refugees, they would lose a political tool with which they could continue prodding Israel. Had there been an outcry for resettlement from the Palestinians, the Arab states no doubt would have been more willing to integrate some refugees. But the pressure all was in the opposite direction.

The one Arab figure who happily would have accepted resettlement schemes was of course King Abdullah. He wanted the Palestinians in his kingdom, and he was anxious to develop it into something beyond a bedouin backwater. But Abdullah was watched carefully by the other Arabs for deviations from common Arab policy. They almost had expelled him from the Arab League for annexing the West Bank and were irate upon learning he had renewed secret negotiations with Israel. Abdullah also was more constrained than his fellow kings and emirs by the wishes of the Palestinian refugees, who were more numerous and more free to speak and to circulate in Jordan than elsewhere. They attacked his government for supporting even small rehabilitation schemes. Whether Abdullah ever would have prevailed in his aspirations for a unified, prosperous country in peace with Israel is doubtful, but he was not granted the time to continue trying. In July 1951, as he walked into the al-Aqsa Mosque in Jerusalem for midday prayers with his grandson Hussein, Abdullah was assassinated by a young Palestinian gunman.

Mahmoud Hamdan was in Amman, where he had taken his quarrying skills to earn a higher wage, when news of Abdullah's death began spreading. Palestinians were targeted for beatings and arrest. "I was afraid because of the intimidation by the Jordanians," he related. "We even heard once that they burned a Palestinian in an oven. They were so mad. They would do anything." Mahmoud hid in the home of a friend for a week, then caught a bus back to Kalandia. Times calmed, and he was able to return to work. But the initial angry reaction of the Jordanian authorities and of common citizens would prove over the years to be merely one reflection of a deep-seated attitude toward the Palestinians. The West Bank had been annexed as one of two supposedly equal parts of Jordan. As the Palestinians became more settled and resigned to living there—as they started building more rooms onto their huts and walling them into compounds—they realized they existed not in a free state but in a territory under Jordanian occupation.

· 19 ·

POROUS
BORDERS

*S*omehow women from the Ishwa families got their hands on a bolt of silk, real silk cloth like that they always had used in the traditional Queen's Dress. They cut it and tenderly embroidered it, then stitched it into a wedding dress for Yusra Khalil. For three nights the men gathered to dance the *dabkey* and the *sabjoy* and to celebrate around the tents and the two-room shack that by now, 1954, Asad Hamdan Asad had built for his family in the Kalandia refugee camp. His oldest boy was getting married. Somebody had a drum, another friend supplied a flute, and the men raised Mahmoud Hamdan to their shoulders and carried the bridegroom over jagged, ragged paths that cut through a welter of huts and tents, bringing cheers from refugees brightened by this rare encounter with gaiety. "It wasn't like in the village when they used to decorate a camel or a horse," Mahmoud said, "but they were very nice days. It used to be like one family. People would come and sing and dance and they would give plays. Things that make your heart very happy."

It had been six years since strafing machine guns and mortars chased the Sorek Valley peasants into the vacuum of a homeless,

stateless existence, and only now were they shaking off the
numbness and orienting themselves to another life. Mahmoud
no longer worked as a day laborer in Amman but with his father
in their own small enterprise of hewing and shaping and selling
stones from the Kalandia quarries, which Jordanian authorities
had thrown open to refugees willing to try the dirty, hard labor.
"We used to carry the stones on our back to the trucks," Mahmoud said. The first tents in the camp of three thousand people
gave way to rough shelters of quarry rocks, roofed with flat-
tened metal barrels supplied by UNRWA. Usually a family
built their shelter in the same spot where they happened to have
dropped their tent perhaps two or three years earlier. Mahmoud
Hamdan's family was fortunate, he said, because his father was
friendly with the camp officer. For their hut he secured a spot
up on a hill toward the back of the camp. It was cleaner and drier
when winter rains washed low-lying paths in mud baths. There
was a breeze and a view of barren hills that weren't pretty, but
proved there still was breathing space not so far outside their
cramped world. Eventually, both with UNRWA's help and by
their own efforts, most families would be able to improve and
expand their two-room shacks into walled compounds. But for
now the combination of tiny hut and tents, plus the work in
quarries, gave enough stability to bring a new bride into the
family, an Ishwa girl, of course.

Jobs, shelters, weddings—the refugees slowly settled into
what they still regarded as temporary homes under the Jordanian regime that they still thought of as their temporary government. The 1950 parliamentary resolution joining the East
and West Bank into one nation had carried the caveat that the
union would not prejudice the final settlement of the issue of
Palestine. The Palestinians preserved the option of returning
and of the West Bank someday being part of a Palestinian state.
But for now they accepted Amman as their governing center.
They watched what the government was doing, and if they
didn't like it they said so. That at least was the habit of Palestinian intellectuals and professionals and businessmen from the
cities, both refugees and native West Bankers who had the time

and energy to think about politics. The new Jordan held nearly 1.5 million people, only about one-third of them original Transjordanians. The other two-thirds were Palestinians, divided almost equally between refugees from Israel and longtime West Bank residents. The leading Palestinians were more educated, political, and sophisticated than the Transjordanians, who largely came from peasant and bedouin stock. Even refugees who never had been politicized stayed angry and concentrated and thus made good targets for political activists. The goals of the Palestinians often were not the goals of Amman. That is at least partly why the West Bank always would remain the stepchild in the Jordanian union, because the government in Amman remained frightened that it one day would be overwhelmed. Over the years, King Abdullah and his grandson King Hussein realized that they had to draw hard limits or these Palestinians would eat up their kingdom.

As the refugees picked up the threads of a new life, their connections to the land and homes they had left in what was now Israel became increasingly theoretical. Infiltration had become a dicey affair. The Israelis got tougher on Palestinians sneaking back to rejoin families or to claim some treasure they had buried or some fruit from the trees they used to own. One reason was that some infiltrators had begun crossing back not just to retrieve their own possessions, but to take revenge by shooting Jews or burning out their new settlements. The Israelis reported that 147 Jewish soldiers and civilians were killed in 1952 in infiltration incidents. So the Israelis were taking no chances. The border police were shooting. In the same year, 1952, the Israelis killed 394 Arabs they believed to be violating borders—an average of more than one a day. They captured an average of seven a day.

Mahmoud Hamdan recollected a clandestine trip back to Ishwa sometime in the early 1950s that was tense enough to make it his last. Knowing that the Israelis had tightened surveillance, he and two friends nonetheless took a bus to Imwas, a town near Latrun on the border. After dark they climbed over the hills and into the Sorek Valley, where they set to liberating some Ishwa olives. They picked in the grove across the valley road from where their village used to be, a grove on a hillside that wasn't bulldozed for a Jewish settlement. Mahmoud and his friends saw no one, filled their sacks, and headed back. As they neared the Bab al-Wad, suddenly they heard an Israeli patrol. About twenty soldiers were going west toward Beit Susin on the Burma Road. The trio slid into a nearby wadi and hunched behind a boulder, not knowing whether the patrol was going somewhere or was just guarding, back and forth, this piece of road near a major intersection. "We were scared to death," Mahmoud remembered. "Besides, it was very very cold and we were freezing, and we were afraid of the wild animals." They also had seen a burned-out bulldozer back in the valley, and they feared they would be blamed for it. After huddling there for what seemed hours, they finally had to run or get caught by the dawn. They made it back to Jordanian territory without becoming Israeli statistics, but it was the last time Mahmoud would sneak back home.

Israel faulted the Jordanian government for not stopping infiltrations and soon turned to retaliatory attacks on the Arab side of the frontier. To stage them the Israelis created a secret unit that had no uniforms and little accountability to anyone except its leader, Ariel Sharon, who had been in military intelligence during the war and was recalled from life as a student to command the new unit. "Unit 101" was in effect a terrorist squad, conducting night raids on Arab police stations and villages believed to harbor infiltrators.

Several months of violent operations ended in international disgrace after Sharon led his commandos into a retaliatory raid on the West Bank village of Khibya. A Jewish mother and two children had been murdered the night before when terrorists from across the border threw a grenade into a house near the Lod (formerly Lydda) airport. Despite a promise by Jordanian authorities to punish the guilty, the army dispatched Unit 101 to mete its brand of justice, along with a regular army paratrooper battalion serving as a backup. Sharon's force stormed Khibya and blew up forty-five houses, burying forty villagers in the wreckage and killing sixty-six Palestinians. Another seventy-five were wounded. After this October 1953 slaughter, Unit 101 disappeared. It was merged with the paratroop battalion and Sharon was named its commander, thus beginning his steady military advancement as a merciless foe of the Palestinians.

Jordan, sharing the longest border with Israel, feared that continued border incidents might lead it back into a disastrous war against Israel's superior weapons and troops. So Jordanian authorities acted to curtail clandestine Palestinian border crossings. Jordan increased security operations, required Palestinians to register guns and ammunition so they could be confiscated, and reduced the population of Palestinian frontier villages, the rural jumping-off spots for infiltration and raids. Young men like Mahmoud Hamdan were deterred as much by Jordan's secret police, who had dozens of informants spread in the refugee camps, as by Israeli guns across the border.

Although Jordan and Israel between them claimed nearly three thousand armistice violations in five years, these were mostly low-level run-ins compared to the troubles on Israel's borders with Syria and Egypt. The Arabs were provocative in some cases, such as when Syrians fired on Israeli fishermen in the Sea of Galilee or Egypt turned a blind eye to infiltrators. But the UN found Israel to be responsible for the biggest confrontations. In the north, the Israelis were trying in 1951 to drain swamps and develop water projects which required them to work in a demilitarized zone where the Palestinians were supposed to live unmolested. When the Palestinian farmers refused to move out for these projects, Israel evicted them and leveled their villages. Syrian troops responded. After twelve days of fighting, the Security Council ordered a cease-fire, then ordered Israel to return the evacuated Palestinians. In the south, Israel was trying to place a military camp disguised as a settlement in the desert DMZ. To do this, Israel expelled six thousand bedouins and destroyed their camps. Israelis forced others to move by taking over their traditional water supplies. By the time Israel got its armed camp in place in 1953, it discovered Egypt also had a military checkpoint in the DMZ. In several relentless drives against the Egyptians, Israeli troops finally pushed them out of the zone. The Israelis were adamant in refusing to back their troops out of the DMZ, even after being censured by the UN Security Council.

Egypt took an approach that was the opposite of Jordan's crackdown policies and won new fidelity from Palestinian refugees. The bloodless Free Officers coup in 1952 had given Egypt a political face-lift, replacing the corrupt King Farouk with a young cadre of military officers who acted partly out of disgust with Egypt's humiliation in the 1948 war. In 1954 Colonel Gamal Abdul Nasser took over the premiership and quickly adopted the Palestinian cause as one political rallying point for his pan-Arab philosophy. His military intelligence unit began training fedayeen and directing these Arab commandos in harassing raids on Israeli targets. The attack squads usually were Palestinian refugees based in the Egyptian-controlled Gaza Strip, although some crossed into Jordan to stage assaults from Jordanian territory. They mined roads and bridges, stole livestock, and killed Israeli settlers, making life dangerous enough that some Israelis began leaving the Negev. The fedayeen and Nasser became idolized by Palestinian refugees, including those in the West Bank whom the Jordanian authorities had strived to contain. Israel's counterpunches into the Gaza Strip produced demonstrations in Kalandia and elsewhere in the West Bank. "They were brothers and when one brother is attacked the others should defend them," remembered Diab Abu Latifah.

Goaded by Egypt, the refugees soon engaged in another round of demonstrations, this time against the Baghdad Pact, a Western-oriented defense alliance already joined by Iraq, Iran, Pakistan, and Turkey. The pact was guided by Britain with the United States in the wings. To Nasser, who finally had nudged the British out of Egypt, the pact threatened even more Western influence and an assault on his own efforts to lead a purely Arab confederation. As soon as the Jordanian prime minister started talking about membership in the Baghdad Pact in December 1955, riots exploded all over the East and West Banks. Even without their hero Nasser fulminating against the pact on Radio

Cairo, Palestinian refugees had their own reasons for fighting it. The British and the Americans were the two governments the Palestinians felt were most responsible for the creation of the enemy Israel and for their own losses. They interpreted membership in this association as abandonment of their cause. After a refugee delegation informed the young King Hussein that his crown was in danger, he dissolved the government and called elections. This flexing of refugee power was a red flasher to Hussein, who would be much less conciliatory when challenged again.

For now, Jordan returned to the pan-Arab fold. King Hussein dismissed the Briton Sir John Glubb as head of the Arab Legion and began removing other British officers. This elicited overwhelming support from his Palestinian subjects. Jordan and Syria announced a new "United Frontier" plan soon to be followed by creation of a joint military command, linking Jordan indirectly to the military alliance among Egypt, Syria, and Saudi Arabia. Israel read these developments as groundwork for a new assault by the surrounding Arab countries. Scare stories appeared in the Israeli press, such as one in May 1956 that described the Palestinian refugees as buoyed by new hope of a "march back into the forsaken land" that would spell the end of their exile.

Israeli leaders had been pondering a preemptive war for months, but they were targeting what they considered the locus of agitation—Egypt. Nasser had become their primary threat when the Soviet Union, dismayed at Israel's growing tilt toward the West, jumped off the Zionist bandwagon and arranged a $320 million sale of Czech arms to Egypt. Israel also was stirred into action by the continuing fedayeen raids and by Egypt's blockage of Israeli shipping through both the Suez Canal and the Strait of Tiran. The time for Israeli action finally arrived when Britain and France, too, found Nasser's nationalism and pan-Arab activism interfering with their interests. He had alienated France by backing the Algerian independence movement and alarmed Britain by nationalizing the British-operated Suez Canal. France, Great Britain, and Israel plotted an attack, in which

Israeli troops fortified by French weapons would be the advance assault force.

While Israel mobilized to attack Egypt, it created the false impression that it was preparing an offensive against Jordan. King Hussein had been worried enough by several intense Israeli raids in September and October to invoke the Anglo-Jordanian defense treaty. Tension magnified in late October, when Israel laid its cover for troop mobilizations. Avi Nachshon, one of the Israeli soldiers who had cleared out the Sorek Valley villages in 1948, now was in charge of moving troops and vehicles to confuse the nervous Jordanians. "We tried to make it look as though we were going to attack Jordan," Nachshon said. These diversionary tactics and rumors spread by Israeli intelligence were convincing enough to draw two telegrams from President Eisenhower asking Israel not to attack Jordan. Prime Minister Ben-Gurion didn't bring his own cabinet into the decision to invade Egypt until October 27, two days after he called up troops and two days before the operation began.

Jordan bolstered its defenses, putting on alert the Arab Legion and Palestinian refugees it recruited into the National Guard. Some Palestinians clamored to be armed and trained and allowed to fight, not for Jordan, but to settle their own personal scores with Israel. Others had no faith in the Jordanian regime and refused to fight for it. Diab Abu Latifah, a mujahid fighting the Jews in 1948, was not willing to fight Israel on Jordan's behalf. At thirty-seven, he was so disenchanted with Jordanian rule that he spent months working in the Jordanian port of Aqaba to avoid the pressures put on camp residents to join the National Guard. By contrast, twenty-one-year-old Mahmoud Hamdan served as a single-striper in charge of eight men and a machine gun in a bunker at En Nabi-Samwil, a West Bank hill town just northwest of Jerusalem. Such was the anxiety on the Jordanian side that Mahmoud's commander forbade his unit to take any initiative. "We had orders. They would not allow anyone to attack the Israelis. Once a plane came to take a look. We opened fire," he said. "We were fined and detained." The young Palestinian guardsmen, wanting nothing more ardently than to see the united Arab nations forge a victory over Israel, had to pay the equivalent of around $10 each, forfeited two weeks' pay, and spent a week in confinement for shooting at the enemy. Their respect for the Jordanians went down another notch.

While Jordanian Private First Class Mahmoud Hamdan was waiting to be attacked by Israel, Israeli Major Yoshko Levy was on alert twenty-five miles away, ready to defend the Sorek Valley in case the Jordanians attacked. His defenses were rather improved over the days when a few dozen troops were isolated in one small Jewish colony. Now the valley was part of Israel, and the state was preparing for the contingency of Jordan entering the war on behalf of Egypt. Yoshko Levy had given up his Jewish Agency job helping new immigrants settle in the valley and had returned to regular military service earlier in 1956, persuaded by repeated call-ups for reserve duty to become a full-time soldier again. As a major, he commanded the troops guarding a strip of twenty settlements that stretched from the old Ishwa to Latrun, a strip facing Mahmoud Hamdan and the Jordanian front. It was called the Ramle block and contained about two thousand soldiers, including two battalions of regulars and the reservists who lived in what were designated A settlements because of their border positions. "The plan was that in the event of an attack, settlements were to defend the line until the army came," he said. "Each settlement was considered a platoon and had its own storehouse of weapons."

The Sorek Valley, seized eight years earlier by the Israelis to protect a jeep track through the hills, had grown in importance in the minds of Israelis. The valley was the connection between the Jewish state and the capital it had proclaimed in West Jerusalem. Through it ran the main Jerusalem–Tel Aviv road, the replacement of Route 1, the old main road that Israelis had not been able to capture in full in 1948. Girls from Kibbutz Tsora hitchhiking to Jerusalem used to hope to be picked up by the glamorous Moshe Dayan, the army chief of staff, who frequently traveled the road from Tel Aviv. Or they might be lucky enough to catch a glimpse of Dayan and cabinet members at the Shimshon Restaurant, where they often met for informal talks en route to Jerusalem. It turned out that the old Hartuvians who had returned to the valley, the Iraqi Jews building their new apartments at Beth Shemesh, and the Yemenite chicken farmers at Eshtaol didn't need to worry. No Arab army came to cut the new lifeline to Jerusalem, to burn down the thousands of Jewish National Fund seedlings taking root on the hills just as their settlements were doing. Indeed, their anxiety was misplaced at a time when Jordanian officers not only had drawn no plans for assault, but were punishing their troops for shooting a machine gun at an enemy airplane they believed to be on a raiding mission.

In one impulsive moment, King Hussein did propose attacking Israel to help the Egyptians, who quickly were overwhelmed. His offer was too late. Nasser urged him not to join battle, because he knew the war already was lost. The Egyptians initially had believed, as Israeli war planners intended, that the October 29 attack was just another reprisal for fedayeen raids and that Israeli troops would back off. By the time Nasser realized this was full-scale war and ordered reinforcements, Israeli forces already were snaking their columns deep into the Sinai, north, center, and south. Nasser's air force was disabled under attacks by two hundred French and British fighter-bombers, which also provided cover for Israeli paratroop drops, and the coast was shelled by Anglo-French ships that covered their troop landings at the canal. The Egyptians were overrun.

The French and British governments made transparent claims that their intervention was merely an attempt to stop the fighting between Egypt and Israel and to protect the Suez Canal. An outraged United Nations, led by the United States, on November 2 demanded an immediate cease-fire and withdrawal of all aggressor troops, British, French, and Israeli. It took days for the truce to be accepted and months for the invading nations to withdraw all their troops, which were replaced by a United Nations Emergency Force. In the end Israel won its major short-term objectives—UN and American guarantees of free shipping and a UN presence in Gaza and at the Strait of Tiran. The UN troops were insurance against both fedayeen attacks and blockades.

One aftershock of the war was the obliteration of a scheme

that had been the last reasonable chance for resettling concentrations of homeless Palestinians like the refugees at Kalandia camp. The Eisenhower administration had envisioned its Johnston Plan as a ticket for regional cooperation, economic development, and the resettlement of refugees in an irrigated Sinai desert. The water development plan would have brought immense economic gains to Israel, Egypt, Jordan, Syria, and Lebanon, creating jobs for their nationals as well as for refugees. In 1955, before political tensions ensnared all the parties, they almost reached agreement. It was Nasser, seeing the rewards that would accrue to Egypt, who was urging the other Arab countries to compromise. Prospects became more tenuous in the months leading up to hostilities, and by the time the war was finished, the notion of any cooperative action with Israel was doomed. So were major development schemes to disperse and resettle refugees. Palestinians did become more receptive after the war to improvements to their lives inside the camps and to UNRWA's expanding programs of training and education. The crushing of the Egyptian military made them realize the return was not near. But dispersal such as the Johnston Plan envisioned would have dimmed the Palestinian identity and the issue of their lost homes and homeland. They remained unwilling to give that up.

Israel had miscalculated that a humiliating defeat of Egyptian forces would crush Nasser's prestige, end his rule, and bring into power a replacement who would see the wisdom of accommodation with Israel. In fact, Nasser emerged an even greater hero, as a righteous leader who had survived the whipping of a gang of powerful bullies. His popularity among the Palestinian refugees could not have been greater, and other Arab nationals were almost as devoted. Nasser had new impetus for his drive to influence, if not control, the Arab states of the Middle East.

The Jordanian government quickly reduced Jordan's remaining ties with Britain, began talking about an Arab federation, and strode toward diplomatic relations with the Soviet Union. The prime minister and much of the new parliament had been elected just before the war and were leftist admirers of Nasser and his allies the Syrians. King Hussein, who had allowed the free elections which produced this radical government, decided it had gone too far. Shortly after he dissolved the government in April 1957, the king easily put down an attempted military coup. Concessions to the opposition parties, largely made up of upper-class Palestinians, ended abruptly and were replaced with repression. Political parties were banished and internal security attempted to bleed all pro-Nasser propaganda out of both the East and West Banks. Martial law was declared.

Palestinian refugees in the camps came under close watch and fast, hard discipline. They seldom had been involved in formal party politics. That was the reserve of city intellectuals and property owners, teachers and students who didn't have to bust their knuckles in rock quarries all day long. Many refugees like Mahmoud Hamdan concentrated on making a living. But the mass of refugees was concentrated and angry and so potentially disruptive that the regime felt it essential to assert control. Even the refugees who never joined political parties or demonstrations were dazzled by Nasser. Mahmoud Hamdan described the sentiments:

> He was like the leader of the whole Arab world. So whenever he gave a speech and it was on the radio, no matter what you were doing, no matter how important the work, you would stop and listen to him. Whatever happened, you would listen to him. We were very angry. Under the Jordanians we were not happy. We had the belief that they were against each other, the Jordanians and the Egyptians. So we came to feel more for the Egyptians. . . . They were the only ones with us and our cause. . . . Whenever the Jordanians would see anyone listening to Egyptian radio, they would come in and smash everything and break the radio and beat the people.

Most Palestinian refugees who lived in refugee camps under Jordan control can relate tale after tale of Jordanian security police breaking into their homes in the 1957 crackdown in search of books or pamphlets or radios tuned to a forbidden station. One night Mahmoud's family, for instance, was listening to the

9:00 P.M. Egyptian news. He speculates that someone informed on them to Jordan's formidable secret police, the *mubabarrat.* At the first sound of approaching strangers, the battery-operated radio was switched to Israeli news. A senior Jordanian officer and two plainclothesmen barged into the shelter, but found only a group quietly listening to the Tel Aviv broadcast, which was not banned. They had no proof of violation, so all they could do was speak intimidating words and leave. The Abu Latifah family was even more political and just as cautious. The family owned several books on the Egyptian leader that in the late 1950s they would hide outside the house under a wooden feeding trough for goats. The Jordanians raided the family's home more than once, but they never thought to search under the trough. Had Mahmoud Hamdan's family been slower to react to the sound of footsteps, or Diab Abu Latifah less clever in secreting a library, they could have spent long stretches in prison. Many Palestinians did. One refugee at a camp outside Amman was sentenced in military court to fifteen years in prison for possessing communist propaganda. He was caught with a single pamphlet.

Repression would wax and wane over the years, as the Jordanian monarch felt the threat to his stability rise and fall. Throughout two decades of Jordanian rule, however, West Bankers always would feel they were the stepchildren. They had high schools and got to vote and weren't treated much more harshly by security services than native East Bankers. But Amman effectively restrained them from building an independent power base, at the same time it retarded the West Bank's economic development. Palestinian merchants received fewer export and import licenses, for example, and West Bankers generally suffered under policies that discouraged investment in commerce and industry. Men like Mahmoud Hamdan seldom found opportunities under Jordanian rule to turn their skills— in agriculture, construction, or commerce—into profit-making enterprises.

One crackdown came against a young, militant Palestinian organization that for decades would draw vacillating responses from King Hussein, whose embraces would alternate with blows. The Palestine Liberation Organization was conceived at an Arab summit meeting in January 1964, by Arab kings and presidents who finally decided there should be an entity to organize the Palestinians in their struggle to return. King Hussein initially supported it and allowed the PLO to hold its founding conference in East Jerusalem. It was the charter of the PLO that convinced Israelis there could be no compromise with this organization that within a decade would become the preeminent representative of the Palestinian people. The charter does not in so many words call for "the destruction of Israel," as Israelis have often contended. But that was the implication of several of the articles when taken together. The PLO charter declared the 1947 partition and the creation of the state of Israel "entirely illegal," defined pre-1948 Palestine as an "indivisible territorial unit," and called for "the retrieval of Palestine and its liberation by armed struggle." The first PLO chairman, Ahmad Shukeiry, alienated Hussein by trying to collect taxes from the king's Palestinian subjects and by suggesting that all of Jordan, including the East Bank, was part of Palestine and thus a candidate for PLO liberation.

A rival Palestinian organization, not under the thumb of the Arab League, had been secretly formed in Kuwait in 1962. It called itself Fatah, and from the start one of its leaders was Yasser Arafat. The members were Palestinian refugees scattered from Kuwait to Germany and Spain. Their presence so far abroad meant they were offspring of wealthier Palestinian families, generally from the cities and larger towns, rather than children of poor fellaheen who had no choice in 1948 but to settle in refugee camps. The vanguard of Fatah was composed of university students and those already graduated into professional jobs, not stonemasons from the Sorek Valley. Although the Fatah leadership threw in with the larger PLO in 1964, Arafat's group remained separate and carried out its own military assaults on Israel. It claimed thirty-nine successful guerrilla raids in 1965.

Syria provided some support and a staging base to Fatah, but the Palestinian commandos were not the only ones to mount operations across this increasingly volatile border. Both the Arabs and the Israelis launched cross-border attacks aimed at each other's water development projects between 1965 and 1967. And shelling from Syria's Golan Heights turned farming into a deadly occupation for Israelis in the valley below. Raids grew into firefights, then into a major air battle in April 1967 and finally into concentrations of troops and artillery at both sides of the border zone in May. The Soviet Union, which had grown close to the leftist Syrian regime, messaged its old friend Egypt that Israel was about to attack Syria and the Egyptians must "take the necessary steps" to aid their Arab brother. Egypt too began concentrating troops as though readying a drive into Israel.

Until then, Egypt had been refraining from direct confrontations with Israel. The movement of troops, however, emboldened Nasser to go further. When Egypt kicked out the UN peacekeeping forces from Gaza and down in the Sinai, then reimposed a blockade on Israeli ships trying to navigate the Strait of Tiran, Israel began to mobilize its entire population. Even Jordan, after several years of sour relations with its Arab neighbors, now got swept back into the brotherhood of Arab nationalism. King Hussein had been under growing pressure at home for six months, since Israel destroyed the West Bank village of As Samu in one of its most vicious of a series of reprisals on Jordan-held territory. The Israelis had acted in spite of Hussein's efforts to stifle terrorist forays from his side of the border. Now the king felt he could no longer stay detached from the belligerent swell of Arab nationalism that was arching toward a crest. At the end of May 1967, Hussein flew to Cairo and signed a mutual defense pact with Nasser, making Jordan an ally of Egypt, Syria, Saudi Arabia, and, within days, Iraq.

The Israelis saw the Arab regimes rattling their imposing sabers and decided they must make a preemptive assault. Israeli military tacticians had believed for years that their only chance of winning a war against the array of potential Arab enemies was to strike first and strike hard. They were ready. Israel perfectly executed its opening move, taking out most of the Egyptian air force in a series of sorties that began the morning of June 5, 1967. Rather than admit the truth, Egyptian officers began reporting they had scored fabulous successes against the Israeli planes. This deception brought both Jordan and Syria into the air war with expectations of quick victories, and both ended up instead with decimated air corps. Monopolizing the skies, Israeli aircraft gave close cover to ground troops heading out in all directions. Within six days Israeli troops had conquered all of the Sinai, the Gaza Strip, Syria's Golan Heights, and the West Bank, including the Old City of Jerusalem. By the time all parties had accepted a UN cease-fire the evening of June 10, Israel had managed to punch great holes in the military forces of Egypt, Jordan, and Syria and to take enough land from each to make its porous borders more secure. Israel now found itself in control of an additional 28,000 square miles of land and more than a million new subjects, most of them hostile. They included 670,000 Palestinians on the West Bank and in East Jerusalem, 356,000 Palestinians in the Gaza Strip, 33,000 Egyptians in the Sinai, and almost 6,000 Syrian Druse on the Golan Heights.

The international community, acting through the UN, resolved that Israel must give up most, if not all, of this captured Arab land along with its population. In exchange the UN expected the Arab countries to give Israel peace. That was the formula that finally emerged in UN Resolution 242 in November 1967, after months of disagreement in the halls of diplomacy. The main provisions stated that "a just and lasting peace in the Middle East" required application of two principles:

1. Withdrawal of Israeli armed forces from territories occupied in the recent conflict:

2. Termination of all claims or states of belligerency and respect for and acknowledgment of the sovereignty, territorial integrity and political independence of every State in the area and their right to live in peace within secure and recognized boundaries free from threats or acts of force.

For years, however, most of the Arabs remained unwilling to accept the terms of Resolution 242 because they couldn't bring themselves to recognize Israel. Eventually in 1979 Egypt and Israel would agree to trade land for peace, but that would not happen until after a decade of arm-twisting by Secretary of State Henry Kissinger and President Jimmy Carter. The Palestinians would be pawns in this diplomatic drama. By the time the mainstream of the PLO became a player in the 1980s by agreeing to live by Resolution 242, Israel's leaders would balk at the notion of giving back any more land.

• 20 •

"THEY ACTED LIKE TOURISTS"

ighter planes bombed Ramallah just up the road, then tanks rolled toward them from Jerusalem. That's when the Palestinian refugees in the Kalandia camp ran. All of them. For the elders from the Sorek Valley and the other refugees, the Israeli advance into the West Bank was a terrifying scene of déjà vu. It was a replay of 1948, except this time the Israelis were armed with Mirage jets and Sherman tanks. Mahmoud Hamdan, who was once again working over on the East Bank when the 1967 war began, was tormented about the fate of his family. How could he know that his wife and five children had made it safely into the unpopulated hills behind the refugee camp? His wife, Yusra, was just as worried about him, as she and the rest of the family waited in a cave and faced what to do next. An UNRWA officer described the scene on June 9, two days after the tanks ground past Kalandia: "There was nobody in the camp, absolutely nobody in the camp. The whole population had fled because of fighting in the area."

Within days, quiet returned to the West Bank, and soon clusters of refugees walked gingerly toward the camp, gambling that they wouldn't be shot or taken prisoner. When they weren't, more quickly joined them. The family of Mahmoud Hamdan, waving a white flag on a stick, came back home.

The refugees of Kalandia returned to a different life—life as a captive people behind the Israeli front lines. The coming years would bring layers of surprises, some genial and others provoking rage. There would be new economic opportunities, but they were opened to a stateless population held in a political limbo by an arsenal of repressive tactics. The most bizarre change of all was that they no longer had to infiltrate through the Israeli border to reach the Sorek Valley. Given the first chance in nearly twenty years to visit the places they left behind, the Palestinians would find their old homes now inexorably Israeli, almost too changed to recognize and incompatible with the remembered object of their yearnings. This combination of stunning changes would pacify many adult Palestinians. For their children, the mix of modest opportunity and oppressive controls was a mulch that would enrich new shoots of rebellion.

The Six-Day War wrought entirely different changes on the valley and its ten thousand Jewish inhabitants. For the first time, Kibbutz Tsora and Beth Shemesh were no longer on the front lines of the Arab-Israeli conflict. Before the Israelis launched their thunderbolt, the Jordanian frontier was only three miles away at Latrun. Now, after one giddy week, the nearest patch of unoccupied Jordan was thirty-five miles away. There was another change which in time would be just as mesmerizing. By capturing the West Bank, the Israelis had struck water. The occupied territories would become a backup reservoir, promising a green future to dry farmland like the Sorek Valley.

The most immediate change, though, was the upheaval that dislodged the West Bank Palestinians from their moorings and caused upwards of 150,000 of them to flee to Jordan. For almost twenty years the Palestinians had been oriented east toward Jordan. Now they were adrift again, for how long no one knew, just as no one knew how the victorious Israelis would treat them. At first, Palestinians had reason to fear a repetition of 1948-style mass evictions. During the second day of the '67 war,

Israeli warplanes bombed and napalmed three UNRWA refugee camps along the Jordan River, causing nearly sixty thousand Palestinian inhabitants of the camps to escape into Jordan. But once the fighting stopped, the feared pattern of mass expulsions was averted, in part because of international pressure. One provable exception was the Old City of Jerusalem, where the Israelis announced they were evicting eighty Palestinian families to make way for the reconstruction of the Jewish Quarter. In some other parts of the West Bank, the Israelis did their best to encourage voluntary flight, organizing free bus transportation to the Jordan River bridges for refugees who would sign statements saying they were going on their own volition.

After briefly leaving the Jordan River bridges open in both directions, the Israelis stopped letting Palestinians return to their homes. Faced with foreign appeals, the government made a modest concession and allowed the return of twenty thousand, out of more than one hundred thousand who applied. Mahmoud Hamdan, who was working across the river when the war started, didn't wait to see if Israel would accept him back. He infiltrated across the river, lying low every time he saw a soldier till he got back to his family in Kalandia.

After the shuffling of refugees ended, Israelis tried to normalize and even to better life for those who were compliant. Military administrators continued the use of Jordanian law in the West Bank, supplementing it with their own system of summary punishment. They kept the Jordanian school system, censoring what they considered anti-Israeli books and adding Hebrew as a compulsory foreign language course. They allowed the use of Jordanian currency and banking, although the Israeli pound became a second official currency. Israel also allowed the West Bankers' produce to be transported and sold in the normal East Bank markets, even though Jordan was beyond the military lines.

General Moshe Dayan, the Israeli defense minister, tried to develop policies that would soften the obtrusiveness of occupation and make life easier for cooperative Palestinians. He placed military offices out of sight and tried to keep Israeli bureaucrats and the occupying soldiers at low profile. Dayan himself wandered the territories freely and was wont to stop and chat with Palestinians. Awad Ibrahim Awad, one of the Ishwa refugees in the Kalandia camp, told of a visit by Dayan not long after the war. Awad and his brothers, who had escaped from the Sorek Valley in a truck back in 1948, were making their living in the 1960s hauling gravel to Jerusalem. However, once the Israelis arrived with their soldiers and roadblocks, Awad found himself repeatedly stopped and forced to dump his gravel. One day Awad was among a group sitting at a Kalandia coffee house when General Dayan came by and asked to talk with them. "We said fine, come in and have some coffee with us. So he came in and he asked us how can we live together," Awad recalled. "We said we can't, because your people won't let us work." Dayan expressed some surprise and asked if the Palestinians really would be willing to come and work with the Israelis. The men said yes, pointing out there were large numbers of available workers in the West Bank, many of whom had worked in Jordan. "He said he would try to fix it."

Whether it was the plaintive talk of unemployed refugees or the need for manual labor, Israel did open up to Palestinian workers. First the territories were opened to Israelis, who were allowed free access to what had been an exclusively Arab world. Then by the end of 1967, some Palestinians were given permits to travel across the "green line" separating the occupied lands from Israel, to visit or even to work. By 1970, the need for permits gave way to virtual free access for Palestinians to travel almost anywhere in Israel. Before long, 150,000 Palestinians in the occupied territories were working in Israel and East Jerusalem. This new force of workers did construction and other menial jobs known as "black labor," the nasty work like mopping floors that Israelis did not want to do.

Mahmoud Hamdan was one of the first and most enterprising of the black laborers. His talents as a stonemason were in high demand as Israel acted quickly to "establish fact"—to move in and build a presence that would be hard to dislodge. The most immediate changes came in Jerusalem, where the Israelis moved quickly to impose Israeli law on the entire city including its eastern suburbs that were packed with Palestinians. Israel did not call it annexation, but the United Nations General Assembly saw it as an invalid change of status, and by a vote of 99 to 0 it called on Israel to rescind the action. One "fact" Mahmoud helped establish was the construction of the first Jewish housing project on the Arab side of the "green line." This sprawling stone suburb built to buttress Jerusalem was named Ramot Eshkol, after Prime Minister Levi Eshkol. It grew into a maze of high-rise apartment buildings for fifteen thousand Israelis, filling hillsides that had been loaded with barbed wire and mines and had separated Arab from Jewish territory. When the first Ramot Eshkol apartments were finished in 1970, it took low prices and subsidized loans to attract residents. "It seemed so far from the center of town," said a civil engineer who moved to the project after helping to plan it. "And most of us were afraid that Ramot Eshkol would be given back to Jordan." But the building didn't stop there. Thousands more apartments were raised in concentric rings so far beyond Ramot Eshkol that what was once a suburb is today considered part of the city core. Little more than a decade later, an Israeli newspaper could safely report that "no one—not even the political minimalists—believes that Israel will relinquish Ramot Eshkol to its former occupier."

Mahmoud Hamdan, now in his mid-thirties, established his own financial independence while helping Israel establish its facts. For nearly five years he worked building apartment houses for Israelis, employed by a Jewish contractor known by the workers as "King Stone." It was a reliable job, six days a week at what he considered a good wage. After Ramot Eshkol came his work on the apartments near Hadassah Hospital on Mount Scopus. If a strain of political tension attached to the job, a feeling of building Israel at the expense of Palestine, it was not strong enough to prevent him and tens of thousands of other Palestinians from grabbing jobs like these. "It was difficult, but everyone needed something to live," explained Mahmoud Hamdan. "And also they were treating us in a human way. We had the same rights as the Jews who were working with us."

The work brought tangible changes to refugee life. By the end of 1969, UNRWA officers were beginning to notice "small minor improvement" in living conditions at Kalandia camp because of the wages earned in Israel. The first thing most families did was put in a latrine so they wouldn't have to use a public outhouse. After almost two years of labor, Mahmoud Hamdan could afford to bring electricity to his home in 1970, a time when more than three-quarters of the camp households still did without it. In another two years, a group of families decided they were doing well enough to explore the logistics of extending piped water to their homes. They had to raise all the money themselves for the pipes, trenches, and concrete platforms for their water connections. It took them almost four more years, but in the middle of 1976 Mamhoud Hamdan's household and another 161 Kalandia families had piped water. They were the minority. Like the vast majority of other refugee camp residents, the remaining eight hundred Kalandia families still carried water in buckets from public spigots.

The new jobs made a better life possible, but something else seems to have resigned the Palestinian refugees to taking root in the West Bank after 1967 on land that was not the land of their forefathers. They went back to that land and found an alien world. The Sorek Valley fellaheen found their old hillsides filled with Yemenites and Iraqis and Moroccans and a few Sabra farmers. They felt envy, admiration, revulsion—a spectrum as complex as the changes they saw before them. On the bottomland beside the Brook of Sorek, they could watch sprinklers irrigating Kibbutz Tsora's cotton fields and peach orchards. With sprinklers like those they would never have lost their wheat crop. And young trees were growing on every incline. In the lushness of the Jewish forests they admired the coolness and shade spread over the hillsides. But they were jolted to see all their grazing land gone.

The abundance of water was the most astonishing change brought about by the Israelis. It didn't all arrive overnight, of course. A giant aqueduct from northern Israel, completed in 1964 with heavy American funding, had brought one early infusion of outside water not only to the valley but to thirsty settlements as far south as the Negev desert. Now after 1967, with Syrian howitzers driven off the Golan Heights, Israel was free to divert one-third more water into the aqueduct by channeling more of the Jordan River's northern headwaters. In the years to come, Israeli hydrologists would tap more and more water for Israeli agriculture from aquifers that lay under the West Bank. By the mid-1980s, Israel was deriving no less than one-fourth of its entire water supply from watersheds in the West Bank, at the same time it was restricting West Bank Palestinians from drilling new wells that would cut into the supply. Even with water tightly controlled throughout Israel, the ambitious farmers of Kibbutz Tsora were able by 1988 to use at least sixteen hundred gallons a day for every kibbutz resident for watering and drinking. The average Israeli was allowed four times as much as the average West Bank Palestinian. Kibbutz Tsora had discovered an additional source, the treated sewage water from metropolitan Jerusalem, which they used in great quantities to irrigate their cotton. Beginning in about 1967, the Brook of Sorek started for the first time to flow all year long. Treated but smelly waste water coursed down the stream bed to the valley, where it was contained in an artificial pond built by Kibbutz Tsora.

Mahmoud Hamdan was drawn for repeated visits, driving back as often as two or three times a year just to look and sometimes to talk with the Yemenites living where his family used to live in the village that used to be called Ishwa. "I tell them it's my land," Mahmoud said of his trips to Eshtaol. "They say no, it's theirs. Only their mukhtar comes and speaks. Once he said, 'They put us here, so we built our houses and stayed. It's not our fault.' " These visits disturbed Mahmoud, but what could he do? "It made me angry," he said. "I could only keep it inside my heart." Awad Ibrahim Awad also drove back to the Sorek Valley in 1967. He was perplexed to find the valley transformed and populated by normal people who had troubles like people everywhere. "We could not tell where our house had been," Awad said. "I talked to a Yemeni Jew. He was very old. He had two wives, and one of his wives was weeping all the time. He said it was because she had one son who died in the

Suez. I told her we are all going to die, to try and calm her down."

To the Yemenites who now lived in Eshtaol, these Arabs seemed quite out of place. "They acted like tourists," remembered Ovediah Aqwa, one of the Yemenite elders. His wife, Rachel, heard them saying that this used to be their land, but she wasn't upset by it. "They walk and they look," she said. "They come to see how much we have done here and that it is a different world altogether."

The most wrenching encounters were the reunions between the Palestinians who had lived in Artuf and the lone Hartuv Jew who still held out in the valley, seventy-two-year-old Ben-Zion Gueron. Ismail Rahhal, the Artufi who became a merchant in Bethlehem, rode the train to the Sorek Valley after the Six-Day War and found a Yemenite sitting in the very same building that had been his house. Two rooms had not been destroyed, and one was in use as an office of the Nahum settlement. The Yemenite gave him directions to the house of the last original Hartuvian who remained there. Ismail Rahhal found Ben-Zion Gueron looking much as he had nineteen years earlier. "We shook hands. I said I was the son of the mukhtar. We drank coffee and he offered us cucumbers," said Ismail, who was then thirty-seven. "We were so confused and sad. Both of us cried when we saw each other."

After 1967, Mahmoud Hamdan and Awad Ibrahim Awad started thinking about building bigger houses at Kalandia camp. In Bethlehem Ismail Rahhal thought the same.

There was one Sorek Valley Jew who was still on the front lines of the Arab-Israeli conflict. That was Yoshko Levy. The Levy family and the other Hartuvians, all but Ben-Zion Gueron, had left the valley back in 1957. Gueron continued to farm the old Hartuv land until he was eighty-two, too old to hang on any longer by himself. Yoshko and Gita Levy left partly because of the risk of war, but mostly because daily life was a trial in the absence of a school they considered suitable for their children. They never worked out a deal with the school at Kibbutz Tsora, and never became resigned to a school overflowing

with Moroccan and Yemenite immigrants who had just stepped
out of a cultural time warp. The Levys and most of the former
Hartuvians had transplanted themselves to a lush little backwater called Udim, about fifteen miles north of Tel Aviv. Still in
the army, Yoshko Levy was sent to Ecuador in 1964 as a military
adviser to help establish settlements similar to the soldier-settler
bases Israel had planted in the Negev and after 1967 in its new
territories. In Ecuador they wanted fortified settlements to combat communism in the countryside. After four years the Levy
family came back to Israel, and Lieutenant Colonel Yoshko Levy
was dispatched to the West Bank as deputy commander of the
military administration in the Nablus district. By then, August
1968, the military government was well entrenched, and excited
talk of more settlements was rife. Yoshko Levy's early—and
continuing—impression was that Israel did not plan to leave the
territories.

While Foreign Minister Abba Eban made conciliatory statements about Israel's willingness to negotiate a peace with the
Arab countries, other leaders were rejoicing in the resumption
of historic Jewish ties not just to Jerusalem, but to Nablus,
Hebron, and Jericho. Before a year elapsed, Israeli settlements
were going up on the Golan Heights, in Hebron, and at the site
of the old Etzion block, the group of Jewish colonies in the West
Bank that the Jordanians had vanquished in the 1948 war. Labor-
ite Prime Minister Eshkol, introducing a catchphrase that
would ring through Israeli political debates for decades to come,
called for new waves of Jewish immigration to settle "Greater
Israel." Meanwhile, General Yigal Allon developed a security
scheme called the Allon Plan which envisioned the annexation
of a strip twelve miles wide along the Jordan River, in addition
to greater Jerusalem, the Judean Desert, and the southern three-
quarters of the Gaza Strip. The fast takeover of Arab East Jerusalem and immediate settlement activities did not encourage the
Arab governments to enter peace negotiations, and they weren't
so inclined in the first place.

What filtered down to Israelis assigned to police the West
Bank was a sense not that this occupied land was being held in

trust for some future trade, but that it would be held for ever. Yoshko Levy certainly had that feeling. As an old-time settler who grew up among Arabs and spoke their language, Levy talked often with West Bank notables during his eighteen months as Nablus deputy commander. There were invitations to tea or dinner, but they never talked much about the future of the occupation. "We figured that one day they would be part of Israel. We had the idea that people would just get used to it. They would learn to live with us," Levy would remember. "What the final status would be we weren't discussing. They weren't talking about a Palestinian state at that time." Looking back on that period, Levy figured that Moshe Dayan was trying to win over the Palestinians to the side of Israel with enlightened policies such as opening the bridges to Jordan for commerce and letting Palestinians work inside Israel. Viewed from his headquarters, the heart of UN Resolution 242—giving land for peace—was not at the heart of this occupation. "That was a political level above us," he said. Yoshko Levy's wife, Gita, helped explain the prevailing sentiment toward United Nations formulas: "Ben-Gurion used to say, 'Let the goyim talk all they want, but we will do what we think best.' That was our thinking. They will talk and we will do."

Yoshko Levy did talk about the future sometimes with one Palestinian leader in Nablus, Hikmat al-Masri, who had been a member of the Jordanian Parliament and a Nasserite. "He would tell me, 'You're not going to be able to hold all those territories in the long run.' Me, in my naiveté, I said, 'I think we can hold it as long as we want, that the only thing that can get us out is force.' "

Keeping the territories would require more force than the Israelis ever anticipated. At the start, Dayan and his troops could quell any resistance with occasional demonstrations of Israeli power. They meted out swift and summary punishment whenever Palestinians resisted by violent means. Suspects were arrested and held without charge, deported without trial. Their houses were blown up to show that whole families must shoulder the blame for radical children. Collective punishment, in which the uninvolved suffered the same as the guilty, usually worked. Yoshko Levy sometimes ran into demonstrations on his drives around Nablus, when an entire school would seem to burst open and spew out yelling students. "I would run out toward the crowd of kids with my gun and they would run away. I never had to shoot. I never had to fire one shot," he said. If a demonstration didn't quickly disperse or if problems threatened to escalate, Levy would put a town or refugee camp under an around-the-clock curfew. No one was to leave the house, not for work or for groceries. The punishments that cowed some Palestinians fed the anger of others.

The kernel of violent opposition after the war was Yasser Arafat's Fatah, which was trying to foment a rebellion from inside the territories. The army and the Shin Bet, Israel's domestic secret police, hunted down and killed at least two hundred Palestinians they suspected of being terrorists and locked up without trial another thousand suspects by the end of 1967. They drove Arafat and Fatah out of the West Bank. Regrouping across the river in Jordan, Fatah scored one success that would win it a lasting reputation among younger West Bank Palestinians. When the Israeli army tried to demolish Fatah's command center at the East Bank town of Karameh, the guerrilla fighters pushed back the attack with the help of Jordanian artillery. Following the abysmal Arab performance in the 1967 war, this stalwart stand by a Palestinian unit brought Fatah thousands of young volunteers, largely from the populations of the grim refugee camps in Lebanon, Syria, and Jordan. Within a year, Fatah had taken control of the PLO and Yasser Arafat was its chairman. The sojourn in Jordan did not last long, however, once the more radical Palestinian factions began agitating against King Hussein. He finally responded with a drive against the PLO that started in September 1970 and turned into virtual civil war before Jordanian troops expelled the guerrillas, killing an estimated three thousand Palestinians over the next nine months while purging Jordan of the PLO presence.

Despite sporadic intrusions by PLO guerrillas who concentrated next in Syria and Lebanon, the Israelis had the territories under control by the early 1970s. Israel was absorbed in maintaining its new growth spurt brought on by the 1967 war. The occupied territories were a captive market, and by 1972 Israel was selling three times as much to the territories as it was buying from the Palestinian residents. The waves of Jewish immigrants who landed in Israel in the years after 1948 were now mostly engaged in productive work, farming, or making consumer goods or perhaps in the burgeoning defense industry that was trying to keep pace with Soviet supplies to the Arab neighbors.

Kalandia camp, home of many Sorek Valley refugees, was also absorbed in advancement. Because it was close to Jerusalem, Kalandia became a model that was displayed to hundreds of Israeli and foreign visitors through the mid-1970s. American congressmen, British peers, priests, and students from all over the world took the Kalandia tour. The refugees there not only were quiescent, they also worked together for the common good. They undertook self-help projects, expanding their mosque and building new classrooms that eliminated double shifts in the elementary school. The women started a sewing cooperative and then a store to sell pillows and hangings and gowns covered with the intricate embroidery with which Palestinian women have decorated their own dresses for generations.

Resistance quieted, but not all its strains were eliminated, not even in the model camp Kalandia. When the lash of reprisal fell, it fell heavily. One Kalandia family of fifteen learned that after one sixteen-year-old member was arrested, but not yet tried, for resistance activities. An internal report by the Jerusalem area officer of UNRWA told what happened to the family and their poultry business:

> They [the Israeli soldiers] requested all people in the area to open windows of their shelters and to move out of them. This they did very hurriedly and through the blaring announcements of loudspeakers. . . . They gave the family . . . half an hour to vacate their living compound. Before the elapse of the 30 minutes and before the family had had the opportunity to remove all of

their furniture and belongings, the explosives were placed in several places within the compound and the whole place was blown up. . . . Besides losing their compound, the family lost 10 turkeys, 25 egg-laying hens, 13 ducks, 50 rabbits, and an incubator, capacity 350 eggs.

To the Israelis and to the outside world, episodes like these were too small and scattered to cause much worry. Security was a much bigger problem outside of Israel, as Palestinian terrorists targeted Israeli airplanes and embassies around the world. In one spectacular episode in September 1970, the Popular Front for the Liberation of Palestine, a rival of Fatah, seized three commercial airliners and forced them to land at one small field in Jordan. In 1972, the attack by "Black September" guerrillas at the Munich Olympics resulted in the deaths of eleven Israeli athletes and raised new questions about the safety of Israeli citizens. Perhaps Israeli authorities were diverted by these attacks, or perhaps they were just less vigilant after their own superior performance on the field of battle during six days one June. They were not ready for the 1973 war.

The Yom Kippur War was the creation of Anwar Sadat, the Egyptian president who took over when Nasser died of a heart attack in 1970. Sadat and Syrian President Hafez al-Asad employed secrecy, subterfuge, and a buildup of Soviet aircraft and missiles to stun Israel into recognizing its continued vulnerability. The strategy was to gain a battlefield advantage and then win through diplomatic means the return of Syrian and Egyptian territory that Israel had captured in the 1967 war. Egypt and Syria did gain the upper hand for several days after the surprise attack on October 6, 1973, the Jewish holy day of Yom Kippur. But the Israelis fought doggedly north and south, and President Nixon's emergency airlift of $825 million worth of American military equipment saved them. By the time the Syrians and Egyptians agreed to a cease-fire almost three weeks later, Israel had gained back roughly the same territory the Arabs had retaken in the first days of fighting. The Arabs had lost the war, but restored their honor by fighting well. Israel had won, but the war called into question whether it could endure forever by military preparedness alone. And it had suffered more than 2,500 dead, almost four times as many as in the Six-Day War. The 1973 war hit home in the Sorek Valley, where Kibbutz Tsora mourned seven men, the youngest nineteen and the oldest twenty-nine. During the Six-Day War, Kibbutz Tsora did not lose a single soldier.

Already wounded by events of the 1973 war, the Israelis were in no mood to encourage the new spurt of Palestinian political activism that was beginning to appear. The PLO had set up a new Palestinian National Front inside the territories to coordinate the work of the factions organizing in the West Bank and Gaza. King Hussein's failure to join the Yom Kippur War had compounded the betrayal Palestinians felt after he drove the PLO from Jordan. Activists now were convinced that if somehow Israel could be dislodged, the West Bank should not be rejoined to Jordan. Instead, the new National Front was trying to lay foundations for a Palestinian state. Israel tried to nip off that possibility by deporting eight of its members. The Palestinians responded with demonstrations, just as they would do over the next few years whenever there came a PLO action and what they considered Israeli repression in answer. Students marched and merchants closed shops to mark the appearance of Yasser Arafat before the UN General Assembly in November 1974. Israel's next move was to deport five leading Palestinians, including Hanna Nasir, the president of Bir Zeit University, one of the new West Bank universities seeding nationalistic sentiment. In 1976 Palestinians turned out in force for local elections and filled their councils and mayoralties with pro-PLO candidates. By 1981, Israel would have removed all the activist mayors from office.

The revival of dormant strains of resistance happened in Kalandia, too. The same thoroughfare that placed Kalandia adults close to jobs in Jerusalem placed Kalandia youths in ideal position to lob rocks at passing settlers and at soldiers en route to their headquarters up the road. Israelis countered demonstrations, here as elsewhere, by shutting down schools for a cool-off break or harassing young people wherever they concentrated.

Mahmoud Hamdan made his own quiet stand for personal—if not territorial—independence when he stopped working for the Israelis. He and a coworker who had some savings didn't like the new attitude of Israeli bosses to Palestinian workers after the 1973 war. "There were some problems," Mahmoud said. "And we were apprehensive. They were insulting us. We didn't like it, so we just left." The pair bought some lumber and other building materials and started their own construction business, working only on West Bank projects for Palestinians. An after-hours project was expanding the old two-room shelter he and his father had built in the 1950s, adding rooms and another small building for his growing family. Mahmoud Hamdan enclosed it all with a cement-covered wall of cinder blocks, as though he could encapsulate his family from the conflict bubbling up with new frequency now, like spits of fire from volcanic gases roiling underground.

· 21 ·

A SHOT
IN THE FACE

fter thirty years, the last filaments of their hope to regain the old soil were disappearing. For most of the middle-aged Sorek Valley exiles, the years had bent their rage into a kind of nostalgia. Their land was the best land in Palestine, they told their children. Some of the Palestinian refugees still motored back to the valley every harvest season to pay the Yemenites for the privilege of picking olives from the old Ishwa groves and from the newer olive trees the Jewish National Fund had planted. One season, Mahmoud Hamdan's cousin joined five other Ishwa old-timers in picking enough of the bitter green fruit to make six hundred kilos of olive oil.

Just when the rage of the middle-aged refugees was cooling, along came their sons and daughters to restoke the embers. Hassan Hamdan, Mahmoud's son, was in the first generation of Sorek Valley refugees to try to fight back. In 1979, Hassan threw his first rock at an Israeli soldier. He was twelve years old. "We used to go out from school to the main street of the camp, where the Israeli patrols were waiting," Hassan remembered. "We would clash with them. We used to demonstrate on national days, like the anniversary of the Balfour Declaration." The world paid no attention at the time, but defiance was a clue to the mood of a new generation. What would happen to Hassan Hamdan in the early and middle 1980s would help to explain the intifada, the Palestinian uprising that seemed to burst with no warning at the end of the decade. It is the story of one boy's intifada.

The toil of Mahmoud Hamdan's generation had given their children the luxuries of time and of education that are so often prerequisites for revolutionary thought. When Mahmoud was twelve, he had finished the fifth grade at the Sorek Valley school-house and he was tending goats. When he was thirteen he would be driven out of his village to begin a life of cutting stones in quarries and lifting them at construction sites. His effort, combined with UNRWA's, had freed his children from privation. "Before, the people were poorer," Mahmoud said. "They only wanted something to eat. Now they can live. So that allows them to think." His son Hassan would also come to that realization. "In the beginning," Hassan said, "people were so traumatized by tragedies. All they were thinking of was something to feed their children. They were not thinking of occupation or liberating themselves, getting a state of their own. But the new generation is educated. You cannot find one house where the young people are not educated."

When Hassan began in the Kalandia boys' grammar school in the mid-1970s, Israeli troops were inconspicuous on the West Bank. What worried Israelis then about the UNRWA camps was that they sometimes harbored PLO guerrillas. Early in 1979, the Israelis arrested one Fatah ring in Kalandia which had six kilograms of Semtex, enough of the plastic explosive to smash the biggest building in Jerusalem. But as long as the Shin Bet could keep the few terrorist cells under surveillance, the army didn't worry much about occasional rock throwing. Typically, the first foray in which Hassan participated, the Balfour Day protest in 1979, drew no Israeli gunfire and no reprisals. It would be another five months before the next outbreak of stone-throwing at Kalandia. That time, the military governor told UNRWA

that it would have to cancel a cross-country running race the
Kalandia staff was planning.

By the time Hassan threw his first rock, events were already
combining to start a stronger cycle of Palestinian demonstration and Israeli repression. The victory of Menachem Begin's
right-wing Likud bloc in the 1977 election had brought militant
Jewish settlers to previously all-Arab portions of the West
Bank, Gaza, and Sinai. The 1978 Camp David agreement meant
they had to give up their designs to colonize the Sinai, which
Prime Minister Begin had agreed to turn back to Egypt in
exchange for a peace treaty. To the settlers, Camp David was
a stimulus to plant their roots even deeper on the West Bank
and Gaza. To the Palestinians, Camp David meant they had
lost the support of Egypt and were being pressured by the
Americans to accept subservience to Israel for the indefinite
future under the name of "autonomy." As they saw it, "autonomy" meant nothing more than granting the Palestinians the
right to collect taxes and supervise their own garbage collec-
tion.

One confrontation followed another as the Israelis bought up
or simply confiscated West Bank land and water sources. To the
more ideological of the Israeli settlers, taking the West Bank was
justified because Moses had told his followers that God had
promised the land of Canaan to the Israelites. They viewed the
word of Moses as a "higher law" which overrode any man-made
codes, such as the bans in the Hague and Geneva conventions
against an occupying power grabbing the wealth of an occupied
country. To the younger Palestinians, the spread of ideological
settlements in the West Bank and Gaza looked exactly like the
creeping encroachment that cost their grandfathers the other
four-fifths of Palestine between 1920 and 1948.

The drumbeat of these controversies resonated among local
Palestinian activists, causing many of them to see the West
Bank and Gaza for the first time as the crux of the Palestinian
claim to nationhood. For this generation of Palestinians, it
seemed less important to pine about the old villages inside Israel than to "liberate" the refugee camps and villages where

Palestinian nationalism still had a toehold. This led to a gain in sympathy for the PLO and a fall in the popularity of the traditional West Bank Arab notables who were amenable to cooperating with both King Hussein and with Israeli occupation authorities.

The violence was set off by the founding of a settlement inside the Arab city of Hebron, a city long permeated by Arab nationalistic fervor. The settlers were members of Gush Emunim, a messianic offshoot of Israel's National Religious Party whose name literally meant "Block of the Faithful." The only way for Jews to reach their destiny, they believed, was to settle the "whole land of Israel." They chose to build in Hebron's downtown Casbah in order to re-establish a Jewish presence and to avenge the murder of sixty Jews in Hebron during the 1929 riots. After months of tit-for-tat incidents between Hebron Arabs and Gush Emunim settlers, six Jews were murdered in May 1980 in an ambush. A month later, Jewish vigilantes retaliated by planting bombs in the cars of three West Bank Palestinian mayors suspected of PLO sympathies. The mayor of Nablus had both legs blown off, and the mayor of Ramallah lost one foot. Both refused Israeli medical treatment and were taken to hospitals in Jordan. They would return to the West Bank as Palestinian heroes.

Hassan's life was touched at this time by an obscure change of tactics by Yasser Arafat's Fatah branch of the PLO. One Kalandia Fatah member a few years older than Hassan recalled what happened: "In 1980, there were instructions from the outside to organize a youth movement. Before that, Fatah only had secret cells." The Fatah youth groups which took shape in various refugee camps and villages were called Shabiba—an Arabic word meaning "youth." Fatah's Shabiba bore a certain resemblance to the labor Zionists' Pioneer Movement which attracted Ikki Nir in the 1940s, in that both were patriotic boys' clubs with ties to an illegal underground fighting force. There were differences between the Shabiba and the Pioneers, of course. One of them was that the Shabiba was never quite accepted by the older generations of Palestinians because Shabiba was itself a fighting

force, even if the weapons were only stones. When the thirteen-
or fourteen-year-old Hassan began mixing with Shabiba groups,
he never told his father.

As the Shabiba groups were springing up in the camps, a
change in the direction of the Israeli government gave Hassan's
life a further push toward activism. Just as the Hebron controversy was developing, the resignations of two relative moderates
removed an element of restraint from the Begin cabinet. With
the departures of Foreign Minister Moshe Dayan in late 1979
and Defense Minister Ezer Weizman in the spring of 1980, the
government became increasingly dominated by zealots led by
Begin himself and Agriculture Minister Ariel Sharon.

The Sorek Valley—Hassan's parents' birthplace—provided
some of the earliest indications that Israel's swing to the right
was not an aberration soon to be reversed. A new Israeli election
was called for the summer of 1981. In the previous election four
years earlier, Israeli Jews had parted along class and religious
lines. The Sephardic lower-middle class had given Begin's
Likud bloc its first victory over the European Ashkenazi Jews
who spearheaded the old-line Labor Alliance. As the campaign
of 1981 unfolded, Labor candidate Shimon Peres remained the
darling of Kibbutz Tsora, the old Palmach settlement on one
side of the valley which was still populated by the Ashkenazi
elite. But for every Ashkenazi Jew in Tsora, about twenty-five
Moroccan, Yemenite, and other Oriental Jews lived on the other
side of the valley in Beth Shemesh. Begin received a rhapsodic
welcome in Beth Shemesh, as crowds of lower-middle-class
Moroccans chanted "Begin, King of the Jews." By contrast,
Peres was heckled by claques of rowdies and pelted with
tomatoes at a Beth Shemesh rally. Later, Moroccan activists
from Beth Shemesh were among the hecklers who pursued
Peres to his big outdoor rally in Jerusalem, booing and shouting
and throwing vegetables until Peres was forced to stop speaking. Exasperated, he later called some hecklers "Khomeinistis"
and said they ought to return to their home countries. It was a
slur which Israel's Oriental Jews would never forgive Peres. By
the early 1980s, 60 percent of Israeli Jews traced their heritage

to Morocco, Yemen, Iran, Iraq, and other Moslem countries. Voting almost solidly for Begin, they gave Likud a thin plurality. Begin went on to form a "narrow" coalition with three Jewish religious parties, pushing Israel even farther to the right.

Israeli writer and novelist Amos Oz visited Beth Shemesh after the election to find out more about the enmity which seemed to be wrenching one class of Jews from another. In Beth Shemesh people spilled their bitterness against "whites"—the Ashkenazim who had dominated Israeli culture and politics since independence. A good deal of it was aimed across the valley at Kibbutz Tsora. "Before every election," one Moroccan told him, "the kibbutzniks show up here—Tsora and all the others—to ask for our votes. You go tell your friends: unless they let us come to Kibbutz Tsora when we want, to swim in their pool and play tennis and go out with their daughters; until they accept the children of Beth Shemesh in their school or bring their kids to school here instead of dragging them a hundred kilometers by bus to some white school; until they stop being so snooty, they've got nothing to look for here. We're for Begin."

Oz found that the lower-middle-class Beth Shemeshites were not only envious of those above them but also afraid that they would get pushed down into an economic underclass if the Ashkenazi establishment had its way. What Oz wrote in his notebook revealed a fear of losing their hold on the economic ladder if Israel traded away the occupied territories in a peace settlement:

> In the army, we Moroccans are the corporals and the officers are from the kibbutz. All my life I've been on the bottom and you've been on the top. . . . What did they bring my parents to Israel for? . . . Wasn't it to do your dirty work? You didn't have Arabs then, so you needed our parents to do your cleaning and be your servants and your laborers. And policemen, too. You brought our parents to be your Arabs. But now I'm supervisor. . . . If they give back the territories, the Arabs will stop coming to work and then and there you'll put us back into the dead-end jobs, like before. If for no other reason, we won't let you give back

those territories. Not to mention the rights we have from the Bible, or security. Look at my daughter: she works in a bank now, and every evening an Arab comes to clean the building. All you want is to dump her back from the bank into some textile factory, or have her wash the floors instead of the Arab. The way my mother used to clean for you. That's why we hate you here. As long as Begin's in power, my daughter's secure at the bank. If you guys come back in, you'll pull her down first thing.

His mandate secure, Begin moved defiantly toward annexing "Judea and Samaria"—the biblical names he always applied when talking about the Israeli-occupied West Bank. Begin announced late in 1981 that he was placing Judea and Samaria under a "civilian administration." In practical terms, it meant the land would no longer be administered as a temporary conquest but as a permanent part of Israel. Begin also turned the defense ministry over to two ultra-hawks who believed that the Palestinians should be suppressed, not accommodated the way Moshe Dayan had tried when he was defense minister fifteen years earlier. As defense minister, Begin named Ariel Sharon, an ex-general whose army career had been clouded by charges of insubordination and brutality to Palestinians in the Gaza Strip. Begin and Sharon went on to retain the incumbent Lieutenant General "Raful" Eytan as chief of staff—a position he held already under the first Begin cabinet.

Hassan, the son of a Sorek Valley refugee, was now on a collision course with one of the Sorek Valley's captors. Raful was the platoon leader who captured the Hartuv police station in 1948. Since then, he had risen to the top of the army. He was the first paratrooper to jump when Israel seized the Mitla Pass from Egypt in the 1956 war. In 1968, he led the Israeli commando team which blew up thirteen Arab-owned airliners in Beirut after the hijacking of an El Al jet. During the 1973 war, he commanded the tank breakthrough that saved the Golan Heights from being recaptured by Syria. As chief of staff, his duty was to defend Israel from all comers, even if the foes were boys throwing rocks.

When the Begin government began to impose its "civilian

administration" on the West Bank, Palestinian activists organized a "mini-uprising." Though it lasted only three months, it
was the most sustained show of homegrown Palestinian resistance in fifteen years of Israeli occupation. The protests began at
Bir Zeit University, many of whose student leaders and professors were PLO sympathizers. In February, some students struck
an Israeli civilian official who entered the Bir Zeit campus. The
army ordered Bir Zeit shut down for two months. Dismissed
from their campuses, the Bir Zeit students organized a few more
protests at other West Bank colleges and in their own villages
and refugee camps. Israeli authorities thought they could contain this first ripple of demonstrations by outlawing the National Guidance Committee, an alliance of the nationalist-
minded West Bank mayors who had been elected in 1976. A week
later, the Israelis deposed the mayor of al-Bireh, a town two
miles from Kalandia, for refusing to deal with the civil administration.

Leaders of other West Bank municipalities called a three-day
general strike, leading to a burst of nationalist demonstrations
and clashes with settlers. Kalandia was in the forefront. Hassan
and other teenagers burned tires, blocked roads, and drew
bursts of gunfire from Israeli troops. After arresting a dozen
Kalandia teenagers, the soldiers tried to teach the camp a lesson
by shooting holes in solar panels and water reservoirs on the
roofs of ten refugees' houses. Hassan escaped without a scratch,
and so did his father's house. But elsewhere in the West Bank,
troops shot and killed six Palestinian demonstrators. Demonstrations echoed into the Gaza Strip and even into a few Arab
communities inside Israel. Menachem Milson, the Israeli "civilian administrator" of the West Bank, was quoted as calling the
disturbances "the most significant battle Israel has had to wage
politically since its creation in 1948."

As low-level protests dragged on, Eytan ordered a new crackdown. He called for large-scale arrests and specified that there
must be no more advance warnings to the local Arab notables.
For "problematic localities" there must be "extensive use of
economic sanctions," including cutoffs of fuel oil and cement

deliveries. Inciters must be "harassed": they should be arrested, detained for the allowable eighteen days of preventive detention, and then released, only to be rearrested a few days later. Furthermore, Arabs must be told that the settlers had guns and were authorized to use them.

Despite the crackdown, teenagers kept throwing stones and blocking roads, even after a dozen Palestinians had been killed and nearly two hundred wounded. The impudence of the Arabs was too much for Alan Harry Goodman, a thirty-eight-year-old Israeli soldier who had emigrated from Baltimore and come under the influence of Rabbi Meir Kahane's extremist Kach Movement. On Easter Sunday, Goodman went on a rampage at the al-Aqsa Mosque, killing two Palestinians with his M-16 rifle and wounding more than a dozen others. "I had to do it," Goodman told an Israeli policeman. "They are killing my friends and family." The Goodman shootings set off several more weeks of Palestinian demonstrations in East Jerusalem and the West Bank, with youngsters holding up Palestinian flags and chanting "Palestine is Arab," "Jews out," and "God is great."

Three decades had passed without any Palestinian from the Sorek Valley writing an Op-Ed piece in the *New York Times*, hijacking an airplane, or otherwise getting noticed. But now Hassan was about to attract his instant of attention. The pro-PLO underground in the West Bank had designated April 25 as a strike day, and the Kalandia Shabiba responded. An Israeli newspaper described the scene: "Crowds of youths waving Palestinian flags and wielding staves and knives clashed with border policemen in the early afternoon." When the border policemen started shooting, Hassan and other demonstrators ran up the winding alleys toward the back of the camp. The border policemen, carrying out Eytan's order for large-scale arrests, gave chase while a military helicopter flew overhead. The border policemen pursued Hassan and other teenagers more than half a mile until they reached a valley beyond the camp's rear boundary. There the Palestinians regrouped. Some of the boys began throwing more stones at the border police, an UNRWA camp employee reported. Hassan glimpsed an Israeli sharpshooter about fifty meters away. The Israeli seemed to be taking aim directly at him.

The bullet plowed into his right cheek an inch below his eye. Bleeding and unconscious, Hassan was driven to the al-Makassed Hospital in East Jerusalem, where a spokesman told Israeli reporters his condition was "very serious." He had avoided being killed or blinded by about half an inch. What he didn't avoid was disfigurement. The bullet shattered his cheekbone, and the surgeon had no time for fancy operations to repair it. When Hassan later took off his bandages, he found a permanent indentation big enough to hold the pit of a plum beside his right eye. The surgeon also left a ragged crow's-foot scar about four inches long on his right temple. Hassan could still see, but his right eye had a tendency to roll back into its socket. He was deaf in his right ear.

For a boy from a refugee camp, plastic surgery and psychological counseling were not available. The therapy he chose was the same one that hundreds of other wounded Palestinians would choose during the intifada of the late 1980s—to fight harder. "When I was wounded, I lost everything," Hassan would explain. "The face is the most beautiful thing. The only course left to me was to continue struggling."

The Israelis thought they had the answer to unrest: eliminate the sanctuaries in Lebanon where the PLO had concentrated after its eviction from Jordan. Hassan was still recuperating on June 6, 1982, the day Sharon sent tanks into Lebanon for "Operation Peace for the Galilee." Sharon and Eytan had been preparing to invade Lebanon for at least six months. They had reached an understanding with one Lebanese politician who hated the PLO almost as much as they did, Bashir Gemayel, who was commander of the neofascist Christian militia called the Phalange. Sharon told Gemayel he was thinking of moving Israeli troops to the edge of Beirut provided the Phalangists would cooperate by taking over the heart of the city. Gemayel said yes. Now all Sharon needed was a pretext to overcome the inevitable objections of the Reagan administration. The pretext came when Israel's ambassador in London was shot and wounded by a hit team sent by Palestinian Abu Nidal's free-lance terrorist organization.

Israeli intelligence learned that the object of Abu Nidal's "hit" was to provoke Israel to attack the Lebanese base camps of his enemy Yasser Arafat. Whatever the motivation, Begin and Sharon seized the opportunity to strike at Arafat. The Israelis rolled into the PLO's stronghold in southern Lebanon and kept advancing north toward Beirut. Israeli forces pushed on to link up with the Phalangists on the outskirts of Beirut, thus trapping fifteen thousand of Arafat's guerrillas in West Beirut. After two months of Israeli bombing and shelling, Arafat agreed to withdraw his fighters under an American-mediated deal that dispersed the PLO cadres to Tunisia and ten other countries.

On September 12, 1982, Sharon's master plan moved another notch forward. His Lebanese protégé, Bashir Gemayel, now president-elect of Lebanon, assured Sharon in person that the Phalangists would "clean out" some two thousand PLO guerrillas they suspected were still hiding in West Beirut Palestinian refugee camps. Two days later, Gemayel was blown to bits in East Beirut by a pro-Syrian assassin. Shaken, Sharon ordered Eytan to arrange for Phalangist militiamen to enter the Sabra and Shatila refugee camps. Over the next two days, the Christian Phalangists methodically killed between seven hundred and three thousand men, women, and children while Israeli troops held positions outside the camps. Later, an Israeli inquiry commission blamed Sharon, Eytan, and Yitzhak Shamir, future Israeli prime minister and at the time the foreign minister, for failing to act once they had been told that a massacre was occurring.

The Palestinian university students who had led the West Bank's "mini-uprising" were stunned by Lebanon. Large-scale demonstrations quieted almost overnight, and the scattering of smaller protests was lost in the blur of more dramatic developments in Lebanon. By all outward appearances, the 1982 demonstrations ended in total victory for Sharon and Eytan. But other forces were at work. Among Israeli Jews, Sabra and Shatila swelled the followers of the small "Peace Now" movement until

400,000 people—one-eighth of the country's Jewish population—turned out for a rally in Tel Aviv. Then Lebanese Shia
militias began to fight back, swelling the list of Israeli service-
men killed in Lebanon to nearly five hundred in six months of
combat. Israeli revulsion against the war forced the resignations
of Sharon and then Begin, who had been certain the war would
last only a few days. Following an indecisive Israeli national
election in 1984, most Israeli forces withdrew from Lebanon in
1985.

As long as Israel was in the grip of the war in Lebanon, few
outsiders noticed the West Bank and Gaza. But the coals of
Palestinian resistance were still glowing. From 1982 onward,
there wouldn't be another year in the decade without at least
three thousand incidents of rock-throwing, tire-burning, or
other violent protests—six times the pace of such incidents in
the late 1970s. Meron Benvenisti, an Israeli researcher who followed the West Bank, noticed a trend as the decade progressed.
For every "terrorist" incident engineered by the PLO outside
the occupied territories, homegrown Palestinians were causing
more and more "spontaneous" disturbances. "Violence is
largely carried out in broad daylight by individuals and groups
who spontaneously express their feelings, undeterred by the
consequence of their actions," Benvenisti remarked.

Thousands of boys had been drawn into Fatah's youth corps
and the rival youth affiliates of other PLO and Moslem funda-
mentalist factions. The angriest of the 1982 stone-throwers went
underground and kept up the fight. One of these was Hassan.
The disfigured teenager and six other Kalandia youths continued their affiliation with the Shabiba and went on to form
what they called a Fatah cell. It included two boys with Sorek
Valley roots, Hassan and his friend Abdullah Abu Latifah,
whose parents had lived up the hill in Saraa. "The beginning
was with my friends," Hassan said. "We used to encourage each
other to clash with the soldiers by throwing stones at patrols."
Once in the spring of 1983, boys from his and other camps and
towns along the Jerusalem-to-Nablus road threw enough rocks
to cause Knesset members to question General Eytan in a closed

session. Hassan and his friends were the ones Eytan was talking about when he made his memorably crude pronouncement to the committee: "We shall create facts, the settlements will be established, and then the Arab stone-throwers will scurry around like cockroaches in a bottle."

Hassan and his friends did more than scurry. "We got training on making Molotov cocktails and on arms and on organizing others," he said. They found an older youth from Kalandia who taught them how to stuff wicks in gasoline bottles to make Molotovs. Someone else told them about a place in Jerusalem where they could buy pistols. They talked about how the Palestinians would never win until they got rid of "collaborators." They were sure that Shin Bet found its informers in the camp by penetrating a small-scale hashish ring which operated there. Hassan and his friends decided there was only one thing to do: bomb it. "There was a little shop at the entrance to the camp where there were drug traffickers and collaborators," Hassan said. "It was a place that was bad for the morals of the people, so we threw a Molotov cocktail on it." After causing a small fire in the shop, Hassan and his friends planned another attack on a Number 42 Egged Bus, a line used by Israeli setters. "We did not succeed," he remembered. "For some reason the bus did not pass." Another frustration was that they wanted to find a way to contact the PLO, now headquartered in Tunis, but they didn't know how. Throughout these years of activism, Hassan did not have much sympathy at home for his exploits. His father, Mahmoud, who wanted only to continue what had become a peaceful and relatively prosperous life, knew virtually nothing about Hassan's activities until he was shot. Afterward, he failed in his pained attempts to keep him away from danger. "I didn't know what he was. He used to go out and come back and say he was with his friends," Mahmoud recalled. "It was only when he was injured that I realized. I used to try to convince him to calm down. It was of no use."

On April 22, 1984, about thirty Israeli troops surrounded his father's house in Kalandia. They knocked down the door and arrested Hassan, who had just passed his seventeenth birthday.

Within twenty-four hours, five of his six companions in the Fatah cell were captured and the three revolvers they had bought in Jerusalem were seized. The seventh member of their cell was picked up later as he was returning from college in Rumania. "It seems they had collaborators," Hassan said later. Hassan was confined and questioned for fifty-one days at the Ramallah jail. By his account, his Israeli plainclothes interrogators forced him to stand dripping wet in the cold, punched him in the head, and kicked him in the groin. He said one Israeli gave him an injection in the abdomen and told him it would make him sterile. Over and over, he was told there was only one way to make the questions stop. That was to agree to become an informer for Shin Bet. Hassan refused. Eventually, he did break down and admit he was a member of Fatah. An Israeli military trial later convicted him of possessing arms, making Molotov cocktails, throwing stones, and belonging to Fatah, which Israel considered an illegal terrorist organization. He was sentenced to serve three years in Jnaid Prison, with another four years suspended.

Yasser Arafat couldn't have designed a better PLO training camp. With the possible exception of Bir Zeit University, Jnaid and other military prisons were the largest collections of impressionable young Palestinian activists anywhere in the occupied territories. In the course of the Israelis' efforts to eradicate the unrest of the early 1980s, they removed hundreds of teenagers from their parents' restraining influence and dumped them into an environment where adult PLO militants had the upper hand. Just as the British prisons had hardened the fiber of the Zionists in the 1940s, so Israeli prisons helped incubate the intifada of the late 1980s. For Hassan, as for many other children from peasant backgrounds, Jnaid Prison was the first exposure to the intellectual basis of Palestinian nationalism. "The national feeling and enthusiasm is born inside us," Hassan said, "but the details of the political cause of the Palestinian revolution came during the time I was in prison."

One lesson in nationalism was the Jnaid prison hunger strike in the fall of 1984. Hassan would remember the strike as a time when Fatah and its rival PLO factions worked together in a unified prisoner organization to demand better prison conditions. To their surprise, the committee actually won some concessions. The prisoners held out until Chaim Bar-Lev, a Labor Party member who was prisons minister, listened personally to complaints of prisoners' representatives. In the minds of the prisoners, it meant that Israel had "recognized" their committee, an event which they celebrated as unprecedented recognition of a PLO-affiliated organization. The prison administrators also allowed prisoners to possess transistor radios—one of the few demands which could be met without constructing a new prison. Whether or not Bar-Lev realized it, the main consequence was that the Palestinian prisoners could now listen to the daily broadcasts of the Voice of the Revolution, the PLO's radio in Baghdad.

Following its first success, the Jnaid prison committee went on to organize a clandestine "unified leadership" within the prison. This and comparable prisoner organizations in other Israeli military prisons went largely unnoticed. But as Hassan has described the Jnaid organization, it bore a striking resemblance to the "Unified National Leadership" that would spring to life three years later to guide the uprising in the West Bank and Gaza. "On the top there was a central committee composed of representatives of each of the factions," Hassan remembered. "The central committee members were from sixteen to forty years old. Below it were other branches, among them an administrative committee, a cultural committee, and a security committee. In each cell block, the cultural committee and the other committees would have a branch. In fact, there was a representative of the prison committee in each cell."

Hassan achieved more in prison than learning nationalist slogans. He also finished high school and even dreamed of going to college and becoming a doctor. The Israeli prison authorities allowed well-behaved inmates to take high school examinations in prison, which were administered throughout the West Bank by the Jordanian education ministry. Hassan passed the *tawjihi*, as the comprehensive exams are called, with an above-average grade in the 80s.

In April 1987, Hassan Hamdan returned to Kalandia with a longer list of heroes. One thing hadn't changed: he still called "Abu Ammar"—the PLO *nom de guerre* of Yasser Arafat—his "idol." But three years in prison had added two more Palestinians to his list. One was Sheikh Izzed Din al-Kassam, the charismatic Palestinian religious figure who began a Palestinian peasant uprising and was killed by British police in 1935. The second was a convicted PLO commando named Mohammed Lufti Yassin, whom he had met in prison. Yassin had been in prison since he was captured by the Israelis during a raid on Israel in the mid-1960s. During the Jnaid hunger strike, Yassin had been one of the chief organizers.

"I admired him," said Hassan. "He spent eighteen years in prison and then he refused to leave when he had the chance to get out in a prisoner exchange. Finally, the Israelis had to deport him to get him to leave."

· 22 ·

"WE'LL
FALL APART
BEFORE THEY WILL"

*J*amal Abu Latifah, an invisible minnow of the Palestinian struggle, was about to help start a tidal wave. This unexpected uprising would reach every one of the valley's exile families—the Palestinians and the Jews of Hartuv as well. The vibrations would reach even into the Sorek Valley, though the valley was well inside the bounds of Israel.

Geographic coincidence put Jamal in a place where the weight of one minnow could make a difference. More than a decade earlier, UNRWA had built a boys' vocational school on one corner of Kalandia camp. Now when a refugee boy anywhere in the occupied territories wanted to become an auto mechanic he would apply to the Kalandia Vocational Training Center. The Kalandia VTC—that was its nickname—was a quarter of a mile from the refugee shelter where Jamal lived with his family. This meant Jamal was one of the few underground PLO leaders on the West Bank who could meet face to face with comrades from the Gaza Strip on the first day of the intifada.

Already Jamal was a revolutionary-in-waiting. Unlike his friend Hassan Hamdan and most other Palestinian youngsters,

Jamal had been encouraged since childhood to keep the Palestinian cause alive. His father, Diab, boiled with determination
that his nine sons and a daughter would never forget what the
family had lost when they were evicted from the Sorek Valley.
To Diab, 1948 was still a crimson scar. Decades after the family
had moved out of their UNRWA tent, Diab kept his first two
tent poles displayed in the front yard in honor of France and
India, the countries that supplied them. Diab liked to say that
except for a few foreign aid workers, nobody ever gave anything
to the Palestinians. Anything else they wanted, Diab said, they
would have to take for themselves. In 1983, Diab hired a bus to
transport his children, grandchildren, and in-laws for a visit to
the ruins of Saraa, his destroyed village now inside Israel. Why
did he do it? Because, he once explained, he wanted his kin to
remember always "that this is my land, this is my father's land,
and my grandfather's land and his grandfather's."

Diab's wife, Sabiha, worried sometimes that her sons would
soak up too much of his rage. Not that she didn't have her own
daydreams about the valley: about the china dishes she had left
behind, about fields of grain and vines loaded with sweet grapes.
But for her children's safety, she tried to put a sour coating on
the memories. "We didn't have any land or any house in Saraa,
we lived in caves," she would sometimes claim. Her stories
never lulled Jamal. At the age of thirteen he had been caught
belonging to a Fatah cell which was hiding explosives. That first
time, the Israelis sent him to prison for a year and a half. He
went to jail twice more while he was growing up.

Now, at the age of twenty-four, Jamal was home in Kalandia
a third time, struggling on as one of the two leaders of the
camp's underground Fatah faction. His above-ground job was
working part-time as a journalist. Young, nationalistic prison
veterans like Jamal were the camp's leaders, replacing the older
refugees who had agitated in the 1970s for better rations and
paved roads. "They became our parents, so to speak," remembered one Kalandia student then going to Bir Zeit University.
"When they came out of jail, they were the ones who instructed
us on what is right and what is wrong, what to do and what not

to do, and what is good for Palestinian nationalism. They became the nucleus of the leadership of the camp."

On December 8, 1987, the news reached Kalandia that an Israeli semi-trailer had plowed into a line of cars in the Gaza Strip, killing four Palestinians returning from work in Israel. The radio called it an accident, but rumors slid from one knot of refugees to another that it was some kind of revenge. The dominant rumor in Gaza was that the truck had been driven by a cousin of an Israeli stabbed to death while shopping in Gaza City. Kalandia heard an entirely different rumor. Kalandia heard that settlers were avenging the "night of the glider," in which six Israeli soldiers had been killed by a PLO commando who penetrated into northern Israel aboard a motorized hang glider.

The day after the Gaza truck episode, the radio reported that another Gazan had been killed, this one shot by an Israeli soldier. He was among a crowd of mourners who threw rocks at an Israeli patrol truck near the Jabalya refugee camp where the four truck victims lived. An Israeli junior officer and several of his soldiers jumped out to pursue the stone-throwers into Jabalya. Inside the camp, the Israelis found themselves surrounded by jeering refugees. The officer saw two flying bottles and assumed they were Molotov cocktails. Rather than wait to see if one would clink at his feet and explode, he fired into the crowd. Hatem al-Sisi, seventeen, died with a bullet through the heart, the first casualty of the intifada.

Sixty miles to the northwest, several young Gaza Palestinians studying at the Kalandia VTC heard about Sisi's death. They slipped out a gate and walked into the twisted alleys of Kalandia camp. Since the Gaza students were members of Fatah, it was only natural that they found Jamal Abu Latifah. There in Kalandia, Jamal and the Gazans and a few other obscure Fatah sublieutenants held the first known meeting of an "underground leadership" of the intifada. They had no sense that they were doing something historic, but they were full of spunk. "We had an extremely nationalistic feeling," remembered Abu Nour, one of the participants. By his recollection, Jamal and the others were inspired by the bravery of "the Palestinian Rambo," their name for the pilot in the glider raid. They were also enraged about the recent Arab summit meeting in Amman, which had all but ignored the Palestinian question. Without waiting to see whether Yasser Arafat might issue some directive from afar, they decided to take nationalism in their own hands. "We decided to close the main road to Ramallah," remembered Abu Nour.

Early the next morning, there was hubbub inside the Kalandia VTC as the Gaza student activists marched around the walled schoolyard, some shouting PLO chants and others chiming in with rival slogans of Islamic fundamentalist student organizations. Meanwhile, camp activists ran from one tiny storefront shop to the next, telling proprietors to close immediately for a one-day strike. After the UNRWA staff canceled classes, the released students joined the activists and found abundant ammunition in the schoolyard. "I looked out and there were a hundred people in the VTC throwing stones at Israeli cars," Abu Nour remembered. "All of a sudden the youths of the camp responded." Rocks flew from the training center on one side of the road and from Kalandia camp on the other. The road they had in a crossfire was a main thoroughfare used by Israelis for traveling between Jerusalem and Jewish settlements north of Ramallah. In minutes, Israeli border policemen and Jerusalem municipal police converged on the VTC. Six policemen were "lightly injured" by flying stones, the *Jerusalem Post* recorded. "Several" Palestinian students were also injured as the police broke into the school "using clubs and tear gas to break up the disturbance." On the Palestinian side of the lines, the episode would be remembered as more like a Kalandian Fort Sumter. "I am honored to say we had more than twenty injuries here in Kalandia camp, mostly from tear gas and some from rubber bullets," said Abu Nour.

Kalandia was one of the two or three places where the uprising breached the breakwater at the Gaza Strip boundary and began overflowing into the West Bank. On the same day as the first Kalandia protest, demonstrators also streamed through Nablus and the nearby Balata refugee camp. To contain them, Israeli troops shot live bullets which left four Palestinians dead in two days. Meanwhile, the protests began to spread into West Bank villages, which were home to Palestinian families native to the West Bank. It was only a day or two before young men in Arroura, a village a few miles from Kalandia camp, put on their own local protest against the raid on the Kalandia VTC. The Arroura villagers raised Palestinian flags, put up stone barricades, and painted PLO slogans on the walls. More demonstrations and more shooting followed in Gaza, elevating the body count to twenty Palestinians in the first nine days of disturbances.

Years of repressed anger burst forth throughout the occupied territories. First it shook the crowded refugee camps, which were home to only about one of five of the Palestinians living in the occupied territories. Then it edged into the Palestinian towns and the villages off the main roads. Throughout their twenty years as an occupying power, Israel had never been forced to deal with such a broad-based revolt. It spread through all parts of their occupied domain at once, drawing at least passive support from Palestinians of every age, background, and political shade. This wasn't like the early 1980s, when Israeli forces could contain the student-led "mini-uprising" on the West Bank because it was ignored by the Islamic fundamentalists in Gaza. And it wasn't like 1971, when General Ariel Sharon crushed a Gaza revolt without having to worry much about the West Bank. This time, the Israelis would face a genuine popular rebellion, the first full awakening of the Palestinian masses since the 1936–39 revolt against the British.

There were fewer young followers in those early days, and the leaders like Jamal Abu Latifah threw their own rocks. Naturally, everyone in the camps, including tipsters for Shin Bet, knew who the leaders were. That is why Jamal was arrested only seventeen days into the uprising and locked up in a detention center. During 1988, he and another Kalandia underground leader were deported, dropped off in southern Lebanon by an Israeli helicopter, and told they could never return. Their uprising lasted less than three weeks, but that was long enough. With their rocks and Molotovs, this first crop of "underground lead-ers" showed other Palestinians that the rest of the world was watching. More and more Palestinians joined, from children to marching women in traditional ankle-length dresses. To televi-sion viewers in the outside world, the intifada came through as the *cri de coeur* of a downtrodden minority. For the first time, Palestinians looked not like terrorists but like humans getting clubbed by colonialists.

Soon, Palestinian university professors, lawyers, and journal-ists rushed in to broaden what came to be called the Unified National Leadership of the Uprising. The most prominent fig-ure associated with the movement was Faisal al-Husseini, head of the Arab Studies Society in Jerusalem. For a people without many heroes, Husseini was a fitting symbol. He had spent months in prison for speaking out for Palestinian independence, and—even more important—he was the son of the 1948 guerrilla leader Abdul Khader al-Husseini. Faisal al-Husseini, like many in the homegrown leadership in the occupied territories, proved to be more pragmatic and willing to compromise with Israel than the outside PLO. The local leaders were smart enough to know that they could not win by bullets. Instead, they chose to rely on such forms of civil disobedience as refusing to renew business licenses. Rather than trying to mount a full "armed struggle," they spread the word that the approved weapons against the Israeli occupation would be the stone and the Molo-tov. The Palestinian leadership reached down into the camps and villages by distributing clandestine leaflets which bore the initials of the leaders of Fatah and other PLO and Islamic funda-mentalist factions. If villagers didn't see a leaflet, they could often hear it rebroadcast on PLO radio from Baghdad. For while the leadership of the intifada was based inside the occupied territories, it generally accepted the PLO's supremacy as the "sole and legitimate representative of the Palestinian people." Through messages passed by travelers and even cryptic ex-changes on Israeli long-distance telephones, the local under-ground leaders stayed in contact with PLO leaders and other Palestinian intellectuals from Tunis to New York.

At first, the Israeli defense establishment had no doubts that it could quickly crush the intifada. "The disturbances in the territories will not occur again," Defense Minister Yitzhak Rabin said three weeks after it started. "Even if we are forced to use massive force, under no circumstances will we allow last week's events to repeat themselves." Army Chief of Staff Dan Shomron confidently told Israeli journalists that Israel had deployed more troops in the Gaza Strip alone than it took to conquer armed enemy soldiers in both the West Bank and the Gaza Strip in the 1967 war. Even when the protests dragged into their second month, Rabin said on television that Israel could surely stifle the protests. "We shall prove to them, even if it takes two months, that they will achieve nothing by violence." He added, however, that his troops were following a new, surefire policy that would quell the troubles—a policy of "force, might, beatings." The new policy was working, he confidently announced: the number of protests had declined to "nearly zero." There were few Israelis, even among critics of the government's policy toward Palestinians, who doubted the army would prevail. "The Israeli army is very strong," said Israeli scholar Meron Benvenisti, "and its new tactic, containment, will work."

Nearly three years later, the intifada was still alive, and television's glimpses from the Holy Land looked a lot like Beirut or Belfast. Nine hundred Palestinians and more than forty Israelis had been killed, thousands were in prison, West Bank schools had been closed on and off for two years. The underground leadership was still trying to prevent the use of firearms against Israelis, but guns and knives were being used by squads of young Palestinians trying to silence Shin Bet collaborators. As a consequence, there was a continuing risk of shootouts between the Israeli troops trying to protect their informers and the Palestinians en route to kill them. That wasn't the only prospect for increased violence. Among Palestinians in the territories, the strains increased between pragmatic pro-PLO leaders who said civil disobedience was working and the hard-line Moslem fundamentalists who said the PLO was too soft. Among Israelis, fanatical settlers and their supporters—many of them recent immigrants from the United States—were increasingly taking the law into their own hands.

By the summer of 1989, the senior Israeli general had come to doubt that the army could crush the intifada. Chief of Staff Shomron used remarkably stark language to spell out Israel's options. "People ask why we don't end the intifada," Shomron said. "Anyone who wants to end the intifada must remember that there are only three ways to achieve this: transfer of the Arab population of the areas, starvation, or physical elimination—that is genocide." By "transfer," Shomron meant mass expulsions of Palestinians from the occupied territories. Shomron, who had been attacked by right-wingers for not wiping out the uprising, went on to say that no weapons could excise the desire for a Palestinian state from the heads of the Palestinian people. Force could help reduce the level of violence, he said, but Israeli army commanders had to take care not to destroy the delicate "consensus" that bound together the army in its daily battles against civilians.

The evolution of one Sorek Valley family revealed why this uprising had proved impossible to suppress without granting the Palestinians their own independent state. Before the uprising, middle-aged breadwinners like Mahmoud Hamdan, the stonecutter born in Ishwa, applied much of the pressure that allowed Israel to keep the lid on the occupied territories. Like many first-generation immigrants all over the world, these former fellaheen sent their children to school, worked with their hands, paid their taxes, and didn't care much about politics. They were the silent majority who went along with the occupation. For every flinty old diehard like Diab Abu Latifah in the camp, there were a dozen get-alongers like Mahmoud Hamdan.

Mahmoud had done only one thing to undermine Israel. That was to raise a family. In the four decades while the Palestinian question remained unresolved, demography had been ticking. Mahmoud and his parents and his brothers and sisters were a family of nine when they landed in Kalandia camp in 1950. While Jordan ruled the West Bank, Mahmoud got married and had five children, but most of his siblings were below marriage age. It was during the next twenty years of Israeli occupation that they had their population explosion. Mahmoud and his wife, Yusra, saw their household grow to ten children and eight grandchildren. Mahmoud's brothers and sisters had another thirty-eight children and five grandchildren. By the start of the intifada, their family in Kalandia spanned four generations, from his parents in their seventies to their toddler grandchildren. Just counting the descendants of Mahmoud's parents, the family numbered seventy. One branch of the family had moved east to Amman, Jordan. Another branch moved out of the Middle East entirely when one of Mahmoud's brothers emigrated to Brazil in 1957 to become a shopkeeper. But the core of the family—fifty-three people in all—still lived in the Kalandia refugee camp. As in most Palestinian families, the average age was well under twenty-five.

At the start of the uprising, Mahmoud, like many in the silent majority, pressured his children to stay at home. When his son Hassan got out of prison in the spring of 1987, Mahmoud assumed the role of a traditional Palestinian father and virtually ordered Hassan to distance himself from Fatah. If they all pulled together as a family, Mahmoud said, they could build a home for Hassan and his brothers and their future wives. Hassan, the former Fatah conspirator, acquiesced and took a job cleaning floors at a school for Hasidic Jews in Jerusalem. That is where he was working when his friend Jamal Abu Latifah promoted the first camp protest.

Mahmoud didn't approve of the intifada, not at first. "The situation is out of control," he said during its second month. "If I say to somebody, 'Come back and don't throw stones,' he will throw stones at me. It's like sheep without a shepherd." He felt that the Palestinians should try to live in peace with the Israelis rather than try to fight them. Though the intifada worried him, he still had high hopes that his sons would prosper. "I have two sons who are drivers," he said. "One drives a bus and one drives a truck." Then, pointing to his sandy-haired, blue-eyed son Yusef, he said, "This one is going to be a teacher." He said Yusef tried to get a permit from the Israelis to teach in Jordan for one year and return, but was refused. "They wanted him to collaborate with them," Mahmoud explained.

Yusef grimaced. "It's only a war of nerves," he said, insisting he would work as a laborer rather than tell the Israelis anything. He gently disagreed with his father about the intifada. "It will make the people aware," he said. "It will help find a solution more quickly. It's for our benefit that international public opinion be aware of us."

Over the months Mahmoud would pass through despair, resignation, indignation, and finally optimism, as he eventually joined his sons in believing that the Palestinians could persevere long enough to have their own independent state. As five of his sons were beaten up or jailed, Mahmoud himself would join a new Palestinian silent majority, one that utterly rejects the Israeli occupation.

Hassan, the twenty-one-year-old former Fatah conspirator, sat subdued all the time Mahmoud spoke. When his father left the room, Hassan talked animatedly about the dream he had brought back from prison that one day he would live in an independent Palestinian nation. It wouldn't have to be a very big state, not at first anyway. But it would have to be really independent. "If they [the Israelis] gave us the land they occupied in 1967 we wouldn't say no," Hassan said. "Even if we had just Jericho, we could start." Hassan was the first in the family to be touched by the intifada. One afternoon as he was coming out of his father's courtyard, he was spotted by an Israeli soldier and ordered to freeze. He was handcuffed, punched in the face, and interrogated for four hours about why some "strangers" had been visiting his house. After that, Hassan never would talk about what, if anything, he was doing to help the intifada. The only act of protest he ever acknowledged was joining in a general strike called by the leadership of the uprising. "I stayed out a week," he said. "When I went back, I found somebody else in my job."

Three months into the intifada, Mahmoud no longer was describing the young demonstrators as "sheep without a shepherd." He was beginning to understand what they were pursuing, but he was unsettled because he didn't know where events were leading. "Our generation has suffered, from the British and the Israelis and even some from the Jordanians," he said.

"So we don't have any hope. But my sons' generation does have hope. They did not suffer as much as we did. They have had a better life. They did not suffer yet. If we were not a very, very hard people, we would have disappeared."

Tear-gassing and stone-throwing and beating got to be so commonplace in the camp that people fell into thinking that nothing had really happened unless somebody went to the hospital. Mahmoud tried to keep his boys out of trouble by keeping them pouring cement for the new addition to his house. One day in March, that didn't work. Secretary of State George Shultz was in Jerusalem. The underground leadership called for a general strike to show Shultz that Palestinians would reject any peace talks that did not involve the PLO. Young stone-throwers at Kalandia transmitted that message by arcing their rocks over the new twenty-five-foot-high barricade the Israelis had made from cement-filled oil drums. That day, Israeli police introduced a new tactic to stop the stones. They set up a roadblock just outside the camp and halted cars with the blue West Bank license plates so the stones would fall on Palestinian drivers instead of on Israelis. That brought shouting, more rocks, and then tear gas. Mahmoud's sons put down their tools and climbed to the roof of their uncle's house, which was just next door to their work site. They were way beyond stone-throwing range from the road, but anyone on a roof attracted the soldiers' suspicion. After a few minutes, an Israeli patrol jogged into sight and lobbed a tear-gas canister into Mahmoud's courtyard. The soldiers burst in and hustled away two sons, Tarek, twenty-five, and Khaled, twenty.

Yusra, Mahmoud's wife, never had been bold enough to take part in sit-ins and marches like some of the other camp women. But seeing them take her sons was too much. "I ran out into the street after them and followed them," she said later. "I tried to get them back. The soldiers put them on a bus parked on the main road outside the camp. I tried to get on the bus, but they wouldn't let me. They told me to get out or they would shoot me. I saw them beating them inside the bus. One pushed me away with his gun." The soldiers drove Khaled and Tarek to the

Ramallah police station. On the way, according to Tarek, he and his brother were worked over with boots, elbows, and rifle butts. "They kept saying that Abu Ammar [Yasser Arafat's code name] is a bastard, and that the troops of the Golani Brigade are strong," Tarek said. When he was released eight hours later, his mother was aghast to see that his skin had turned a deep purple, just like the deep purple in her embroidered dress.

All along, the family's greatest hopes for the future hung on Yusef, the most educated of the children. Yusef was twenty-three when the uprising started. He had gone through high school and two years of teacher training. Mahmoud and Yusra were determined to keep him from getting arrested so that the Israelis might still grant him travel documents to teach abroad and then return to the West Bank. But while Tarek was being interrogated, he learned that the Israelis had Yusef under suspicion. The Israeli interrogator told Tarek he had a file on each of the brothers in the Hamdan family. When Tarek asked whether his brother would be held in jail, the Israeli answered in Arabic, "You mean Yusef?" Tarek had been referring to Khaled, the brother hauled in with him from the rooftop. Because of the interrogator's hint, the Hamdans had to figure Yusef would be next. One day during an Israeli curfew, Yusra saw a soldier chasing Yusef down an alley. It could be fatal to go outside her house during the curfew, but Yusra rushed out after the soldiers. This time she ran smack into an Israeli patrol. She was released after brief questioning, and Yusef got away.

Relief gave way to the feeling they were trapped. The camp was locked in a twenty-four-hour curfew for two straight weeks in the spring of 1988. "I become so fed up with all the men in the house and all the children," Yusra said at the time. "And I even get bored with myself. And yet every time you go to sleep you know they [soldiers] are out there, watching. It's like they are strangling you. You can't breathe."

Of all their sons, the one who seemed the least likely to join the intifada was Mohammed. He was a bus driver, not an agitator. He was thirty years old and had a wife and baby. But as the uprising rumbled on through the months, it took many forms besides throwing rocks. There were popular committees to grow vegetables, popular committees to provide vaccinations, popular committees to teach school now that the official schools were closed. Some of the bolder refugees refused to pay taxes. Mohammed, the bus driver, showed his defiance by driving camp residents in and out of a back road during curfews so they could get to work. For that Mohammed was stopped at a road-block and beaten by soldiers, the fourth of Mahmoud and Yusra's seven sons to be roughed up so far.

Almost all of their neighbors had at least one child shot or sent to a detention camp. One neighbor's child, sixteen-year-old Atta Ayyad, had died in Dahriyeh military prison. The boy was a great-grandson of a supervisor on the Goldberg Estate in the Sorek Valley during the 1930s. The Israelis said Atta Ayyad committed suicide. His fellow prisoners claimed that he was tortured during an interrogation until he went crazy, tearing up his mattress and beating his hands against the wall until he finally died. Whether it was murder, accident, or suicide, his death galvanized the people of Kalandia. Israeli authorities re-turned his body to his family in the middle of the night and ordered them to bury him immediately. The next morning, family members and local PLO activists defied the camp curfew and dug up the body. They reburied him with the four-colored PLO flag draped across his body and with hundreds of mourn-ers near the gravesite. From then on, his mother, Amna Ayyad, came to be known through the camp as "Mother of the Martyr." Sometimes the boys of the camp would sing a nationalist song to her: "Oh, Mother of the Martyr, all the boys are your sons. . . ."

That wasn't an honor Yusra coveted. But about the time of the Atta Ayyad funeral, her son Yusef, the educated one, was ar-rested and sent to the Ansar 3 detention camp in the Negev desert. Emergency regulations didn't require specific charges, and none were placed against him. "They broke the door down and left a summons and said if Yusef doesn't come, they will take Tarek," Mahmoud remembered. After some family debate, Yusef turned himself in.

It was during the six months while Yusef was at Ansar 3 that Mahmoud came around to approving of the intifada. Much had happened outside the West Bank to encourage a reluctant fatalist like Mahmoud to change his mind. An Israeli commando squad murdered deputy PLO chief Abu Jihad in Tunis. King Hussein had renounced his claims to the West Bank. Yasser Arafat, following the wishes of the intifada's underground leadership, had recognized Israel and renounced terrorism. The United States had responded by assigning an ambassador to talk to the PLO. Israel, after inconclusive elections in 1988, formed a hard-line government unified only by its determination to stop the uprising. Prime Minister Yitzhak Shamir put forward a sketchy plan for West Bank elections.

Yet it was the self-reliance among West Bankers that swept Mahmoud along. "Now people are more organized," he said as the uprising shook on toward its third year. "People are more aware of their political rights. My generation grew up having to concentrate entirely on the need for food. This generation after 1967 was more aware of their political rights. And even I am full of hope that a Palestinian state will take place. If there is no political solution, things will deteriorate and go to the opposite side, and there even could be a third world war. But if there is a peace settlement and we can have two states, both of us can live together the same as we did before 1948."

◆ ◆ ◆

It fell to Israeli soldiers like Yuval Levy to try to contain the tidal wave. "What you see on TV, that is what I do in the reserves," Yuval Levy said. "Call it policing activities, enforcing order, clearing away roadblocks, when they throw rocks, throwing back at them . . . the regular things."

Yuval Levy was one of the bulwarks on which Israel rested, the citizen-soldier. There weren't many others in the army whose roots in Israel extended back nearly a century. His great-grandfather Yosef was among the Bulgarian pioneers who started Hartuv out of religious Zionism. His grandfather Gavriel clung to to the valley through droughts and locust plagues and Arab raids. His father, Yoshko, fought to put Israel on the map and later helped pacify the West Bank. Now, on the eve of the 1990s, it was up to Yuval's generation to carry out a much grubbier duty. Like the Vietnam generation in America and the Afghanistan generation in the Soviet Union, they were battling little people in funny clothes who didn't know when to stop dying.

As a reservist, Yuval alternated patrols in the occupied territories with raising a family and building a career in marketing. He had been drafted into the army for three years right after high school, just like every young Israeli Jew who doesn't claim a deferment for religious studies. When the intifada started, he was twenty-nine, married and the father of a two-year-old daughter. His infantry reserve unit was called up for three of the first eighteen months of the intifada. The first year, he pulled one-month tours in Khan Younis in the Gaza Strip and Hebron on the West Bank. In the spring of 1989 he drew his third tour at Kalkilya, a Palestinian town in the West Bank which happens to be only ten miles from his home in Israel.

Like a lot of Israeli reserve soldiers, Yuval Levy didn't like what the intifada did to the troops. Some guys just followed orders and tried to avoid having to shoot. But he found to his consternation that other guys enjoyed it. "When they shoot, they shoot to kill, because it's a sport, it's hunting," he said. "It looks funny the way the water spurts out of the water tanks on the roofs of the homes when you shoot at them, so they shoot at a whole bunch of tanks. Or they continue beating a suspect after he has already been caught and handcuffed."

Yuval had to work through his own honor code. "For some, shooting is very easy," he said, "whereas for others, kicking an old lady or making her clear away a roadblock is very hard." His personal guideline was trying hard to avoid situations in which he had to beat up or shoot someone. "Many situations can be handled in such a way so that you never have to get to the point where you have to decide whether to open fire or not, to beat or not, and so on. Not always, of course—sometimes you have no choice—but most of the time you do. That's my method, and thus far I have luckily not been forced to do really difficult things."

The looks of hatred on the faces of Palestinians, and the words they spoke to him in Hebrew, left Yuval with feelings he couldn't have anticipated. "We belittle them, their abilities and talents, we only give them the menial jobs," he said. "Not that I want it otherwise—I mean, I prefer that they live separately from me. It's not that I love them, you understand me? But I still respect them. They are human beings, also—a nation, humans—there's no getting around it."

Before long, the intifada blew Mahmoud Hamdan and Yuval Levy in the same direction: they started thinking that maybe a Palestinian state was the only answer.

"I want to be freed of them—not because I want them to have a state, but because it is good for us," Yuval said. "I don't want to live so close to them, but on the other hand, I'm not willing to kill them, or push them into the sea, that's unacceptable. I want to disengage myself from them for our sake, not theirs. It [the occupation] is ruining us, the army, the state, the people, morale, lots of things. We who grew up in Israel don't see the IDF as an army that should be doing these things. I mean, maybe for a short interim period, but military rule as a way of life, I don't think that's the way we see the IDF, that's not what I meant when I 'made my vows' to the army.

"All conquerors, in the final analysis, failed. Throughout history, no empire or country succeeded in holding, over time, populated territories. I don't believe we can do this either. My concern is first and foremost for us, and not humanitarian. We'll fall apart before they will."

· 23 ·

"I WANT
MY PEACE"

*C*urlicues of smoke drifted up over the forested hillside, joined here and there by grayish puff-clouds that meant a bigger fire was burning below. On a hot dry day in May the heavy smell of wood smoke seemed odd, out of place. Wood smoke was a late-autumn scent that evoked nostalgic feelings of cycles coming to a close. This was the time for ebullient summer growth, not the time for endings. Two Israeli foresters stood at the hilltop observation post, a fire tower on spindle legs planted in the remnants of a house of the old Palestinian village of Saraa. They ranged their binoculars over vast tracts of pines and cypress and acacia, watching as the intifada claimed ten acres of the forest below. Their two-way radio alternated Hebrew and static crackles as they fed coordinates to the pilot circling above in his small airplane, looking for red flashes to douse with his load of water. Foresters would spend many more hours in the fire tower over coming months. The mistimed smell of wood smoke would hover over the Sorek Valley all summer long.

Almost one year later, in April 1989, kibbutznik Avi Hector roamed across the same hilltop on a quiet Sabbath and pointed out stretches of land where shoots of grass and wild flowers and pine seedlings already were sprouting from the ashes. Avi Hector had come to love the fields and hills of the Sorek Valley in the thirty-five years since he immigrated to Israel and joined Kibbutz Tsora. That was why he was so distracted at the notion that some Palestinians chose to pursue the intifada by setting fires in this valley. "That's a terrible thing," he said. "The land is the land. You can fight about it, but why destroy it?"

The land was the land and had been fought over for five millennia. Settlements here had been destroyed, but never the land. This hilltop dominating the heart of the Sorek Valley showed fewer scars from the battles than imprints left from the times of peaceable life. It was a place to stand and look and acknowledge the longevity of the land and the brevity of cultures. The first permanent settlers had come to this valley about 5,300 years ago. What made these Canaanites exchange their nomadic life for a town and a temple? What made them stop? When they stood on this hill, they looked down on a place that was truly empty. It never would look quite the same again to any of the successors who climbed to the top to survey the broad sweep of country undulating east, toward the inland hills where Jerusalem would arise in fifteen hundred years. This place looked different to the following generations of Canaanites, who gazed out on their own city looming on the western edge of the valley, and then to Samson, the warrior-judge who was born on this hillside when the Israelites were beginning to conquer the land of Canaan. The Egyptians, the Philistines, the Jews, the Romans, the Byzantines, the Arabs, the Crusaders, the Turks— they all would get their chance to look down from here. By the time explorer Edward Robinson got to this hilltop in the middle of the nineteenth century, the valley would be peppered with Arab villages and cultivated fields, but he would imagine it to be much the same as it appeared in Samson's time.

Some came to this hilltop not just to view the panorama but to stay and leave their marks. The old winepress gouged into the bedrock may have been used by Samson's mother at the ancient town of Zorah, or by the Canaanites who lived in Zorah before

her. Long after they were gone, later inhabitants of the place cut
a network of cisterns into the rock big enough to hold thousands
of gallons of water. Whoever dug them a millennium or more
ago also patiently chiseled a latticework of broad stone pans and
connecting channels that still funneled the winter cloudbursts
into abandoned cisterns centuries later. The weathered rock-
works bespoke patient labor by a people whose town no one had
bothered to excavate. And there were more recent, living remnants of a people gone from this hilltop. They were the flora of
a centuries-old Palestinian village whose buildings were erased
only four decades ago. Near this site of Palestinian Saraa, green
cactus grew wild and huge along what was left of a deteriorating
stone wall. This cactus that the Israelis call *sabra* was a typical
border of Palestinian villages. They took the same name for
their native-born sons and daughters, Sabra Jews whom they
said were tender inside and prickly tough on the surface. Near
the sabra there was still a grove of olive trees that could be a
thousand years old, their presence so ponderous and fat and
rooted in the past that they seemed to be daring someone to
knock them from the continuum of history. Scattered around
them were trees from which the Arabs used to pick almonds and
apples and pomegranates, figs, peaches, plums, and mulberries.
And of course there were the vines of the sweet grape that
Sabiha Abu Latifah remembered, the vines with precursors
thousands of years old, brought perhaps by invading Egyptians
who were the vintners of the ancient world. These grapes ex-
celled and gave the valley its name.

When the Palestinians left, the view from the hilltop didn't
look very different than it did in biblical times. But in forty
years the change was monumental, from the lusciousness of the
new forests to the stink of Off Yerushalayim, the factory that
processed chickens in the valley bottom where Arab wheat fields
used to be. Most of the alterations made the valley greener, more
livable, more productive. The one change that dismayed Avi
Hector was that the springs which had dotted the hillsides when
he arrived thirty-five years ago were now dry; the millions of
roots from the new stands of pines had drunk up the water.

The proximity of structures separated by ages was bewildering to see, impossible to comprehend. In a patch of scrubby weeds and purple star thistles near the Brook of Sorek sat a line of stone slabs, upright, still in the positions they held five thousand years ago when the world's ancestors worshiped them. Dug out from a shallow covering of dirt were the remnants of the newly uncovered Canaanite village, only a fraction of it excavated but enough to discern that this was a place of assemblage—a village and a temple in a time before there were cities in this part of the world. It was a time before there was bronze to wage battles of the flesh or alphabets to wage battles of the mind. When these people left, they weren't driven away but went to join a bigger town that was emerging as a city. After intervening centuries cycled in battle and in peace, the silhouettes of Israeli high-rise apartments towered over the ruins from the southern lip of the valley half a mile away. They were the modern city of Beth Shemesh, so modern that one of its main employers was a factory that built jet engines for Israel's fighter planes. The jet craft weren't much of a defense against young Palestinians fighting with rocks or forest fires, the kind of weapons those first Canaanite settlers must also have used.

Sitting in the lounge of Kibbutz Tsora after the communal dinner one night, some middle-aged Israelis ruminated about what relics future generations would uncover to define this age. There would be nothing like the ancient winepress up at old Saraa or the slabs of stone that were worshiped at the proto-urban village in the valley bottom. Maybe it would be bank vaults, one cynically suggested, since that seemed to be one of today's most solidly constructed objects.

The talk continued pessimistic as the kibbutzniks moved from the physical legacy to the moral legacy, not of the entire age, but of just their own Israeli people in this one conflicted time. It was April 1989 and the battle of the moment was not being waged on their own space of land. The battle was being fought by their children against people who used to live in their valley and in other bits of former Palestine. The intifada troubled them, especially the tactics their government employed in what seemed to be failing efforts to contain it. The kibbutzniks had been disturbed by the Rabin policy of breaking bones, and disturbed again by soldiers sometimes shooting too quickly at civilians. Now they were even more disturbed by Israel's inability to come together on what to do with the occupied territories and the Palestinians living in them. Aliza Tibon, one of the Sabra founders of Kibbutz Tsora, said the moral dilemma of this conflict was tearing Israel apart. "Look what happened just the other day," she said, referring to an incident at the West Bank village of Nahalin, where Israeli border police staged a predawn raid and ended up killing five Palestinians. "Sometimes it's so bad," she said, "you want to go on the street and scream."

No one in the small group disagreed when Aliza's husband, Yoav, predicted it would get worse before getting better, that force would not resolve the conflict. "It is a political problem, not a military problem," he said. "The only answer is that we've got to give them some land of their own." Wouldn't that place Tsora practically on the frontier again, less than five miles away from the boundary of a Palestinian state? "Yes," he said, "we have no other choice."

One lesson of 1948 was being reinvented, the lesson that you can get what you want if you are strong enough and are willing to pay the price. In this round called the intifada, the Palestinians had upped the price. Now the price, in the judgment of General Dan Shomron, was starvation, expulsion, or genocide—wreaked not on the Israelis but by them. For these people at Kibbutz Tsora, it was too high to pay for the miserable turf called the West Bank. They came, after all, from a liberal Jewish tradition wrapped round utopian ideas about sharing and caring and the extended family of community. For these kibbutzniks, these were not simply ideas but the only way to practice life.

Their ideals did not make them naive. They knew that at the moment you kiss an enemy's cheek he may take the opportunity to stab you. They worried about that with the Palestinians. "We want to believe in peace," said Avi Hector. "We have the Western idea that—well, you remember, after World War II, the Europeans made peace with the Germans, and the Americans and the Japanese made peace, and it worked. People [on the outside] think the Arabs and the Israelis can make peace too, but the hatred is so ingrained, I'm not sure that it's possible.'' Just as some Israelis said they must have the original Eretz Israel— the biblical vision of a homeland from the Euphrates to the Mediterranean—so some Palestinians said they wouldn't be satisfied until there was no Israel at all. These Israelis at Kibbutz Tsora wanted peace, but the line had to be drawn somewhere. For them the line would have to be someplace beyond this place, beyond their place at Kibbutz Tsora. They didn't talk about going all the way back to Israel's pre-1967 boundaries and certainly not back to the 1947 UN partition borders by which the world community tried to set up Jewish and Arab states in Palestine. Under that plan, the Sorek Valley would have been Palestinian all along, but for these kibbutzniks—and for the outside world as well—it was much too late for that.

In her living room across the valley, Ester Shulim was also troubled. The Polish immigrant whose family was among the first at Beth Shemesh was an elementary-school principal in 1989 with a complex of concerns. She was worried about her son and where he would be sent each time he reported for army reserve duty. It was not as she had envisioned, when he was four years old and she thought how proud she would be when he was eighteen. She had wanted him to be ''a chocolate soldier,'' she confessed, the kind they have in peaceful countries like Switzerland. ''You are at home . . . and you go and march for a week or two and that's all. That's our dream.'' These days, she worried not only about his staying alive, but about the possibility that he would have to beat or shoot protesters, this child brought up to love people. Like the others across the valley, she, too, wondered about the moral legacy of these days.

The explosive times, she thought, were made only worse by the right-wing radicals—the people such as followers of Rabbi Meir Kahane, who would like to rid the occupied territories of Arabs and maybe take Jordan too. There were two hundred hard-core Kahane followers in Beth Shemesh, she said sadly. Much of the anger of the 1970s, the anger of the Sephardim toward the Ashkenazim, had been tempered, but in the Kahane people it still raged. Ester Shulim, whose uncles died at Auschwitz, heard the talk of the Kahane people as a failure of the schools, of education. As for her, she had no designs on an Israel reaching up to Damascus or even over to the Jordan River.

"Look, I don't need it," she said. "I am now surer than ever. I don't need their Western Bank. I don't need one million Arabs. . . . I am ready to give them their rights, if I get my rights. And my rights, first of all I mean, are to live in peace. Not to be afraid to turn on the radio. Not to be afraid to open the newspaper. Not be afraid to watch television. Enough. That's enough upheaval in this country. *I want my peace.*"

Like Ester Shulim and the kibbutzniks of Tsora, the old Hartuvians Yoshko and Gita Levy made no claim to Greater Israel. They would not feel spiritually unfulfilled if the Jews did not gain sovereignty over Abraham's tomb in Hebron or the spot in Nablus where his tribe built an altar. In 1989, in the middle of the intifada, Yoshko Levy remembered the Palestinian notable who had told him twenty years before that Israel would not be able to keep all the territory it had conquered. Yoshko remembered disagreeing. "Today I think he was right and I was wrong," Levy said. "Now I believe that a country as small as Israel can't in the long run hold a territory from Suez to the Golan. Maybe if history had been different and if another ten million Jews had come, maybe. But now it is not possible. Now where the border should run exactly is a difficult question."

The Levys were convinced the border should run outside the Sorek Valley, a place that still held some mystical lure for the surviving Hartuvians, and outside the lush greenery of Udim, the Levys' place of the moment. Their family lived in Udim in a spacious home filled with the oddly soft yet geometric designs of South America, adopted during his two assignments there. The years in Ecuador for the army were followed in the early 1970s by a mission to Chile, working this time for the Jewish Agency. After that, the Levys never tried to go back again to farm in the Sorek Valley, but the appeal of the earth led them to run a greenhouse. They have done well enough to send two of their five children to study in America.

Yoshko Levy, like most Israelis in 1989, was worried. Young Palestinians were willing to die for a Palestinian state, he said, and the Israeli army, the soldiers like his son Yuval, couldn't simply kill them all. The Palestinians must have autonomy or a state or something, Yoshko said. "We must live together. There are all kinds of possible solutions, but what I see as the main problem is the lack of mutual faith." He remembered that the Hartuvians and the Palestinians of the valley were great friends, that they shared weddings and celebrations. But he also remembered when his moshava was burned and besieged. "How can we be sure they will not start firing on us again? Tulkarm is only ten kilometers from our house," he said, talking about the West Bank Palestinian town which was closest to his greenhouse. "We don't want to have to go through it all again. We don't want to have to conquer them again."

Yoshko Levy said he was willing to trade territories for peace, as long as it was real peace. He wanted peace for Udim, but also for the Sorek Valley, where his grandfather sank his stake when he came to live among the Arabs in the last century. Yoshko and Gita Levy plan to go back someday to one small plot of land, near the place his parents and grandparents lay in the old cemetery. They have told Yuval that this was where they want to be buried.

For the Palestinians on the eve of the 1990s, the Sorek Valley was a dissipating memory. Parents still drove back for visits, but seldom did their daughters and sons. Old Hajj Diab still said that as long as any Abu Latifahs survived, he wanted them to remember Saraa was theirs. His son Ibrahim heard his father, but said he did not really feel Saraa was his land. "My attachment is to the camp," said Ibrahim, a thirty-four-year-old who had been in and out of Israeli prisons for the previous sixteen years. "This is where I was born," he said. "This is where I had my childhood." When there is a Palestinian state, Ibrahim said, he will stay in Kalandia. "This is my place," said this man whose younger brother had been deported for helping ignite the intifada. For most in the new generation of Palestinians, the lesson of 1948 was sinking in: know when you must compromise.

Of all the Palestinians who had lived in the valley, Ismail

Rahhal, the son of the last Artuf mukhtar, was among the earliest to compromise. His powers of recall were more vivid than anyone's, but he did not share Hajj Diab's lust to reclaim the ancient land. With the 1990s approaching, he had worked himself into a big house and grain business, not just at his store in the old Bethlehem souk but as wholesale supplier to other West Bank businessmen. A practical, persistent man, Ismail Rahhal had decided long ago that his children's future must not be captivated by the past. The children of Ismail Rahhal had gone to a private school in Jerusalem and never had been in trouble. Rahhal himself spoke words of perfunctory support for the intifada after it had ground on for more than a year. "The intifada is a message of peace, a message of freedom, that everyone should live in peace in their own country," he said. But would it result in a state for Palestinians? "Maybe," he replied.

Ismail Rahhal had done exceedingly well for a man with a fifth-grade education from a fellaheen school. Under the circumstances of Israeli occupation, he did not want to count on new opportunities spreading before his children. Hajj Diab Abu Latifah taught his children to keep fighting. Ismail Rahhal took the other path open to Palestinians, if they have the money. He sent his children away. "It is more important for me to eat less, but to educate my children," he said. And so these Sorek Valley descendants would not throw stones and be shot by soldiers, not these four Rahhal children who had become a computer expert in California, a chemistry professor in Virginia, and university students in Pescara and Siena, Italy. The six others were on the West Bank raising families or studying too hard to be stone-throwers.

Somewhere between the passions of Diab Abu Latifah and the rationality of Ismail Rahhal lay the heart of Mahmoud Hamdan. He spent more time than most Palestinians going back to look and to walk on the land of his ancestors. When he was thirteen, Mahmoud Hamdan sometimes carried a rifle, but forty years later all he carried was a chisel to carve building stone. Mahmoud had no intention of fighting to reclaim the land of Ishwa and did not want his sons dying for it either. Perhaps he went back out of a need to set free the anger he had stored deep, the anger about what had happened to his people when he was thirteen. For him, that anger was finally allowed to vent when his people gathered their pride and spirit forty years later and threw them like a gauntlet in front of Israel and the world. It took half a lifetime for Mahmoud Hamdan to let go of the anger, but he did. The intifada was a gauntlet for him, too. He accepted both the challenge and the release when he spurned Israeli occupation and committed himself to a Palestinian state in the West Bank and Gaza.

"It is not realistic demanding all of Palestine back," he said. "The many slogans—like throwing the Jews to the sea or taking all of Palestine—these are slogans and don't exist anymore." It was for him a question not of suddenly loving the Israelis, but of acknowledging limits that the Palestinian leaders of 1948 were not ready to accept. His old home of Ishwa was one example. Before 1967 he held hopes of going back there, he said, but the war and the transformation of the land killed those hopes. Going back to Ishwa would mean another war. "Now it is unimaginable that we can beat the Israelis. The only way is maybe a third world war and everything will be destroyed."

Mahmoud Hamdan did not want to destroy the valley any more than Avi Hector and Ester Shulim and Aliza and Yoav Tibon wanted it destroyed. They were the moderates of both sides, not the hotheads who sometimes monopolize the ears of decision-makers. For sure, there were still some Palestinians who would never rest until they drove out the Israelis and reclaimed their particular spot of land, as those who torched the woods in the Sorek Valley may have been trying to warn. And for sure, there were some Israelis who would never be satisfied without extending Israel's frontier farther and farther toward the widest bounds of King David's biblical domain.

Such a man was retired General Rafael "Raful" Eytan, who started his military career helping clear the Sorek Valley of Palestinians, then went on to commando fighting in Egypt and Lebanon. His flinty political views made him the leader of a right-wing Knesset faction. Now, he said, the West Bank was just as integral to Israel as California was to the United States. "The first step must be massive settlement," he said. "You have to let the Arabs understand they have no chance to win." As he saw things, the army had been too soft, too dainty, in its response to the Palestinian intifada. Economic sanctions, expulsions, and collective punishments—those would show them who was boss. If Palestinians wanted to vote, he said, let them vote in Jordan, not in the territories that belonged to Israel.

The same kind of roughneck talk could be heard in refugee camps ten miles from the Knesset, especially from some of the young militants who think the Unified National Leadership of the Uprising has been too soft, too dainty in refraining from "the armed struggle." Such talk came, for instance, from twenty-one-year-old Jamil Shahin from Kalandia camp, whose grandfather was part of the Awad clan of Ishwa. "I don't want Ishwa back," he said, "I want all of Palestine."

But for the first time in years, the middle ranges of Palestinians and Israelis were converging. The intifada had made Palestinians much less dogmatic, and it had made the Israelis recognize that they could no longer ignore 1.7 million Palestinians in their backyard. As the 1990s approached, the average people in the middle, men like Yoshko Levy and Mahmoud Hamdan, were closer in their thinking than they or almost everyone else realized. Even so, history had left them separated by a minefield of corroding, explosive questions, none of which was going to be easy to defuse. The Israelis had to think very hard about Jerusalem, whose Jewish and Palestinian quarters were now an integral part of the state of Israel. If there is a Palestinian state, would the Palestinians get East Jerusalem? And there was the problem of a growing population sharing the same overpumped water aquifers. How can water be apportioned so well-drilling on one side does not steal water from the other? Will some outside nation pay for enough desalting equipment to replace the water that Palestinians in their own state will rightly demand for their own fields and vineyards? And what about air rights, ports, and markets? If the Israelis turn their backs on the minefield and try to go it alone, they will be staring a fundamental question in the face: what happens if they do manage to keep the territories and extend sovereignty over them? What happens to the Palestinians living in them? If the Palestinians are allowed to vote as Israeli Arabs do, the Jews in Israel will be outvoted by Arabs and Palestinians within a generation. Yet if they aren't made citizens of Israel, can soldiers like Yuval Levy subjugate them forever—and will they do it? Ultimately the Palestinians, too, have to face some fundamental questions more squarely than they have. Do they really accept the existence of Israel forever? Are they willing to forswear tanks and fighter planes, as Israel will surely demand in a peace settlement, even though such weapons are among the first accoutrements of sovereignty for most new countries? Will the Palestinians be satisfied with just a state in the West Bank and Gaza Strip, or will they continue agitating to move the frontiers little by little, like stone fences between two fields? And finally, what will happen to the two-thirds of the Palestinians who live outside the occupied territories, from Lebanon to New Jersey? How can their demands for a "right to return" be finessed?

On a plot of land in the Kalandia refugee camp, one man was starting to apply the lessons of the past to find his own way through the minefield. Mahmoud Hamdan, the man who used to daydream about renewed war leading him back to the valley of his ancestors, was building a place for his descendants. Slowly over many, many months the house of whitish-gray rocks dappled with chisel marks rose two stories high. Rooms were partitioned off and allotted to each of the four oldest boys, one-quarter of the house for each boy and a bride. "I don't think our people will move again," Mahmoud said, "even if the people will die here." Before the house was finished, Mahmoud Hamdan did something that Palestinian families do only at the place they consider home, something the Palestinians for years refused to do at the refugee camps. He planted trees in the small dirt yard: a fig and a pomegranate and an olive. For now, this plot was enough of a promised land.

NOTES

The first paragraph for each chapter's notes will indicate persons interviewed by the authors and directly quoted in that chapter.

CHAPTER 1

Quotations from Mahmoud Asad Hamdan and Yoshko Levy are from extensive interviews in their homes and during visits to the Sorek Valley.

5   1945 village population statistics: Government of Palestine, *Village Statistics as of 4-1-1945* (London).

CHAPTER 2

12   Samson and Delilah story: Judges 13–16; *Encyclopaedia Judaica*, Vol. 14, p. 771, and Vol. 5, p. 1473, citing Talmud, Sot. 9b–10a; Lev. R. 8:2. *Encyclopaedia Judaica* states (Vol. 5, p. 1473): "In order to wrest his secret from him she disengaged herself from him at the moment of sexual consummation (Sot. 9b). She realized that Samson was finally telling the truth when he said: 'I have been a Nazarene unto God' (Judg. 16:17), because she knew that he would not take the Lord's name in vain."

13   Canaanite village two thousand years before Samson: Prof. Amihai Mazar, Hebrew University archaeology department, interviewed by the authors. Also, an account of Mazar's findings in *Hebrew University News,* Autumn 1988.

13   Canaanite history: Yohanan Aharoni, *The Land of the Bible: A Historical Geography* (London, 1979), pp. 133ff; Ilene Beatty, "The Land of Canaan," in Walid Khalidi, *From Haven to Conquest* (Washington, 1987), pp. 3ff; W. F. Albright, *Archaeology of Palestine and the Bible* (New York, 1931), pp. 60–85.

13 Canaanites in Sorek Valley 3300 B.C.: Prof. Amihai Mazar, Hebrew University archaeology department, interviewed by authors. The site was discovered by a team headed by Mazar and Prof. Pierre de Miroschedji of the French Research Center in Jerusalem in an expedition funded by the National Geographic Society of the U.S. First accounts of the results appeared in *Hebrew University News,* Autumn 1988, p. 8, and *Jerusalem Post,* Jan. 6, 1989.

13 Later Canaanite town in Sorek Valley: Description of 1929–33 American excavation of site now called Tel Beit Shemesh is in Elihu Grant and C. Ernest Wright, *Ain Shems Excavations (Palestine),* 5 vols. (Haverford, Pa., 1931–39). A more current scholarly appraisal of the findings is in *Encyclopaedia of Archaeological Excavations* (London, 1975), Vol. 1, pp. 248–52.

13 Earliest name: Archaeologists have no clue to what Ir-Shemesh was called from 2200 B.C. until the arrival of the Israelites. Ir-Shemesh is the name given in Joshua 19:42.

13 Estimated seven hundred inhabitants: Archaeologists use a rule of thumb to estimate ancient population based on the size of the excavated site. This estimate derives from the authors' interviews with Professor Amitai Mazar of Hebrew University and Professor Zvi Getlin of Albright Archaeological Institute, Jerusalem.

14 Yahweh's promise: Genesis 12:7.

14 Habirus, Yahweh, Abram: Genesis 12–17, 23.

14 Sarah, Hagar, Isaac, and Ishmael: Genesis 16, 21, 25.

14 Islamic teaching on Abraham: Among many references in the Koran is Surah xxi.52: "We bestowed on Ibrahim his rectitude before, for We knew him well." There are also many references in the Koran to Ishmael, including Surah xix.55: "And commemorate Ishmael in 'The Book'; for he was true to his promise, and he was an Apostle, a prophet." Reference to construction of Kaaba: Surah ii.119.

15 Internal threat: Exodus 1:8–12.

15 ". . . *more than a hornet's sting.*" Hori to the Pharaoh, Amarna letters, cited in Grant, Part 3, p. 230.

15 "*Oh King my lord behold . . .*" Queen Basmatu to Pharaoh, Tel Amarna No. 137B, as quoted in C. R. Condor, *The Tel Amarna Tablets* (London, 1894), p. 155.

16 "*If there are no archers . . .*" King of Jerusalem to the Pharaoh, Amarna Letter No. 290, cited in Yohanan Aharoni and Michael Avi-Yonah, *The Macmillan Bible Atlas* (New York, 1977), p. 39.

16 "*They utterly destroyed . . .*" Joshua 6:20–21.

16 "*I shall spread . . .*" Exodus 23:27–31.

17 Sorek Valley apportioned to Tribe of Dan: Joshua 19:40.

17   Danites forced into the mountain: Judges 1:34.

17   *"begin to rescue"* Judges 13:5.

18   Ir-Shemesh renamed Beth Shemesh: Joshua 15 describes territory allocated to the sons of Judah as having a boundary line which passed through Beth Shemesh. Later Joshua (19:40) says the inheritance of the Tribe of Dan includes the towns of Eshtaol, Ir-Shemesh, and Zorah. According to Aharoni and Avi-Yonah, p. 106, this listing must refer to the period 980 B.C., during the time of King David, since this region was outside Israelite control prior to then.

18   Beth Shemesh as administrative center: I Kings 4.

19   *"fled every man to his tent"* II Chronicles 25:30. Also see II Kings 14:11–13.

19   Gigantic idol: Talmud's Aggudath, cited in *Encyclopaedia Judaica*, Vol. 11, p. 851.

19   Destruction of Beth Shemesh in sixth century B.C.: Grant and Wright, Part 5, p. 12.

20   Talmud on Moabite woman Ruth: Aggudath, Yev. 77a.

20   David's seven hundred wives, three hundred concubines: I Kings 11:3.

20   Canaanite cults: II Kings 21:7 says of Manasseh, king of Judah: "He did what was wrong in the eyes of the Lord. . . . He rebuilt the hill-shrines which his father Hezekiah had destroyed, he erected altars to Baal. . . . He built altars in the House of the Lord . . . and the image that he had made of the goddess Asherah he put in the house. . . ."

20   Asherah inscription: Ruth Hestrin, "The Lachish Ewer and the 'Asherah," *Israel Exploration Journal*, Vol. 37, No. 4 (1987).

20   Inhabitants of Palestine after Babylonian conquest: Uriel Rappaport, "Jewish-Pagan Relations and the Revolt Against Rome in 66–70 CE," *Jerusalem Cathedra*, No. 1 (1981), pp. 81–95.

20   Saint Stephen: Acts of the Apostles 6:8–7:60; Zeev Vilnay, *Israel Guide* (Jerusalem, 1985), p. 200.

21   Bar-Kokhba revolt and expulsion of Jews from Jerusalem Hills: Amos Kloner, "The Subterranean Hideaways of the Judean Foothills and the Bar-Kokhba Revolt," *Jerusalem Cathedra*, No. 4 (1983), pp. 114–36; Michael Avi-Yonah, *The Holy Land from the Persian to the Arab Conquests (536 B.C. to A.D. 640): A Historical Geography* (Grand Rapids, Mich., 1966), p. 215.

22   Coins as evidence of habitation after expulsion of Jews: Grant and Wright, Part 5, p. 85.

22   Eusebius geography: *The Onomasticon of Eusebius* (Leipzig, 1904), p. 160. Bishop Eusebius (A.D. 260–339) originally wrote the book in about 324.

22   Saint Stephen's relics: Vilnay, p. 200.

22   Arab victory in A.D. 634: Phillip K. Hitti, *History of Syria Including Lebanon and Palestine* (London, 1951), pp. 412–15.

23   Crusader settlement in Sorek Valley: Meron Benvenisti, *The Crusaders in the Holy Land* (Jerusalem, 1970), p. 187.

23   Beth Shemesh called Ain Schemes: J.C.M. Laurent, ed., *Peregrinatores Medii Aevi Quatuor* (J. C. Hinrichs, 1864), p. 77.

23   Blue-eyed Palestinians: Charles Cleremont-Ganneau, "On the Arabs of Palestine," *Palestine Exploration Fund Quarterly* (London, Oct. 1885), p. 199.

23   Zorah and Eshtaol still existed: Isaac Estori ha-Parhi, "Kaftor va Ferah," *Jerusalem Yearbook* (Jerusalem, 1897), p. 293.

24   *"It is a very ancient . . ."* Rabbi Itzhak Chelo, "The Path of Jerusalem," written in 1322 and reissued in 1919 in *Jerusalem Yearbook*, ed., A. M. Luncz, Vol. 5568, p. 96.

CHAPTER 3

26   *"Coffee was served for us. . . ."* Edward Robinson, *Biblical Researches in Palestine and in the Adjacent Regions* (Boston, 1874), Vol. 1, pp. 152–55; Vol. 2, p. 13.

27   Climate change in Palestine: A study by Israeli geographer Zipora Klein is cited in Haim Gerber, *The Social Origins of the Modern Middle East* (Boulder, Colo., 1987), p. 16.

29   Turkish tax system: The most authoritative description of the effect of Turkish taxes on Palestine is Amnon Cohen, *Palestine in the 18th Century: Patterns of Government and Administration* (Jerusalem, 1973), pp. 299ff.

30   List of Arab villages: In the sixteenth century their respective names were Artuf, Deir Aban, Shawa, Aslin, Rafat, and Saraa. Shawa apparently referred to the village of Ishwa. Names taken from the Turkish tax registers for the Jerusalem area for 1526 and 1562, as translated and described in E. Toledano, "The Sanjaq of Jerusalem in the 16th Century: Aspects of Topography and Population," in *Archivum Ottomanicum*, Vol. 9, Wiesbaden, 1984, p. 279.

30   Artuf population about a hundred: Demographers studying the old Ottoman "adult-males-only" census figures generally assume that for every adult male there were four other residents not counted because they were too young or female.

30   1596 tax rolls: Wolf-Dieter Huetteroth and Kamal Abdelfattah, *Historical Geography of Palestine, Transjordan and Southern Syria in the late 16th Century* (Erlangen, 1977), p. 122.

30 Deir Aban in 1596: Toledano, p. 279.
30 Deir Aban tax controversy: Amnon Cohen, *Palestine in the 18th Century: Patterns of Government and Administration* (Jerusalem, 1973), pp. 299ff.
31 Turkish financial problems: Aharon Cohen, *Israel and the Arab World* (New York, 1970), p. 54.
33 Turkish tax system: Gerber, p. 54.
34 An "angel" appears: Austrian Consulate Document 78, October 30, 1883, as cited in Mordechai Eliav, *Under the Patronage of the Kingdom of Austria: From the Archives of the Consulate of Jerusalem, 1849–1917* (Jerusalem, 1986; in Hebrew). The document refers to the buyer as "Effendi (the Honorable) Iskandar." The family name Eifulend was listed in a subsequent land document found at the Central Zionist Archives, Jerusalem, in File A109/25.

CHAPTER 4

36 London Society and its history: The Rev. W. T. Gidney, *The History of the London Society for Promoting Christianity Amongst The Jews, from 1809 to 1908* (London, 1908), pp. 452–55.
38 Pines's early career, Petah Tikvah, and the significance of the network of Zionist colonies: Howard M. Sachar, *A History of Israel from the Rise of Zionism to Our Time* (New York, 1979), p. 87; Central Zionist Archives (referred to below as CZA), Jerusalem, File A109/25; Israel Klausner, *A Nation Awakens: The First Aliyah from Russia* (Jerusalem, 1962; in Hebrew), p. 305; *Encyclopaedia Judaica*, Vol. XIII, p. 535.
39 470,000 Arabs: Sachar, p. 87.
39 Sold to Jewish land broker: Yechiel Brill, *The Immigration of Eleven Farmers from Russia in 1883* (Jerusalem, 1978; in Hebrew), pp. 68–70.
39 *"The fellaheen who live . . ."* The contract drafted by Pines was found in CZA file A109/25.
39 Brill and the Russian farmers visit Artuf: Brill, pp. 68–70.
41 *"dependent on the Jerusalem rabbinate."* From Austrian Consulate, Jerusalem, to Vienna, Letter No. 70, Oct. 30, 1883, reproduced in Mordechai Eliav, *Under the Patronage of the Kingdom of Austria; Selections from the Archives of the Consulate of Jerusalem, 1849–1917* (Jerusalem, 1986; in Hebrew), p. 202.
41 45,000 francs: Austrian consulate, Jerusalem, to Vienna, Oct. 30, 1883, in Eliav, p. 202. Gidney's history of the London Society, pp.

454–56, cites a price in pounds that would have been equivalent at 1880s exchange rates.

42   One-third of Jewish colonists: *Tidings from Zion: A Monthly Statement of the London Society's Work Among the Jews of Palestine*, Vol. 2, No. 5 (Nov. 15, 1883).

42   150 Jewish refugees at Artuf: Kelk, *Tidings of Zion*, Jan. 15, 1884; *"It requires a stout heart,"* Friedlander, *ibid.*, based on his visit to Artuf of Jan. 4, 1884.

42   *"in an apparent state of serfdom"* *Tidings from Zion*, Aug. 1, 1884.

42   Request for firearms: Friedlander, *Tidings from Zion*, Jan. 15, 1884.

43   *"one of the usual miserable places . . ."* *Tidings from Zion*, Nov. 15, 1883.

43   Mounds of manure: Friedlander, *Tidings from Zion*, Mar. 15, 1884.

43   *". . . really making its way."* Gidney, p. 454.

44   Closing of Christian settlement: Jossi Ben-Artzi, *Hartuv: The History of a Jewish Settlement* (Jerusalem, 1984; in Hebrew), p. 351; Klausner, p. 301.

44   *"They were very angry . . ."* Binyamin Cohen, quoted in the reminiscences of Yehuda Appel. CZA file A6/30, "Observations of Yehuda Appel" (in Hebrew).

44   Saraa tax sale: The Rev. James Joseph Beltriti, patriarch emeritus of Deir Rafat convent, interviewed by the authors; CZA file Z4/771/1.

44   Jaffa-Jerusalem railway: Paul Cottrell, *The Railways of Palestine and Israel* (Abbington, England, 1984), pp. 2–7.

45   The word "Zion": *Encyclopaedia Britannica* (Chicago, 1985), Vol. 12, p. 922, says the word "appears to be a pre-Israelite Canaanite name of the hill upon which Jerusalem was built. . . . In biblical usage, however, 'Mount Zion' often means the city rather than the hill itself."

46   Rejection of Tel Aviv land: Interview with Shabtai Gueron, a grandson of the first Bulgarian settlers, in *Ma'ariv*, May 16, 1986.

46   Price Christians paid: Gidney, p. 454.

46   Founding of Hartuv: Ben-Artzi, pp. 351ff.

47   *"all people of means . . ."* An undated dispatch by the Jerusalem correspondent of the *Jewish Chronicle* (London), cited in *Jewish Missionary Intelligence* ("The Monthly Record of the London Society for Promoting Christianity Amongst the Jews"), Vol. III, Jan. 1897, p. 15. (Cited later as *JMI.*)

47   *"For what reason do you expel . . ."* *Jewish Chronicle* correspondent, cited in *JMI*, Jan. 1897.

48   *"These Jews are Turkish citizens. . . ."* Interview with Ben-Zion Gueron in *Ma'ariv*, Sept. 9, 1977. Another settler born in the 1890s, Avraham Behor, has said that Musa Kasem al-Husseini sent

messages to the neighboring villages putting Hartuv under his protection. See interview with Behor in *Ma'ariv*, Sept. 20, 1968; also, Behor, *Memoirs of Hartuv*, pamphlet (Jerusalem, 1970; in Hebrew).

48　*"Thanks to the baksheesh . . ."* Behor, *Memoirs.*

48　Uprooting of mulberry bushes: Avraham Behor, interviewed in *Ma'ariv*, Sept. 20, 1968.

48　*". . . exploiters of their lands."* Appel history, CZA file A6/30.

48　Argument over land near streambed: Archives of Department of Revival of Islamic Heritage (IHJ), Jerusalem, file 3/1,9/315/13.

49　Partition of valley land: An 1897 Turkish memorandum recounts that a Turkish district official in charge of *waqf* land summoned the Sorek Valley's Jewish and Arab village leaders to a meeting on April 23, 1897. "There was an agreement between the two parties [the moshava leaders and the Turkish department] on the partition of the *waqf* land . . . [and an agreement] to delimit and make a map of it," according to the Turkish document, which was uncovered in an Islamic archive in Jerusalem. It reported that the Jewish mukhtar, along with a half-dozen elders and mukhtars from the villages of Artuf, Ishwa, and Deir Aban took part in the discussion and "agreed on the partition." IHJ file 3/1,9/315/13.

CHAPTER 5

51　*"The Arabs were the ones to guide us . . ."* Avraham Behor, *Memoirs of Hartuv*, pamphlet (Jerusalem, 1970; in Hebrew).

52　*". . . the water is the property of Allah . . ."* Use of Ishwa well by Jews, from Behor, *Memoirs of Hartuv.* Description of well from Mahmoud Hamdan, interviewed by authors.

52　*". . . worst of all the settlements . . ."* Achad HaAm, quoted in Jossi Ben-Artzi, *Hartuv: The History of a Jewish Settlement* (Jerusalem, 1984; in Hebrew), pp. 351ff.

53　1907 land dispute: Archives of Department of Revival of Islamic Heritage, Jerusalem, File 3/1,9/315/13.

53　Allegation that Arabs cheated the Turkish court: Raphael Ben-Aroya, interviewed by authors.

53　*". . . I will slaughter twenty goats."* Interview with Avraham Behor in *Ma'ariv*, Sept. 20, 1968.

54　*"all these last ones would emigrate . . ."* This and other quotations from this letter cited below are from Albert Antebi to Jewish Colonization Association, Paris, Sept. 15, 1909, to which Antebi attached a copy of a letter to him signed by the nine Hartuv colonists. Central Zionist Archives, Jerusalem, file J15/6271.

55   ". . . *Arie or Alajem* . . ." Alajem is probably a reference to the family of Chaim Alajem, one of the original settlers who later returned to Bulgaria but retained his land ownership. The reference to Arie is unclear.

55   Hartuvians find a patron: Behor, *Memoirs.*

56   "*We received him with bread* . . ." Behor, *Memoirs.*

56   1883 Palestine population: Howard M. Sachar, *A History of Israel from the Rise of Zionism to Our Time* (New York, 1986), p. 87. While there is general agreement about the Jewish population in 1870, scholars differ on the 1870 Arab population, with estimates ranging from 350,000 to more than 500,000. Sachar, a middle-of-the-road pro-Zionist historian, gives the figure 470,000.

57   1914 Palestine population: British Mandatory Government, *A Survey of Palestine, Prepared in December 1945–1946 for Information of Anglo-American Committee of Inquiry,* Vol. 1 (Palestine, 1946); Sachar, p. 88.

57   Jewish holdings in 1914: Aharon Cohen, *Israel and the Arab World* (New York, 1970), pp. 40–41.

57   Hartuv during World War I: Unless otherwise cited, all descriptions and quotations are taken from Behor, *Memoirs.*

58   Hussein-McMahon correspondence: Texts are in George Antonius, *The Arab Awakening* (New York, 1946), pp. 413–28.

59   "*was never fully understood by him* . . ." Maj. Hubert Young of the Middle East Department, minute on telegram of Feb. 11, 1923, cited in William B. Quandt, Fuad Jabber, and Ann Mosely Lesch, *The Politics of Palestinian Nationalism* (Berkeley, 1973), p. 10.

60   ". . . *a definite promise* . . ." Cited by Sachar, p. 108.

61   ". . . *he is entirely in sympathy* . . ." Quoted in Conor Cruise O'Brien, *The Siege* (New York, 1986), p. 128.

61   Allies take Artuf: Gen. Sir Edmund Allenby, *A Brief Record of the Advance of the Egyptian Expeditionary Forces* (London, 1919), p. 51.

62   Jewish population decline 1914–18: Sachar, p. 118. Christian and Moslem population declines: O'Brien, p. 133.

62   "*My father was a contractor* . . ." Yoshko Levy, interviewed by authors.

63   Wartime rail and road building: Allenby, p. 91; Paul Cottrell, *The Railways of Palestine and Israel* (Abingdon, England, 1984), p. 25.

63   Hebrew University dedication: Aharon Cohen, *Israel and the Arab World* (New York, 1970), pp. 146–47.

64   "the civil and religious rights . . ." Also other mandate terms cited. Mandatory Government of Palestine, *A Survey of Palestine,* Vol. 1, pp. 4–5.

64   ". . . *without our being consulted* . . ." Cited in Quandt et al., p. 16.

CHAPTER 6

65   Accounts of the 1929 attack on Hartuv by Yoshko Levy, Hajj Diab
      Abu Latifah, Mahmoud Hamdan, and Alia Mohammed Daher
      are from interviews.

65   Saraa and Deir Ayub neighborliness: Avraham Behor, *Memoirs of
      Hartuv,* pamphlet (Jerusalem, 1970; in Hebrew).

66   Forty-seven Jews and forty-eight Arabs killed: Mandatory Gov-
      ernment of Palestine, *A Survey of Palestine, Prepared in December
      1945 and January 1946 for the Information of the Anglo-American Com-
      mittee of Inquiry,* Vol. 1 (Palestine, 1946), p. 18.

66   *"would become so highly organized . . ."* Report of the Commission of
      Inquiry on the Disturbances in May, 1921, in Palestine (London, 1921),
      p. 57.

67   *"If it was raining . . ."* Ben-Zion Gueron, interviewed in *Ma'ariv,*
      Sept. 9, 1977.

67   Olive press, flower drying, and other enterprises: Central Zionist
      Archives (CZA), File S15/614b, "Points of Settlement and Mosha-
      vot in the Land of Israel."

68   *"All the mukhtars . . ."* Avraham Behor, interviewed in *Ma'ariv,*
      Sept. 20, 1968.

68   Friends would warn: Ben-Zion Gueron, interviewed in *Ma'ariv,*
      Sept. 9, 1977.

68   Letter from Levy to Goldberg: Aug. 8, 1926, in French, CZA, File
      A6/9.

69   Forty to eighty times: Kenneth Stein, *The Land Question in Pales-
      tine, 1917–1939* (Chapel Hill and London, 1984), p. 65.

69   Jezreel Valley purchases and effect on Arab farmers: Stein, p. 60.

69   Palestinian Arabs sell about a fourth: Stein, pp. 66–67.

70   *"exceptional volume of immigrants"* Mandatory Government of
      Palestine, *A Survey of Palestine,* Vol. 1, p. 23.

70   Arabs' new tactics: Ann Mosely Lesch, "The Palestine Arab
      Nationalist Movement Under the Mandate," in William B.
      Quandt, Fuad Jabber, and Ann Mosely Lesch, *The Politics of Pales-
      tinian Nationalism* (Berkeley, 1973), pp. 27–28.

71   A new Palestine Arab Executive: Quandt et al., p. 29.

71   Jews take opposite course: Mandatory Government of Palestine,
      A Survey of Palestine, p. 16.

72   Hajj Amin's power base: Philip Mattar, *The Mufti of Jerusalem:
      al-Hajj Amin al-Husayni and the Palestinian National Movement*
      (New York, 1988), pp. 29–30.

73   Talk of buying the wall: Mattar, p. 37.

74   Ben-Gurion urged restraint: Shabtai Teveth, *Ben-Gurion: The
      Burning Ground, 1886–1948* (Boston, 1987), p. 372.

74   Youth demonstration: Teveth, p. 373.

74   First deaths recorded: This sequence of events was noted by American correspondent Vincent Sheean, who was on the scene. From Vincent Sheean, *Personal History* (New York, 1935), pp. 333–39, cited in Walid Khalidi, ed., *From Haven to Conquest* (Washington, D.C., 1987), pp. 295–96.

74   Hajj Amin's effort to calm crowds: Mattar, p. 47.

75   Arab elders moved to save: *Palestine Commission on the Disturbances of August 1929, Evidence Heard by the Commission* (London, 1929), p. 42.

75   *"Fellows, what are we . . ."* Behor, *Memoirs.*

75   *"They only had five weapons . . ."* This and subsequent Levy quotations on the 1929 attack, Yoshko Levy, interviewed by authors.

76   Playfair's role: *Palestine Commission on the Disturbances of August 1929,* p. 135.

76   Attack on Hartuv: Yoshko Levy, interviewed by authors; Ben-Zion Gueron, interviewed in *Ma'ariv,* Sept. 9, 1977; an article in *Ma'ariv,* May 16, 1986; Behor, *Memoirs.*

77   Behor believed: Behor, *Memoirs.*

78   Fisher's record: University Museum Archives, University of Pennsylvania, RG Near East/Syro Palestine Subgroup Ain Shems Container 7 Folder 8—C. S. Fisher, Notes of C. S. Fisher on 1929 expedition to Ain Shems (Beth Shemesh)—Expedition Records.

79   Commissioner disarmed Constables: British Foreign Office 371/13751, TG 123 from Officer Administering, Government of Palestine to Colonial Secretary, Aug. 28, 1929, copy found in Israel State Archives.

79   *"Their position . . ."* and summary of recommendations: *A Survey of Palestine,* pp. 24–25, and Sachar, p. 175.

CHAPTER 7

Descriptions of the Sorek Valley in early 1930s and local Arab-Jewish relations are from interviews with Yoshko Levy, Raphael Ben-Aroya, Alia Mohammed Daher, Awad Ibrahim Awad, and Sabiha Abu Latifah.

81   *"Arab neighbors from Hartuv . . ."* Avraham Behor, *Memoirs of Hartuv,* pamphlet (Jerusalem, 1970; in Hebrew), p. 19.

81   Murder of a Hartuvian: Raphael Ben-Aroya, interviewed by authors.

82   *"In Tel Aviv people suddenly . . ."* Chaim Levy, interviewed in *Ma'ariv,* May 16, 1986.

83   *"as a free nation of workers"* Shabtai Teveth, *Ben-Gurion: The Burn-ing Ground, 1886–1948* (Boston, 1987), p. 360.

84   Meeting in January 1930: Central Zionist Archives (CZA), S15/614b, "Points of Settlements and Moshavot in the Land of Israel," minutes of a meeting on Jan. 2, 1930, of Committee for Investigating Settlement of Hartuv at Agricultural Experiment Station in Tel Aviv.

84   *"lush valley . . ."* University Museum Archives, University of Pennsylvania, RG Near East/Syro Palestine Subgroup Ain Shems Container 7 Folder 8—C. S. Fisher, notes of C. S. Fisher on 1929 expedition to Ain Shems (Beth Shemesh)—Expedition Records.

84   Architect's recommendation: CZA, S15/614b, Letter July 27, 1930, from Jewish Agency Agricultural Settlement Department to Mr. Passman of Emergency Fund.

85   *"very undesirable for sanitary . . ."* CZA, S15/614b, Letter dated Aug. 4, 1930, from Mr. Passman, Emergency Fund for Palestine, Jerusalem, to Mr. Bawly, Colonization Department of Palestine Zionist Executive.

85   Jewish Agency loans and plan: CZA, S15/614b, undated list of loans to Hartuv settlers.

86   Assessment of damages: CZA, S15/614b, Mar. 24, 1930, Report for Emergency Fund.

86   Field inspectors found some crops: CZA, S15/614b, Reports dated 11/24/30, 12/19/30 and 12/21/30 to Agricultural Settlement Dept. of Jewish Agency, on visits by agents to Hartuv.

86   *"Their land does not supply . . ."* CZA, S15-2220, 1931, Report Dec. 3, 1931, from Shlomo Tzemach, Jewish Agency for Palestine, Agricultural Station, Extension Division, Palestine.

87   *"In the first day . . ."* CZA, S15/614b, undated letter from Yehuda Behor to Emergency Fund.

88   *"an important experiment"* CZA S15/614b, Report dated Feb. 18, 1930, to Colonization Dept. of Palestine Zionist Executive (Jewish Agency), Jerusalem, from R. Riftin.

88   They bored 985 feet: Great Britain, "Report by HMG on Administration of Palestine and Transjordan for 1933," p. 231.

89   *"Amounts to about 5,000 . . ."* CZA, A6/9, Petition from Mukhtars of Artuf, Ishwa, and surrounding villages.

90   Number of homes and people in 1931: Census by Mandatory Administration, 1931, available on microfiche in Hebrew University Library, Mount Scopus Campus, Jerusalem.

90   Displaced Arabs: Pamela Ann Smith, *Palestine and the Palestinians 1876–1983* (New York, 1984), pp. 50–54.

92   Alarming policies: Sir John Hope-Simpson, "On the Employ-

ment of Arab Labour," in Walid Khalidi, ed., *From Haven to Conquest* (Washington, D.C., 1987), pp. 304–5.

93   No margin of land: Howard Sachar, *A History of Israel from the Rise of Zionism to Our Time* (New York, 1986), pp. 176–77.

94   *"then our destructive force . . ."* David Ben-Gurion, quoted in Teveth, p. 396.

94   By-election: Allan Bullock, "The Passfield White Paper and the Politics of Whitechapel 1930–1931," in Khalidi, pp. 313–14.

94   *"obligation to facilitate . . ."* Prime Minister James Ramsay Mac-Donald, letter dated Feb. 13, 1931, to Dr. Chaim Weizmann, published in Walter Laqueur and Barry Rubin, eds., *The Israel-Arab Reader: A Documentary History of the Middle East Conflict* (New York, 1969), pp. 53–54.

95   *"has ruined hope . . ."* Sachar, p. 178.

CHAPTER 8

Much of the description of how the Sorek Valley got sucked into the whirlwind of the 1936–39 Arab rebellion was drawn from interviews with Yoshko Levy, Itzhak "Levitza" Levi, Raphael Ben-Aroya, Hamed Odeh Faraj, Mahmoud Hamdan, Hajj Diab Abu Latifah, and Sabiha Abu Latifah. It was Yoshko Levy who recalled Sadeh training the Hartuvians. Itzhak Levi told of the unsanctioned Haganah squad.

97   Immigration and population: Howard Sachar, *A History of Israel from the Rise of Zionism to Our Time* (New York, 1986), p. 189.

98   Jewish leaders moving to concentrate forces: Kenneth W. Stein, *The Land Question in Palestine, 1917–1939* (Chapel Hill and London, 1984), pp. 93, 174–75.

98   Settlement patterns: Stein, p. 220.

99   Background of Shimshon factory: Yoshko Levy, interviewed by authors, and Avraham Behor, *Memoirs of Hartuv,* pamphlet (Jerusalem, 1970; in Hebrew).

99   Divide-and-rule tactics: Pamela Ann Smith, *Palestine and the Palestinians 1876–1983* (New York, 1984), p. 60.

100   Arabs' appearance before commissioner: High Commissioner Sir Arthur Wauchope expressed some understanding of Arab complaints. He wrote to the colonial secretary after meeting the joint delegation that Arab hostility was anchored in belief that the British had promised them independence after the war. "To this sense of injustice must now be added a genuine feeling of fear that the Jews will succeed in establishing themselves in such large numbers that in the not distant future they will gain eco-

nomic and political control over the country," he wrote. Quoted in William B. Quandt, Fuad Jabber, and Ann Mosely Lesch, *The Politics of Palestinian Nationalism* (Berkeley, 1973), p. 16.

100 Legislative scheme killed: British Mandatory Government, *A Survey of Palestine, Prepared in December 1945 and January 1946 for the Information of the Anglo-American Committee of Inquiry*, Vol. 1 (Palestine, 1946), p. 34.

100 Isolated incidents: Smith, p. 63.

102 Lawlessness; trains wrecked: *Report by His Majesty's Government in the United Kingdom of Great Britain and Northern Ireland to the Council of the League of Nations on the Administration of Palestine and Transjordan for the Year 1936* (London, 1937), pp. 12–14; Paul Cottrell, *The Railroads of Palestine and Israel* (Abingdon, England, 1984), p. 64.

105 Raghib Nashashibi envisioned himself prime minister: Quandt, p. 37.

105 Galilee Jewish population: Lesch describes Jews as "a minute proportion" of the population of Galilee at this time, and cites a British report that Jews were .001 percent of rural population of Acre subdistrict and 4 percent of Safad subdistrict. Quandt, Jabber, and Lesch, p. 37.

105 Amin preparing to restoke: Philip Mattar, *The Mufti of Jerusalem: al-Hajj Amin al-Husayni and the Palestinian National Movement* (New York, 1988), p. 81.

106 Absorb 100,000 immigrants: Sachar, p. 207.

106 "I do not doubt . . ." Shabtai Teveth, *Ben-Gurion: The Burning Ground, 1886–1948* (Boston, 1987), p. 612.

108 Behor's conversation with police commander: Behor, *Memoirs.*

109 Water-pipe anecdote: Behor, *Memoirs.*

109 Behor's conversation with British officer: Behor, *Memoirs.*

111 Rifles and pistols anecdote: Behor, *Memoirs.*

CHAPTER 9

Contrasting glimpses of Palestine and the Sorek Valley in the late 1930s and early 1940s emerged from interviews with Hajj Diab Abu Latifah, Mahmoud Hamdan, Alia Mohammed Daher, Raphael Ben-Aroya, Yoshko Levy, Ariyeh Nir, Avizohar Nachshon, and Rafi Horowitz. It was Abu Latifah who recalled local Arabs' reaction to hearing of Jewish military training.

A first-hand account of Palestinian leaders' frustration with Hajj Amin al-Husseini's rejection of the British White Paper came in an interview with Izzat Tannous, the long-retired treasurer of the Arab Higher Committee, who is believed to be the only surviving Palestinian participant in the 1939 Beirut meeting with Hajj Amin.

113 Surveyors chased from mountain: Ismail Abdul Fattah Rahhal, interviewed by authors. Judging from records of the Jewish National Fund, this episode probably occurred in early 1941. JNF records for 1940–46 carry details of multiple land disputes along the boundaries of Hartuv. In a May 1941 letter a JNF lawyer writes of arranging police protection so a surveyor could finish surveying the lands, "which he was stopped from doing earlier due to the conflict with the Arabs" (Central Zionist Archives, KKL5, 11385). Also, former Hartuv residents recall an incident around this time in which Artuf villagers chased away a surveyor and broke his equipment.

113 British curfew, military operations: Ann Mosely Lesch, "The Palestine Arab Nationalist Movement Under the Mandate," in William Quandt, Fuad Jabber, and Ann Mosely Lesch, *The Politics of Palestinian Nationalism* (London, 1973), p. 38. Also, Mandatory Government of Palestine, *A Survey of Palestine,* reported that 2,543 people were interned in 1938, while only 382 people were tried in military courts.

115 *"However, before we take . . ."* Avraham Behor, letter to Haganah, CZA, S15/3006.

116 *"Don't let the rumor . . ."* Avraham Behor, letter to Haganah, CZA, S15/3006.

116 Denials of discrimination: Letter from D. Stern of Jewish Agency to Committee of Hartuv, Aug. 6, 1939, CZA, S15/3006.

116 $600 loan: Letter from L. Pinnar of Jewish Agency to Weitz at JNF, Feb. 27, 1940, CZA, S15/3005.

116 Formation of cooperative: Report from Shimon Meckler to Jewish Agency, Mar. 4, 1940, CZA, S15/3006.

117 *"I hear today . . ."* L. Pinnar, letter to Weitz, Feb. 27, 1940, CZA, S15/3006.

117 *"Among ourselves . . ."* Weitz diary entry, June 22, 1941, quoted in Israel Shahak, "A History of the Concept of 'Transfer' in Zionism," *Journal of Palestine Studies,* Vol. 18, No. 3 (Spring 1989), p. 26.

118 *"With all the farming . . ."* Shimon Meckler, letter to Jewish Agency, Mar. 4, 1940, CZA, S15/3006.

118 *"After working for . . ."* Avraham Behor, quoted in court hearing transcript, found in Israel State Archives (ISA), RG23 file 854/M/31, District Commissioner of Jerusalem, Government of Palestine 20/35/14 "Land Dispute-Artuf."

118   *"This land in dispute..."* Complaint filed Jan. 20, 1941, to district commissioner of Jerusalem, ISA, RG23 file 854/M/31.

119   Judge ordered Arabs to get off land: Avraham Behor, *Memoirs of Hartuv,* pamphlet (Jerusalem, 1970, in Hebrew).

119   *"It is not true..."* Complaint filed Jan. 20, 1941, to district commissioner of Jerusalem, ISA, RG23 file 854/M/31.

119   *"We have had grazing..."* Testimony of 'Eissa Hassan Ahmad, ISA, RG23 file 854/M/31.

119   *"I find the Arab inhabitants..."* Order of W. R. McGeagh, ISA, RG23 file 854/M/31.

119   Disagreement over police: Details of argument between the JNF (Keren Keyemeth Leisrael) and the mandatory government are from ISA, File 3330: Israel, the Mandatory Government, Tagart Scheme Police Post, Har Tuv, Jerusalem s/d.

120   *"It made me more important..."* Behor, *Memoirs.*

121   No success increasing price: ISA, File 3330: Israel, the Mandatory Government, Tagart Scheme Police Post, Har Tuv, Jerusalem s/d.

123   *"the kids who just roll..."* D. Eidelson, Tel Aviv child welfare official, in letter to Weitz, Dec. 14, 1944, CZA, KKL5/13448, "Hartuv Transferring the Land" Part 2.

123   Colonization company project: CZA, KKL5/13448 (1944–45), "Hartuv, Transferring the Land," memorandum of visit to Hartuv, Aug. 21, 1944, by Banim Ligulam Colonization Company Ltd. Also, copy of news article from *Haaretz,* Aug. 23, 1945, in same file.

123   Shimshon cement plant: CZA, KKL5/15011 (1945–47), "Hartuv, Transferring the Land," letter from Hiram Danin of JNF to Committee of Hartuv, June 17, 1946.

123   Boomlet from British demands: Pamela Ann Smith, *Palestine and Palestinians* (New York, 1984), p. 70, and Howard Sachar, *A History of Israel from the Rise of Zionism to Our Time* (New York, 1986), p. 230.

CHAPTER 10

126   *"were second to none in regretting..."* Resolution of Arab states at October 1944 preparatory meeting for the founding of the Arab League, cited in Egyptian Ministry of Foreign Affairs, *Performance Report: Egypt and the Palestinian Question, 1945–1983* (Cairo, 1984), p. 8.

126   Anshass meeting: Walid Khalidi, "The Arab Perspective," in William R. Louis and Robert W. Stookey, eds., *The End of the Palestine Mandate* (Austin, Tex., 1986), p. 110.

127   Bludan meeting: Khalidi, in Louis and Stookey, p. iii.
128   Hajj Amin's escape and Farouk's reception: Philip Mattar, *The Mufti of Jerusalem: al-Hajj Amin al-Husayni and the Palestinian National Movement* (New York, 1988), p. 110.
129   "Judaea" and "Abdallia": Avi Shlaim, *Collusion Across the Jordan: King Abdullah, the Zionist Movement and the Partition of Palestine* (New York, 1988), p. 79.
129   Kohn comments: Memo from U.S. diplomat William J. Porter to his superior, Gordon Merriam of State Department Near East Bureau, June 26, 1946, U.S. National Archives 867N.01/6-2646.
130   1946 Jewish Agency plan: Nahum Goldmann letter to Dean Acheson, July 10, 1946, U.S. National Archives 867N.01/7-1046.
131   Sasson-Abdullah meeting: For text of Sasson's reports to Jewish Agency on meetings with King Abdullah, see Neil Caplan, *Futile Diplomacy: Arab-Zionist Negotiations and the End of the Mandate*, Vol. 2 (London, 1986), p. 268. Further details in Shlaim, p. 76.
132   King David Hotel bombing: Howard Sachar, *A History of Israel from the Rise of Zionism to Our Time* (New York, 1986), p. 267.
132   "... *unable to accept*..." This quotation and its British domestic context are well described in Michael J. Cohen, *Palestine and the Great Powers—1945–1948* (Princeton, N.J., 1982), p. 223.
133   "... *This was my first Hora*..." Jorge García-Grenados, *The Birth of Israel: The Drama As I Saw It* (New York, 1949), p. 100.
133   "*are entitled to Palestine as a whole*..." Jewish Agency for Palestine, *The Jewish Plan for Palestine: Memoranda and Statements Presented to UNSCOP* (Jerusalem, 1947), p. 355.
134   "... *fear of false news*" Quoted in *Palestine Post*, June 16, 1947, p. 3.
134   "... *convincing argument for partition.*" García-Grenados, p. 39. The Guatemalan delegate's memoirs also describe the incidents of discrimination against Jewish reporters.
135   Abdullah's off-the-record statements to UNSCOP: García-Grenados, p. 209.
135   Abdullah's message to Bevin: Quoted in Cohen, p. 266. For more on Abdullah's role, see Mary Wilson, *King Abdullah, Britain and the Making of Jordan* (Cambridge, 1987), pp. 162–63, and Shlaim, p. 93.
136   Sasson's call to suspend Abdullah's subsidies: Shlaim, p. 95. By Shlaim's account, Abdullah had received no follow-up payments after Sasson's £5,000 down payment in August 1946.
136   "... *still in control.*" Jon Kimche, *Jerusalem Post*, July 4, 1947.
136   "... *rather as a joke.*" Sir Henry Gurney, British chief secretary

in Palestine, to Colonial Office, Sept. 8, 1947, as reproduced in Michael J. Cohen, *The Rise of Israel: United Nations Discussions on Palestine, 1947* (New York, 1987), pp. 8off.

138 *"... grasp at any possibility ..."* Comar letter to Bernard Gering of South African Zionist Federation, Dec. 3, 1947, reproduced in Cohen, pp. 2ooff. Comay's letter also documents the last-minute Truman administration intervention, which American officials at the time denied.

138 Statistics on final partition plan, as well as events leading up to it: Sachar, p. 292.

138 Less than 8 percent: Kenneth W. Stein, *The Land Question in Palestine, 1917–1939* (Chapel Hill, N.C., 1984), p. 227.

139 *"I want to be the rider ..."* Report of Ezra Danin to Jewish Agency on meeting with King Abdullah, Nov. 17, 1947, reproduced in full in Caplan, p. 277.

139 *"will not allow his forces ..."* Sasson telegram to Moshe Shertok, Nov. 20, 1947, quoted in Shlaim, p. 115.

140 *"What were the Zionists conceding? ..."* Walid Khalidi, *From Haven to Conquest* (Washington, 1987), p. lxix. The book was published first in Beirut in 1971.

CHAPTER 11

In interviews, Itzhak "Levitza" Levi, Raphael Ben-Aroya, Mahmoud Hamdan, and Hajj Diab Abu Latifah provided details on how the Sorek Valley was touched by fighting between November 1947 and March 1948. Levi spoke of how the valley fit into the Haganah's military planning. Levi remembered, and Mahmoud Hamdan confirmed, the participation of Haroun Ibn Jazzi in the valley fighting. Recollections of Abdul Khader al-Husseini's forays to Saraa came from Hajj Diab.

143 Casualty summary for early December: Martin Gilbert, *The Arab-Israeli Conflict: Its History in Maps* (London, 1974), pp. 39–40.

143 Irgun attacks: *Palestine Post*, Dec. 14, 1947.

143 Khissas raid: *New York Times*, Dec. 21, 1947.

144 Haifa refinery attacks: *New York Times*, Dec. 31, 1947. Ben-Zion Dinur, Yehuda Slucki, Shaul Avigur, Itzhak Ben-Zvi, and Yisrael Galili, *Sefer Toldot Ha-Haganah* ("The History of the Haganah") (Tel Aviv, 1972; in Hebrew), Vol. 3, Part 2, p. 1383, describes the Irgun attack as "an irresponsible act of revenge"; it also details the reprisal at Balad ash-Sheikh. The operations order and oral instruction to kill a hundred males is reported in a review by

Benny Morris of Uri Milstein, *History of the War of Independence,*
12 vols. (Tel Aviv, 1989; in Hebrew). The Morris review of the
first three volumes of Milstein's work appeared in the *Jerusalem
Post International Edition,* May 20, 1989.

143   Tit-for-tat violence: The *Palestine Post* (Jan. 2, 1948) reported that
in the month after the UN partition vote, the official death count
included 208 Arabs, 204 Jews, twelve British soldiers, six foreign
civilians, and five policemen.

144   *"There is a sporting chance . . . "* U.S. Embassy London to Washington, Jan. 6, 1948, enclosing memo of conversation among Clayton, Harold Beeley of the Foreign Office, and U.S. diplomat
Lewis Jones, U.S. National Archives 867N.01/1-648.

145   December 26 convoy: Itzhak "Levitza" Levi, *Jerusalem in the War
of Independence* (Tel Aviv, 1986; in Hebrew), pp. 120ff.

145   Ben-Aroya's instinct: Four decades later, Israeli military historian Uri Milstein found his instinct had considerable validity.
Milstein's twelve-volume *History of the War of Independence* con-
cludes that Dani Mack's commander, Amos Horev, had chosen
"the worst" possible route to reach the Etzion block, and that it
was a mistake to send the platoon to Hartuv in the first place
because most of the troopers were exhausted from the previous
night's fighting. Milstein's findings were initially reported in a
review of the first three volumes of Milstein's work. The review,
by Benny Morris, appeared in the *Jerusalem Post International
Edition,* May 20, 1989, p. 12.

146   Palmach unit wiped out: Levi, p. 89, gives details of the battle and
casualties on both sides.

146   *"I was mad at myself . . ."* Raphael Ben-Aroya, interviewed in
Ma'ariv, May 16, 1986.

147   Death of Ben-Besset: Raphael Ben-Aroya, interviewed by authors. Ben-Aroya, who has spent a decade researching and writing a memoir of Hartuv, said the only other Hartuvian killed up
to then in conflict with the Arabs was a man murdered while
walking on the beach in Jaffa in 1929.

147   Panic and retreat of rescue column: Levi, pp. 120ff.

147   *"I wanted to finish him."* Raphael Ben-Aroya, interviewed by authors.

147   *"Okay, go."* Raphael Ben-Aroya, interviewed by authors.

148   Armory inventory: Levi, pp. 120ff.

148   Plan D. The text, which has never appeared in English, is in the
authorized history of the Haganah, *History of the Haganah,* Vol.
3, Part 2, p. 1473.

148   Inclusion of Hartuv station in Plan D: Levi, pp. 215ff.

150   Twenty-five rifles: Walid Khalidi, *From Haven to Conquest* (Wash-

ington, 1987), p. 858. Professor Khalidi cites unpublished files of the Arab Higher Committee as his source.

150 "... *too small for the talents of the mufti.*" Consulate General, Jerusalem, to Washington, Dec. 30, 1947, U.S. National Archives 867N.01/12-3047.

151 Arab League deliberations and Safwat warning: Walid Khalidi, "The Arab Perspective," in William R. Louis and Robert W. Stookey, eds., *The End of the Palestine Mandate* (Austin, 1986), pp. 118ff. Khalidi, who has had access to private papers of Syrian Prime Minister Jamil Mardam, provides the most authoritative account of Arab League debates in 1947–48.

151 Saudi knowledge of Abdullah taking bribe: Terry Duce, an official of the Arabian-American Oil Company, learned from Saudi officials about bribes to Abdullah "by the Sasson family" and informed the U.S. Legation in Saudi Arabia. U.S. Legation, Jidda, to Washington, Jan. 3, 1948, U.S. National Archives 867N.01/1-1348.

151 Saudi oil revenues: U.S. Legation, Jidda, to Washington, Jan. 22, 1947, U.S. National Archives 867N.01/1-2247.

152 Sharabati comments after three old-fashioneds: U.S. Legation Damascus to Washington, Oct. 10, 1947, U.S. National Archives 867N.01/10-1047.

152 *"the prospect of doing some looting ..."* Azzam remark at luncheon conversation in Baghdad, quoted by American diplomat Edmund J. Dorsz. U.S. Legation Baghdad to Washington, Nov. 6, 1947, U.S. National Archives 867N.01/11-647.

152 Strength of Arab irregulars: The figures are taken from Khalidi, *From Haven to Conquest*, pp. 858–60. Khalidi had access to unpublished figures from Arab sources.

153 *"inflict crushing defeats ..."* U.S. Legation Beirut to Washington, Oct. 8, 1847, U.S. National Archives 867N.01/10-847.

154 Ibn Jazzi's involvement in Bab al-Wad fighting: Aref al-Aref, *The Tragedy of the Holy Land and the Loss of Paradise* (Sidon, 1956; in Arabic), Vol. 1, p. 161; Dominique Lapierre and Larry Collins, *O Jerusalem!* (New York, 1972), p. 142. Also, Itzhak "Levitza" Levi (the chief of intelligence of Haganah in Jerusalem in 1947–48), interviewed by authors.

155 Details on the convoy attack: Report analyzing failure of the convoy by an unnamed Haganah officer. The file—"Summary of reports between 18.3.48 and 8.4.48"—was found in IDF Archives, Tel Aviv. Also, unidentified 1948 news clipping on the incident from a Hebrew language newspaper, reproduced in Raphael Ben-Aroya, "Hartuv As It Used to Be," photocopied manuscript (Evan Yehuda, Israel, 1989; in Hebrew), appendix.

155   Report of Piper Cub pilot: Relayed in message from Chief of Operations Yigael Yadin to Jerusalem, March 18, 1948, 2120 hours, IDF Archives.

CHAPTER 12

Yoshko Levy, a survivor of the Hartuv siege, provided the fullest oral account during several interviews. Other details about the siege emerged in interviews with Itzhak "Levitza" Levi, and Mahmoud Hamdan. The account of Asad Hamdan Asad's role in the Ishwa battle against the British came from his son, Mahmoud Hamdan. For his part, Asad Haman Asad said the 1948 war was too painful to discuss.

157   Intelligence warning: Itzhak "Levitza" Levi, *Jerusalem in the War of Independence* (Tel Aviv, 1986; in Hebrew), p. 90ff. Additional details from Levi, interviewed by authors.

157   Attack on Shimshon: Mattityahu Peled, "Hartuv Under Siege," *Ma'arachot* (official journal of the Israel Defence Forces), No. 61 (February 1950); also written account of Yosef "Yoshko" Levy, included in Raphael Ben-Aroya, "Hartuv As It Used to Be," photocopied manuscript (Evan Yehuda, Israel, 1989; in Hebrew), appendix.

158   *"The situation is serious . . ."* Radio messages of Hartuv garrison to Haganah, Jerusalem, Mar. 21, 1948, 1900 and 2230 hours, IDF archives, Tel Aviv.

158   *". . . They instill fear in each other."* This and other details of the siege, including from Peled, *Ma'arachot*, No. 61. Peled went on to become a general in the IDF and later a dovish member of the Knesset.

158   *". . . otherwise we'll all go to hell."* Yosef "Yoshko" Levy, interviewed by authors. His recollections, quoted throughout this chapter, generally support Peled's version of the siege.

159   *". . . one hundred Arabs there."* Hartuv garrison to Jerusalem, Mar. 22, 1948, 0800 hours, IDF archives.

159   Fifty Arabs killed or wounded: *New York Times*, Mar. 23, 1948.

160   Description of Britishers ambushed in Ishwa: *New York Times*, Mar. 23 and 24, 1948; Mahmoud Hamdan, interviewed by authors. Estimate of twenty Arabs killed or wounded is from an unidentified 1948 clipping in a Hebrew-language newspaper. The clipping is photocopied in Ben-Aroya, appendix.

159   Account of British raid and driving out Arabs: *New York Times*, Mar. 24, 1948. It was this article which briefly reported an "alle-

gation" that British soldiers were beaten to death in Ishwa. The story did not say who made the allegation or provide any other details. The *Times* of London, which gave daily coverage to Palestine developments, carried a Reuters dispatch on the incident on March 23 which reported that two Warwickshire soldiers had been killed during the battle. It did not mention an allegation that the soldiers were stoned to death. When interviewed many years later, Palestinians from Ishwa maintained that the two British soldiers were killed in an exchange of gunfire.

160   *". . . resist being evacuated. "* Visit by British armored car described in Peled, *Ma'arachot,* No. 61.

161   *"U.S. Abandons Jewish State . . ." Palestine Post,* Mar. 21, 1948.

161   *". . . not accept any trusteeship . . ."* Quoted in Amos Perlmutter, *The Life and Times of Menachem Begin* (Garden City, N.Y., 1987), p. 212.

161   *". . . replaced by others."* Haganah headquarters, Jerusalem, to Haganah chief of operations, enclosing telegram from Hartuv garrison, Mar. 27, 1948, 1430 hours, IDF archives.

161   *". . . it is zero. "* Hartuv garrison to Haganah headquarters, Jerusalem, Mar. 29, 1948, 0800 hours, IDF archives.

162   Casualty statistics: *Palestine Post,* Apr. 4, 1948.

162   Kfar Etzion convoy attack and booty: Izzat Tannous, *The Palestinians* (New York, 1988), p. 493.

163   Dhubiya raid: *Palestine Post,* Mar. 16, 1948.

163   Negev attack: *Palestine Post,* Mar. 22, 1948.

163   *"friendly advice"* The attack was on the village of Qira wa Qamun in the Galilee, according to Yehuda Burstein, who was quoted in Benny Morris, "The Causes and Character of the Arab Exodus from Palestine: The Israel Defense Forces Intelligence Branch Analysis of June 1948," *Middle East Studies,* Vol. 22, No. 1 (January 1986), p. 6.

163   Radio messages: Hartuv garrison to Haganah headquarters, Jerusalem, Mar. 30–Apr. 1, 1948, IDF archives.

164   Piper Cubs: Figures from Walid Khalidi's detailed analysis of writings by Israeli military historians in Khalidi, *From Haven to Conquest* (Washington, 1987), pp. 881–86.

164   Sixty-six rifles and Stens: Levi, p. 120ff. 250 rifles: Khalidi, p. 859.

164   27,000 veterans: Edward N. Luttwak and Daniel Horowitz, *The Israeli Army, 1948–1973* (New York, 1983), p. 24.

164   Strength of Haganah and Arab irregular forces: Khalidi, pp. 865ff., estimates the various Arab irregular forces, including the Arab Liberation Army, as totaling fewer than seven thousand.

Khalidi attributed his figures to his study of documents made available to him by Palestinian and other Arab officials involved in the 1948 war. Pro-Israeli scholars have put Arab irregular strength higher; Arab irregulars and volunteers totaled fourteen thousand, according to Howard Sachar, *A History of Israel from the Rise of Zionism to Our Time* (New York, 1986), p. 300. As for the Haganah, Luttwak and Horowitz estimate (p. 23) that as of mid-1947, the Haganah numbered 43,000, of which 32,000 were from the static Home Guard and the rest were from Field Force and mobile Palmach units. A much higher estimate comes from a UNSCOP delegate, who has written that in July 1947, Haganah officials privately told UNSCOP that Haganah's "trained and armed strength" numbered 55,000 without reserves, or some 90,-000 counting reserves. See Jorge García-Grenados, *The Birth of Israel* (New York, 1949), p. 183. All sources agree that Haganah increased its strength between 1947 and May 1948.

165 $114 million: The United Jewish Appeal targets were disclosed to the State Department on Dec. 16, 1947 by Eliazer Kaplan, treasurer of the Jewish Agency. Memo of conversation between Kaplan and Fraser Wilkins of Near East Bureau, U.S. National Archives 867N.01/12-1648.

165 $50 million: Jacques Derogy and Hesi Carmel, *The Untold History of Israel* (New York, 1979), p. 80.

165 Czech purchases: Arnold Krammer, "Arms for Independence: When the Soviet Bloc Supported Israel," reprinted in Khalidi, p. 745.

165 Fund-raising of Arab Higher Committee: Tannous, pp. 391–92.

166 *"operations of conquest . . ."* Benny Morris, *The Birth of the Palestinian Refugee Problem, 1947–1949* (Cambridge, 1987), p. 304.

166 Contents of April 2 airdrop: Hartuv Garrison to Jerusalem, Apr. 2, 1948, 1600 hours, IDF archives.
". . . assembly or jumping-off bases." Operational order cited in Morris, *Birth*, p. 111.

167 Sweeping terms of Plan D. Text of the plan in the official Israeli military history of this period, *Sefer Toldot Ha-Haganah* ("The History of the Haganah") (Tel Aviv, 1972; in Hebrew), Part 2, p. 1473.

167 *". . . can't execute it efficiently . . ."* Hartuv garrison to Jerusalem, Apr. 3, 1948, 1720 hours, IDF archives.

168 *"Hi, boys."* This version comes from the then chief of Haganah intelligence in Jerusalem, Itzhak "Levitza" Levi, in interviews with the authors. Collins and Lapierre, *O Jerusalem!* (New York, 1972), p. 262, contends that Abdul Khader's reply was "It's us,

boys" in Arabic. According to Herzog (p. 31), Abdul Khader was killed "as he approached a position he thought had already been taken by Arab forces."

CHAPTER 13

The last days of Hartuv and rescue of the garrison were described in interviews by Yoshko Levy, Shlomo Lahat, and Sabiha Abu Latifah. Recollections of how the Burma Road sliced through the edge of the valley were provided by Itzhak "Levitza" Levi, one of the first Haganah officers to traverse the jeep trail. Zeev Eytan, later to become a prominent Israeli military analyst, told of the 1948 attack on Beit Susin.

172   British departure: Because of conflicting recollections and the absence of records, it is impossible to know whether the last British policeman departed the Hartuv station before or after the March 21–22, 1948, attack on Hartuv.

173   ". . . the legion would capture Jerusalem . . ." Chaim Levy, interviewed in Ma'ariv, May 16, 1986.

173   "the tipping of the scales" This and other details of the latter stages of the siege taken mainly from a reconstruction in 1950 by Lieutenant Mati Peled. See Mattiyahu Peled, "Hartuv Under Siege" (in Hebrew), Ma'arachot, No. 61 (Feb. 1950).

173   Jewish doctor visits Artuf during siege: Ismail Rahhal, interviewed by authors. He was apparently referring to Miriam Dukker, a physician who lived at Hartuv in the 1940s.

174   Yoshko Levy's recollections: Quoted from his written account in Raphael Ben-Aroya, "Hartuv As It Used to Be," photocopied manuscript (Evan Yehuda, Israel, 1989; in Hebrew).

174   Destruction of Beit Mahsir: Documented from Palmach reports and logbooks in Benny Morris, The Birth of the Palestinian Refugee Problem, 1947–1949 (Cambridge, 1988), pp. xviii, 158, 333.

175   ". . . joy and happiness . . ." Peled, Ma'arachot.

176   "such forces as are available." Walid Khalidi, "The Arab Perspective," in Robert W. Stookey, ed., The End of the Palestine Mandate (Austin, Tex., 1986), pp. 129ff.

176   Abdullah-Golda Meir meeting: Avi Shlaim, Collusion Across the Jordan (New York, 1988), pp. 205–14, 236.

176   Kfar Etzion battle: Martin Gilbert, The Arab-Israeli Conflict: Its History in Maps (London, 1979), p. 45; Larry Collins and Dominique Lapierre, O Jerusalem! (New York, 1972), p. 363; Chaim Herzog, The Arab-Israeli Wars (New York, 1984), p. 42.

177   Woman saved from rape: Collins and Lapierre, p. 364.

177   "*. . . the despair ate everything. . . .*" Peled, *Ma'arachot.*

177   "*It was decided on evacuating Hartuv. . . .*" Yadin message, [May 14?], 1948, IDF archives, Tel Aviv.

178   "*. . . We will walk.*" Shepach-Lahat exchange from Shlomo Lahat, interviewed by authors.

179   Jewish eyewitness: Quotations are from "Heroic Withdrawal from Hartuv," a June 1, 1948, article by Uri Avineri in *Yom Yom* ("The Daily"), an Israeli newspaper. A photocopy of the article appears in Ben-Aroya, appendix.

179   "*. . . would not enjoy it.*" Chaim Levy, interviewed in *Ma'ariv,* May 16, 1986. In the same article Chaim Levy describes going out to the fields and killing the animals.

180   "*. . . The baby was wiggling . . .*" Chaim Levy, interviewed in *Ma'ariv,* May 16, 1986.

180   Morphine injection: *Yom Yom,* June 1, 1948.

180   "*We left by foot . . .*" Telegram from Hartuv commander, quoted in Itzhak Levi, *Jerusalem in the War of Independence* (Tel Aviv, 1986; in Hebrew), pp. 120–22.

181   Relative strengths of Arab and Jewish forces. Neither the Arab countries nor the Israelis have published detailed, accurate figures on their armies in 1948. However, Chaim Herzog, an intelligence officer in the 1948 war and later the president of Israel, has written that "approximately 40,000" Jewish troops were available to fight on May 15. See Herzog, p. 48. As for the Arab forces, Walid Khalidi, who has had access to Arab military documents from 1948, wrote in *From Haven to Conquest* (Washington, 1987), p. 867, that the total Arab expeditionary forces sent to Palestine on May 15 totaled 13,876.

181   "*Not one word . . .*" Sir John Bagot Glubb, *A Soldier with the Arabs* (London, 1957), p. 94.

182   Situation at Hartuv on May 19–20, 1948: From a report by that night's Transjordanian patrol to Hartuv, later quoted in a book by Colonel Mahmoud al-Rusan, an Arab Legion intelligence officer stationed at Latrun. Rusan's book, *Battles of Bab al-Wad and Latrun* (Damascus, 1950), appeared first in Arabic and was later translated into Hebrew by the Israeli army intelligence: see Capt. S. Sahaj, translator, *In the Eyes of the Enemy* (Tel Aviv, 1955), p. 160. The number of the Arab Legion troops at Hartuv is taken from Abdallah al-Tall, *The Tragedy of Palestine* (Cairo, 1959; in Arabic), p. 266. Supplementary details from Mahmoud Hamdan and Ismail Rahhal, interviewed by authors.

182   About fifty Egyptians: Tall, p. 266. The leader of the fifty Egyptians is thought to have been a young Egyptian officer named Hassan al-Tohami. Three decades later, Tohami would serve as

President Anwar Sadat's main intermediary in the stealthy talks leading up to his trip to Jerusalem.

182   Arafat in 1948 war: Alan Hart, *Arafat—Terrorist or Peacemaker?* (London, 1984), p. 75.

183   "*. . . lose our capital.*" Ben-Gurion diary entry and account of Ben-Gurion–Yadin meeting, from Collins and Lapierre, pp. 465–66.

185   "*Under no condition . . .*" Lapierre and Collins, p. 525, citing the memoirs of the Arab League adjutant.

185   Roseate battle communiqués: This explanation of why Egypt accepted the cease-fire when its troops seemed poised for victory comes from the memoirs of a member of the UN mediation team who was in Cairo: Pablo de Azcarte, *Mission in Palestine—1948–1952* (Washington, 1966), p. 99.

186   "*. . . end of our rope.*" Lapierre and Collins, p. 527.

186   "*We have checked out . . .*" Ben-Gurion diary, June 10, 1948, in David Ben-Gurion, *The War of Independence* (Tel Aviv, 1982; in Hebrew), p. 502.

CHAPTER 14

Some details on how the valley fared in June and early July, 1948, came from interviews with Sabiha Abu Latifah, Awad Ibrahim Awad, Itzhak "Levitza" Levi, Avizohar Nachshon, Ariyeh Nir, and Ismail Abdul Fattah Rahhal.

188   No resupplies: Sir John Bagot Glubb, *A Soldier with the Arabs* (London, 1957), pp. 148–49.

189   Commandeering trucks and buses: U.S. Legation, Damascus, to Washington, June 26, 1948, U.S. National Archives 501.BB-Palestine/6-2648.

189   Enemy fires first: Glubb, p. 150.

189   "*There won't be . . .*" Transjordanian Prime Minister Tawfiq Abul Huda, quoted in Glubb, p. 145.

189   "*If I were to drive . . .*" King Abdullah, quoted in Glubb, pp. 151–52.

190   Syrian and others oppose plan: U.S. Embassy, Cairo, to Washington, *Foreign Relations in the United States (FRUS)* 1948, Vol. 5, Part 2, p. 1159.

190   "*The Arabs are living . . .*" Acting U.S. representative at UN to Washington, *FRUS,* 1948, Vol. 5, Part 2, p. 1206.

190   Arab rulers believed Arabs had right: For example, see *FRUS,* 1948, Vol. 5, Part 2, p. 1184; and Glubb, p. 152.

191   *"Presumably the politicians . . ."* Glubb, p. 151.

191   Nearly 400,000 refugees: Benny Morris, "The Causes and Character of the Arab Exodus from Palestine: The Israel Defence Forces Intelligence Branch Analysis of June 1948," *Middle Eastern Studies*, Vol. 22, No. 1 (January 1986), pp. 6–10. See also Benny Morris, *The Birth of the Palestinian Refugee Problem, 1947–1949* (Cambridge, 1987), pp. 68–69, regarding efforts by Arab leaders to convince Palestinians to remain.

191   Arab League feared: *Economist*, June 12, 1948, p. 962.

192   *"As for the return . . ."* Howard Sachar, *A History of Israel from the Rise of Zionism to Our Time* (New York, 1986), p. 335.

193   *"The factor of surprise . . ."* Morris, "Causes and Character," pp. 6–7.

193   *"Every enemy field . . ."* Benny Morris, "The Harvest of 1948 and the Creation of the Palestinian Refugee Problem," *Middle East Journal*, Vol. 40, No. 4 (Autumn 1986), pp. 675–78.

193   One ship delivered: Larry Collins and Dominique Lapierre, *O Jerusalem!* (New York, 1972), p. 543.

194   Food and weapons stocks: Itzhak Levi, *Jerusalem in the War of Independence* (Tel Aviv, 1986; in Hebrew), p. 292.

194   CIA analysis. *FRUS*, 1948, Vol. 5, Part 2, pp. 1244–45.

196   *"We have not succeeded . . ."* David Ben-Gurion, *The War of Independence* (Ben-Gurion's War Diary), G. Rivlin and Dr. E. Orren, eds. (Tel Aviv, 1982) p. 525.

196   Glubb pulled out troops: Glubb, pp. 163–64.

197   *" 'Driving out' is a term . . ."* David Shipler, *Arab and Jew* (New York, 1986), p. 34.

197   *"Ben-Gurion made . . ."* Morris, *Birth*, p. 207.

198   Arab Legion pulled out immediately: Abdullah al-Tall, *The Tragedy of Palestine* (Cairo, 1959; in Arabic), pp. 266–67.

CHAPTER 15

The account of how the Palestinians came to flee from the Sorek Valley in mid-July 1948 was pieced together primarily from the recollections of four Palmach soldiers who participated in the Jewish attack on the valley: Ariyeh Nir, Avizohar Nachshon, Penina Yariv and retired Lt. Gen. Rafael Eytan. Their stories, provided in interviews, were supplemented and crosschecked against interviews with eight former Palestinian residents of the valley: Sabiha Abu Latifah, Hajj Diab Abu Latifah, Awad Ibrahim Awad, Amira Shahin, Asad Hamdan Asad, Alia Mohammed Daher, Mahmoud Hamdan, and Ismail Abdul Fattah Rahhal.

201 Bayonets piercing: Larry Collins and Dominique Lapierre, *O Jerusalem!* (New York, 1972), p. 275, quotes a young woman, Haleem Eid, as saying she was at Deir Yassin and saw her pregnant sister killed and then her stomach cut open with a butcher's knife.

201 Israeli argument discredited: See, for example, Howard Sachar, *A History of Israel from the Rise of Zionism to Our Time* (New York, 1986), p. 332: "This was a frequently repeated Israeli claim after the war. Yet no such order for evacuation was ever found in any release of the Arab League or in any military communiqués of the period. Rather, the evidence in the Arab press and radio of the time was to the contrary." Benny Morris, *The Birth of the Palestinian Refugee Problem, 1947–1949* (Cambridge, 1987), pp. 286–96, makes a persuasive case that the Palestinian flight began as a by-product of war, and once the flight began, the Israelis acted to accelerate it.

202 July 14, 1948: The dates that Saraa and other valley villages were captured were obtained from a 1948 chronology maintained at the IDF Archives in Tel Aviv.

202 Suba and Saraa: David Ben-Gurion, *The War of Independence* (Tel Aviv, 1982; in Hebrew), p. 585. A footnote says the capture of Saraa took two nights, which agrees with accounts given to the authors by villagers.

204 *"The people were fleeing . . ."* Awad Ibrahim Awad and his wife, Amira Shahin, interviewed by authors.

207 *"With the break of dawn . . ."* An undated 1948 account in an Israeli newspaper, reproduced in the form of a photocopy in Raphael Ben-Aroya, "Hartuv As It Used to Be," photocopied manuscript (Israel, 1988). Cited below as war correspondent's dispatch.

208 Correspondent's account confirms mortar fire: War correspondent's dispatch, in Ben-Aroya.

209 *"Twenty rebels concentrated . . ."* War correspondent's dispatch, in Ben-Aroya.

211 *". . . Mr. Friedman . . ."* Eytan's recollection was in error about the name on the letter. The contemporaneous war correspondent's dispatch, reproduced in Ben-Aroya, reported that the name of the employer mentioned in the letter was a "Mr. Green." This was probably a reference to one of the Gueron family from Hartuv. The fact that a letter was left was confirmed by Ismail Rahhal, one of the fleeing Artufis, when interviewed by the authors.

214   *"He started weeping."* Ismail Abdul Fattah Rahhal, interviewed by
      authors. War correspondent's dispatch, Ben-Aroya, also de-
      scribes Artuf homes being exploded by Israeli demolitions ex-
      perts.

      CHAPTER 16

      While written sources provided the broad outlines of the history
      of the exodus of the Palestinian people, the story of what hap-
      pened to the Sorek Valley residents came mainly from interviews
      with six participants in the flight: Mahmoud Hamdan, Asad
      Hamdan Asad, Alia Mohammed Daher, Ismail Abdul Fattah
      Rahhal, Diab Abu Latifah, and Sabiha Abu Latifah.

218   At least 750,000 refugees: Most Arab sources say the number
      was higher; most Israeli sources say it was lower. The figure
      used here comes from the "First Interim Report of the United
      Nations Economic Survey Mission for the Middle East," UN
      Document A/1106, Nov. 7, 1949. It estimated 774,000 people
      were refugees, including 48,000 in Israel (17,000 Jews and 31,-
      000 Palestinian Arabs). This meant that 726,000 were Pales-
      tinian refugees outside the boundaries Israel occupied. The
      UN daily ration count at the time was 940,000. The report said
      such a high number could not be reconciled with its statistical
      analysis of the Arab population of prewar Palestine. It sug-
      gested that the ration figure was bloated by impoverished non-
      refugees claiming rations. Despite this, Arab leaders have in-
      sisted the war created 900,000 to 1,000,000 Palestinian refugees.
      Israel has estimated the refugee total was 520,000. Benny Mor-
      ris, *The Birth of the Palestinian Refugee Problem, 1947–1949* (Cam-
      bridge, 1987), p. 297, cites the view of the director-general of
      the Israel Foreign Ministry in late 1950 that the real number
      was around 800,000.

218   About one-third: According to the authors' estimate, the 1949
      UN figure of 726,000 refugees outside of Israel included about
      235,000 Palestinians from regions the UN had designated ei-
      ther for the Arab partition zone or for internationalized Jeru-
      salem. This estimate is derived as follows. As of December
      1946, 804,000 Arabs lived in the Arab partition zone, according
      to UN figures. By December 1947, natural population increase
      (at 2.5 percent a year, the figure used by UN statisticians at the
      time) raised the Arab population of the Arab zone to 825,000.
      According to the 1949 UN Economic Survey mission report,

530,000 Arabs lived (as of December 1947) in the portion of Palestine which Israel did not capture in the 1948–49 war— namely, the West Bank and Gaza. By subtraction, the remaining 295,000 can be assumed to have lived in the portions of the Arab partition zone which Israel did capture. Of these 295,000, the authors estimated that 100,000 remained in Israel to become Israeli citizens. (Israel's non-Jewish population totaled 108,000 in early 1949, according to Israeli estimates. Most lived in the UN-designated Arab partition zone.) The rest— 195,000—thus were refugees who had lived in the Arab zone. These, plus the roughly 40,000 Arabs (estimate cited in *Palestine Post*, May 17, 1948) who fled the international zone of Jerusalem, yield the authors' estimate of 235,000.

218 *"Sanitation practically nonexistent. . . . "* U.S. Consulate, Jerusalem, to Washington, Aug. 12, 1948, National Archives 867N.49/8-1248.

218 *"There is no food . . ." Palestine Post,* July 28, 1948.

218 Syrian expenditure: U.S. Legation Damascus to Washington, July 29, 1948, National Archives 867N.48/7-2948.

219 Spending on refugees: State Department memorandum, Feb. 9, 1949, National Archives 867N.48/2-949. The three governments together spent a total of more than $8 million. The Arab League in September 1947 had pledged $3 million to the war.

219 British concerns: U.S. Embassy London to Washington, July 24, 1948, National Archives 501.BB-Palestine/7-2448.

219 Bernadotte proposal and Israeli response: *Palestine Post,* July 28, 1948.

219 *". . . at expense former Arab inhabitants. "* Marshall to U.S. Embassy in London, Aug. 9, 1948 (enclosing instructions to U.S. mission to UN), *FRUS,* 1948, p. 1310.

219 Reports of confiscations of Arab property for Jewish immigrants: For instance, on August 5, 1948, the U.S. embassy in Cairo cabled an account of a meeting between Bernadotte and a U.S. diplomat. Bernadotte was reported as saying: ". . . he himself had seen in Ramle the Haganah organizing and supervising the removal by trucks of the contents of Arab homes. This loot was, he understood, being distributed among the newly arrived Jewish immigrants." U.S. Embassy Cairo to Washington, National Archives 501.BB-Palestine/8-548. See also U.S. Consulate Jerusalem to Washington, July 27, 1948, 867N.48/7-2748.

219 Marshall view: In an Aug. 16, 1948, memorandum, Marshall proposed warning the Israelis that if they did not become less "ag-

gressive," they might face trouble in getting *de jure* recognition from the United States, in obtaining a $100 million loan from the Export-Import Bank, and in securing United Nations membership. He later toned down his recommendation, suggesting only that Israel alter its loan application by detailing specific projects it wished to finance. *FRUS*, 1948, Vol. 5, Part 2, pp. 1313–15, 1320, 1345–48.

219 Consensus: Morris, *Birth*, p. 141.

220 Reported decision not to allow refugees' return: The *Times* article cited in U.S. Embassy London to Washington, July 26, 1948, National Archives 867N.48/7-2648.

220 "*a politically explosive . . .*" *Palestine Post*, Aug. 2, 1948.

220 "*a large and well-organized . . .*" U.S. mission in Tel Aviv to Washington, Aug. 2, 1948, National Archives 867N.48/8-248.

220 "*It was a miraculous . . .*" David Lamb, *The Arabs* (New York, 1987), p. 212.

221 "*We went up the hill . . .*" Yosef Weitz, *My Diary and Letters to the Children*, Vol. 3, *Watching the Walls* (Israel, 1965), pp. 327–28.

221 Kaplan discusses confiscation: Weitz, p. 312.

222 Troubling thoughts: Weitz, pp. 327–28. In one passage Weitz suggested the deal wouldn't work, that the state would have to return the money the JNF paid it for Arab land, if the state was unable to transfer title to the JNF.

222 Weitz and settlements: Benny Morris, *Birth*. Also Benny Morris, "Yosef Weitz and the Transfer Committees, 1948–49," *Middle Eastern Studies*, Vol. 22, No. 4 (Oct. 1986).

222 "*Can we afford . . .*" Cited in Morris, *Birth*, p. 141.

223 Complaints about army actions: Israel State Archives, FM 2401/21, "Property of Absentees," Minutes of Ministerial Committee on Abandoned Property, July 26, 1948.

223 "*Jerusalem will be established . . .*" and following quotations: Weitz, pp. 329–30.

224 "*The view . . .*" Morris, *Birth*, p. 148. Morris also provides details of the August 18 meeting and list of settlements.

224 "*As for the Arabs . . .*" ISA, FM2401/21, "Property of Absentees," Minutes of Ministerial Committee on Abandoned Property, Aug. 20, 1948.

225 "*In his opinion . . .*" Also description of meeting on settlements, ISA FM 2401/21.

225 Sasson's actions: Avi Shlaim, *Collusion Across the Jordan* (New York, 1988), pp. 280–85.

226 "*uprooted from their homes . . .*" *FRUS*, 1948, p. 1403.

226 Ben-Gurion meeting with envoy. *FRUS*, 1948, p. 1385.

226   Ben-Gurion's proposal: Shlaim, pp. 306–8.
228   Negev fighting: Chaim Herzog, *The Arab-Israeli Wars* (New York, 1984), pp. 92–96.

CHAPTER 17

In interviews Aliza Tibon and Yoav Tibon told about the founding and early years of Kibbutz Tsora. Ovediah Aqwa reminisced about the early years of the Yemenite settlement at Eshtaol. Ester Shulim told of growing up in the Hartuv-B transit camp. Yoshko Levy supplied the perspective of the veteran Hartuvians trying in the 1950s to re-establish their destroyed settlement.

236   Eshtaol and Nahum population, 1961: Central Bureau of Statistics, State of Israel.
236   Fistfights at Eshtaol: Central Zionist Archives, KKL 5, 502, Oct. 1, 1949–51, "Eshtaol, Delivering the Land," Letter from Shimon Meckler to Yosef Weitz, Jan. 28, 1951, and Letter from [Eshtaol] Committee of Organization to Management of KKL, Jerusalem, May 12, 1951.
237   JNF frustration with Yemenites: CZA, KKL 5, 502, Oct. 1, 1949–51, "Eshtaol, Delivering the Land," Letters from Shimon Meckler to Committee of Eshtaol, July 11, 1951, and July 17, 1951. For a contemporaneous description of Yemenites in 1949–50, see Shlomo Barer, *The Magic Carpet* (London, 1952), pp. 256–67.
237   Yemenites clustered near borders: Absolam Rokah, retired from Settlement Department of Jewish Agency, and Jacob Barmore, public relations director of JNF (1988), interviewed by authors.
238   *"When my father . . ."* Ester Shulim, interviewed by the authors, told of early years of Hartuv-B. Further details came from another early resident, Meir Cohen, who was interviewed for the authors by Daniel Shapiro, and from Barer, pp. 256–67.
240   *"The big difference . . ."* Yoshko Levy, interviewed by authors. Further accounts of the problems the Hartuvians encountered returning to Hartuv after 1948 came from Gita Levy, and from *Ma'ariv*, Sept. 9, 1977, and May 16, 1986.
240   Settling in abandoned homes: Tom Segev, *1949: The First Israelis* (New York, 1986), p. 76.
240   Settlements raised: Howard M. Sachar, *A History of Israel from the Rise of Zionism to Our Time* (New York, 1986), p. 438.
241   Ishwa land purchase: As of 1989, files at the Israeli land office in Jerusalem showed 3,120 dunams (=780 acres) of Ishwa land were first registered to the state of Israel on Jan. 7, 1953. Records also

showed that 2,402 dunams (=600 acres) of Ishwa land were registered to the Custodian of Abandoned Property on Jan. 1, 1953. Both were new registrations and no purchase payment was shown. In a transaction on Feb. 24, 1953, the state sold 3,045 dunams (=761 acres) of Ishwa land to the Jewish National Fund for 8,144 Israeli pounds. In another transaction on March 10, 1953, the Development Authority sold 2,402 dunams (=600 acres) to the JNF for 28,446 Israeli pounds. None of these funds were turned over to the former Arab owners.

241 Attempt to give confiscation legal basis; see, for example, Sachar, which calls the Development Authority a "legal fiction," p. 438.

241 *"This point . . ."* Dr. Abraham Granovsky, "The Measure of the Task," speech delivered to JNF of America conference, March 4–6, 1949, JNF archives, New York.

242 Jackhammers and bulldozers: Barer, pp. 256–67.

242 U.S. donations: JNF publication "Facts and Figures," Activities of the JNF, Oct. 1950 to Sept. 1951, JNF archives, New York.

243 Housing: *Jerusalem Post*, July 10, 1951.

243 Shimshon refurbished: *Jerusalem Post*, April 12, 1954.

243 *"feast of light" Jerusalem Post*, May 2, 1955.

244 Accounts of shooting and capture: *Jerusalem Post*, Mar. 11 and 13, 1956.

245 Thefts: CZA, JNF 502, "Land Acquiring," April 4, 1951, letter from Tony Marcus to JNF.

CHAPTER 18

The wandering of the Sorek Valley refugees and their early years in Kalandia refugee camp were recounted in interviews with Labiba Suleiman, Mahmoud Hamdan, Asad Hamdan Asad, and Hajj Diab Abu Latifah. A retired UNRWA official, Antranig "Tony" Bakerjian, recalled the growth of Kalandia from the perspective of a sympathetic outsider.

248 Dec. 11, 1948, resolution: *FRUS*, 1948, Vol. 5, pp. 1661–62.

250 *"Jericho in 1948 . . ."* Antranig "Tony" Bakerjian (who would become an UNRWA official), interviewed by authors.

250 Attack on soldiers: *Palestine Post*, Jan. 31, 1949.
Coups and other disruptions: In December 1949 the Syrian government resigned amid riots, and the shuffled cabinet was ousted in a coup the following March. Also in December 1949, Egypt declared a state of emergency and outlawed the activist Moslem Brotherhood to still unrest. This did not prevent the assassination of Prime Minister Nokrashi Pasha.

251 Royal visits: Clinton Bailey, "The Participation of the Palestini-
     ans in the Politics of Jordan," doctoral thesis, Columbia Univer-
     sity, 1966, pp. 72–73.
251 Abdullah named Palestinian monarch: *Palestine Post*, Dec. 2, 1948.
251 *"creeping annexation"* See, for example, Mary C. Wilson, *King Abdul-
     lah, Britain and the Making of Jordan* (Cambridge, 1987), p. 194.
253 Zaim's proposal: Avi Shlaim, *Collusion Across the Jordan* (New
     York, 1988), pp. 427–28.
253 Conquering the Negev to Aqaba: Chaim Herzog, *The Arab-Israeli
     Wars* (New York, 1984), p. 104.
253 Narrow strip where Syrian troops were lodged: This territory in
     the northern West Bank actually was occupied by Iraqi forces,
     but the Iraqis had agreed to pull out and leave it in Abdullah's
     control. The Iraqis had ten thousand troops there, but Transjor-
     dan's Arab Legion could only afford to send two thousand sol-
     diers, not enough to withstand an Israeli assault.
254 Armistice: For details of talks with Abdullah and threats, see
     FRUS, 1949, Vol. 6 (Washington, D.C., 1977), pp. 861–62; Wilson,
     p. 188; and Shlaim, Chapter 13.
257 Camp petitions: Avi Plascov, *The Palestinian Refugees in Jordan,
     1948–57* (London, 1981), p. 52.
258 Ethridge's efforts: *FRUS*, 1949, Vol. 6. See, for example, pp. 776–
     77, 825–26, 876–78, and 911–16.
258 U.S. 1949 pressure on Israel: *FRUS*, 1949, Vol. 6. See, for exam-
     ple, pp. 853–56, 880–81, 890, 964.
258 Truman message and Ben-Gurion response: *FRUS*, 1949, Vol. 6,
     pp. 1073–75.
259 Informal peace offers: These include Israeli talks in 1949 and 1950
     with leaders of Syria, Egypt, and Jordan. For the most detailed
     account see Shlaim, Chapters 14 and 15. Also see Tom Segev,
     1949: The First Israelis (New York, 1986), pp. 15–17, 23–24, 40; and
     Wilson, pp. 201–2.
259 Water diversion: John K. Cooley, "The War Over Water," *Foreign
     Policy*, Vol. 54 (Spring 1984), p. 10.
260 $11 million: State Department memorandum, Feb. 9, 1949, Na-
     tional Archives 867N.48/2-949.
260 Abdullah more constrained: Plascov, p. 62.

CHAPTER 19

The events of the 1950s, including the 1956 war, were recalled by
Mahmoud Hamdan, Hajj Diab Abu Latifah, Avizohar Nach-

shon, and Yoshko Levy. Aliza Tibon and Yoav Tibon told of
Moshe Dayan stopping for coffee in the Sorek Valley.

263 Shelter construction: "Information on Kalandia Camp,
UNRWA, Jerusalem Area," a January 1979 report from
UNRWA files, supplied by a private source.

263 1950 resolution: Reprinted in Avi Shlaim, *Collusion Across the Jordan* (New York, 1988), p. 559.

264 Population figures and characteristics: Mary Wilson, *King Abdullah, Britain and the Making of Jordan* (London, 1987), p. 198. Also
see Avi Plascov, *The Palestinian Refugees in Jordan, 1948–1957* (London, 1981), p. 32.

264 147 Jews killed in 1952: Edward W. Luttwak and Daniel Horowitz, *The Israeli Army, 1948–1973* (Lanham, Md., 1983), p. 108.

264 Statistics of Arab killed and captured: Howard M. Sachar, *A
History of Israel from the Rise of Zionism to Our Time* (New York,
1986), p. 444.

265 Khibya incident: Luttwak and Horowitz, pp. 110–11; Sachar, pp.
444–45.

266 Moved to curtail: Plascov, pp. 76–77.

266 Camp informants: Mahmoud Hamdan and retired UNRWA officer Antranig Bakerjian, interviewed by authors. Also, Israel
State Archives hold Jordanian West Bank files that now are
closed to the public, but were used by Israeli historian Amnon
Cohen in his book *Political Parties in the West Bank Under the Jordanian Regime, 1949–1967* (Ithaca, 1982). Cohen found in them
information about West Bank activities obtained from an extensive Jordanian spy network.

266 Armistice violations, major confrontations: Sachar, pp. 444–49.

268 Refugee riots and delegation: *Jerusalem Post*, Jan. 22, 1956, describing events in December 1955.

268 Overwhelming Palestinian support of Hussein: Plascov, p. 101.

268 "*march back into . . .*" *Jerusalem Post*, May 27, 1956.

269 Telegrams from Eisenhower: Sachar, p. 494.

271 Hussein proposed attacking: Richard Nyrop, ed., *Jordan: A Country Study* (Washington, D.C., 1980), p. 30.

271 Two hundred fighter-bombers: Sachar, p. 499.

272 Johnston Plan: John Cooley, "The War over Water," *Foreign Policy*, Vol. 54 (Spring 1984), pp. 10–12.

272 Palestinians receptive to improvements but unwilling to disperse: Plascov, p. 70. Also, retired UNRWA officer Antranig
Bakerjian and Ismail Abdul Fattah Rahhal, interviewed by authors.

273 Concessions replaced with repression: Shaul Mishal, *West Bank/*

East Bank: The Palestinians in Jordan, 1949–1967 (New Haven and London, 1978), pp. 47–48.

274 Refugee caught with pamphlet: *Jerusalem Post,* May 13, 1957.

274 Policies that discouraged investment: Pamela Ann Smith, *Palestine and the Palestinians 1876–1983* (New York, 1982), p. 170.

275 "*entirely illegal . . .*" The Palestinian National Covenant, as translated from Arabic to English by the PLO, has been reprinted in full in a U.S.-funded study on Jordan; see Nyrop, p. 267. The same translation was provided to Western correspondents in the early 1980s by the Israel Information Centre, an organization in Jerusalem with close ties to the Israeli government.

275 Shukeiry alienated Hussein: Helena Cobban, *The Palestinian Liberation Organization* (Cambridge, 1984), pp. 30–31.

275 Thirty-nine raids claimed: Cobban, p. 33.

276 "*take the necessary steps*" Sachar, p. 622.

277 New land and subjects: Sachar, p. 667.

CHAPTER 20

Personal stories about the 1967 war and its aftermath were provided in interviews by Mahmoud Hamdan, Awad Ibrahim Awad, Ovediah and Rachel Aqwa, Ismail Abdul Fattah Rahhal, and Yoshko and Gita Levy.

279 "*There was nobody . . .*" Antranig Bakerjian, interviewed by authors.

281 Evictions from the Old City: *New York Times,* June 19, 1967.

281 Compulsory Hebrew course: Howard Sachar, *A History of Israel from the Rise of Zionism to Our Time* (New York, 1986), p. 672.

283 "*It seemed so far . . .*" Ralph Hyman, quoted in *Jerusalem Post,* May 13, 1983.

283 ". . . *relinquish Ramot Eshkol . . .*" *Jerusalem Post,* May 13, 1983.

284 Piping water to Kalandia: UNRWA report, supplied by a private source.

285 One-third more water: Sachar, p. 703.

285 One-fourth of its water supply: David Kahan, *Agriculture and Water Resources in the West Bank and Gaza (1967–1987)* (Jerusalem, 1987), p. 20, says: "The water resources of the West Bank are rather limited. About one-quarter of Israel's annual water potential originates from beyond the 'green line,' i.e. some 475 million cubic feet." The water reaches Israel either by natural underground flow or from pumped springs and wells on the West Bank. Meron Benvenisti and Shlomo Khayat, *The West Bank and*

Gaza Atlas (Jerusalem, 1988), says annual consumption by Palestinians on the West Bank totals 115 million cubic feet, while Jewish settlements in the West Bank use 40–50 million cubic feet.

285   Sixteen hundred gallons a day. By comparison, two other farm settlements in the valley, Nahum and Eshtaol, used about 1,100 gallons per person per day. In the late 1980s, the combined urban and rural population of Israel used about 320 gallons of water per person per day, compared to about 80 gallons used by rural and urban Palestinians on the West Bank. Each Israeli settler on the West Bank used an average of 500 gallons a day. Sources: populations of the Israeli settlements in the valley are based on the Central Bureau of Statistics 1983 census of local areas. Local water consumption figures were provided by Mordecai Yakobovich, spokesman of Israel's Mekorot Water Co. Ltd., who told the authors that in 1988, Kibbutz Tsora consumed 1,756,000 cubic meters of water a day of fresh water from Israel's main aqueduct system. He had no figures available on additional water used by Tsora from local groundwater and from Jerusalem's treated sewage. Comparisons to the West Bank were calculated by the authors from population and water use figures published in 1988 by the West Bank Data Project, a research project funded by the Rockefeller Foundation and Ford Foundation in Jerusalem.

286   Gueron farmed until he was eighty-two: Gueron, who was an infant when Hartuv was founded, moved in with relatives in Tel Aviv in 1977, and died seven years later at the age of eighty-nine. *Ma'ariv*, May 16, 1986.

287   Talk of settlements: Sachar, p. 677.

287   Call to settle "Greater Israel": Eshkol, quoted in Sachar, p. 674.

287   Allon Plan: Meron Benvenisti, *The West Bank Handbook: A Political Lexicon* (Jerusalem, 1986), p. 5. The Allon Plan would have left three uncontiguous Arab cantons which were to be parts of a Jordanian-Palestinian state under King Hussein. The plan never was adopted by an Israeli cabinet, though versions of it still were being discussed by Israelis sympathetic to the Labor Party in the late 1980s.

288   *". . . That was our thinking. . . ."* Gita Levy, interviewed by the authors. By the time Levy was assigned to the West Bank, the aging Ben-Gurion was leader of a small opposition party in the Knesset. He retired from politics in 1970.

289   Terrorists killed and locked up: Helena Cobban, *The Palestinian Liberation Organisation* (Cambridge, 1984), p. 38.

289   Estimated three thousand Palestinians killed: Cobban, p. 52.

290 Report on destruction of shelter in Kalandia: UNRWA Jerusalem Area officer, memo to A/Dir of UNRWA ops, West Bank,
May 14, 1970, supplied by a private source. The report did not
specify the charges against the 16-year-old, explaining that he had
not been brought before a military tribunal.

291 Eleven Israeli athletes: Israeli security officials have contended
that Black September was an arm of Fatah. PLO officials have
said it was a splinter group of guerrillas from Fatah and other
factions who were embittered over the PLO's expulsion from
Jordan.

291 War called Israel's endurance into question: Chaim Herzog, *The
Arab-Israeli Wars* (New York, 1984), p. 321.

292 PNF organization and deportations: Cobban, p. 173.

292 Israelis countered demonstrations: UNRWA Situation Reports,
Apr. 9, 1975 and July 8, 1976, provided by a private source.

CHAPTER 21

Mahmoud Hamdan told of his cousin returning to the Sorek
Valley to pick olives. He and his son Hassan Hamdan gave detailed interviews about the wounding of Hassan Hamdan in
1982, about Hassan's teenage years in prison and about his return
to Kalandia.

295 Discovery of Semtex: *Jerusalem Post*, Mar. 2, 1979.

295 Israeli reaction to 1979–80 rock-throwing: UNRWA records,
from a private source.

296 For this generation of Palestinians unimportant to pine about old
villages: Examples of the greater emphasis by younger activists
on preserving the West Bank rather than on trying to reclaim
former Palestinian land inside Israel include Jonathan Kuttab
and Rajah Shehadeh, *The West Bank and the Rule of Law* (Ramallah,
West Bank, 1980), and Rajah Shehadeh, *Occupier's Law: Israel and
the West Bank* (Washington, 1985).

297 Hebron murders and surrounding events: Howard M. Sachar,
A History of Israel (New York, 1987), Vol. 2, p. 162.

297 Jewish vengeance against Palestinian mayors: Sachar, Vol. 2, p.
162; Emile Sahliyeh, *In Search of Leadership: West Bank Politics Since
1967* (Washington, 1988), p. 83.

297 "... *instructions from the outside* ..." Abu Nour, the underground
Fatah leader of Kalandia camp during the Palestinian uprising of
the late 1980s, interviewed by the authors.

299 "... *We're for Begin.*" This and other quotations in Beth She-

mesh from Amos Oz, *In the Land of Israel* (New York, 1983), p. 35.

300 Eytan's career: *Jerusalem Post,* Mar. 2, 1982.

301 1982 Bir Zeit events: Sachar, Vol. 2, p. 162.

301 Kalandia in the forefront: UNRWA reports Mar. 21 and 22, 1982, furnished by a private source.

301 *"the most significant battle . . ."* Milson, quoted in Helena Cobban, *The Palestine Liberation Organization* (Cambridge, 1987), p. 119.

301 Order to harass inciters: Text of Eytan order, as disclosed in a 1983 trial of Israeli officers accused of mistreating Palestinians in Hebron, *Jerusalem Post,* Jan. 21, 1983.

302 *"I had to do it. . . ."* Goodman's quotation and details of the attack from *New York Times,* Apr. 12–13, 1982.

302 *". . . waving Palestinian flags . . ." Jerusalem Post,* Apr. 26, 1989

302 Palestinians stoning border policemen in the valley: An UNRWA report of Apr. 25, 1982, supplied by a private source, said: "It is reported . . . the soldiers . . . were stoned."

303 *"very serious" Jerusalem Post,* Apr. 26, 1982.

303 Israel's Lebanon war of 1982: For more details, see Sachar, Vol. 2, pp. 165–210; Herzog, pp. 339–60; Thomas L. Friedman, *From Beirut to Jerusalem* (New York, 1989), pp. 126ff.

303 Sharon and Eytan preparing for at least six months: Sachar, Vol. 2, p. 172.

304 Israeli-Syrian air battle: Herzog, p. 347.

304 Death toll at Sabra and Shatila: A Reuters report, Feb. 8, 1983, cited an Israeli intelligence estimate that some 700 Palestinians were killed. Friedman, p. 163, cited an estimate of the Red Cross that 800 to 1,000 were killed. Cobban, p. 130, quoted Israeli journalist Amnon Kapeliouk as estimating that about 3,000 were killed.

305 *". . . in broad daylight . . ."* This quotation and the incident totals are from Meron Benvenisti, *The West Bank Data Base Project 1987 Report* (Jerusalem, 1987), p. 41.

306 *". . . cockroaches in a bottle."* Lt. Gen. Rafael Eytan to closed meeting of Knesset Foreign Affairs and Defense Committee, Apr. 12, 1983. Several variations of this quotation have been published. This version is taken from *Jerusalem Post,* Apr. 15, 1983. Several other sources, including Sachar, Vol. 2, p. 194, said Eytan compared the stone-throwers to "drugged cockroaches" instead of merely "cockroaches."

306 Arrest, detention, treatment in jail, and trial of Hassan: Confirmation that Hassan and five others were arrested on April 21 and 22 was found in an UNRWA camp official's report of Apr. 26,

1984, provided by a private source. Hassan Hamdan and his father, Mahmoud, provided details of the charges and sentence in interviews with the authors. The authors' written request to Israeli authorities for comment or access to the files on Hassan Hamdan's case did not elicit a response. While the details of his account remain unsubstantiated, they are hardly implausible. A special Israeli judicial commission reported in 1987 that for many years Shin Bet had used psychological and physical pressures to obtain confessions in security cases. See U.S. State Department, *Human Rights Report for 1988* (Washington, 1989), pp. 1376ff.

CHAPTER 22

The description of Kalandia camp during the intifada relied almost entirely on interviews inside the camp during or soon after the events unfolded. The account of Jamal Abu Latifah's role in the first days of the intifada was drawn mainly from an interview with Abu Nour, the code name of a ranking Fatah leader in the Kalandia camp. Abu Nour, who was twenty-four when interviewed in 1989, was the son of a refugee from Lydda. Others who shared their feelings and recollections included Hajj Diab Abu Latifah and Sabiha Abu Latifah (parents of Jamal Abu Latifah); Mahmoud Hamdan and eight members of his family; and Amna Ayyad, mother of the late Atta Ayyad. The quotations from Israeli reservist Yuval Levy came from an interview conducted with him on behalf of the authors by Israeli journalist-translator Daniel Shapiro.

312   First casualty of the uprising: For more on the early events in Gaza, see Thomas L. Friedman, *From Beirut to Jerusalem* (New York, 1989), pp. 370–71.

313   *"lightly injured" Jerusalem Post*, Dec. 11, 1987.

313   Refugee camps home to only about one out of five: Since there has been no census in the occupied territories since 1967, the proportion can only be approximated on the basis of published estimates. In June 1987, UNRWA's estimate of Palestinians still in refugee camps was 244,416 in Gaza and 94,824 in the West Bank (UNRWA, *Guide to UNRWA* [Vienna, 1988], pp. 7–8). In 1987, the total "permanent" Palestinian population was estimated by the West Bank Data Project, an Israeli research center, as 1,067,000 in the West Bank and 633,000 in the Gaza Strip (Meron Benvenisti and Shlomo Khayat, *The West Bank and Gaza Atlas* [Jerusalem, 1988], pp. 27, 109).

314 Jamal Abu Latifah deported: He was arrested Dec. 29, 1987, and dropped off in southern Lebanon by an Israeli helicopter on Aug. 1, 1988. Jamal and other deportees were later given heroes' welcomes at the November 1988 meeting of the Palestine National Congress, the PLO's parliament in exile, in Algiers. His family later heard that he was working for the PLO in Iraq.

316 ". . . *will not occur again* . . ." *New York Times,* Dec. 30, 1987.

316 *"We shall prove to them.* . . ." *Jerusalem Post,* Jan. 14, 1988.

316 *"force, might, beatings"* Several translations of Rabin's phrase have appeared. This translation comes from U.S. State Department, *Country Reports on Human Rights Practices for 1988, "The Occupied Territories"* (Washington, 1989), pp. 1367–87.

316 *"nearly zero" Washington Post,* Jan. 23, 1988.

316 ". . . *new tactic . . . will work. "* Meron Benvenisti, interviewed by Anthony Lewis, *New York Times,* Jan. 24, 1988.

317 ". . . *transfer . . . starvation, or physical elimination . . ."* *New York Times,* June 17, 1989; *Jerusalem Post International Edition,* June 24, 1989.

320 Tear-gassing, stone-throwing, beating so commonplace: Even sympathetic outsiders soon came to accept stones and tear gas as the norm. For instance, one UNRWA report on Feb. 24, 1988, supplied to the authors by a private source, said: "At 1400 hours at Kalandia Camp stoning and firing tear gas bombs took place between Israeli soldiers and youths of the camp. No incidents reported."

322 *"Oh, Mother of the Martyr . . ."* Death and burial of Atta Ayyad: Amna Ayyad and Abu Nour, interviewed by authors. Also, *Davar* (Tel Aviv), Aug. 31, 1988, on what Ayyad's fellow prisoners heard. On Apr. 7, 1989, Captain Ira Barakat, a press spokesman for the Israel Defence Forces, told the authors that Israeli army investigators had just finished a report which concluded that Ayyad's death was a suicide. Barakat said the report was forwarded to the IDF's office of the military prosecutor for a final decision on whether there were grounds to prosecute anyone at Dahriyeh prison in connection with Ayyad's death. Ayyad's death was among the cases to which the U.S. State Department was alluding when it reported in its 1988 human rights report on the Israeli-occupied territories that there were five instances in 1988 when "unarmed Palestinians in detention died under questionable circumstances or were clearly killed by detaining authorities."

CHAPTER 2 3

Developments at Kibbutz Tsora in the late 1980s and concerns of the kibbutzniks about the intifada were related in interviews with Avi Hector, Yoav Tibon, Aliza Tibon, Aharon Avraham, and Maoz Haviv. Other Israeli perspectives in this period came from interviews with Ester Shulim, Yoshko Levy, and Gita Levy. Palestinian viewpoints cited included those of Mahmoud Hamdan, Ismail Abdul Fattah Rahhal, Hajj Diab Abu Latifah, Ibrahim Abu Latifah, and Jamil Shahin.

326 Mistimed smell of wood smoke: In the first summer of the intifada, some 2,500 acres of woodland in Israel were burned in fires blamed by Israelis on the intifada, according to *Jerusalem Post International Edition*, May 6, 1989. Arson-related fires in Israeli forests were on the decline in 1989, partly because of heightened precautions by foresters, the newspaper reported.

329 When these people left: Prof. Amihai Mazar, Hebrew University archaeology department, interviewed by authors.

329 Jet-engine factory: The factory, Beit Shemesh Engine Company, produced parts for the engines of Israeli F-15 and F-16 fighter planes, mostly under licenses from U.S. companies. In addition, some of the engine parts it produced were purchased by the United States for American F-15s and F-16s under an "offset" agreement between Israel and the U.S. Defense Department. The plant, which employed about four hundred Israeli workers in the late 1980s, was partly owned by Pratt & Whitney, a subsidiary of United Technologies of Connecticut. Its work force dropped in the mid-1980s after the Israeli government decided to cancel production of the Lavi fighter, which Israel had designed as a substitute for U.S.-made jets. Source: authors' interview with Pratt & Whitney public information staff in Florida.

SELECTED
BIBLIOGRAPHY

Here are twenty-five books in English that are recommended by the authors for further reading.

Aharoni, Yohanan, and Michael Avi-Yonah. *The Macmillan Bible Atlas.* New York: Macmillan, 1977.

Antonius, George. *The Arab Awakening.* New York: G.P. Putnam's Sons, 1946.

Cohen, Michael. *Palestine and the Great Powers—1945–1948.* Princeton, N.J.: Princeton University Press, 1982.

Elon, Amos. *Herzl.* New York: Holt, Rinehart & Winston, 1975.

Flappan, Simha. *The Birth of Israel: Myths and Realities.* New York: Pantheon, 1987.

Friedman, Thomas L. *From Beirut to Jerusalem.* New York: Farrar, Straus & Giroux, 1989.

Herzog, Chaim. *The Arab-Israeli Wars.* New York: Vintage, 1984.

Hitti, Phillip K. *History of the Arabs from the Earliest Times to the Present.* New York: St. Martin's Press, 1946.

Hurwitz, J. C. *The Struggle for Palestine.* New York: W. W. Norton, 1950.

Jaffee Center for Strategic Studies. *The West Bank and Gaza: Israel's Options for Peace.* Tel Aviv: Tel Aviv University, 1989.

Khalidi, Walid, ed. *From Haven to Conquest: Readings in Zionism and the Palestinian Problem Until 1948.* Washington: Institute for Palestine Studies, 1987.

Laqueur, Walter, and Barry Rubin, eds. *The Israel-Arab Reader, A Documentary History of the Middle East Conflict.* New York: Penguin, 1969.

Louis, William R., and Robert W. Stookey, eds. *The End of the Palestine Mandate.* Austin: University of Texas, 1986.

Mattar, Philip. *The Mufti of Jerusalem.* New York: Columbia University Press, 1988.

Morris, Benny. *The Birth of the Palestinian Refugee Problem, 1947–1949.* Cambridge: Cambridge University Press, 1987.

O'Brien, Connor Cruise. *The Siege.* New York: Simon & Schuster, 1986.

Quandt, William B., Fuad Jabber, and Ann Mosely Lesch. *The Politics of Palestinian Nationalism.* Berkeley: University of California Press, 1973.

Sachar, Howard M. *A History of Israel from the Rise of Zionism to Our Time.* New York: Knopf, 1986.

Sahliyeh, Emile. *In Search of Leadership: West Bank Politics Since 1967.* Washington: Brookings Institution, 1988.

Shipler, David K. *Arab and Jew.* New York: Times Books, 1986.

Shlaim, Avi. *Collusion Across the Jordan: King Abdullah, the Zionist Movement and the Partition of Palestine.* New York: Columbia University Press, 1988.

Smith, Pamela Ann. *Palestine and the Palestinians 1876–1983.* New York: St. Martin's Press, 1984.

Stein, Kenneth. *The Land Question in Palestine, 1917–1939.* Chapel Hill, N.C.: University of North Carolina Press, 1984.

Viorst, Milton. *Sands of Sorrow.* New York: Harper & Row, 1987.

Wilson, Mary. *King Abdullah, Britain and the Making of Jordan.* Cambridge: Cambridge University Press, 1987.

ACKNOWLEDGMENTS

The people who made it possible for us to write this book are half a dozen families of Palestinians and Israelis who agreed to share hour upon hour with us on repeated visits, as we probed their memories and their records for events that help explain the conflict as it touched their homes. It happened that we arrived in Israel to begin our interviewing about six weeks into the intifada, the Palestinian uprising, after research that began in the United States months earlier. Even during the intifada these Israelis and Palestinians were forthcoming and were courageous enough to allow us to use their names, without imposing any conditions. These are the people we thank the most. But they were not the only ones who helped us.

We are among the small multitude of journalists aided and abetted by the late Howard Simons, who encouraged us to do this book and helped us find an academic home for our research. For granting us this stimulating opportunity we thank the Center for International Studies of the Massachusetts Institute of Technology, where we were visiting scholars in 1987–88. At MIT, Dean Philip Khoury gave us guidance, friendship, and the chance to participate in the Bustany Middle East Seminars. His wife, Mary Wilson, like him a scholar of the Middle East, helped us especially on the history of Transjordan. Also in Cambridge we owe special gratitude to Walid Khalidi, who shared his insight developed after years of thought and study into Palestinian issues. We thank our employer, the Cox Newspapers, for granting leaves of absence for research and concerted writing.

Other American research centers whose staffs helped us dig out information include the U.S. National Archives in Washington, D.C., the University Museum Archives of the University of Pennsylvania in Philadelphia (for the notes of an archaeological expedition), the Harry S Truman Library in Independence, the University of North Carolina Library in Chapel Hill (for Mark Ethridge papers), the Jewish National Fund archives in New York, and the Institute for Palestine Studies in Washington, D.C.

But most of the story was in Israel and the occupied territories. We found a wealth of documents at the Central Zionist Archives in Jerusalem, and we owe much to its staff and its director, Michael Heymann, who seems to have filed in his own mind most of what is stored in the archives. And we are grateful to the Ben Zvi Institute and librarian Yochi Goele; to the Israel Defence Forces Archives and archivist Micha Kaufman, who showed us recently declassified military documents on 1948; to the Hebrew University libraries at both the Mount Scopus and Givat Ram campuses; and to the Israel State Archives.

We also thank the present mufti of Jerusalem for granting us access to the Archives of the Department of Revival of Islamic Heritage, and Fahmi Ansari and others who helped us there. The Arab Studies Center in Jerusalem also opened its bookshelves and records to us. From the United Nations Relief and Works Agency in East Jerusalem, Bill Lee gave us valuable help, as did retired UNRWA officer Antranig "Tony" Bakerjian. Our friend and colleague Michael Widlanski contributed perceptive insights.

Others who shared memories of events important to our work include former Palmach soldier Rafi Horowitz, who also extended to us the assistance of the Government Press Office, and historian Itzhak "Levitza" Levi, the former Haganah intelligence chief for Jerusalem. We have also consulted scholars Sharif Cana'ni, Nadim Rouhana, and El Hannan Reiner on various historical puzzles. Our Israeli and Palestinian translators, whose interest and contributions far exceeded translating, included Ruba Hussary, Daniel Shapiro, and Nadia Bilbasi.

We are indebted to three scholars who read and commented on points of accuracy and interpretation in our draft. They are

Dr. Mohammed Muslih and Dr. Lester Vogel, specialists in the history of modern Palestine, and biblical historian Dr. Murray Newman. We accepted many of their suggestions, but in the end we are responsible for what appears in print.

Finally, we owe much to our editor—Barbara Grossman, who encouraged us from our first conversation, and James Wade, who saw us through to the finish.

INDEX

The Hamdan Family

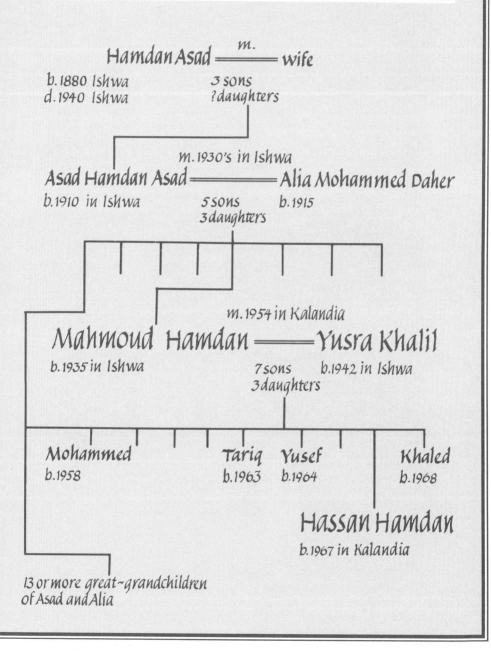

Hamdan Asad === m. === wife
b. 1880 Ishwa   3 sons
d. 1940 Ishwa   ? daughters

m. 1930's in Ishwa
Asad Hamdan Asad === Alia Mohammed Daher
b. 1910 in Ishwa   5 sons   b. 1915
                         3 daughters

m. 1954 in Kalandia
Mahmoud Hamdan === Yusra Khalil
b. 1935 in Ishwa   7 sons   b. 1942 in Ishwa
                         3 daughters

Mohammed   Tariq   Yusef   Khaled
b. 1958   b. 1963   b. 1964   b. 1968

Hassan Hamdan
b. 1967 in Kalandia

13 or more great-grandchildren
of Asad and Alia